Lecture Notes in Computer

Commenced Publication in 1973
Founding and Former Series Editors:
Gerhard Goos, Juris Hartmanis, and Jan van Leeuwen

Norbert Eisinger   Jan Małuszyński (Eds.)

Reasoning Web

First International Summer School 2005
Msida, Malta, July 25-29, 2005
Tutorial Lectures

 Springer

Volume Editors

Norbert Eisinger
Ludwig-Maximilians-Universität München, Institut für Informatik
Oettingenstr. 67, 80538 München, Germany
E-mail: norbert.eisinger@ifi.lmu.de

Jan Małuszyński
Linköping University, Department of Computer and Information Science
58183 Linköping, Sweden
E-mail: janma@ida.liu.se

Library of Congress Control Number: 2005928809

CR Subject Classification (1998): H.4, H.3, C.2, H.5, J.1, K.4, K.6, I.2.11

ISSN   0302-9743
ISBN-10   3-540-27828-1 Springer Berlin Heidelberg New York
ISBN-13   978-3-540-27828-3 Springer Berlin Heidelberg New York

Springer is a part of Springer Science+Business Media

springeronline.com

© Springer-Verlag Berlin Heidelberg 2005
Printed in Germany

Typesetting: Camera-ready by author, data conversion by Scientific Publishing Services, Chennai, India
Printed on acid-free paper   SPIN: 11526988   06/3142   5 4 3 2 1 0

Preface

This volume contains the tutorial papers of the Summer School "Reasoning Web," July 25–29, 2005 (http://reasoningweb.org). The School was hosted by the University of Malta and was organized by the Network of Excellence REWERSE "Reasoning on the Web with Rules and Semantics" (http://rewerse. net), funded by the EU Commission and by the Swiss Federal Office for Education and Science within the 6th Framework Programme under the project reference number 506779. The objective of the school was to provide an introduction into methods and issues of the Semantic Web, a major endeavor in current Web research, where the World Wide Web Consortium W3C plays an important role.

The main idea of the Semantic Web is to enrich Web data with meta-data carrying a "meaning" of the data and allowing Web-based systems to reason about data (and meta-data). The meta-data used in Semantic Web applications is usually linked to a conceptualization of the application domain shared by different applications. Such a conceptualization is called an ontology and specifies classes of objects and relations between them. Ontologies are defined by ontology languages, based on logic and supporting formal reasoning. Just as the current Web is inherently heterogeneous in data formats and data semantics, the Semantic Web will be inherently heterogeneous in its reasoning forms. Indeed, any single form of reasoning turns out to be insufficient in the Semantic Web. For instance, ontology reasoning in general relies on monotonic negation, while databases, Web databases, and Web-based information systems call for non-monotonic reasoning. Constraint reasoning is needed in dealing with time (for time intervals are to be dealt with). Reasoning with topologies, e.g., in mobile computing applications, requires planning methods. On the other hand (forward and/or backward) chaining is the reasoning of choice in coping with database-like views (for views, i.e., virtual data, can be derived from actual data by operations such as join and projections).

The programme of the school and the selection of the lecturers was discussed and approved by the REWERSE Steering Committee. This volume contains 10 papers written or co-authored by the lecturers. The papers present some well-established fundamentals of the Semantic Web and selected research issues addressed by REWERSE.

The first two papers concern the ontology level of the Semantic Web. The paper by Grigoris Antoniou, Enrico Franconi, and Frank van Harmelen gives an introduction to Semantic Web ontology languages and discusses their relation to description logics. An alternative foundation for Semantic Web reasoning is F-logic, as discussed in the paper by Michael Kifer.

The next two papers take the perspective of the Web as an information system. The first of them, co-authored by James Bailey, François Bry, Tim Furche, and Sebastian Schaffert, surveys most Web and Semantic Web query languages so far proposed for the major representation formalisms of the standard and Semantic Web: XML, RDF and topic maps. The survey stresses the necessity of an integrated access to the data on the Web that is represented in various formalisms and discusses the role of reasoning in querying Web data. The size of this paper is larger than the other ones in this volume. This was necessary in order to provide a comprehensive and focused survey of numerous Web query languages. The second paper, by José Júlio Alferes and Wolfgang May, addresses the issue of evolution of Web data and reactivity to events. The paper first discusses logical foundations of evolution and reactive languages in general and then focuses on issues specific to evolution and reactivity in the Web and in the Semantic Web.

User-friendliness of the Web is addressed by the next two papers. The first of them, by Matteo Baldoni, Cristina Baroglio, and Nicola Henze discusses the issue of personalization for the Semantic Web. Personalization techniques aim at giving the user optimal support in accessing, retrieving and storing information, where solutions are built so as to fit the preferences, the characteristics, and the taste of the individual. The objective of the paper is to provide a coherent introduction into issues and methods for realizing personalization in the Semantic Web. It shows that reasoning is essential for personalization. The paper by Norbert Fuchs, Stefan Höfler, Kaarel Kaljurand, Fabio Rinaldi, and Gerold Schneider gives a systematic introduction into Attempto Controlled English (ACE) a knowledge representation language readable by human and machine. ACE can be seen as a first-order logic language with the syntax of a non-ambiguous subset of English. It has already been used as an interface language to formal systems, and due to its ability to express business and policy rules it is of prime interest for Semantic Web applications.

The remaining papers in this volume show potentially important links between the Semantic Web and some well-established techniques. The paper by Gerd Wagner addresses several issues of rule modeling on the basis of the Unified Modeling Language (UML) proposed by the Object Management Group (OMG). It discusses similarities and differences between UML class models and vocabularies of the W3C ontology language OWL. It also shows how UML can be used for specifying rules and for providing concise descriptions of the abstract syntax of Semantic Web languages, such as RDF, OWL, and emerging Semantic Web rule languages. The paper by Robert Baumgartner, Thomas Eiter, Georg Gottlob, Marcus Herzog, and Christoph Koch surveys the state of the art and techniques in Web information extraction and explains their importance for creation of input data for Semantic Web applications. The paper by Uwe Aßmann shows that employing ontologies can help to enlarge the software reuse factor and concludes that ontologies will play an important role in the construction of software applications, both singular and product lines. This concerns standard applications as well as Web applications, including Web services. Finally, the paper by Włodzimierz Drabent argues that type checking is needed for Web rule and query languages. For that purpose the paper presents a formalism for describing sets of semistructured data. Such sets, to be used as types, are related to XML schemata described in schema languages such as DTD or XML Schema. Research on their application to typechecking of REWERSE rule languages is in progress.

July 2005   Norbert Eisinger and Jan Małuszyński
                              Co-ordinators of REWERSE Education and Training

Table of Contents

Introduction to Semantic Web Ontology Languages
Grigoris Antoniou, Enrico Franconi, Frank van Harmelen 1

Rules and Ontologies in F-Logic
Michael Kifer 22

Web and Semantic Web Query Languages: A Survey
James Bailey, François Bry, Tim Furche, Sebastian Schaffert 35

Evolution and Reactivity for the Web
José Júlio Alferes, Wolfgang May 134

Personalization for the Semantic Web
Matteo Baldoni, Cristina Baroglio, Nicola Henze 173

Attempto Controlled English: A Knowledge Representation Language
Readable by Humans and Machines
Norbert E. Fuchs, Stefan Höfler, Kaarel Kaljurand, Fabio Rinaldi,
Gerold Schneider 213

Rule Modeling and Markup
Gerd Wagner 251

Information Extraction for the Semantic Web
Robert Baumgartner, Thomas Eiter, Georg Gottlob, Marcus Herzog,
Christoph Koch 275

Reuse in Semantic Applications
Uwe Aßmann 290

Towards Types for Web Rule Languages
Włodzimierz Drabent 305

Author Index 319

Introduction to Semantic Web Ontology Languages

Grigoris Antoniou[1], Enrico Franconi[2], and Frank van Harmelen[3]

[1] ICS-FORTH, Greece
antoniou@icsforth.gr
[2] Faculty of Computer Science, Free University of Bozen–Bolzano, Italy
franconi@inf.unibz.it
[3] Department of Computer Science, Vrije Universiteti Amsterdam, Netherlands
frankh@cs.vu.nl

Abstract. The aim of this chapter is to give a general introduction to some of the ontology languages that play a prominent role on the Semantic Web, and to discuss the formal foundations of these languages. Web ontology languages will be the main carriers of the information that we will want to share and integrate.

1 Organisation of This Chapter

In section 2 we discuss general issues and requirements for Web ontology languages, including the semantics issues. We then describe briefly the most important ontology languages in the design of the Semantic Web, namely RDF Schema in section 3 and OWL in section 4. Section 5 contains a brief comparison with other ontology languages. A brief introduction to description logics and their relation to the OWL family of web ontology languages is included. The chapter is concluded by a discussion on the importance of having correct and complete inference engines for web ontology languages.

2 On Web Ontology Languages

Even though ontologies have a long history in Artificial Intelligence (AI), the meaning of this concept still generates a lot of controversy in discussions, both within and outside of AI. We follow the classical AI definition: an ontology is a *formal specification of a conceptualisation*, that is, an abstract and simplified view of the world that we wish to represent, described in a language that is equipped with a formal semantics. In knowledge representation, an ontology is a description of the concepts and relationships in an application domain. Depending on the users of this ontology, such a description must be understandable by humans and/or by software agents. In many other field – such as in information systems and databases, and in software engineering – an ontology would be called a *conceptual schema*. An ontology is formal, since its understanding

N. Eisinger and J. Małuszyński (Eds.): Reasoning Web 2005, LNCS 3564, pp. 1–21, 2005.

should be non ambiguous, both from the syntactic and the semantic point of views.

Researchers in AI were the first to develop ontologies with the purpose of facilitating automated knowledge sharing. Since the beginning of the 90's, ontologies have become a popular research topic, and several AI research communities, including knowledge engineering, knowledge acquisition, natural language processing, and knowledge representation, have investigated them. More recently, the notion of an ontology is becoming widespread in fields such as intelligent information integration, cooperative information systems, information retrieval, digital libraries, e-commerce, and knowledge management. Ontologies are widely regarded as one of the foundational technologies for the Semantic Web: when annotating web documents with machine-interpretable information concerning their *content*, the meaning of the terms used in such an annotation should be fixed in a (shared) ontology. Research in the Semantic Web has led to the standardisation of specific web ontology languages.

An ontology language is a mean to specify at an abstract level – that is, at a *conceptual* level – what is necessarily true in the domain of interest. More precisely, we can say that an ontology language should be able to express *constraints*, which declare what should necessarily hold in any possible concrete instantiation of the domain. In the following, we will introduce various ways to impose constraints over domains, by means of statements expressed is some suitable ontology language.

2.1   What Are Ontology Languages

How do we describe a particular domain? Let us consider the domain of courses and lecturers at Griffith University. First we have to specify the "things" we want to talk about. Here we will make a first, fundamental distinction. On one hand we want to talk about particular lecturers, such as David Billington, and particular courses, such as Discrete Mathematics. But we also want to talk about courses, first year courses, lecturers, professors etc. What is the difference? In the first case we talk about *individual objects* (resources), in the second we talk about *classes* (also called *concepts*) which define types of objects.

A class can be thought of as a set of elements, called the *extension* of the class. Individual objects that belong to a class are referred to as *instances* of that class.

An important use of classes is to *impose restrictions* on what can be stated. In programming languages, *typing* is used to prevent nonsense from being written (such as $A + 1$, where A is an array; we lay down that the arguments of + must be numbers). The same is needed in RDF. After all, we would like to disallow statements such as:

- Discrete Mathematics is taught by Concrete Mathematics.
- Room MZH5760 is taught by David Billington.

The first statement is non-sensical because we want courses to be taught by lecturers only. This imposes a restriction on the values of the property "is taught by". In mathematical terms, we restrict the *range* of the property.

The second statement is non-sensical because only courses can be taught. This imposes a restriction on the objects to which the property can be applied. In mathematical terms, we restrict the *domain* of the property.

Class Hierarchies. Once we have classes we would also like to establish relationships between them. For example, suppose that we have classes for

- staff members
- academic staff members
- professors
- associate professors
- assistant professors
- administrative staff members
- technical support staff members.

These classes are not unrelated to each other. For example, every professor is an academic staff member. We say that professor is a *subclass* of academic staff member, or equivalently, that academic staff member is a *superclass* of professor. The subclass relationship is also called *subsumption*.

The subclass relationship defines a hierarchy of classes. In general, A is a subclass of B if every instance of A is also an instance of B.

A hierarchical organisation of classes has a very important practical significance, which we outline now. Consider the range restriction

Courses must be taught by academic staff members only.

Suppose Michael Maher was defined as a professor. Then, according to the restriction above, he is not allowed to teach courses. The reason is that there is no statement which specifies that Michael Maher is also an academic staff member. Obviously it would be highly counterintuitive to overcome this difficulty by adding that statement to our description. Instead we would like Michael Maher to *inherit* the ability to teach from the class of academic staff members.

Property Hierarchies. We saw that hierarchical relationships between classes can be defined. The same can be done for properties. For example, "is taught by" is a *subproperty* of "involves". If a course c is taught by an academic staff member a, then c also involves a. The converse is not necessarily true. For example, a may be the convenor of the course, or a tutor who marks student homework, but does not teach c.

In general, P is a subproperty of Q if two objects are related by Q whenever they are related by P.

Summary. As a consequence of the discussion above, (Web) ontology languages consist of:

- the important concepts (classes) of a domain
- important relationships between these concepts. These can be hierarchical (subclass relationships), other predefined relationships contained in the ontology language, or user defined (properties).
- further constraints on what can be expressed (e.g. domain and range restrictions, cardinality constraints etc.).

2.2 Formal Semantics

Ontology languages allow users to write explicit, formal conceptualisations of domains models. The main requirements are:

1. a well-defined syntax
2. a well-defined semantics
3. efficient reasoning support
4. sufficient expressive power
5. convenience of expression.

The importance of a *well-defined syntax* is clear, and known from the area of programming languages; it is a necessary condition for *machine-processing* of information. Web ontology languages have a syntax based on XML, though they may also have other kinds of syntaxes.

Of course it is questionable whether the XML-based syntax is very user-friendly, there are alternatives better suitable for humans. However this drawback is not very significant, because ultimately users will be developing their ontologies using authoring tools, or more generally *ontology development tools*, instead of writing them directly in the Web ontology language.

Formal semantics describes precisely the meaning of knowledge. "Precisely" here means that the semantics does not refer to subjective intuitions, nor is it open to different interpretations by different persons (or machines). The importance of formal semantics is well-established in the domain of mathematical logic. In the context of ontology languages, the semantics enforces the meaning of the expressed knowledge as a set of constraints over the domain. Any possible instantiation of the domain should necessarily conform to the constraints expressed by the ontology.

Given a statement in an ontology, the role of the semantics is to devise precisely which are the *models* of the statement, i.e., all the possible instantiations of the domain that are compatible with the statement. We say that a statement is *true* in an instantiation of the domain if this instantiation is compatible with the statement; the instantiation of the domain in which a statement is true is of course a model of the statement, and viceversa. So, an ontology will itself devise a set of models, which is the intersection among all the models of each statement in the ontology. The models of an ontology represent the only possible realisable situations.

For example, if an ontology states that professor is a subclass of academic staff member (i.e., in any possible situation, each professor is also an academic staff member), and if it is known that Michael Maher is a professor (i.e., Michael

Maher is an instance of the professor class), then in any possible situation it is necessarily true that Michael Maher is an academic staff member, since the situation in which he would not be an academic staff member is incompatible with the constraints expressed in the ontology.

If we understand that an ontology language talks basically about classes, properties and objects of a domain, then a model (i.e., a specific instantiation of the domain) is nothing else than the precise characterisation for each objects of the classes it is instance of, and of the properties it participates to. So, in the above example, in any model of the ontology Michael Maher should be an instance of the academic staff member class.

2.3   Reasoning

The fact that the formal semantics associates to an ontology a set of models, allows us to define the notion of *deduction*. Given an ontology, we say that an additional statement can be deduced from the ontology if it is true in all the models of the ontology. This definition of deduction comes from logic and it is very general but also very strict: if a statement is not true in all the models of an ontology, then it is not a valid deduction from it. The process of deriving valid deductions from an ontology is called *reasoning*.

If we consider the typical statements of web ontology languages, the following deductions ("inferences") can be introduced:

– *Class membership.* We want to deduce whether an object is instance of a class. For example, if in the ontology it is stated that Michael Maher is an instance of a class Professor, and that Professor is a subclass of the Academic Staff Member class, then we can infer that Michael Maher is an instance of Academic Staff Member, because this latter statement is true in all the models of the ontology, as we have explained above.
– *Classification:* We want to deduce all the subclass relationships between the existing classes in the ontology. For example, if in the ontology it is stated that the class Teaching Assistant is a subclass of the Professor class, and that Professor is a subclass of the Academic Staff Member class, then we can infer that Teaching Assistant is a subclass of Academic Staff Member. This deduction holds since in any model of the ontology the extension of Teaching Assistant is a subset of the extension of Professor, and the extension of Professor is a subset of the extension of Academic Staff Member. Therefore, in any model the extension of Teaching Assistant is a subset of the extension of Academic Staff Member, and in any model the statement that Teaching Assistant is a subclass of Academic Staff Member is true.
– *Equivalence of classes.* We want to deduce whether two classes are equivalent, i.e., they have the same extension. For example, if class Professor is equivalent to class Lecturer, and class Lecturer is equivalent to class Teacher, then Professor is equivalent to Teacher, too.
– *Consistency of a class.* We want to check that some class does not have necessarily an empty extension. For example, given an ontology in which the class Working-Student is defined to be a subclass of two disjoint classes

Student and Professor, it can be inferred that the class Working-Student is inconsistent, since in every model of the ontology its extension is empty. In fact, any instance of Working-Student would violate the constraints imposed by the ontology (namely, that there is no common instance between the two classes). In this case, it would be possible to remove the inconsistency for the Working-Student class by removing from the ontology the disjointness statement between Student and Professor.

- *Consistency of the ontology.* We want to check that the ontology admits at least a model, i.e., there is at least a possibility to have an instantiation of the domain compatible with the ontology. For example, suppose we have declared in the ontology

  1. that John is an instance of both the class Student and the class Professor, and
  2. that Student and Professor are two disjoint classes.

  Then we have an inconsistency because the two constraints can not be satisfied simultaneously. Statement 2 says that the extensions of the two classes can not have any element in common, since they are disjoint, but statement 1 says that John is an instance of both classes. This clearly indicates that there is an error in the ontology, since it does not represent any possible situation.

In designing an ontology language one should be aware of the *tradeoff between expressive power and efficiency of reasoning.* Generally speaking, the richer the language is, the more inefficient the reasoning support becomes, often crossing the border of non-computability. Thus we need a compromise, a language that can be supported by reasonably efficient reasoners, while being sufficiently expressive to express large classes of ontologies and knowledge.

Various methodologies are being developed on how to build a "good" ontology. These approaches may differ in many aspects, e.g., in the underlying representation formalism, and whether they are equipped with an explicit notion of quality, but most of them rely on reasoning mechanisms to support the design of the ontology. Semantics is a prerequisite for *reasoning support*: derivations such as the above can be made mechanically, instead of being made by hand. Logic-based reasoning is employed by the tools to verify the specification, infer implicit statements and facts, and manifest any inconsistencies. Reasoning support is important because it allows one to

- check the consistency of the ontology and the knowledge;
- check for unintended relationships between classes;
- derive explicitly all the statements that are true in the ontology, to better understand its properties;
- reduce the redundancy of an ontology, discover equivalent descriptions, reuse concept descriptions, and refine the definitions;
- automatically classify instances in classes.

In addition to the so called *standard* reasoning support listed above, non-standard inference for ontologies are of great practical impact in ontology-based applications. In particular, tools for building and maintaining large knowledge bases also requires system services that cannot be provided by the standard reasoning techniques. These non-standard reasoning problems encompass matching and unification of concepts (useful, e.g., for browsing ontologies and detecting redundancies), least-common-subsumer and most-specific-concept computation (useful to support the definition of new concepts), and approximation of concepts (useful for approximate reasoning and for a comprehensible presentation of ontologies to non-expert users).

Automated reasoning support allows one to check many more cases than what can be done manually. Checks like the above are valuable for

- *designing* large ontologies, where multiple authors are involved;
- *integrating and sharing* ontologies from various sources.

Formal semantics and reasoning support is usually provided by mapping an ontology language to a known logical formalism, and by using automated reasoners that already exist for those formalisms.

3   The Key Semantic Web Ontology Languages

We now turn to a discussion of specific ontology languages that are based on the abstract view from the previous version: RDF Schema and OWL. Quite a few other sources already exist that give general introductions to these languages. Some parts of the RDF and OWL specifications are intended as such introductions (in particular [13], [9] and [10]), and also didactic material such as [12] and [11].

Our presentation is structured along the so-called layering of OWL: OWL Lite, OWL DL and OWL Full. This layering is motivated by different requirements that different users have for a Web ontology language:

- RDF(S) is intended for those users primarily needing a classification hierarchy with typing of properties and meta-modelling facilities;
- OWL Lite adds the possibility to express definitions and axioms, together with a limited use of properties to define classes;
- OWL DL supports those users who want the maximum expressiveness while retaining good computational properties;
- OWL Full is meant for users who want maximum expressiveness with no computational guarantees.

Before discussing the language primitives of OWL Lite, we first discuss language elements from RDF and RDF Schema (RDF(S) for short). With the only purpose to simplify the presentation in this tutorial by obtaining a strict layering between RDF(S) and OWL Lite, we will restrict our discussion of RDF(S) to the case where the vocabulary is strictly partitioned, the meta-modelling and reification facilities are forbidden, as described in [12], also called "type separation" in [9]:

"Any resource is allowed to be only a class, a data type, a data type property, an object property, an individual, a data value, or part of the built-in vocabulary, and not more than one of these. This means that, for example, a class cannot at the same time be an individual, [...]"

Under this restriction, we have the following strict language inclusion relationship:

$$RDF(S) \subset OWL \text{ Lite} \subset OWL \text{ DL},$$

where $\subset$ stands for both syntactic and semantic language inclusion, in other words: every syntactically correct RDF(S) statement is also a correct OWL Lite statement, and every model of a RDF(S) ontology is also a model for the same ontology expressed in OWL Lite (and similarly for the other case). A similar but less strong restriction was proposed with RDFS(FA) [7], which does allow a class to be an instance of another class, as long as this is done in a stratified fashion. When dropping the restriction of a partitioned or stratified vocabulary for RDF(S), the first inclusion relationship no longer holds. In that case, RDF(S) is only a sublanguage of OWL Full. However, note that even in the general case when the inclusion does not hold RDF(S) and OWL Lite/DL can still easily inter-operate. Also note that the inclusion between OWL DL and OWL Full does not hold, intuitively due to the lack of reification in OWL DL and OWL Lite.

Before we discuss the different language primitives that we encounter along this set of inclusions, we first list some of our notational conventions.

We use the normative abstract syntax for OWL as defined in [15]. While this syntax in only meant for OWL itself, we use the same syntax for introducing RDF(S) in order to clarify the relation between the languages[1]. We will use symbols c_i for classes, e_i for objects, p_i for properties between objects, and o_i for ontologies. Whenever useful, we will prefix classes and instances with pseudo-namespaces to indicate the ontology in which these symbols occur, e.g. $o_1 e_1$ and $o_2 e_1$ are two different instances, the first occurring in ontology o_1, the second in ontology o_2.

Note that the XML-based syntax is far better known, but arguably not as readable. In fact, the XML-syntax is clearly geared towards machine processing, while the abstract syntax is tailored to human reading, thus our choice in this section. The reader should keep in mind that the characteristics of the ontology languages are independent of the syntax used.

3.1   RDF Schema

The most elementary building block of RDF(S) is a class, which defines a group of individuals that belong together because they share some properties. The following states that an instance e belongs to a class c:

Individual(e type(c)) ("e is of type c").

---

[1] Note that the semantics of the same constructs in RDF(S) and OWL can differ.

The second elementary statement of RDF(S) is the subsumption relation between classes: subClassOf:

$$\mathtt{subClassOf}(c_i\ c_j)$$

In RDF, instances are related to other instances through properties:

$$\mathtt{Individual}(e_i\ \mathtt{value}(p\ e_j))$$

Properties are characterised by their domain and range:

$$\mathtt{ObjectProperty}(p\ \mathtt{domain}(c_i)\mathtt{range}(c_j))$$

Finally, just as with classes, properties are organised in a subsumption hierarchy:

$$\mathtt{SubPropertyOf}(o_1 : p_i\ o_2 : p_j)$$

RDF and RDFS allow the representation of *some* ontological knowledge. The main modelling primitives of RDF/RDFS concern the organisation of vocabularies in typed hierarchies: subclass and subproperty relationships, domain and range restrictions, and instances of classes. However a number of other features are missing. Here we list a few:

- *Local scope of properties:* rdfs:domain and fs:range define a unique domain/range of a property for all classes. Thus in RDF Schema we cannot declare domain/range restrictions that apply to some classes only. For example, for the property "father of", the father of elephants are elephants, while the fathers of mice are mice.
- *Disjointness of classes:* Sometimes we wish to say that classes are disjoint. For example, male and female are disjoint. But in RDF Schema we can only state subclass relationships, e.g. female is a subclass of person.
- *Boolean combinations of classes:* Sometimes we wish to build new classes by combining other classes using union, intersection and complement. For example, we may wish to define the class person to be the disjoint union of the classes male and female. RDF Schema does not allow such definitions.
- *Cardinality restrictions:* Sometimes we wish to place restrictions on how many distinct values a property may take. For example, we would like to say that a car has at most four wheels. Again such restrictions are impossible to express in RDF Schema. Note that min cardinality restrictions can be expressed *for individuals* in RDF(S) by making use of the b-nodes.
- *Special characteristics of properties:* Sometimes it is useful to say that a property is *transitive* (like "greater than"), *unique* (like "has mother"), or the *inverse* of another property (like "eats" and "is eaten by").

Summary of Basic Features of RDF Schema.

- Classes and their instances
- Binary properties between objects
- Organisation of classes and properties in hierarchies
- Types for properties: domain and range restrictions

4   Web Ontology Language OWL

4.1   OWL Lite

One of the significant limitations of RDF Schema is the inability to make equality claims between individuals. Such equality claims are possible in OWL Lite:

$$\text{SameIndividual}(e_i \; e_j)$$

Besides equality between instances, OWL Lite also introduces constructions to state equality between classes and between properties. Although such equalities could already be expressed in an indirect way in RDF(S) (e.g., through a pair of mutual `Subclassof` or `SubPropertyOf` statements), this can be done directly in OWL Lite:

$$\text{EquivalentClasses}(c_1 \; c_j)$$
$$\text{EquivalentProperties}(p_1 \; p_j)$$

Just as importantly, as making positive claims about equality or subsumption relationships, is stating negative information about inequalities. A significant limitation of RDF(S)[2] is the inability to state such inequalities. Since OWL does not make the unique name assumption, two instances e_i and e_j are not automatically regarded as different. Such an inequality must be explicitly stated, as:

$$\text{DifferentIndividuals}(e_i \; e_j)$$

Because inequality between individuals is an often occurring and important statement (in many ontologies, all differently named individuals are assumed to be different, i.e. they embrace the unique name assumption), OWL Lite provides an abbreviated form:

$$\text{DifferentIndividuals}(e_1 \; ... \; e_4)$$

abbreviates the six `DifferentIndividuals` statements that would have been required for this.

Whereas the above constructions are aimed at instances and classes, OWL Lite also has constructs specifically aimed at properties. An often occurring phenomenon is that a property can be modelled in two directions. Examples are *ownerOf* vs. *ownedBy*, *contains* vs. *isContainedIn*, *childOf* vs. *parentOf* and countless others. The relationship between such pairs of properties is established by stating

$$\text{ObjectProperty}(p_i \; \text{inverseOf}(p_j))$$

Other vocabulary in OWL Lite (`TransitiveProperty` and `SymmetricProperty` are modifying a single property, rather then establishing a relation between two properties:

---

[2] But motivated by a deliberate design decision concerning the computational and conceptual complexity of the language.

$$\text{ObjectProperty}(o_1 : p_i \text{ Transitive})$$
$$\text{ObjectProperty}(o_1 : p_i \text{ Symmetric})$$

The main limitation of RDF(S) to represent knowledge in terms of concepts and their properties, is its inability to use properties in the local context of a class. As we have already noted, a property has a unique definition for its domain and for its range, and moreover the participation constraints of the instances of the domain and range classes to the property are not specifiable in RDF(S). So, in RDF(S) it is impossible to state whether a property is optional or required for the instances of the class (in other words: should it have at least one value or not), and whether it is single- or multi-valued (in other words: is it allowed to have more than one value or not). Technically, these restrictions constitute 0/1-cardinality constraints on the property. The case where a property is allowed to have at most one value for a given instance (i.e. a max-cardinality of 1) has a special name: FunctionalProperty. The case where the value of a property uniquely identifies the instance of which it is a value (i.e. the inverse property has a max-cardinality of 1) is called InverseFunctionalProperty. These two constructions allow for some interesting derivations under the OWL semantics: If an ontology models that any object can only have a single "age":

$$(\text{ObjectProperty age Functional})$$

then different age-values for two instances e_i and e_j allow us to infer that

$$\text{DifferentIndividuals}(e_i \ e_j)$$

(if two objects e_i and e_j have a different age, they must be different objects). Similarly, if an ontology states that social security numbers uniquely identify individuals, i.e.

$$\text{ObjectProperty}(\text{hasSSN InverseFunctional})$$

then the two facts

$$\text{Individual}(e_i \ \text{value}(\text{hasSSN 12345}))$$
$$\text{Individual}(e_j \ \text{value}(\text{hasSSN 12345}))$$

sanction the derivation of the fact

$$\text{SameIndividuals}(e_i \ e_j)$$

Although RDF(S) already allows to state domain and range restrictions, these are very limited. OWL Lite allows more refined version of these, local to the definition of a class:

$$\text{Class}(c_i \ \text{restriction}(p_i \ \text{allValuesFrom}(c_j)))$$

says that all p_i-values (if any) *for each member of* c_i must be members of c_j. This differs from the RDF(S) range restriction

$$\text{ObjectProperty}(p \ \text{range}(c_j))$$

which says that all p_i-values must be members of c_j, irrespective of whether they are members of c_i or not. This allows us to use the same property-name p_i with different range restrictions c_j depending on the class c_i to which p_i is applied. For example, take for p_i the property Parent. Then Parents of cats are cats, while Parents of dogs are dogs. An RDF(S) range restriction would not be able to capture this.

Similarly, although in RDF(S) we can define the range of a property, we cannot enforce that properties actually do have a value: we can state the authors write books:

$$\texttt{ObjectProperty(write domain(author) range(book))}$$

but we cannot enforce in RDF(S) that every author must have written at least one book. This is possible in OWL Lite:

$$\texttt{Class(author restriction(write someValuesFrom(book)))}$$

Technically speaking, these are just special cases of the general cardinality constraints allowed in OWL DL. The someValuesFrom corresponds to a min-cardinality constraint with value 1, and the functional property constraint mentioned above can be rewritten in this context with a max-cardinality constraint with value 1. These can also be stated directly:

$$\texttt{Class(author restriction(write minCardinality(1)))}$$
$$\texttt{Class(object restriction(age maxCardinality(1)))}$$

When a property has a minCardinality and maxCardinality constraints with the same value, these can be summarised by a single exact Cardinality constraint.

4.2   OWL DL

With the step from OWL Lite to OWL DL, we obtain a number of additional language constructs, which simplify the writing of an ontology, even if most of them could be written anyway in OWL Lite as macros. It is often useful to say that two classes are disjoint (which is much stronger than saying they are merely not equal):

$$\texttt{DisjointClasses}(c_i \; c_j)$$

OWL DL allows arbitrary Boolean algebraic expressions on either side of an equality of subsumption relation. For example

$$\texttt{SubClassOf}(c_i \; \texttt{unionOf}(c_j \; c_k))$$

In other words: c_i is not subsumed by either c_j or c_k, but is subsumed by their union. Similarly

$$\texttt{EquivalentClasses}(c_i \; \texttt{intersectionOf}(c_j c_k))$$

in other words: although c_i is subsumed by c_j and c_k (a statement already expressible in RDF(S)), stating that c_i is equivalent to their intersection is much stronger. An obvious example to think of here is "old men": "old men" are not just both old and men, but they are *exactly* the intersection of these two properties.

Of course, the `unionOf` and `intersectionOf` may be taken over more than two classes, and may occur in arbitrary Boolean combinations.

Besides disjunction (`unionOf`) and conjunction (`intersectionOf`), OWL DL completes the Boolean algebra by providing a construct for negation: `complementOf`:

$$\texttt{complementOf}(c_i\ c_j)$$

In fact, arbitrary class expressions can be used on either side of subsumption or equivalence axioms.

Note that all the additional OWL DL constructs introduced so far, are also indirectly expressible already in OWL Lite. For example, the disjointness between two classes c_i and $c_j$can be expressed by means of the following two statements in OWL Lite, for some fresh new property p:

$$\texttt{SubClassOf}(c_i\ \texttt{restriction}(p\ \texttt{minCardinality}(1)))$$
$$\texttt{SubClassOf}(c_j\ \texttt{restriction}(p\ \texttt{maxCardinality}(0)))$$

There are cases where it is not possible to define a class in terms of such algebraic expressions. This can be either impossible in principle. In such cases it is sometimes useful to simply enumerate sets of individuals to define a class. This is done in OWL DL with the `oneOf` construct:

$$\texttt{EquivalentClasses}(c_j\ \texttt{oneOf}(e_1\ \dots\ e_n))$$

Similar to defining a class by enumeration, we can define a property to have a specific value by stating the value:

$$\texttt{Class}(c_i\ \texttt{restriction}(p_j\ \texttt{hasValue}\ e_k))$$

The extension from OWL Lite to OWL DL also lifts the restriction on cardinality constraints to have only 0/1 values.

4.3   OWL Full

OWL Lite and DL are based on a strict segmentation of the vocabulary: no term can be both an instance and a class, or a class and a property, etc. Full RDF(S) is much more liberal: a class c_1 can have both a `type` and a `subClassOf` relation to a class c_2, and a class can even be an instance of itself. In fact, the class `Class` is a member of itself. OWL Full inherits from RDF(S) this liberal approach. This feature is crucial for using OWL as a meta-modelling language.

Schreiber [14] argues that this is exactly what is needed in many cases of practical ontology integration. When integrating two ontologies, opposite commitments have often been made in the two ontologies on whether something is modelled as a class or an instance. This is less unlikely than it may sound: is "747" an *instance* of the class of all airplane-types made by Boeing or is "747" a *subclass* of the class of all airplanes made by Boeing, and are particular jet planes instances of this subclass? Both points of view are defensible. In OWL Full, it is possible to have equality statements between a class and an instance.

In fact, just as in RDF Schema, OWL Full allows us even to apply the constructions of the language to themselves. It is perfectly legal to (say) apply a max-cardinality constraint of 2 on the subClassOf relationship. For this reason, OWL Full does not include OWL DL, in which the constructions of the language are not semantic objects. Of course, building any complete and terminating reasoning tools that support this very liberal self-application of the language is out of the question. In fact, the theory shows that it is impossible to build a correct and complete inference engine for OWL Full.

5   Other Web-Based Ontology Languages

Besides the two standards RDF Schema and OWL discussed above, a number of other approaches for encoding ontologies on the World Wide Web have been proposed in the past. A comparison of these older languages is reported in [16]. We will now briefly review the results of this comparison and discuss implications for our work.

Besides RDF Schema and OWL[3], which have been introduced above, the comparison reported in [16] includes the following languages that have been selected on the basis of their aim of supporting knowledge representation on the Web and their compatibility to the Web standards XML or RDF.

- *XOL (XML-based ontology language)*. XOL [4] has been proposed as a language for exchanging formal knowledge models in the domain of bio-informatics. The development of XOL has been guided by the representational needs of the domain and by existing frame-based knowledge representation languages.
- *SHOE (simple HTML ontology extension)*. SHOE[6] was created as an extension of HTML for the purpose of defining machine-readable semantic knowledge. The aim of SHOE is to enable intelligent Web agents to retrieve and gather knowledge more precisely than it is possible in the presence of plain HTML documents.
- *OML: (ontology markup language)*. OML [5] is an ontology language that has initially been developed as an XML serialisation of SHOE. Meanwhile, the language consists of different layers with increasing expressiveness. The semantics especially of the higher levels is largely based on the notion of conceptual graphs. In the comparison, however, only a less expressive subset of OML (simple OML) is considered.

---

[3] Actually, [16] discuss DAML+OIL instead of OWL. DAML+OIL [8] is the direct precursor of OWL, and all of the conclusions from [16] about DAML+OIL are also valid for OWL.

Table 1. Comparison of web ontology languages with respect to concepts and taxonomies (taken from [16])

	XOL	SHOE	OML	RDF/S	OIL	DAML+OIL
Partitions	–	–	+	–	+	+
Attributes						
Instance attr.	+	+	+	+	+	+
Class attr.	+	–	+	–	+	+
Local scope	+	+	+	+	+	+
Global scope	+	–	+	+	+	+
Facets						
Default values	+	–	–	–	–	–
Type constr.	+	+	+	+	+	+
Cardinalities	+	–	–	–	+	+
Taxonomies						
Subclass of	+	+	+	+	+	+
Exhaustive comp.	–	–	+	–	+	+
Disjoint comp.	–	–	+	–	+	+
Not subclass of	–	–	–	–	+	+

– *OIL (ontology inference layer)*. OIL [3] is an attempt to develop an ontology
language for the Web that has a well defined semantics and sophisticated
reasoning support for ontology development and use. The language is constructed in a layered way starting with core-OIL, providing a formal semantics for RDF Schema, standard-OIL, which is equivalent to an expressive
description logic with reasoning support, and Instance OIL that adds the
possibility of defining instances.

We have to mention that there is a strong relationship between the OIL language
and RDF Schema as well as DAML+OIL. OIL extends RDF Schema and has
been the main influence in the development if DAML+OIL. The main difference
between OIL and DAML+OIL is an extended expressiveness of DAML+OIL
in terms of complex definitions of individuals and data types. DAML+OIL in
turn has been the basis for the development of OWL, which carries the stamp
of an official W3C recommendation. All observations on DAML+OIL in this
comparison also apply to OWL.

6 Description Logics

We briefly now introduce description logics, which is the logic-based formalism
which is behind the OWL family of web ontology languages. From this brief
Section the parallel with the OWL family of web ontology languages will appear
clear. An extensive treatment of description logics, from friendly introductory
chapters, to the theoretical results, up to the description of applications and
systems, can be found in the Handbook of Description Logics [1]. Consistently

with the informal notion of semantics introduced above for the web ontology languages, description logics are considered as a *structured* fragment of predicate logic. $\mathcal{ALC}$ is the minimal description language including full negation and disjunction—i.e., propositional calculus.

The basic types of a DL language are *concepts*, *roles*, and *features*. A concept is a description gathering the common properties among a collection of individuals; from a logical point of view it is a unary predicate ranging over the domain of individuals. A concept corresponds to a class in the web ontology languages. Inter-relationships between these individuals are represented either by means of roles (which are interpreted as binary relations over the domain of individuals) or by means of features (which are interpreted as partial functions over the domain of individuals). Roles correspond to properties of RDF and OWL, while features correspond to functional properties. In this Section, we will consider the Description Logic $\mathcal{ALCQI}$, extending $\mathcal{ALC}$ with qualified cardinality restrictions and inverse roles.

According to the syntax rules of Figure 1, $\mathcal{ALCQI}$ concepts (denoted by the letters C and D) are built out of *primitive concepts* (denoted by the letter A), *roles* (denoted by the letter R), and *primitive features* (denoted by the letter f); roles are built out of *primitive roles* (denoted by the letter P) and *primitive features*. The top part of Figure 1 defines the $\mathcal{ALC}$ sublanguage. Please also note that features are introduced as shortcuts; in fact, they can be expressed by means of axioms using cardinality restrictions, as we already noticed for OWL DL.

$$
\begin{aligned}
C, D \rightarrow \ & A \mid & A & \qquad \text{(primitive conc.)} \\
& \top \mid & \texttt{top} & \qquad \text{(top)} \\
& \bot \mid & \texttt{bottom} & \qquad \text{(bottom)} \\
& \neg C \mid & (\texttt{not } C) & \qquad \text{(complement)} \\
& C \sqcap D \mid & (\texttt{and } C\ D\ \ldots) & \qquad \text{(conjunction)} \\
& C \sqcup D \mid & (\texttt{or } C\ D\ \ldots) & \qquad \text{(disjunction)} \\
& \forall R.\,C \mid & (\texttt{all } R\ C) & \qquad \text{(univ. quantifier)} \\
& \exists R.\,C \mid & (\texttt{some } R\ C) & \qquad \text{(exist. quantifier)} \\[1em]
& f{\uparrow} \mid & (\texttt{undefined } f) & \qquad \text{(undefinedness)} \\
& f : C \mid & (\texttt{in } f\ C) & \qquad \text{(selection)} \\
& {\geq}n\,R.\,C \mid & (\texttt{atleast } n\ R\ C) & \qquad \text{(min cardinality)} \\
& {\leq}n\,R.\,C & (\texttt{atmost } n\ R\ C) & \qquad \text{(max cardinality)} \\[1em]
R \rightarrow \ & P \mid & P & \qquad \text{(primitive role)} \\
& f \mid & f & \qquad \text{(primitive feature)} \\
& R^{-1} & (\texttt{inverse } R) & \qquad \text{(inverse role)}
\end{aligned}
$$

Fig. 1. Syntax rules for $\mathcal{ALCQI}$

$$\top^{\mathcal{I}} = \Delta^{\mathcal{I}}$$
$$\bot^{\mathcal{I}} = \emptyset$$
$$(\neg C)^{\mathcal{I}} = \Delta^{\mathcal{I}} \setminus C^{\mathcal{I}}$$
$$(C \sqcap D)^{\mathcal{I}} = C^{\mathcal{I}} \cap D^{\mathcal{I}}$$
$$(C \sqcup D)^{\mathcal{I}} = C^{\mathcal{I}} \cup D^{\mathcal{I}}$$
$$(\forall R.\, C)^{\mathcal{I}} = \{i \in \Delta^{\mathcal{I}} \mid \forall j.\, R^{\mathcal{I}}(i,j) \Rightarrow C^{\mathcal{I}}(j)\}$$
$$(\exists R.\, C)^{\mathcal{I}} = \{i \in \Delta^{\mathcal{I}} \mid \exists j.\, R^{\mathcal{I}}(i,j) \wedge C^{\mathcal{I}}(j)\}$$
$$(f\uparrow)^{\mathcal{I}} = \Delta^{\mathcal{I}} \setminus \operatorname{dom} f^{\mathcal{I}}$$
$$(f : C)^{\mathcal{I}} = \{i \in \operatorname{dom} f^{\mathcal{I}} \mid C^{\mathcal{I}}(f^{\mathcal{I}}(i))\}$$
$$(\geq n\, R.\, C)^{\mathcal{I}} = \{i \in \Delta^{\mathcal{I}} \mid \sharp\{j \in \Delta^{\mathcal{I}} \mid R^{\mathcal{I}}(i,j) \wedge C^{\mathcal{I}}(j)\} \geq n\}$$
$$(\leq n\, R.\, C)^{\mathcal{I}} = \{i \in \Delta^{\mathcal{I}} \mid \sharp\{j \in \Delta^{\mathcal{I}} \mid R^{\mathcal{I}}(i,j) \wedge C^{\mathcal{I}}(j)\} \leq n\}$$
$$(R^{-1})^{\mathcal{I}} = \{(i,j) \in \Delta^{\mathcal{I}} \times \Delta^{\mathcal{I}} \mid R^{\mathcal{I}}(j,i)\}$$

Fig. 2. Extensional semantics of $\mathcal{ALCQI}$

Let us now consider the formal semantics of $\mathcal{ALCQI}$. We define the *meaning* of concepts as sets of individuals—as for unary predicates—and the meaning of roles as sets of pairs of individuals—as for binary predicates. This is the formalised notion of instantiation of the domain we introduced at the beginning of this chapter. Formally, an *interpretation* is a pair $\mathcal{I} = (\Delta^{\mathcal{I}}, \cdot^{\mathcal{I}})$ consisting of a set $\Delta^{\mathcal{I}}$ of individuals (the *domain* of $\mathcal{I}$) and a function $\cdot^{\mathcal{I}}$ (the *interpretation function* of $\mathcal{I}$) mapping every concept to a subset of $\Delta^{\mathcal{I}}$, every role to a subset of $\Delta^{\mathcal{I}} \times \Delta^{\mathcal{I}}$, and every feature to a partial function from $\Delta^{\mathcal{I}}$ to $\Delta^{\mathcal{I}}$, such that the equations in Figure 2 are satisfied. The semantics of the language can also be given by stating equivalences among expressions of the language and First Order Logic formulae. An atomic concept A, an atomic role P, and an atomic feature f, are mapped respectively to the open formulae $A(\gamma)$, $P(\alpha, \beta)$, and $f(\alpha, \beta)$ – with f a functional relation, also written $f(\alpha) = \beta$. Figure 3 gives the transformational semantics of $\mathcal{ALCQI}$ expressions in terms of equivalent FOL well-formed formulae. A concept C and a role R correspond to the FOL open formulae $F_C(\gamma)$ and $F_R(\alpha, \beta)$ respectively. It is worth noting that, using the standard model-theoretic semantics, the extensional semantics of Figure 2 can be derived from the transformational semantics of Figure 3.

For example, we can consider the concept of HAPPY FATHERS, defined using the primitive concepts Man, Doctor, Rich, Famous and the roles CHILD, FRIEND. The concept HAPPY FATHERS can be expressed in $\mathcal{ALCQI}$ as

Man $\sqcap$ ($\exists$CHILD. $\top$)$\sqcap$
$\forall$CHILD. (Doctor $\sqcap$ $\exists$FRIEND. (Rich $\sqcup$ Famous)),

i.e., those men having some child and all of whose children are doctors having some friend who is rich or famous.

An ontology is called in DL a *knowledge base*, and formally it is a finite set Σ of *terminological axioms* – these are the ontology statements; it can also be called a *terminology* or TBox. For a concept name A, and (possibly complex)

$$\top^{\mathcal{I}} \sim \text{true}$$
$$\bot^{\mathcal{I}} \sim \text{false}$$
$$(\neg C)^{\mathcal{I}} \sim \neg F_C(\gamma)$$
$$(C \sqcap D)^{\mathcal{I}} \sim F_C(\gamma) \wedge F_D(\gamma)$$
$$(C \sqcup D)^{\mathcal{I}} \sim F_C(\gamma) \vee F_D(\gamma)$$
$$(\exists R.\, C)^{\mathcal{I}} \sim \exists x.\, F_R(\gamma, x) \wedge F_C(x)$$
$$(\forall R.\, C)^{\mathcal{I}} \sim \forall x.\, F_R(\gamma, x) \Rightarrow F_C(x)$$
$$(f \uparrow)^{\mathcal{I}} \sim \neg \exists x.\, f(\gamma, x)$$
$$(f : C)^{\mathcal{I}} \sim \exists x.\, f(\gamma, x) \wedge F_C(x)$$
$$(\geq n\, R.\, C)^{\mathcal{I}} \sim \exists^{\geq n} x.\, F_R(\gamma, x) \wedge F_C(x)$$
$$(\leq n\, R.\, C)^{\mathcal{I}} \sim \exists^{\leq n} x.\, F_R(\gamma, x) \wedge F_C(x)$$
$$(R^{-1})^{\mathcal{I}} \sim F_R(\beta, \alpha)$$

Fig. 3. FOL semantics of $\mathcal{ALCQI}$

concepts C, D, terminological axioms are of the form $A \doteq C$ (concept definition), $A \sqsubseteq C$ (primitive concept definition), $C \sqsubseteq D$ (general inclusion statement). An interpretation $\mathcal{I}$ satisfies $C \sqsubseteq D$ if and only if the interpretation of C is included in the interpretation of D, i.e., $C^{\mathcal{I}} \subseteq D^{\mathcal{I}}$. It is clear that the last kind of axiom is a generalisation of the first two: concept definitions of the type $A \doteq C$ – where A is an atomic concept – can be reduced to the pair of axioms $(A \sqsubseteq C)$ and $(C \sqsubseteq A)$. Another class of terminological axioms – pertaining to roles R, S – are of the form $R \sqsubseteq S$. Again, an interpretation $\mathcal{I}$ satisfies $R \sqsubseteq S$ if and only if the interpretation of R – which is now a set of *pairs* of individuals – is included in the interpretation of S, i.e., $R^{\mathcal{I}} \subseteq S^{\mathcal{I}}$. An interpretation $\mathcal{I}$ is a *model* of a knowledge base Σ iff every terminological axiom of Σ is satisfied by $\mathcal{I}$. If Σ has a model, then it is *satisfiable*; thus, checking for KB satisfiability is deciding whether there is at least one model for the knowledge base. Σ *logically implies* an axiom α (written $\Sigma \models \alpha$) if α is satisfied by every model of Σ. We say that a concept C is *subsumed* by a concept D in a knowledge base Σ (written $\Sigma \models C \sqsubseteq D$) if $C^{\mathcal{I}} \subseteq D^{\mathcal{I}}$ for every model $\mathcal{I}$ of Σ. For example, the concept

> Person $\sqcap$ ($\exists$CHILD. Person)

denoting the class of PARENTS—i.e., the persons having at least a child which is a person—subsumes the concept

> Man $\sqcap$ ($\exists$CHILD. $\top$)$\sqcap$
> $\forall$CHILD. (Doctor $\sqcap$ $\exists$FRIEND. (Rich $\sqcup$ Famous))

denoting the class of HAPPY FATHERS – with respect to the following knowledge base Σ:

> Doctor $\doteq$ Person $\sqcap$ $\exists$DEGREE. Phd,
> Man $\doteq$ Person $\sqcap$ sex : Male,

i.e., every happy father is also a person having at least one child, given the background knowledge that men are male persons, and that doctors are persons.

A concept C is satisfiable, given a knowledge base Σ, if there is at least one model $\mathcal{I}$ of Σ such that $C^{\mathcal{I}} \neq \emptyset$, i.e. $\Sigma \not\models C \equiv \bot$. For example, the concept

$$(\exists \texttt{CHILD.Man}) \sqcap (\forall \texttt{CHILD.}(\texttt{sex} : \neg \texttt{Male}))$$

is unsatisfiable with respect to the above knowledge base Σ. In fact, an individual whose children are not male cannot have a child being a man.

7   The Importance of Correct Inference

An ontology inference engine based on description logics (such as iFaCT or Racer) can offer a reasoning service to applications willing to properly use an ontology. As we have already noticed, the inferential process's complexity depends strictly on the adopted ontology language's expressivity: the inference engine becomes increasingly complex as the ontology language becomes more expressive. In fact, theoreticians have proved that you can't build a complete inference engine for OWL Full, although it's possible to use existing description logic systems as inference engines for OWL Lite and OWL DL.

Designing and implementing complete inference engines for expressive ontology languages isn't easy. As a prerequisite, you must have formal proof that the algorithms are complete with respect to the ontology language's declared semantics. The description logics community – which provides the theoretical foundations to the OWL family of web ontology languages – has 20-plus years of experience to help provide theoretical results, algorithms, and efficient inference systems for all but the most expressive OWL languages. We can understand how important it is for an inference engine to be complete with the following example.

Suppose a military agency asks you to write an ontology to recognise whether a particular individual description indicates some sort of "enemy" concept so that an application can take appropriate automatic action (such as shooting) given the inference engine's answer. If the inference engine is sound but incomplete, it will recognise most but not all enemies because it isn't a complete reasoner. Because it is sound, however, it won't confuse a friendly soldier with an enemy. So, the application will start the automatic shooting procedure only when the system recognises without doubt that someone is an enemy. The application could fail to shoot an enemy, but field soldiers can take traditional backup (nonautomatic) action. Soundness is more important because you don't want to shoot your own soldiers. So far, so good.

The agency has another application strictly related to the first one. The task is now to recognise an individual description as an allied soldier to activate automatic procedures that will alert the soldier to the headquarters' secret position. Again, the system must have a sound inference engine because the agency doesn't want to disclose secret information to enemies. Moreover, incompleteness is not a major problem because the defence system can still be valid even if a soldier doesn't know where the headquarters is located.

The agency decides, of course, to use the same shared ontology for both applications. After all, the task in one case is to decide whether a soldier is an enemy and in the other case decide whether he or she isn't. So the second application can use the same ontology as the first, but it exploits the outcome in a dual way. Unfortunately, it turns out that the agency can't use the same ontology for both tasks if the ontology language's inference engine is sound but incomplete. If a sound but incomplete reasoning system exists for solving, say, the first problem (recognising enemies), you can't use the same reasoning system as a sound (and possibly incomplete) procedure for solving the second problem (recognising allies). In fact, using the same procedure for solving the second problem would be unsound – it will say an individual isn't an enemy when he or she actually is. Although this is harmless for the first problem, it is bad for the second, dual one. It would disclose valuable military secrets to enemies.

To solve this problem, one must have both a sound and complete inference engine for the ontology language. This rules out using OWL Full for the above application because having a complete inference engine with this language is impossible. The same of course holds for OWL DL inference engines without guaranteed completeness properties.

It is important that Semantic Web application developers consider properly whether such completeness properties are required for their applications.

References

1. F. Baader, D. Calvanese, D. McGuinness, D. Nardi, and P. F. Patel-Schneider, editors. *Description Logic Handbook: Theory, Implementation and Applications.* Cambridge University Press, 2003.
2. F. van Harmelen and D. Fensel. Practical Knowledge Representation for the Web. In *Proc. IJCAI'99 Workshop on Intelligent Information Integration,* 1999
3. D. Fensel, I. Horrocks, F. van Harmelen, D.L. McGuinness and Peter F. Patel-Schneider. OIL: An Ontology Infrastructure for the Semantic Web. *IEEE Intelligent Systems* 16,2 (2001): 38-44
4. P. Karp, V. Chaudri and J. Thomere. An XML-Based Ontology Exchange Language. Available at http://www.ai.sri.com/~ pkarp/xol
5. R. Kent. Conceptual Knowledge Modelling Language. Available at http://www.ontologos.org/CKML/
6. S. Luke and J. Hefflin. SHOE 1.01 Proposal Specification. Available at http://www.cs.umd.edu/projects/plus/SHOE
7. J. Pan and I. Horrocks. (FA) and RDF MT: Two Semantics for RDFS. In *Proc. 2003 International Semantic Web Conference (ISWC 2003),* LNCS 2870, Springer 2003,30-46
8. P. Patel-Schneider, I. Horrocks and F. van Harmelen. Reviewing the Design of DAML+OIL: An Ontology Language for the Semantic Web. In *Proc. Eighteenth National Conference on Artificial Intelligence,* AAAI Pres 2002
9. D.L. McGuinness and F. van Harmelen. OWL Web Ontology Language Overview. Available at http://www.w3.org/TR/owl-features/
10. M.K. Smith, Chris Welty and D.L. McGuinness. OWL Web Ontology Language Guide. Available at http://www.w3.org/TR/owl-guide/
11. G. Antoniou and F. van Harmelen. Web Ontology Language: OWL. In S. Staab and R. Studer (Eds), *Handbook on Ontologies in Information Systems,* Springer 2003

12. G. Antoniou and F. van Harmelen. *A Semantic Web Primer*, MIT Press 2004
13. F. Manola and E. Miller. RDF Primer. Available at http://www.w3c.or.kr/ Translation/PR-rdf-primer-20031215/
14. G. Schreiber. The Web is not well-formed. *IEEE Intelligent Systems* 17,2 (2002)
15. P.F. Patel-Schneider, P. Hayes and I. Horrocks. OWL Web Ontology Language Semantics and Abstract Syntax. Available at http://www.w3.org/TR/owl-semantics/
16. A. Gomez-Perez and O. Corcho. Ontology Languages for the Semantic Web. *IEEE Intelligent Systems* 2002, 54-60

Rules and Ontologies in F-Logic[*]

Department of Computer Science,
State University of New Your at Stony Brook,
Stony Brook, NY 11794, U.S.A.
`kifer@cs.stonybrook.edu`

Abstract. F-logic is a formalism that integrates logic with object-oriented programming in a clean and declarative fashion. It has been successfully used for information integration, ontology modeling, agent-based systems, software engineering, and more. This paper gives a brief overview of F-logic and discusses its features from the point of view of an ontology language.

1 Introduction

F-logic [15] extends classical predicate calculus with the concepts of objects, classes, and types, which are adapted from object-oriented programming. In this way, F-logic integrates the paradigms of logic programming and deductive databases with the object-oriented programming paradigm.

Most of the applications of F-logic have been as a language for intelligent information systems based on the logic programming paradigm, and this was the original motivation for the development of F-logic. More recently, F-logic has been used to represent ontologies and other forms of Semantic Web reasoning [9, 8, 25, 1, 7, 4, 14].

Currently several implementations of the rule-based subset of F-logic are available. Ontobroker [20] is a commercial F-logic based engine developed by Ontoprise. It is designed as a knowledge-base component for a Java application. FLORA-2 [32] is an open-source system that was developed at Stony Brook as part of a research project. Unlike Ontobroker which is designed to serve Java applications, FLORA-2 is a complete programming environment for developing knowledge-intensive applications. It integrates F-logic with other novel formalisms such as HiLog [6] and Transaction Logic [5]. TRIPLE [23] is a partial implementation of F-logic with a particular emphasis on interoperability with RDF. Older systems based on F-logic are also available: SILRI[1] and FLORID.[2]

In this paper we first survey the main features of F-logic and then discuss its use as an ontology language.

---

[*] This work was supported in part by NSF grant CCR-0311512 and by U.S. Army Medical Research Institute under a subcontract through Brookhaven National Lab.
[1] http://ontobroker.semanticweb.org/silri/
[2] http://www.informatik.uni-freiburg.de/ dbis/florid/

N. Eisinger and J. Małuszyński (Eds.): Reasoning Web 2005, LNCS 3564, pp. 22–34, 2005.
© Springer-Verlag Berlin Heidelberg 2005

2   Overview of F-Logic

F-logic extends and subsumes predicate calculus both syntactically and semantically. In particular, it has a monotonic logical entailment relationship, and its proof theory is sound and complete with respect to the semantics. F-logic comes in two flavors: the first-order flavor and the logic programming flavor. The first-order flavor of F-logic can be viewed as a syntactic variant of classical logic, which makes an implementation through source-level translation possible [15, 27, 32]. The logic programming flavor uses a subset of the syntax of F-logic, but gives it a different, non-first-order semantics.

To understand the relationship between the first-order variant of F-logic and its logic programming variant, recall that standard logic programming [17] is built on top of the rule-based subset of the classical predicate calculus by adding non-monotonic extensions. By analogy, object-oriented logic programming is built on the rule-based subset of F-logic by adding the appropriate non-monotonic extensions [31, 32, 20]. These extensions are intended to capture the semantics of negation-as-failure (like in standard logic programming [26]) and the semantics of multiple inheritance with overriding (which does not arise in the standard case).

2.1   Basic Syntax

F-logic uses first-order variable-free terms to represent *object identity* (abbr., OID); for instance, john and father(mary) are possible Ids of objects. Objects can have single-valued or set-valued attributes. For instance,

    mary[spouse → john, children ↠ {alice,nancy}].
    mary[children ↠ {jack}].

Such formulas are called F-logic *molecules*. The first formula says that object mary has an attribute spouse, which is single-valued and whose value is the OID john. It also says that the attribute children is set-valued and its value is a set that *contains* two OIDs: alice and nancy. We emphasize "contains" because sets do not need to be specified all at once. For instance, the second formula above says that mary has an additional child, jack.

While some attributes of an object are specified explicitly, as facts, other attributes can be defined using deductive rules. For instance, we can derive john[children ↠ {alice, nancy, jack}] using the following deductive rule:

    X[children ↠ {C}] :- Y[spouse → X, children ↠ {C}].

Here we adopt the standard convention in logic programming that uppercase symbols denote variables while symbols beginning with a lowercase letter denote constants.

F-logic objects can also have *methods*, which are functions that take arguments. For instance,

    john[grade(cs305,fall2004) → 100, courses(fall2004) ↠ {cs305,cs306}].

says that john has a single-valued method, grade, whose value on the arguments cs305 (a course identifier) and fall2004 (a semester designation) is 100; it also has a set-valued method courses, whose value on the argument fall2004 is a set of OIDs that contains course identifiers cs305 and cs306. Like attributes, methods can be defined using deductive rules.

The F-logic syntax for *class membership* is john:student and for *subclass relationship* it is student::person. Classes are treated as objects and it is possible for the same object to play the role of a class in one formula and of an object in another. For instance, in the formula student:class, the symbol student plays the role of an object, while in student::person it appears in the role of a class.

In addition, F-logic provides the means for specifying schema information through *signature* formulas. For instance, person[name ⇒ string, child ⇒⇒ person] is a signature formula that says that class person has two attributes: a single-valued attribute name and a set-valued attribute child. It further says that, the first attribute returns objects of type string and the second returns sets of objects such that each object in the set is of type person. F-logic also supports first-order predicate syntax and in this way it extends classical predicate calculus and integrates the relational and object-oriented paradigms in knowledge representation.

We remark that attempts are being made to unify the syntax of the various implementations of F-logic, such as Ontobroker [20] and FLORA-2 [32]. Among the more significant forthcoming changes (as far as this overview goes) are that all attributes will be treated as set-valued (for which → will be used instead of ↠). To capture the single-valued attributes of old, cardinality constraints will be introduced. The syntax of variables will also change: instead of capitalization, all variables will be prefixed with the "?" prefix.

2.2   Querying Meta-information

F-logic provides simple and natural means for exploring the structure of object data. Both schema information associated with classes and the structure of individual objects can be queried by simply putting variables in the appropriate syntactic positions. For instance, to find the set-valued methods that are defined in the *schema* of class student and return objects of type person, one can ask the following query:

?- student[M ⇒⇒ person].

The next query is about the type of the results of the attribute name in class student. In addition, the query returns all the superclasses of class student.

?- student::C and student[name ⇒ T].

The above queries are *schema-level meta-queries* because they involve the subclass relationship and the type information (as indicated by the operators ::, ⇒, and ⇒⇒). In contrast, the following queries involve object data (rather than schema); they return the methods that have a known value for the object with the OID john:

```
?- john[SingleM → SomeValue].
?- john[SetM →→ SomeValue].
```

Like the previous queries, the last two deal with meta-information about objects, but they examine object data rather than schema. Therefore, they are called *instance-level meta-queries*. The two kinds of meta-queries can return different results for several reasons. First, in case of semistructured data, schema information might be incomplete, so additional attributes might be defined for individual objects but not mentioned in the schema. Second, even if the schema is complete, the values of some attributes can be undefined for some objects. In this case, the undefined attributes will not be returned by instance-level meta-queries, but they would be returned by schema-level meta-queries.

2.3   Path Expressions

In addition to the basic syntax, F-logic supports so-called *path expressions*, which generalize the dot-notation in object-oriented programming languages such as Java or C++. Path expressions simplify navigation along attribute and method invocations, and help avoid explicit join conditions [10].

A *single-valued* path expression, $O.M$, refers to the *unique* object R for which $O[M \rightarrow R]$ holds; a *set-valued* path expression, $O..M$, refers to some object, R, such that $O[M \twoheadrightarrow \{R\}]$ holds. Here the symbols O and M can be either OIDs or other path expressions. Furthermore, M can be a method with arguments. For instance, $O.M(P_1,\ldots,P_k)$ is a valid path expression that refers to the object R that satisfies $O[M(P_1,\ldots,P_k) \rightarrow R]$.

Since path expressions can occur anywhere an OID is allowed, they can be nested within other F-logic molecules and provide alternative and much more concise ways of addressing objects in a knowledge base. For instance, the path expression

```
Paper[authors →→ {Author[name → john]}].publication..editors
```

refers to all editors of those papers in which john is the name of a coauthor. An equivalent representation in terms of the basic F-logic syntax would be

```
Paper[authors →→ Author] and Author[name → john] and
Paper[publication → P] and P[editor →→ E]
```

The reader has probably noticed the conceptual similarity between the path expressions in F-logic, introduced in [10], and the language of XPath, which was developed later but with a similar purpose in mind.

2.4   Additional Features

F-logic includes a number of other language constructs that can be very useful in knowledge representation in general and on the Semantic Web in particular. One of these important features is the equality predicate, :=:, which can be used to declare two objects to be the same. For instance, mary :=: mother(john) asserts that the object with the OID mary and the object with the OID mother(john) are one and the same object. The presence of explicit equality goes against the grain of standard logic programming, which assumes a particular built-in theory of equality, where two variable-free terms are equal if and only if they are identical. A common use of explicit equality on the Semantic Web is to provide assertions stating that a pair of syntactically different URIs refer to the same document.

Another important feature of some of the F-logic implementations, such as FLORA-2, is integration with HiLog [6]. This allows a higher degree of meta-programming in a clean and logical way. For instance, one can ask a query of the form

?- person[M(Arg) $\Rightarrow$ person].

and obtain a set of all methods that take one argument, are declared to be part of the schema of class person, and return results that are objects belonging to class person. Note that M(Arg) is not a first-order term, since it has a variable in the position of a function symbol; such terms are not allowed in Prolog-based logic programming languages.

Later additions to F-logic include reification and anonymous object identity [30, 14]. Both features are deemed to be important for Semantic Web and are included in RDF [16, 13]. It has been argued, however, that the RDF formalization of these notions is less that optimal and that the proposal requires significant extensions in order to be useful for advanced applications [30]. A convincing use of the extensions provided by F-logic has been given in [14] in the context of Semantic Web Services.

2.5   Inheritance

F-logic supports both *structural* and *behavioral* inheritance. The former refers to inheritance of method types from superclasses to their subclasses and the latter deals with inheritance of method definitions from superclasses to subclasses.

Structural inheritance is defined by very simple inference rules:

If   subcl::cl, cl[attr $\star\Rightarrow$ type]   **then**   subcl[attr $\star\Rightarrow$ type]
If   obj:cl, cl[attr $\star\Rightarrow$ type]   **then**   obj[attr $\Rightarrow$ type]

Similar rules hold for the types of the multi-valued attributes, which are designated using the arrows $\star\Rightarrow\!\!\Rightarrow$ and $\Rightarrow\!\!\Rightarrow$. The statement cl[attr $\star\Rightarrow$ type] in the above rules states that attr is an *inheritable* attribute, which means that both its type and value are inheritable by the subclasses and members of class cl. Inheritability of the type of an attribute is indicated with the star attached to the symbol $\star\Rightarrow$. In all previous examples we have been dealing with *non-inheritable* attributes, which were designated with star-less arrows. Note that when the type of an attribute is inherited to a subclass it remains inheritable. However, when it is inherited to a member of the class it is no longer inheritable.

Type inheritance is not overridable; instead all types accumulate. For instance, from

```
faculty::employee.
manager::employee.
john:faculty.
faculty[reportsTo *⇒ faculty].
employee[reportsTo *⇒ manager].
```

we can derive two statements by inheritance: john[reportsTo *⇒ faculty] and john[reportsTo *⇒ manager]. The type expression for the more specific super-class, faculty, does not override the type expression for the less specific class employee. The intended interpretation is that whoever john reports to must be both a manager and an employee. These two statements can be replaced with a single statement of the form john[reportsTo *⇒ (faculty and manager)].

Behavioral inheritance is more complex. To get a flavour of behavioral inheritance, consider the following small knowledge base:

```
royalElephant::elephant.
clyde:royalElephant.
elephant[color *→ grey].
royalElephant[color *→ white].
```

Like with type definitions, a star attached to the arrow, $\star\!\to$, designates an inheritable method. For instance, color is an inheritable attribute in classes elephant and royalElephant. The inference rule that guides behavioral inheritance can informally be stated as follows. If obj is an object and cl is a class, then

$$\text{obj:cl, cl[attr} \star\!\to \text{value]} \quad \text{should imply} \quad \text{obj[attr} \to \text{value]}$$

unless the inheritance is overwritten by a more specific class. The meaning of the exception here is that the knowledge base should *not* imply the formula obj[attr → value] if there is an intermediate class, cl′, which overrides the inheritance, i.e., if obj : cl′, cl′ :: cl are true and cl′[attr *→ value′] (for some value′ ≠ value) is defined explicitly.[3] A similar exception exists in case of multiple inheritance conflicts. Note that inheritable attributes become non-inheritable after they are inherited by class members. In the above case, inheritance of the grey color is overwritten by the white color and so clyde[color → white] is derived by the rule of inheritance.

2.6   Semantics

The semantics of F-logic is based on the notion of F-structures, which extend the notion of semantic structures in classical predicate calculus. OIDs are interpreted in F-structures as elements of the domain and methods (and attributes) are interpreted as partial functions of suitable arities. The first argument of each such function is the Id of the object in whose context the method or the attribute

---

[3] The notion of an explicit definition seems obvious at first but, in fact, is quite subtle. Details can be found in [28].

is defined. Signature formulas are interpreted by functions whose properties are made to fit the common properties of types. Details of F-structures can be found in [15].

Armed with the notion of the F-structures, a first-order entailment relation is defined in a standard way: $\phi \models \psi$ if and only if every F-structure that satisfies ϕ also satisfies ψ. This entailment together with the sound and complete resolution-based proof theory [15] are the basis of the first-order variant of F-logic.

The semantics of the logic programming variant of F-logic is built by analogy with the corresponding development in deductive databases. The meaning of negation is made non-monotonic and is based on an extension of the well-founded semantics [26]. The interesting and nontrivial aspect of this extension is not due to negation (negation is handled analogously to [26]) but due to the behavioral inheritance with overriding. Earlier we have seen an informal account of inference by inheritance. Although the rules of such inference seem natural, they present subtle problems when behavioral inheritance is used together with deductive rules. To understand the problem, consider the following example.

```
cl[attr *→ v1].
subcl::cl.
obj:subcl.
subcl[attr *→ v2] :- obj[attr → v1].
```

If we apply the rule of inheritance to this knowledge base, then `obj[attr → v1]` should be inherited, since no overriding takes place. However, once `obj[attr →` `v1]` is derived by inheritance, `subcl[attr *→ v2]` can be derived by deduction, and now we have a chicken-and-egg problem. Since `subcl` is a more specific super-class of `obj`, the derivation of `subcl[attr *→ v2]` appears to override the earlier inheritance of `obj[attr → v1]`. But this, in turn, undermines the reason for deriving `subcl[attr *→ v2]`. The above is only one of several suspicious derivation patterns that arise due to interaction of inheritance and deduction. The original solution reported in [15] was not model-theoretic and was problematic in several other respects as well. A satisfactory and completely model-theoretic solution was proposed in [28, 29].

3   F-Logic as an Ontology Language

From the beginning, F-logic has been viewed as a natural candidate for an ontology language due to its direct support for object-oriented concepts, its frame-based syntax, and extensive support for meta-programming [9, 8, 25]. More recently it has been adopted as a basis for ontology languages for Semantic Web Services: WSML and SWSL [7, 4].

3.1   The Basic Techniques

A typical ontology includes three main components:

1. *A taxonomy of classes.* This includes the specification of the class hierarchy, i.e., which classes are subclasses of other classes.

2. *Definitions of concepts.* These definitions specify the allowed attributes of each class, their types, and other properties (like symmetry or transitivity).
3. *Definitions of instances.* Instances (i.e., concrete data objects) are defined by indicating which concepts (i.e., classes) they belong to and by specifying concrete values for the attributes of those instances. Sometimes the values might not be given explicitly, but only their existence may be asserted with various degrees of precision. For instance, $\exists$ F john[father $\rightarrow$ F] or john[father $\rightarrow$ bob] $\vee$ john[father $\rightarrow$ bill]. Some concepts may not have explicitly defined instances. Instead, their instances may be defined by deductive rules. The latter concepts are akin to database views.

In F-logic, class taxonomies are represented directly using the subclass relationship ::. Concept definitions are represented using signature formulas, such as person[name $\star\Rightarrow$ string, spouse $\star\Rightarrow$ person]. Special properties of certain attributes can be expressed using rules. For instance, to state that spouse is a symmetric relationship in class person one can write

   X[spouse $\rightarrow$ Y] :- Y:person and Y[spouse $\rightarrow$ X].

Finally, instance definitions can be specified as facts using data molecules as follows:

   john:student.
   john[name $\rightarrow$ John, address $\rightarrow$ '123 Main St.', spouse $\rightarrow$ Mary].

Derived classes can be defined using rules. For instance, if the concepts of student and employee are already defined, we can define a new concept, workstudy using the following rule:

   X:workstudy :-
         X:(student and employee) and X[jobtype $\rightarrow$ J] and J:clerical.

   Properties can also be defined using rules. For instance, if the properties mother and father are already defined, we can define the properties of parent and ancestor as follows:

X[parent $\rightarrow$ P] :- X[mother $\rightarrow$ P].
X[parent $\rightarrow$ P] :- X[father $\rightarrow$ P].
X[ancestor $\rightarrow$ A] :- X[parent $\rightarrow$ A].
X[ancestor $\rightarrow$ A] :- X[parent $\rightarrow$ P] and P[ancestor $\rightarrow$ A].

Various implementations of F-logic introduced several forms of more concise syntax. For instance, the workstudy rule above can be written as

X:workstudy :- X[jobtype $\rightarrow$ J:clerical]:(student and employee).

the two parent rules can be abbreviated to

X[parent $\rightarrow$ P] :- X[mother $\rightarrow$ P or father $\rightarrow$ P]].

and the second ancestor rule can be written as

   X[ancestor $\rightarrow$ A] :- X[parent $\rightarrow$ P[ancestor $\rightarrow$ A]].

3.2   Relationship to Description Logics

No discussion of F-logic as an ontology language is complete without a comparison with description logics (abbr. DL) [2] and, in particular, with languages such as OWL [24]. Since the first-order flavor of F-logic is an extension of classical predicate logic, it is clear that a description logic subset can be defined within F-logic and, indeed, this has been done [3]. In this sense, F-logic subsumes DLs. However, as mentioned earlier, most applications of F-logic (and all implementations known to us) use the logic programming flavor of the logic so a proper comparison would be made with that flavor.

Unlike DLs, F-logic is computationally complete. This can be a blessing or a curse depending on how one looks at this matter. On one hand, the expressive power of F-logic provides for a simple and clear specification of many problems that are beyond the expressive power of any DL. On the other hand, expressive F-logic knowledge bases provide no computational guarantees. However, many workers in the field dismiss this problem as a non-issue for two reasons:

- The exponential complexity of many problems in description logics provides very little comfort in practice, especially in reasoning with large ontologies.
- A vast class of computational problems in F-logic is decidable and has polynomial complexity. This includes all queries to knowledge bases that do not use function symbols and includes a large subclass of queries that are beyond the expressive power of DLs. Furthermore, research in logic programming and deductive database has identified large classes of knowledge bases *with* function symbols where query answering is decidable (for instance, [19]).

Nevertheless, there are two aspects where DLs provide more flexibility. First, DLs allow the user to represent existential information. For instance, one can say that there is a person with certain properties without specifying any concrete instance of such a person. In F-logic one can express only an approximation of such a statement using Skolem functions. Similarly, DLs admit disjunctive information into the knowledge base. For instance, one can say that John has a book or a bicycle. The corresponding statement in F-logic is only an approximation:

```
john[has → _#:(book or bicycle)].
```

The symbol _# here denotes a unique Skolem constant that does not occur anywhere else in the knowledge base. While this may be an acceptable approximation in some cases, it is still significantly weaker that the corresponding DL statement.

For instance, if upon closer examination it becomes known that John does not have a book, then in DLs we would conclude that John has a bicycle. In the logic programming flavor of F-logic (as in other logic programming systems) we cannot even state that John has no books directly—one has to employ some rather complex tricks. Some extensions of standard logic programming support *explicit negation* and this can make negative information easier to specify. For instance, this problem could be overcome by combining F-logic with Courteous Logic Programming [11, 12]. Other extensions allow disjunctive information in the rule heads [22, 18], which permits statements like john[father → bob] ∨ john[father → bill].

3.3   Example: An OWL-S Profile

We now give a more extensive example of an ontology specified using F-logic—part of an OWL-S profile [21]. OWL-S is an OWL-based Web ontology, which is intended to provide Web service providers with a core set of constructs for describing the properties and capabilities of their Web services. OWL-S often refers to externally defined data types using the namespace notation. Although some implementation of F-logic support URIs and namespaces, our example will omit all namespace definitions and will reference the corresponding external data types and concepts by enclosing them in single quotes, e.g., 'xsd:string'.

```
'service:ServiceProfile' : 'owl:Class'.
'Profile' :: 'service:ServiceProfile'
'Profile'[
    serviceName *=> 'xsd:string',
    textDescription *=> 'xsd:string',
    'rdfs:comment'*->'Definition of Profile',
    contactInformation *=>> 'Actor',
    hasProcess *=> 'process:Process',
    serviceCategory *=>> ServiceCategory,
    serviceParameter *=>> ServiceParameter,
    hasParameter *=>> 'process:Parameter',
    hasInput *=>> 'process:Input',
    hasOutput *=>> 'process:ConditionalOutput',
    hasPrecondition *=>> 'expr:Condition',
    hasEffect *=>> 'process:ConditionalEffect'
].

hasInput[subpropertyof ->> hasParameter].
hasOutput[subPropertyOf ->> hasParameter].

// Definition of subPropertyOf
Obj[P ->> Val] :- S[subPropertyOf ->> P] and Obj[S ->> Val].

'ServiceCategory' : 'owl:Class'.
'ServiceCategory'[
    categoryName *=> 'xsd:string',
    taxonomy *=> 'xsd:string',
    value *=> 'xsd:string',
    code *=> 'xsd:string'
].

'ServiceParameter' : 'owl:Class'.
'ServiceParameter'[
```

```
    serviceParameterName *=> 'xsd:string',
    sParameter *=> 'owl:Thing'
].
```

```
'Actor' : 'owl:Class'.
'process:Process' : 'owl:Class'.
'expr:Condition' : 'owl:Class'.
'process:Input' : 'owl:Class'.
'process:ConditionalOutput' : 'owl:Class'.
'process:ConditionalEffect' : 'owl:Class'.
'process:Parameter' : 'owl:Class'.
```

The above ontology is fairly simple. The frame-based syntax of F-logic enables concise and clear description of the properties of the various classes defined by OWL-S. The only place where a more sophisticated aspect of F-logic is necessary is the definition of subPropertyOf, a property that applies to attributes when they are considered as objects in their own right. To define the meaning of this property we use an F-logic rule.

OWL distinguishes between *object properties* and *data type properties*, and defines two OWL classes for that. The class 'owl:ObjectProperty' is populated by object properties, which are attributes whose range is an OWL class. The class 'owl:DataTypeProperty' is populated by data type properties, which are defined as attributes whose range is an XML type, such as 'xsd:string'. Since OWL-S is an OWL-based ontology, every property must be explicitly specified to be in either the 'owl:ObjectProperty' class or the 'owl:DataTypeProperty' class. In F-logic this can be done much more elegantly using rules:

```
Prop:property(Range) :- Domain[Prop *⇒ Range or Prop *⇒⇒ Range].
Prop:'owl:ObjectProperty' :-
           Prop : property(Range) and Range : 'owl:Class'.
Prop:'owl:DataTypeProperty' :-
           Prop : property(Range) and not Range : 'owl:Class'.
```

This example provides a glimpse on how the ability of F-logic to operate at the meta-level provides significant benefits in terms of conciseness and readability of ontology specifications.

4 Conclusion

We provided an overview of the main concepts underlying F-logic with particular attention to its use as an ontology language. We illustrates the key modeling capabilities of F-logic on a number of examples, which culminated with a larger example of a piece of the OWL-S ontology. Due to lack of space, we could not describe the semantics and the proof theory of the logic—neither of its first-order flavor nor of its logic programming flavor. However, the necessary details can be found in the references.

References

1. J. Angele and G. Lausen. Ontologies in F-logic. In S. Staab and R. Studer, editors, *Handbook on Ontologies in Information Systems*, pages 29–50. Springer Verlag, Berlin, Germany, 2004.
2. F. Baader, D. Calvanese, D. McGuinness, D. Nardi, and P. Patel-Schneider, editors. *The Description Logic Handbook*. Cambridge University Press, 2002.
3. M. Balaban. The F-logic approach for description languages. *Annals of Mathematics and Artificial Intelligence*, 15(1):19–60, 1995.
4. D. Berardi, H. Boley, B. Grosof, M. Gruninger, R. Hull, M. Kifer, D. Martin, S. McIlraith, J. Su, and S. Tabet. SWSL: Semantic Web Services Language. Technical report, Semantic Web Services Initiative, April 2005. http://www.daml.org/services/swsl/.
5. A. Bonner and M. Kifer. A logic for programming database transactions. In J. Chomicki and G. Saake, editors, *Logics for Databases and Information Systems*, chapter 5, pages 117–166. Kluwer Academic Publishers, March 1998.
6. W. Chen, M. Kifer, and D. Warren. HiLog: A foundation for higher-order logic programming. *Journal of Logic Programming*, 15(3):187–230, February 1993.
7. J. de Bruijn, H. Lausen, R. Krummenacher, A. Polleres, L. Predoiu, and D. Fensel. The WSML family of representation languages. Technical report, DERI, March 2005. http://www.wsmo.org/TR/d16/d16.1/.
8. S. Decker, D. Brickley, J. Saarela, and J. Angele. A query and inference service for RDF. In *QL'98 - The Query Languages Workshop*, December 1998.
9. D. Fensel, M. Erdmann, and R. Studer. OntoBroker: How to make the WWW intelligent. In *Proceedings of the 11th Banff Knowledge Acquisition for Knowledge-Based Systems Workshop*, Banff, Canada, 1998.
10. J. Frohn, G. Lausen, and H. Uphoff. Access to objects by path expressions and rules. In *Proceedings of the Intl. Conference on Very Large Databases*, pages 273–284, Santiago, Chile, 1994. Morgan Kaufmann, San Francisco, CA.
11. B. Grosof. Prioritized conflict handling for logic programs. In *International Logic Programming Symposium*, pages 197–211, 1997.
12. B. Grosof. A courteous compiler from generalized courteous logic programs to ordinary logic programs. Technical Report RC 21472, IBM, July 1999.
13. P. Hayes. RDF model theory. W3C Working Draft, 10 October 2003. Available at http://www.w3.org/TR/rdf-mt/.
14. M. Kifer, R. Lara, A. Polleres, and C. Zhao. A logical framework for web service discovery. In *Semantic Web Services Workshop*, November 2004.
15. M. Kifer, G. Lausen, and J. Wu. Logical foundations of object-oriented and frame-based languages. *Journal of ACM*, 42:741–843, July 1995.
16. G. Klyne and J. J. Carroll. Resource description framework (RDF): Concepts and abstract syntax. W3C Working Draft, 10 October 2003. Available at http://www.w3.org/TR/rdf-concepts/.
17. J. W. Lloyd. *Foundations of Logic Programming (Second, extended edition)*. Springer series in symbolic computation. Springer-Verlag, New York, 1987.
18. J. Lobo, J. Minker, and A. Rajasekar. *Foundations of Disjunctive Logic Programming*. MIT Press, Cambridge, Massachusetts, 1992.
19. N.Lindenstrauss and Y. Sagiv. Automatic termination analysis of logic programs. In *International Conference on Logic Programming*, 1997.
20. Ontoprise, GmbH. OntoBroker Manual. http://www.ontoprise.com/.
21. OWL-S Coalition. OWL-S: Semantic markup for Web services. Release 1.1. http://www.daml.org/services/owl-s/1.1/, December 2004.

22. T. Przymusinski. Well-founded and stationary models of logic programs. *Annals of Mathematics and Artificial Intelligence*, 12:141–187, 1994.

23. M. Sintek, S. Decker, and A. Harth. The TRIPLE system. http://triple. semanticweb.org/, 2003.

24. M. K. Smith, C. Welty, and D. L. McGuinness. OWL Web ontology language guide. W3C Candidate Recommendation, 18 August 2003. Available at `http://www.w3.org/TR/owl-guide/`.

25. S. Staab and A. Maedche. Knowledge portals: Ontologies at work. *The AI Magazine*, 22(2):63–75, 2000.

26. A. Van Gelder, K. Ross, and J. S. Schlipf. The well-founded semantics for general logic programs. *J. ACM*, 38(3):620–650, July 1991.

27. G. Yang and M. Kifer. Implementing an efficient DOOD system using a tabling logic engine. In *First International Conference on Computational Logic, DOOD'2000 Stream*, July 2000.

28. G. Yang and M. Kifer. Well-founded optimism: Inheritance in frame-based knowledge bases. In *Intl. Conference on Ontologies, DataBases, and Applications of Semantics for Large Scale Information Systems (ODBASE)*, October 2002.

29. G. Yang and M. Kifer. Inheritance and rules in object-oriented semantic Web languages. In *Rules and Rule Markup Languages for the Semantic Web (RuleML03)*, volume 2876 of *Lecture Notes in Computer Science*. Springer Verlag, November 2003.

30. G. Yang and M. Kifer. Reasoning about anonymous resources and meta statements on the Semantic Web. *Journal on Data Semantics, LNCS 2800*, 1:69–98, September 2003.

31. G. Yang, M. Kifer, and C. Zhao. FLORA-2: A rule-based knowledge representation and inference infrastructure for the Semantic Web. In *International Conference on Ontologies, Databases and Applications of Semantics (ODBASE-2003)*, November 2003.

32. G. Yang, M. Kifer, and C. Zhao. FLORA-2: User's Manual. http://flora. sourceforge.net/, March 2005.

Web and Semantic Web Query Languages: A Survey

James Bailey[1], François Bry[2], Tim Furche[2], and Sebastian Schaffert[2]

[1] NICTA Victoria Laboratory,
Department of Computer Science and Software Engineering,
The University of Melbourne, Victoria 3010, Australia
http://www.cs.mu.oz.au/~jbailey/
[2] Institute for Informatics,University of Munich,
Oettingenstraße 67, 80538 München, Germany
http://pms.ifi.lmu.de/

Abstract. A number of techniques have been developed to facilitate powerful data retrieval on the Web and Semantic Web. Three categories of Web query languages can be distinguished, according to the format of the data they can retrieve: XML, RDF and Topic Maps. This article introduces the spectrum of languages falling into these categories and summarises their salient aspects. The languages are introduced using common sample data and query types. Key aspects of the query languages considered are stressed in a conclusion.

1 Introduction

The Semantic Web Vision

A major endeavour in current Web research is the so-called *Semantic Web*, a term coined by W3C founder Tim Berners-Lee in a Scientific American article describing the future of the Web [37]. The Semantic Web aims at enriching Web data (that is usually represented in (X)HTML or other XML formats) by meta-data and (meta-)data processing specifying the "meaning" of such data and allowing Web based systems to take advantage of "intelligent" reasoning capabilities. To quote Berners-Lee et al. [37]:

> "The Semantic Web will bring structure to the meaningful content of Web pages, creating an environment where software agents roaming from page to page can readily carry out sophisticated tasks for users."

The Semantic Web meta-data added to today's Web can be seen as advanced semantic indices, making the Web into something rather like an encyclopedia. A considerable advantage over conventional encyclopedias printed on paper, however, is that the relationships expressed by Semantic Web meta-data can be followed by computers, very much like hyperlinks can be followed by human readers and programs. Thus, these relationships are well-suited for use in drawing conclusions automatically:

N. Eisinger and J. Małuszyński (Eds.): Reasoning Web 2005, LNCS 3564, pp. 35–133, 2005.

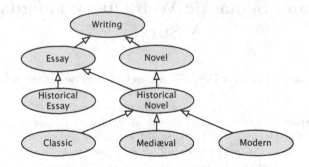

Fig. 1. A categorisation of books as it might occur in a Semantic Web ontology

"For the Semantic Web to function, computers must have access to structured collections of information and sets of inference rules that they can
use to conduct automated reasoning."[37]

A number of formalisms have been proposed for representing Semantic Web
meta-data, in particular RDF [217], Topic Maps [155], and OWL (formerly
known as DAML+OIL) [23, 150]. These formalisms usually allow one to describe
relationships between data items, such as concept hierarchies and relations between concepts. For example, a Semantic Web application for a book store could
assign categories to books as shown in Figure 1. A customer interested in novels
might also get offers for books that are in the subcategory *Historical Novels* and
in the sub-subcategories *Classic*, *Mediæval* and *Modern*, although these books
are not directly contained in the category *Novels*, because the data processing
system has access to the ontology and can thus infer the fact that a book in the
category *Mediæval* is also a *Novel*.

Whereas RDF and Topic Maps merely provide a syntax for representing
assertions like *"Book A is authored by person B"*, schema or ontology languages
such as RDFS [51] and OWL allow one to state properties of the terms used in
such assertions, e.g. *"no 'person' can be a 'text'"*. Building upon descriptions of
resources and their schemas (as detailed in the architectural road map for the
Semantic Web [36]), rules expressed in formalisms like SWRL [151] or RuleML
[43] additionally allow one to specify actions to take, knowledge to derive, or
constraints to enforce.

Importance of Query Languages for the Web and Semantic Web

The enabling requirement for the Semantic Web is an integrated access to the
data on the Web that is represented in any of the above-mentioned formalisms
or in formalisms of the "standard Web", such as (X)HTML, SVG, or any XML
application. This data access is the objective of Web and Semantic Web *query
languages*. A wide range of query languages for the Semantic Web exist, ranging
from pure "selection languages" with only limited expressivity, to full-fledged
reasoning languages capable of expressing complicated programs, and from query

languages restricted to a certain data representation format (e.g. XML or RDF), to general purpose languages supporting several different data representation formats and allowing one to query data on both the standard Web and the Semantic Web at once.

Structure and Goals of This Survey

This survey aims at introducing the query languages proposed for the major representation formalisms of the standard and Semantic Web: XML, RDF, and Topic Maps. The intended audience are students and researchers interested in obtaining a greater understanding of the relatively new area of Semantic Web querying, as well as researchers already working in the field that want a survey of the state of the art in existing query languages. This survey does *not* aim to be a comprehensive tutorial for each of the approximately 50 languages discussed. Instead, it tries to highlight important or noteworthy aspects, only going in depth for some of the more widespread languages. The following three questions are at the heart of this survey:

1. what are the core *data retrieval capabilities* of each query language,
2. to what extent, and what forms of *reasoning* do they offer, and
3. how are they realised?

Structure. After briefly discussing the three different representation formats XML, RDF, and Topic Maps in Section 2.1, each of the languages is introduced with sample queries against a common Semantic Web scenario (cf. Section 2.2). The discussion is divided into three main parts, corresponding to the three different data representation formats XML, RDF, and Topic Maps. The survey concludes with a short summary of language features desirable for Semantic Web query languages. The outline is as follows:

1. Introduction
2. Preliminaries
   2.1 Three Data Formats: XML, RDF and Topic Maps
   2.2 Sample Data: Classification-based Book Recommender
   2.3 Sample Queries
3. XML Query and Transformation Languages
   3.1 W3C's Query Languages:The Navigational Approach
   3.2 Research Prototypes: The Positional Approach to XML Querying
4. RDF Query Languages
   4.1 The SPARQL Family
   4.2 The RQL Family
   4.3 Query Languages inspired from XPath, XSLT or XQuery
   4.4 Metalog: Querying in Controlled English
   4.5 Query Languages with Reactive Rules
   4.6 Deductive Query Languages
   4.7 Other RDF Query Languages

5. Topic Maps Query Languages
   5.1 tolog: Logic Programming for Topic Maps
   5.2 AsTMA?: Functional Style Querying of Topic Maps
   5.3 Toma: Querying Topic Maps inspired from SQL
   5.4 Path-based Access to Topic Maps
6. Conclusion

Selection of Query Languages. This survey focuses on introducing and comparing languages designed primarily for providing efficient and effective access to data on the Web and Semantic Web. In particular, it *excludes* the following types of languages:

- *Programming language tools for XML.* General-purpose programming languages supporting XML as native data type are not considered, e.g. XM-Lambda [205], CDuce [27], XDuce [152], Xtatic (http://www.cis.upenn.edu/~bcpierce/xtatic/), Scriptol (http://www.scriptol.com/), and Cω (http://research.microsoft.com/Comega/ [206]). XML APIs are not considered, e.g.: DOM [9], SAX (http://www.saxproject.org/), and XmlPull (http://www.xmlpull.org/). XML-related language extensions are not considered, e.g.: HaXML [276] for Haskell, XMerL [282] for Erlang, CLP(Flex) [88] for Prolog, or XJ [145] for Java. General-purpose programming languages with Web service support are also not considered, e.g.: XL [116, 117], Scala [218], Water [235].
- *Reactive languages.* A reactive language allows specification of updates and logic describing how to react when events occur. Several proposals have been made for adapting approaches such as ECA (Event-Condition-Action) rules to the Web, cf. [4] for a survey. There is, of course, a close relationship between such reactive languages and query languages, with the latter often being embedded within the former.
- *Rule languages.* Transformations, queries, consequences, and reactive behaviours can be conveniently expressed using rules. The serialisation of rules for their exchange on the Web is investigated in the RuleML [43] initiative. Similar to reactive languages, rule languages are also closely related to query languages.
- *OWL query languages.* Query languages designed for OWL, e.g., OWL-QL [113], are not considered for two reasons: (1) They are still in their infancy, and their small number makes interesting comparisons hardly possible, (2) the languages proposed so far can only query schemas, i.e., meta-data but not data, and access data only through meta-data, e.g., returning the instances of a class.

A pragmatic approach has been adopted in this survey: A language of one of the above-mentioned four kinds is considered if querying is one of its core aspects, or if it offers a unique form of querying not covered by any of the other query languages considered in the survey. Authoring tools, such as visual editors, are only considered with a query language that they are based upon. The storing or indexing of Web data is not covered (for a survey on storage systems for XML cf. [280], for RDF cf. to [190]).

Despite these restrictions, the number of languages is still quite large. This reflects a considerable and growing interest in Web and particularly Semantic Web query languages. Indeed, standardisation bodies have recently started the process of standardisation of query languages for RDF and Topic Maps. It is our hope that this survey will help to give an overview of the current state of the art in these areas.

2   Preliminaries

2.1   Three Data Formats: XML, RDF and Topic Maps

XML. Originally designed as a replacement for the language SGML as a format for representing (structured) text documents, XML nowadays is also widely used as a format for representing and exchanging arbitrary (structured) data:

> The "Extensible Markup Language (XML) is a simple, very flexible text format derived from SGML [...]. Originally designed to meet the challenges of large-scale electronic publishing, XML is also playing an increasingly important role in the exchange of a wide variety of data on the Web and elsewhere."[1]

An "XML document" is a file, or collection of files, that adheres to the general syntax specified in the XML Recommendation [48], independent of the concrete application. XML documents consist of an optional document prologue and a document tree containing elements, character data and attributes, with a distinguished root element.

Elements. Elements are used to "mark up" the document. They are identified by a label (called tag name) and specified by opening and closing tags that enclose the element content. Opening tags are of the form `<label ...>` and contain the label and optionally a set of attributes (see below). Closing tags are of the form `</label>` and contain only the label.

Elements may contain either other elements, character data, or both (mixed content). In analogy with the document tree, such content is often referred to as *children* of an element. Interleaving of the opening and closing tags of different elements (e.g. `<b><i>Text</b></i>`) is forbidden. The order of elements is significant (so-called document order). This is a reasonable requirement for storing text data, but might be too restrictive when storing data items of a database. Applications working with XML data thus often ignore the document order. If an element contains no content, it may be abbreviated as `<label/>`, i.e. the "closing slash" is contained in the start tag.

Attributes. Opening tags of elements may contain a set of key/value pairs called attributes. Attributes are of the form `name = "value"`, where `name` may contain

---

[1] http://www.w3.org/XML/

the same characters as element labels and `value` is a character sequence which is always enclosed in quotes. An opening tag may contain attributes in any order, but each attribute name can occur at most once.

References. References of various kinds, (like ID/IDREF attributes and hypertext links) make it possible to refer to an element instead of explicitly including it.

Document Tree. An XML document can be seen as a rooted, unranked[2], and ordered[3] tree, if one does not consider the various referencing or linking mechanisms of XML. Although this interpretation is that of the data model retained for XML (cf. XML Infoset [94], XQuery, XPath [111]) and most XML query languages, it is too simplistic. Indeed, references (as expressed, e.g. through ID and IDREF attributes or hypertext links) make it possible to express both oriented and non-oriented cycles in an XML document.

RDF and RDFS. *RDF* [25, 172] data is sets of "triples" or "statements" of the form (*Subject, Property, Object*). RDF data is commonly seen as a directed graph, whose nodes correspond to a statement's subject and object and whose arcs correspond to a statement's property (thus relating a subject with an object). For this reason, properties are also often referred to as "predicates". Nodes (i.e. subjects and objects) are labeled by either (1) URIs describing (Web) resources, or (2) literals (i.e. scalar data such as strings or numbers), or (3) are unlabeled, being so-called anonymous or "blank nodes". Blank nodes are commonly used to group or "aggregate" properties. Specific properties are predefined in the RDF and RDFS specifications [51, 148, 172, 194], e.g. `rdf:type` for specifying the type of properties, `rdfs:subClassOf` for specifying class-subclass relationships between subjects/objects, and `rdfs:subPropertyOf` for specifying property-subproperty relationships between properties. Furthermore, RDFS has "meta-classes", e.g. `rdfs:Class`, the class of all classes, and `rdfs:Property`, the class of all properties.[4]

RDFS allows one to define so-called "RDF Schemas" or "ontologies", similar to object-oriented data models. The inheritance model of RDFS exhibits some peculiarities: (1) resources can be classified in different classes that are not related in the class hierarchy, (2) the class hierarchy can be cyclic (so that all classes on the cycle are "subclass equivalent"), (3) properties are first-class objects, and (4) in contrast to most object-oriented formalisms, RDF does not describe which properties can be associated with a class, but instead the domain and range of a property. Based on an RDFS schema, "inference rules" can be specified, for instance the transitivity of the class hierarchy, or the type of an untyped resource that has a property associated with a known domain.

RDF can be *serialised* in various formats, the most frequently being XML. Early approaches to RDF serialisation have raised considerable criticism due to

---

[2] i.e. the number of children of an element is not bounded.

[3] i.e. the children of an element are ordered.

[4] this survey tries to use self-explanatory prefixes for namespaces where possible.

their complexity. As a consequence, a surprisingly large number of RDF seriali-sations have been proposed, cf. [60] for a detailed survey.

OWL [23, 204, 261] extends RDFS with a means for defining description vocabularies for Web resources. OWL is only considered superficially in this survey, cf. Section 1.

Topic Maps. Topic Maps [155, 232] have been inspired from work in library sciences and knowledge indexing. The main concepts of Topic Maps are "topics", "associations", and "occurrences". Topics might have "types" that are topics. Types correspond to the classes of object-oriented formalisms, i.e., a topic is related to each of its types in an instance-class relationship. A topic can have one or more "names". Associations are n-ary relations (with $n \geq 2$) between topics. Associations might have "role types" and "roles". Occurrences are information resources relevant to a topic. An occurrence might have one or several types characterising the occurrence's relevance to a topic, expressed by "occurrence roles" and "occurrence role types" in the formalism HyTM [155], or only by "occurrence types" in the formalism XTM [232].

"Topic characteristics" denote the names a topic has, what associations it partakes in, and what its occurrences are. "Facets" (a concept of HyTM but not of XTM) are attribute-value pairs that can be attached to any kind of topic map component for explanation purposes. Facets are thus a means to attach to Topic Maps meta-data in another formalism. "Subject identifiers" denote URIs of resources (called "subject indicators" or sometimes also "subject identifiers") that describe in a human-readable form the subject of a Topic Map component. Commonly, subjects and topics stand in one-to-one relationships, such that they can be referred to interchangeably.

Like RDF data, Topic Maps can be seen as oriented graphs with labeled nodes and edges. Topic Maps offer richer data modeling primitives than RDF. Topic Maps allow relationships, called associations, of every arity, while RDF only allows binary relationships, called properties. Initial efforts towards integrating RDF and Topic Maps are described in [126, 177]. Interestingly, Topic Maps associations are similar to the "extended links" of the XML linking language XLink (http://www.w3.org/XML/Linking/).

2.2   Running Example: Classification-Based Book Recommender

In the following, we shall consider as a running example queries in a simple book recommender system describing various properties and relationships between books. It consists of a hierarchy (or *ontology*) of the book categories `Writing`, `Novel`, `Essay`, `Historical_Novel`, and `Historical_Essay`, and two books *The First Man in Rome* (a `Historical_Novel` authored by *Colleen McCullough*) and *Bellum Civile* (a `Historical_Essay` authored by *Julius Caesar* and *Aulus Hir-tius*, and translated by *J.M. Carter*). Figure 2 depicts this data as a (simplified) RDF graph [51, 172, 184]. Note in particular that a `Historical_Novel` is both, a `Novel` and an `Essay`, and that books may optionally have a translator, as is the case for *Bellum Civile*. To illustrate the properties of the different kinds of query

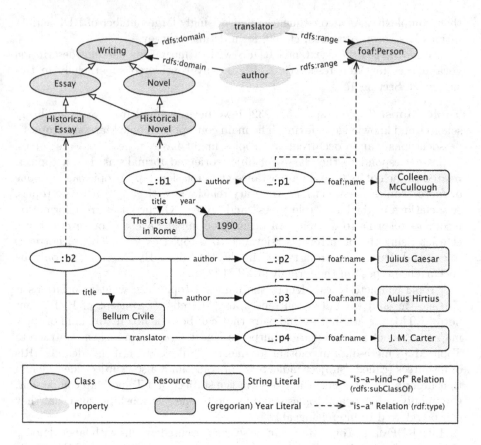

Fig. 2. Sample Data: representation as a (simplified) RDF graph

languages, the data is in the following represented in the three representation formalisms RDF, Topic Maps, and XML.

The simple ontology in the book recommender system only makes use of the subsumption (or "is-a-kind-of") relation `rdfs:subClassOf` and the instance (or "is-a") relation `rdf:type`. Though small and simple, this ontology is sufficient to illustrate the most important aspects of ontology querying. In particular, querying this ontology with query languages for the standard Web already requires one to model and query this data in an *ad hoc* fashion, i.e. there is no unified way to represent this data. A possible representation is shown in the XML example below.

The RDF, Topic Maps, and XML representations of the sample data refer to the "simple datatypes" of XML Schema [39] for scalar data: Book titles and authors' names are "string", (untyped or typed as `xsd:string`), publication years of books are "Gregorian years", `xsd:gYear`. The sample data is assumed to be stored at `http://example.org/books#`, a URL chosen in accordance to RFC 2606 [105] in the use of URLs in sample data. Where useful, e.g when referencing the vocabulary defined in the ontology part of the data, this URL is associated with the prefix books.

Sample Data in RDF. The RDF representation of the book recommender system directly corresponds to the simplified RDF graph in Fig. 2. It is given here in the *Turtle* serialisation [24].

```
@prefix rdf:  <http://www.w3.org/1999/02/22-rdf-syntax-ns#> .
@prefix rdfs: <http://www.w3.org/2000/01/rdf-schema#> .
@prefix xsd:  <http://www.w3.org/2001/XMLSchema#> .
@prefix foaf: <http://xmlns.org/foaf/0.1/> .
:Writing a rdfs:Class ;
         rdfs:label "Novel" .
:Novel   a rdfs:Class ;
         rdfs:label "Novel" ;
         rdfs:subClassOf :Writing .
:Essay   a rdfs:Class ;
         rdfs:label "Essay" ;
         rdfs:subClassOf :Writing .
:Historical_Essay a rdfs:Class ;
         rdfs:label "Historical Essay" ;
         rdfs:subClassOf :Essay .
:Historical_Novel a rdfs:Class ;
         rdfs:label "Historical Novel" ;
         rdfs:subClassOf :Novel ;
         rdfs:subClassOf :Essay .
:author  a rdfs:Property ;
         rdfs:domain :Writing ;
         rdfs:range  foaf:Person .
:translator a rdfs:Property ;
         rdfs:domain :Writing ;
         rdfs:range  foaf:Person .
_:b1     a :Historical_Novel ;
         :title "The First Man in Rome" ;
         :year  "1990"^^xsd:gYear ;
         :author [foaf:name "Colleen McCullough"] .
_:b1     a :Historical_Essay ;
         :title "Bellum Civile" ;
         :author [foaf:name "Julius Caesar"] ;
         :author [foaf:name "Aulus Hirtius"] ;
         :translator [foaf:name "J. M. Carter"] .
```

Books, authors, and translators are represented by blank nodes without identifiers, or with temporary identifiers indicated by the prefix "_:".

Sample Data in Topic Maps. The Topic Map representation of the book recommender system makes use of the Linear Topic Maps syntax [121]. Subclass-superclass associations are identified using the subject identifiers of XTM [232]. For illustration purposes, the title of a book is represented as an occurrence of that book/topic.

```
/* Association and topic types for subclass-superclass hierarchy */
[superclass-subclass = "Superclass-Subclass Association Type"
        @ "http://www.topicmaps.org/xtm/1.0/core.xtm#superclass-subclass" ]
[superclass = "Superclass Role Type"
        @ "http://www.topicmaps.org/xtm/1.0/core.xtm#superclass" ]
[subclass = "Subclass Role Type"
        @ "http://www.topicmaps.org/xtm/1.0/core.xtm#subclass" ]
/* Topic types */
[Writing = "Writing Topic Type" @ "http://example.org/books#Writing" ]
[Novel = "Novel Topic Type"      @ "http://example.org/books#Novel" ]
[Essay = "Essay Topic Type"      @ "http://example.org/books#Essay" ]
[Historical_Essay = "Historical Essay Topic Type"
                        @ "http://example.org/books#Historical_Essay" ]
[Historical_Novel = "Historical Novel Topic Type"
                        @ "http://example.org/books#Historical_Novel" ]
[year = "Topic Type for a Gregorian year following ISO 8601"
                        @ "http://www.w3.org/2001/XMLSchema#gYear" ]
[Person = "Person Topic Type" @ "http://xmlns.org/foaf/0.1/Person"]
[Author                    @ "http://example.org/books#author" ]
[Translator                @ "http://example.org/books#translator" ]
/* Associations among the topic types */
superclass-subclass(Writing: superclass, Novel: subclass)
superclass-subclass(Writing: superclass, Essay: subclass)
superclass-subclass(Novel: superclass, Historical_Novel: subclass)
superclass-subclass(Essay: superclass, Historical_Essay: subclass)
superclass-subclass(Essay: superclass, Historical_Novel: subclass)
superclass-subclass(Person: superclass, Author: subclass)
superclass-subclass(Person: superclass, Translator: subclass)
/* Occurrence types */
[title = "Occurrence Type for Titles" @ "http://example.org/books#title" ]
/* Association types */
[author-for-book = "Association Type associating authors to books"]
[translator-for-book =
                  "Association Type associating translators to books"]
[publication-year-for-book =
                  "Association Type associating translators to books"]

/* Topics, associations, and occurrences */
[p1: Person        = "Colleen McCullough"]
[p2: Person        = "Julius Caesar"]
[p3: Person        = "Aulus Hirtius"]
[p4: Person        = "J. M. Carter"]
[b1: Historical_Essay = "Topic representing the book 'First Man in Rome'"]
author-for-book(b1, p1: author)
publication-year-for-book(b1, y1990)
{b1, title, [[The First Man in Rome]]}
[b2: Historical_Novel = "Topic representing the book 'Bellum Civile'"]
author-for-book(b2, p2: author)
author-for-book(b2, p3: author)
```

```
translator-for-book(b2, p4: translator)
{b2, title, [[Bellum Civile]]}
```

The representation given above has been chosen for illustrating query language features. In reality, a different representation might be more natural. For instance, a ternary association connecting a book with its author(s), translator, and year of publication could be used. Also, instead of separate associations for author and translator, use of a generic association between persons and books, and use of roles for differentiation would be reasonable.

Sample Data in XML. XML has no standard way to express relationships other than parent-child. The following is thus one of many conceivable *ad hoc* XML representations of the data in the book recommender system. Its use is obviously highly application-specific.

```
<bookdata xmlns:xsd="http://www.w3.org/2001/XMLSchema#">
  <book type="Historical_Novel">
    <title>The First Man in Rome</title>
    <year type="xsd:gYear">1990</year>
    <author>  <name>Colleen McCullough</name>  </author>
  </book>
  <book type="Historical_Essay">
    <title>Bellum Civile</title>
    <author>        <name>Julius Caesar</name>   </author>
    <author>        <name>Aulus Hirtius</name>   </author>
    <translator>  <name>J. M. Carter</name>     </translator>
  </book>
  <category id="Writing">
    <label>Writing</label>
    <category id="Novel">
      <label>Novel</label>
      <category id="Historical_Novel">
        <label>Historical Novel</label>
      </category>
    </category>
    <category id="Essay">
      <label>Essay</label>
      <category id="Historical_Essay">
        <label>Historical Essay</label>
      </category>
      <category idref="Historical_Novel" />
    </category>
  </category>
</bookdata>
```

For the sake of brevity, the above representation does not express that authors and translators are persons. Note the use of ID/IDREF references for expressing the types (e.g. "Novel", "Historical_Novel") of books.

One of the XML-based serialisations of the RDF or Topic Maps representations of the sample data could be used for comparing XML query languages.

Instead, in this article, the XML representation given above is used, because these XML-based serialisations of the RDF or Topic Maps representations are awkward, complicated to query, and can yield biased comparisons.

2.3   Sample Queries

The different query languages are illustrated using five types of queries against the sample data. This categorisation is inspired by Maier [192] and Clark [87].

Selection and Extraction Queries. *Selection Queries* simply retrieve parts of the data based on its content, structure, or position. The first query is thus:

Query 1. *"Select all* Essays *together with their* authors *(i.e. author items and corresponding names)"*

Selection Queries are used in the following to illustrate basic properties of query languages, like the basic means of addressing data, the supported *answer formats*, or the way *related information* (like author names or book titles) is selected and delivered (grouping). *Extraction Queries* extract substructures, and can be considered as a special form of Selection Query. Such queries are commonly found on the Semantic Web. The following query extracts a substructure of the sample data (e.g. as an RDF subgraph):

Query 2. *"Select all data items with any relation to the book titled 'Bellum Civile'."*

Reduction Queries. Some queries are more concisely expressed by specifying what parts of the data *not* to include in the answer. On the Semantic Web, such *reduction queries* are e.g. useful for combining information from different sources, or for implementing different levels of trust: It might be desirable to create a simple list of books from the data in the recommender system, leaving out ontology information and translators:

Query 3. *"Select all data items except ontology information and translators."*

Restructuring Queries. In Web applications, it is often desirable to *restructure* data, possibly into different formats/serialisations. For example, the contents of the book recommender system could be restructured to an (X)HTML representation for viewing in a browser, or derived data could be created, like inverting the relation `author`:

Query 4. *"Invert the relation* author *(from a book to an author) into a relation* authored *(from an author to a book)."*

In particular, RDF requires restructuring for *reification*, i.e. expressing "statements about statements". When reifying, a statement is replaced by three new statements specifying the subject, predicate, and object of the old statement. For example, the statement *"Julius Caesar is author of Bellum Civile"* is reified by the three statements "the statement has subject *Julius Caesar*", "the statement has predicate *author*", and "the statement has object *Bellum Civile*".

Aggregation Queries. Restructuring the data also includes *aggregating* several data items into one new data item. As Web data usually consists of tree- or graph-structured data that goes beyond flat relations, we distinguish between *value aggregation* working only on the values (like SQL's max($\cdot$), sum($\cdot$), . . .) and *structural aggregation* working also on structural elements (like "how many nodes"). Query 5 uses the max($\cdot$) value aggregation, while Query 6 uses structural aggregation:

Query 5. *"Return the last year in which an author with name 'Julius Caesar' published something."*

Query 6. *"Return each of the subclasses of 'Writing', together with the average number of authors per publication of that subclass."*

Related to aggregation are *grouping* (collecting several data items at some common position, e.g. a list of authors) and *sorting* (extending grouping by specifying in which order to arrange data items). Note that they are not meaningful for all representation formalisms. For instance, sorting in RDF only makes sense for sequence containers, as RDF data in general does not specify order for statements.

Combination and Inference Queries. It is often necessary to *combine* information that is not not explicitly connected, like information from different sources or substructures. Such queries are useful with ontologies that often specify that names declared at different places are synonymous:

Query 7. *"Combine the information about the book titled 'The Civil War' and authored by 'Julius Caesar' with the information about the book with identifier* `bellum_civile`.*"*

Combination queries are related to inference, because inference refers to combining data, as illustrated by the following example: If the books entitled "Bellum Civile" and "The Civil War" are the same book, and 'if 'Julius Caesar" is an author of "Bellum Civile", then 'Julius Caesar' is also an author of "The Civil War".

Inference queries e.g. compute transitive closures of relations like the RDFS `subClassOf` relation:

Query 8. *"Return the transitive closure of the* `subClassOf` *relation."*

Not all inference queries are combination queries, as the following example illustrates:

Query 9. *"Return the co-author relation between two persons that stand in author relationships with the same book."*

Some query languages have closure operators applicable to any relation, while other query languages have closure operators only for certain, predefined relations, e.g., the RDFS `subClassOf` relation. Some query languages support *general recursion*, making it possible and easy to express the transitive closure of every relation.

3   XML Query and Transformation Languages

Most query and transformation languages for XML specify the structure of the XML data to retrieve using one of the following approaches:

- *Navigational approach.* Path-based navigation through the XML data queried.
- *Positional approach.* Query patterns as "examples" of the XML data queried.
- Relational expressions referring to a "flat" representation of the XML data queried.

Languages already standardized, or currently in the process of standardisation by the W3C, are of the first kind, while many research languages are of the second kind. This article does not consider languages of the third kind, e.g., monadic datalog [128, 130] and LGQ [224]. Such languages have been proposed for formalizing query languages and reasoning about XML queries. This article also does not consider special purpose languages like ELog [21] which are not tailored towards querying by humans. Finally, this article does not consider XML query languages focused on information retrieval, e.g., XirQL [120], EquiX [89], ELIXIR [82], XQuery/IR [49], XXL [270], XirCL [210], XRANK [142], PIX [5], XSEarch [90], FleXPath [8], and TeXQuery [7]. Although these languages propose interesting and novel concepts and constructs for combining XML querying with information retrieval methods, they (a) do not easily compare to the other query languages in this survey and (b) mostly do not provide additonal insight on the non-IR features of query languages.

3.1   W3C's Query Languages: Navigational Approach

Characteristics of the Navigational Approach.   The navigational languages for XML are inspired from path-based query languages designed for relational or object-oriented databases. Most such database query languages (e.g., GEM [286], an extension of QUEL, and OQL [73]) require *fully specified* paths, i.e., paths with explicitly named nodes following only parent-child connections. OQL expresses paths with the "extended dot notation" introduced in GEM [286]: "SELECT b.translator.name FROM Books b" selects the name, or component, of the translator of books (note that there must be at most one translator per book for this expression to be legal).

Generalized Path Expressions. Generalized (or regular) path expressions [83, 119], allow more powerful constructs than the extended dot notation for specifying paths, e.g., the Kleene closure operator on (sub-)paths . As a consequence and in contrast to the extended dot notation, generalized path expressions do not require explicit naming of all nodes along a path.

Lorel. Lorel [2] is an early proposal for a query language originally designed for semistructured data, a data model that was introduced with the "Object Exchange Model (OEM)" [127, 230], and can be seen as a precursor of XML. Lorel's syntax resembles that of SQL and OQL, extending OQL's extended dot notation to generalized path expressions. Lorel provides a means for expressing:

- Optional data: In Lorel, the query SELECT b.translator.name FROM Books b returns an empty answer, whereas in OQL it causes a type error, if there is no translator for a book.
- Set-valued attributes: In Lorel, b.author.name selects the names of all authors of a book, whereas in OQL it is only valid if there is only a single author.
- Regular path expressions, e.g. a (strict) Kleene closure operator for expressing navigation through recursively defined data structures and alternatives in both labeling and structure.

The following Lorel query expresses Query 1 against the sample data (treating attributes as sub-elements since OEM has no attributes):

```
select xml(results:(
  select xml(result:(
    select B, B.author
      from bookdata.book B
      where B.type = bookdata.(category.id)+
  ) ) ) )
```

Lines 1 and 2 are constructors for wrapping the selected books and their authors into XML elements. Note the use of the strict Kleene closure operator + in line 5. Note also that Lorel allows entire (sub-) paths to be repeated, as do most query languages using generalized path expressions.

To illustrate further aspects of Lorel, assume that one is only interested in books having "Julius Caesar" either as author or translator. Assume also that, as in some representations of the sample data, cf. 2.2, the literal giving the name of the author is either wrapped inside a name child of the author element, or directly included in the author element. Selection of such books can be expressed in Lorel by adding the following expression to the query after line 5 B.(author|translator).name? = "Julius Caesar".

StruQL. StruQL [114, 115] relies on path expressions similar to that of Lorel. StruQL is another early (query and) transformation language for semi-structured data using Skolem functions for construction.

Data Selection with XPath. XPath is presented in [86] and [258, 269], as well as many online tutorials. It was defined originally as part of XSL, an activity towards defining a stylesheet language for XML (in replacement of SGML's stylesheet language DSSSL). XPath provides expressions for selecting data in terms of a navigation through an XML document. In contrast to the previous approaches based on generalized path expressions, XPath provides a syntax inspired from file systems, aiming at simplicity and conciseness. Conciseness is an important aspect of XPath, since it is meant to be embedded in host languages, such as XSLT or XPointer. Other aspects such as formal semantics, expressiveness, completeness, and complexity, have not played a central role in the development of XPath but have recently been investigated at length.

Data Model. An XML document is considered as an ordered and rooted tree with nodes for elements, attributes, character data, namespaces declaration, comments and processing instructions. The root of this tree is a special node which has the node for the XML document element as child. In this tree, element nodes are structured reflecting the element nesting in the XML document. Attribute and namespace declaration nodes are children of the node of the element they are specified with. Nodes for character data, for comments, and for processing instructions are children of the node of the element in which they occur, or of the root node if they are outside the document element. Note that a character node is always "maximal", i.e., it is not allowed that two character data nodes are immediate siblings. This model resembles the XML Information Set recommendation [94] and has become the foundation for most activities of the W3C related to query languages.

Path Expressions. The core expressions of XPath are "location steps". A location step specifies where to navigate from the so-called "context node", i.e., the current node of a path traversal. A location step consists of three parts: an "axis", a "node-test", and an optional "predicate". The axis specifies candidate nodes in terms of the tree data model: the base axes `self`, `child`, `following-sibling`, and `following` (selecting the context node, their children, their siblings, or all elements if they occur later in document order, resp.), the transitive and transitive-reflexive closure axes `descendant` and `descendant-or-self` of the axis `child`, and the respective "reverse" (or inverse) axes `parent`, `preceding-sibling`, `preceding`, `ancestor`, and `ancestor-or-self`. Two additional axes, `attributes` and `namespace`, give access to attributes and namespace declarations. Both node-tests and predicates serve to restrict the set of candidate nodes selected by an axis. The node-test can either restrict the label of the node (in case of element and attribute nodes), or the type of the node (e.g., restrict to comment children of an element). Predicates serve to further restrict elements to some neighborhood (which nodes are in the neighborhood of the node selected by an axis and node-test) or using functions (e.g., arithmetic or boolean operators).

Successive location steps are separated by "/" to form a path expression. A path expression can be seen as a nested iteration over the nodes selected by each location step. E.g., the path expression `child::book/descendant::name` expresses: *"for each book child of the context node select its name descendant"*.

XPath compares to generalized path expressions as follows:

- XPath allows navigation in all directions, while generalized path expressions only allow vertical and downwards navigation.
- XPath provides closure axes, but does not allow closure of arbitrary path expressions, e.g. as provided in Lorel.
- XPath has no means for defining variables, as it is intended to be used embedded in a host language that may provide such means. In contrast, Lorel and StruQL offer variables for connecting path expressions, making it possible to specify so-called tree or graph queries. Instead, XPath predicates may contain nested path expressions and thus allow the expression of tree and even some graph queries. However, not all graph queries can be expressed

this way. This has been recognized in XPath 2.0 [31], a revision of XPath currently under development at the W3C.

Reverse navigation has been considered for generalized path expressions, cf. [68, 69]). However, it has been shown in [225] that reverse axes do not increase the expressive power of path navigations.

Without closure of arbitrary path expressions, XPath cannot express regular path expressions such as a.(b.c)*.d (meaning *"select d's that are reached via one a and then arbitrary many repetitions of one b followed by one c"*) and a.b*.c, cf. [199, 200], where also a first-order complete extension to XPath is proposed that can express the second of the above-mentioned path expressions.

Query 1 can only be approximated in XPath as follows:

```
/descendant::book[attribute::type =
              /descendant::category[attribute::id = "Essay"]/
                        descendant-or-self::category/attribute::id]
```

XPath always returns a single set of nodes and provides no construction. Therefore, it is not possible to return authors and their names together with the book.

XPath also has an "abbreviated syntax". In this syntax the above query can more concisely be expressed as:

```
//book[@type = "Essay" or //category[@::id = "Essay"]/
                        descendant-or-self::category/@id]
```

Query 2 can be expressed in (abbreviated) XPath as:

```
//book[title="Bellum Civile"]
```

XPath returns a set of nodes as result of a query, the serialization being left to the host language. Most host languages consider as results the sub-trees rooted at the selected nodes, as desired by this query. The link to the category is not expressed by means of the XML hierarchy and therefore not included in the result.

Query 3 can be approximated in XPath (assuming we identify "ontology information" with category elements):

```
/bookdata//*[name(.) != "translator" and name(.) != "category"]
```

This query returns all descendants of the document element bookdata the labels of which (returned by the XPath function name) are neither "translator" nor "category". While this might at first glance seem to be a convenient solution for Query 3 (the set of nodes returned by the expression indeed does not contain translators and categories), the link between selected book nodes and the excluded translators is not removed and in most host languages of XPath the translators would be included as part of their book parent.

Queries 4 and 7–9 cannot be expressed in XPath because they all require some form of construction.

Aggregations, needed by Query 5, are provided by XPath. Query 5 can be expressed as follows:

```
max(//book[author/name="Julius Caesar"]/year)
```

The aggregation in Query 6 can be expressed analogously. However, Query 6 like Query 1 cannot be expressed in XPath properly due to the lack of construction.

XPath in Industry and Research. Thanks to XPath's ubiquity in W3C standards (in XML Schema [108], in XSLT [85], in XPointer [135], in XQuery [42], in DOM Level 3), XPath has been adopted widely in industry both as part of implementations of the afore-mentioned W3C standards and in contexts not (yet) considered by the W3C, e.g., for policy specifications. It has also been included in a number of APIs for XML processing in languages for providing easy access to data in XML documents.

XPath has also been deeply investigated in research. *Formal semantics* for (more or less complete) fragments for XPath have been proposed in [129, 225, 275]. Surprisingly, most popular implementations of XPath embedded within XSLT processors exhibit exponential behavior, even for fairly small data and large queries. However, the *combined complexity* of XPath query evaluation has been shown to be P-complete [131, 132]. Various sub-languages of XPath (e.g., forward XPath [225], Core or Navigational XPath [132], [26]) and extensions (e.g., CXPath [199]) have been investigated, mostly with regard to expressiveness and complexity for query evaluation. Also, satisfiability of positive XPath expressions is known to be in NP and, even for expressions without boolean operators, NP-hard [149]. Containment of XPath queries (with or without additional constraints, e.g., by means of a document schema) has been investigated as well, cf., e.g., [98, 211, 250, 285]. Several methods providing efficient implementations of XPath relying on standard relational database systems have been published, cf., e.g., [137, 138, 226].

Currently, the W3C is, as part of its activity on specifying the XML query language XQuery, developing a revision of XPath: XPath 2.0 [31]. See [164] for an introduction. The most striking additions in XPath 2.0 are: (1) a facility for defining variables (using `for` expressions), (2) sequences instead of sets as answers, (3) the move from the value typed XPath 1.0 to extensive support for XML schema types in a strongly typed language, (4) a considerably expanded library of functions and operators [193], and (5) a complete formal semantics [104].

Project pages:
    http://www.w3.org/TR/xpath for XPath 1.0
    http://www.w3.org/TR/xpath20/ for XPath 2.0
Implementations:
    numerous, mostly as part of implementations of XPath host languages or APIs for processing XML (e.g., W3C's DOM Level 3)
Online demonstration:
    none (offline XPathTester http://xml.coverpages.org/ni2001-05-25-a.html)

XPathLog. XPathLog [203] is syntactically an extension of XPath but its semantics and evaluation are based on logic programming, more specifically F-Logic and FLORID [188]. XPathLog extends the syntax of XPath as follows: (1) variables may occur in path expressions, e.g., `//book[name` $\rightarrow$ `N]` $\rightarrow$ B binds B to books and N to the names of the books, and (2) both existential and universal quantifiers can be used in Boolean expressions. The data model of XPathLog deviates considerably from XPath's data model: XML documents are viewed in XPathLog as edge-labeled graphs with implicit dereferencing of ID/IDREF references. XPathLog provides means for constructing new or updating the existing XML data, as well as more advanced reactive features such as integrity constraints.

Project page:
    http://dbis.informatik.uni-goettingen.de/lopix/
Implementation:
    With the LoPiX system, available from the project page
Online demonstration:
    none

FnQuery. FnQuery [254] is another approach for combining path expressions with logic programming. Attribute lists are used to define a novel representation of XML in Prolog called "field-notation". Data in this representation can then be queried using FnPath: E.g., the expression

```
D^bookdata^book-[^title:'Bellum Civile', ^year:1992]
```

returns the book with title "Bellum Civile" published in "1990" if the sample data from Section 2.2 is bound to D. As XPathLog FnQuery allows multiple variables in a path expression. It has been used, e.g., for visualizing knowledge bases [256] and querying OWL ontologies [255].

Project page:
    http://www-info1.informatik.uni-wuerzburg.de/database/research_
    seipel.html
Implementation:
    not publicly available
Online demonstration:
    none

The Transformation Language XSLT. XSLT [85], the Extensible Stylesheet Language, is a language for *transforming* XML documents. Transformation is here understood as the process of creating a new XML document based upon a given one. The distinction between querying and transformation has become increasingly blurred as expressiveness of both query and transformation languages increase. Typically, transformation languages are very convenient for expressing selection, restructuring and reduction queries, such as Query 3 above.

XSLT uses an XML syntax with embedded XPath expressions. While the XML syntax makes processing and generation of XSLT stylesheets easier (cf. [279]), it has been criticized as hard to read and overly verbose. Also XPath expressions use a non-XML syntax requiring a specialized parser.

XSLT Computations. An XSLT program (called "stylesheet" reflecting the origin of XSLT as part of the XSL project) is composed of one or more transformation rules (called *templates*) that recursively operate on a single input document. Transformation rules are guarded by XPath expressions. In a template, one can specify (1) the resulting shape of the elements matched by the guard expression and (2) which elements in the input tree to process next with what templates. The selection of the elements to process further is done using an XPath expression. If no specific restriction is given, all templates with guards matching these elements are considered, but one can also specify a single (named) template or a group of templates by changing the so-called *mode* of processing. XSLT allows also recursive templates. However, recursion is limited: except for templates constructing strings only, the result of a template is immutable (a so-called *result tree fragment*) and cannot be input for further templates except for literal copies. This means in particular, that no views can be defined in XSLT. Work in [169] shows that XSLT is nevertheless Turing complete, by using recursive templates with string parameters and XSLT's powerful string processing functions.

XSLT 2.0. Recently this and other limitations (e.g., the ability to process only a single input document, no support for XML Schema, limited support for namespaces, lack of specific grouping constructs) have lead to a revision of XSLT: XSLT 2.0 [167]. As with XQuery 1.0, this language is based upon XPath 2.0 [31]. It addresses the above mentioned concerns, in particular adding XML schema support, powerful grouping constructs, and proper views. The XQuery 1.0 and XPath 2.0 function and operator library [193] is also available in XSLT 2.0.

Sample Queries. All example queries can be expressed in XSLT. Query 2 and 5 to 8 are omitted as their solutions are similar enough to solutions shown in the following.

Query 1 can be expressed in XSLT as follows:

```
<xsl:stylesheet version="1.0"
                xmlns:xsl="http://www.w3.org/1999/XSL/Transform">
  <xsl:template match="/">
    <results>
      <xsl:apply-templates select="//book[@type =
              //category[@id = 'Essay']/descendant-or-self::category/@id]"/>
    </results>
  </xsl:template>
  <xsl:template match="book">
    <result>
      <xsl:copy select = "."/>
      <xsl:apply-templates select="author|author/name" />
```

```
    </result>
  </xsl:template>
  <xsl:template match="author|author/name">
    <xsl:copy-of select="." />
  </xsl:template>
</xsl:stylesheet>
```

This stylesheet can be evaluated as follows:

- try to match the root node (matched by the guard / of the template in line 3) with the guards of templates in the style-sheet (only first template matches)
- create a `<results>` element and within it try to recursively apply the templates to all nodes matched by the XPath expression in the `select` attribute of the `apply-templates` statement in line 5.
- such nodes are book elements matched by the second template which creates a `<result>` element, makes a shallow copy of itself and recursively applies the rules to the book's author children and their name children.
- for each author or name of an author, copy the complete input to the result.

Aside from templates, XSLT also provides explicit iteration, selection, and assignment constructs: `xsl:for-each`, `xsl:if`, `xsl:variable` among others. Using these constructs one can formulate Query 1 alternatively as follows:

```
<results xmlns:xsl="http://www.w3.org/1999/XSL/Transform">
  <xsl:for-each select="//book[@type = //category[@id = 'Essay']/
                                 descendant-or-self::category/@id]">
    <result>
      <xsl:copy select = "."/>
      <xsl:for-each select = "author|author/name">
        <xsl:copy-of select="." />
      </xsl:for-each>
    </result>
  </xsl:for-each>
</results>
```

The `xsl:for-each` expressions iterate over the elements of the node set selected by the XPath expression in their `select` attribute. Aside from the expressions for copying input this very much resembles the solution for Query 1 in XQuery shown in the following section.

Whereas the first style of programming in XSLT is sometimes referred to as rule-based, the latter one is known as the "fill-in-the-blanks" style, as one specifies essentially the shape of the output with "blanks" to be filled with the result of XSLT expressions. Other programming styles in XSLT can be identified, cf. [165].

Query 3 can be expressed in XSLT as follows:

```
<xsl:stylesheet version="1.0"
        xmlns:xsl="http://www.w3.org/1999/XSL/Transform">
```

```
<xsl:template match="@*|node()">
  <xsl:copy>
    <xsl:apply-templates select="@*|node()"/>
  </xsl:copy>
</xsl:template>
<xsl:template match="translator | category" />
</xsl:stylesheet>
```

The first template specifies that for all attributes and nodes, the node itself is copied and their (attribute and node) children are processed recursively. The second template specifies that for translators and category elements, nothing is generated (and their children are *not* processed). Notice that the first template also matches translator and category elements. For such a case where multiple templates match, XSLT uses detailed conflict resolution policies. In this case, the second template is chosen as it is more specific than the first one (for more the details of resolution rules, refer to [85]).

Query 4 can be expressed in XSLT as follows:

```
<xsl:stylesheet version="1.0"
                xmlns:xsl="http://www.w3.org/1999/XSL/Transform">
  <xsl:template match="/">
    <bookdata>
      <xsl:apply-template
          select="//author[not(name = preceding::author/name)]" />
    </bookdata>
  </xsl:template>
  <xsl:template match="author">
    <person>
      <name><xsl:value-of select="name" /></name>
      <authored>
        <xsl:apply-templates
            select="//book[author/name=current()/name]" />
      </authored>
    </person>
  </xsl:template>
  <xsl:template match="book">
    <book>
      <xsl:copy-of select="@*" />
      <xsl:copy-of select="*[name() != 'author']" />
    </book>
  </xsl:template>
</xsl:stylesheet>
```

The preceding axis from XPath is used to avoid duplicates in the result. Also note the use of the current() function in the second template. This function always returns the current node considered by an XSLT expression. Here, it returns the author element last matched by the second template. This function is essentially syntactic sugar to limit the use of variables (cf. solution for Query 9).

Query 9 can be expressed in XSLT as follows:

```
<xsl:stylesheet version="1.0"
                xmlns:xsl="http://www.w3.org/1999/XSL/Transform">
  <xsl:template match="/">
    <results>
      <xsl:for-each select="//author">
        <xsl:variable name="author" select="." />
        <xsl:for-each select="$author/following-sibling::author">
          <co-authors>
            <name> <xsl:value-of select="$author/name" /> </name>
            <name> <xsl:value-of select="current()/name" /> </name>
          </co-authors>
        </xsl:for-each>
      </xsl:for-each>
    </results>
  </xsl:template>
</xsl:stylesheet>
```

Here, the solution is quite similar to the XQuery solution for Query 9 shown below (but can use in `following-sibling` axis that is only optionally available in XQuery), as variables and `xsl:for-each` expressions are used. The solution uses `xsl:for-each`, as the inner and the outer author are processed differently. A solution without `xsl:for-each` is possible but requires parameterized templates and named or grouped templates:

```
<xsl:stylesheet version="1.0"
                xmlns:xsl="http://www.w3.org/1999/XSL/Transform">
  <xsl:template match="/">
    <results>
      <xsl:apply-template select="//author" />
    </results>
  </xsl:template>
  <xsl:template match="author">
    <xsl:apply-template select="following-sibling::author"
                        mode="co-author">
      <xsl:with-param name="first-co-author" select="." />
    </xsl:apply-templates>
  </xsl:template>
  <xsl:template match="author" mode="co-author">
    <xsl:param name="first-co-author" />
    <co-authors>
      <name> <xsl:value-of select="$first-co-author/name" /> </name>
      <name> <xsl:value-of select="name" /> </name>
    </co-authors>
  </xsl:template>
</xsl:stylesheet>
```

Note that for clarity neither of these solutions avoids duplicates if two persons are co-authors of multiple books.

XSLT in Industry and Academia. XSLT has been the first W3C language for transforming and querying XML and thus has been adopted quickly and widely. A multitude of implementations exist (e.g. as part of the standard library for XML processing in Java) as well as good practical introductions (e.g.., [165, 269]).

Research on XSLT has not received the same attention that XPath and XQuery have, in particular not from the database community. A more detailed overview of research issues on XSLT and its connection to reactive rules is given in [13], here only some core results are outlined: Formal semantics for (fragments of) XSLT have been investigated in [38, 171]. [169] gives a proof showing that XSLT is Turing complete. Analysis of XSLT is examined in [103], which proposes four analysis properties and presents an analysis method based on the construction of a template association graph, which conservatively models the control flow of the stylesheet. There is also an important line of theoretical research with regard to analysis of the behaviour of XSLT. Work in [214] presents a theoretical model of XSLT and examines a number of decision questions for fragments of this model. Work in [198] examines the question of whether the output of an XML transformation conforms to a particular document type. Type checking is also addressed in [272].

Efficient evaluation of XSLT programs is also an important topic. In [156, 186], translations to SQL are considered. Work in [274] describes incremental methods for processing multiple transformations. Work in [249] proposes a lazy evaluation for XSLT programs, while [166] describes optimizations based on experiences from the widely used XSLT processor Saxon. Other specific techniques for optimizing XSLT programs and evaluation are described in [102, 134, 143, 273]. Further engineering aspects of XSLT programs have also received attention, namely transformation debugging [12] and automatic stylesheet generation [227, 279].

Project page:
    http://www.w3.org/Style/XSL/
Implementation:
    very numerous, see project page
Online demonstration:
    none

Fxt. fxt [33], the *functional XML transformer*, is a transformation language similar to XSLT, in particular with respect to its syntax. However, instead of XPath expressions *fxt* uses *fxgrep* patterns that are based on an expressive grammar formalisms and can be evaluated very efficiently (cf. [32]). *Fxt*'s computation model is also more restricted than that of XSLT due to the lack of named templates.

Project page:
    http://atseidl2.informatik.tu-muenchen.de/~berlea/Fxt/
Implementation:
    available from the project page

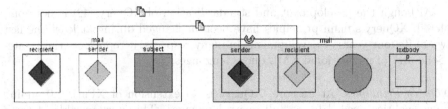

Fig. 3. Treemap representation of a VXT rule(Pietriga et al. [233], © ACM Press)

Online demonstration:
   none

VXT. VXT [233] is a visual language and interactive environment for specifying transformations of XML documents. It is based on the general purpose transformation language Circus[5]: Whereas most other XML query languages employ some form of graph-shaped visualization for both data and queries, VXT uses treemaps [157] for representing hierarchies: the nesting of the elements in the document is reflected by nested of nodes. As XSLT, VXT uses rules to specify transformations. A rule consists in treemap representation of the queried data and the constructed data. The two representations are linked by various typed edges indicating, e.g., the copying of a matching node or its content, cf. 3

Project page:
   none
Implementation:
   not publicly available
Online demonstration:
   none

The Query Language XQuery. Shortly before the publication of the final XPath 1.0 and XSLT 1.0 recommendations, the W3C launched an activity towards specifying an XML query language. In contrast to XSLT, this query language aims at a syntax and semantics making it convenient for database systems. Requirements and use cases for the language have been given in [78, 79, 192]. A number of proposals, e.g., XQL and Quilt, have been published in answer to this activity, each with varying influence on XQuery [42], the language currently under standardisation at the W3C:

   XQL [244, 245] notably influenced the development of XPath. Although XQL did not consider the full range of XPath axes, some language features that have not been included in XPath, e.g., existential and universal quantifiers and an extended range of set operations, are under reconsideration for XPath 2.0.

   Quilt [77] is in spirit already close to the current version of XQuery, mainly lacking the extensive type system developed by the W3C's XML query working group. It can be considered the predecessor of XQuery.

---

[5] http://www.xrce.xerox.com/solutions/circus.html

Although the development and standardisation of XQuery [42] is not completed, XQuery's main principles have been unchanged during at least the last two of its four years of development. In many respects, it represents the "state-of-the-art" of navigational XML query languages.

XQuery Principles. At its core, XQuery is an extension of XPath 2.0 adding functionalities needed by a "full query language". The most notable of these functionalities are:

- *Sequences.* Where in XPath 1.0 the results of path expressions are node sets, XQuery and XPath 2.0 use sequences. Sequences can be constructed or result from the evaluation of an XQuery expression. In contrast to XPath 1.0, sequences cannot only be composed of nodes but also from atomic values, e.g., (1, 2, 3) is a proper XQuery sequence.
- *Strong typing.* Like XPath 2.0, XQuery is a strongly typed language. In particular, most of the (simple and complex) data types of XML Schema are supported. The details of the type system are described in [104]. Furthermore, many XQuery implementations provide (although it is an optional feature) static type checking.
- *Construction, Grouping, and Ordering.* Where XPath is limited to selecting parts of the input data, XQuery provides ample support for constructing new data. Constructors for all node types as well as the simple data types from XML Schema are provided. New elements can be created either by so-called direct element constructors (that look just like XML elements) or by what is referred to as computed element constructors, e.g. allowing the name of a newly constructed element to be the result of a part of the query. For examples on these constructors, see the implementations for Query 1 and 3 below.
- *Variables.* Like XPath 2.0, XQuery has variables defined in so-called FLWOR expressions. A FLWOR expression usually consists in one or more **for**, an optional **where** clause, an optional **order by**, and a **return** clause. The **for** clause iterates over the items in the sequence returned by the path expression in its **in** part: **for $book in //book** iterates over all books selected by the path expression **//book**. The **where** clause specifies conditions on the selected data items, the **order by** clause allows the items to be processed in a certain order, and the **return** clause specifies the result of the entire FLWOR expression (often using constructors as shown above). Additionally, FLWOR expressions may contain, after the **for** clauses, **let** clauses that also bind variables but without iterating over the individual data items in the sequence bound to the variable. FLWOR expressions resemble very much XSLT's explicit iteration, selection, and assignment constructs described above.
- *User-defined functions.* XQuery allows the user to define new functions specified in XQuery (cf. implementation of Query 3 below). Functions may be recursive.
- *Unordered sequences.* As a means for assisting query optimization, XQuery provides the **unordered** keyword, indicating that the order of elements in

sequences that are constructed or returned as result of XQuery expressions is not relevant. E.g., `unordered{for $book in //book return $book/name}` indicates that the nodes selected by `//book` may be processed in any order in the `for` clause and the order of the resulting name nodes also can be arbitrary (implementation dependent). Note that inside unordered query parts, the result of any expressions querying the order of elements in sequences such as `fn:position`, `fn:last` is non-deterministic.

- *Universal and existential quantification.* Both XPath 2.0 and XQuery 1.0 provide `some` and `all` for expressing existentially or universally quantified conditions (see implementation of Query 9 below).
- *Schema validation.* XQuery implementations may (optionally) provide support for schema validation, both of input and of constructed data, using the `validate` expression.
- *Full host language.* XQuery completes XPath with capabilities to set up the context of path expressions, e.g., declaring namespace prefixes and default namespace, importing function libraries and modules (optional), and (again optionally) providing flexible means for serialization that are in fact shared with XSLT 2.0 (cf. [168]).

In at least one respect, XQuery is more restrictive than XPath: not all of XPath's axes are mandatory, `ancestor`, `ancestor-or-self`, `following`, `following-sibling`, `preceding`, and `preceding-sibling` do not have to be supported by an XQuery implementation. This is, however, no restriction to XQuery's expressiveness, as expressions using reverse axes (such as `ancestor`) can be rewritten, cf. [225], and the "horizontal axes", e.g., `following` and `following-sibling`, can be replaced by FLWOR expressions using the `<<` and `>>` operators that compare two nodes with respect to their position in a sequence.

For a formal semantics for XQuery 1.0 (and XPath 2.0) see [104]. Comprehensive but easy to follow introductions to XQuery are given in, e.g., [53, 163].

Sample Queries. All nine sample queries can be expressed in XQuery. In the following, an expression of Query 2 is omitted because it can be expressed as a simplification of the XQuery expression of Query 1 given below. Query 5 can be expressed as for XPath, cf. above. Expressions of Query 8 and 9 are similar. Since the expression for Query 9 in XQuery exhibits an interesting anomaly, it is given below and no expression for Query 8 is given.

Query 1 can be expressed in XQuery as follows (interpreting the phrase "an essay" as a book with type attribute equal to the id of the category "Essay" or one of its sub-categories represented as descendants in the XML structure):

```
<results> {
  let $doc := doc("http://example.org/books")/bookdata
  let $sub-of-essay :=
        $doc//category[@id="Essay"]/descendant-or-self::category
  for $book in $doc//book
  where $book/@type = $sub-of-essay/@id
  return
```

```
    <result>
      { $book }
      { $book/author }
      { $book/author/name }
    </result> }
</results>
```

Note the use of the `let` clause in line 2: the sequence of all sub-categories of the category with `id` "Essay" including that category itself (we use the reflexive transitive axis `descendant-or-self`) is bound to the variable. However, in contrast to a `for` expression, this sequence is not iterated over. Instead of the `where` clause in line 4 a predicate could be added to the path expression in line 3 resulting in the expression `$doc//book[@type = $sub-of-essay/@id]`.

Query 3 requires structural recursion over the tree, while constructing new elements that are identical to the ones encountered, except omitting translator and category nodes. The following implementation shows the use of a user-defined, recursive function that copies the tree rooted at its first parameter `$e`, except all nodes in the sequence given as second parameter.

```
declare function
  local:tree-except($e as element(),
                    $exceptions as node()*) as element()*
{
    element {fn:node-name($e)} {
      $e/@* except $exceptions, (: copy the attributes :)
      for $child in $element/node() except $exceptions
      return
        if $child instance of element()
          (: for elements process them recursively :)
          local:tree-except($section)
        else (: others (text, comments, etc. copy  :)
          $child
    }
};

document {
    let $doc :=  doc("http://example.org/books")/bookdata
    let $exceptions := $doc//translator union $doc//category
    local:tree-except($doc, $exceptions)
  }
```

Note the typing of the parameters: the first parameter is a single element, the second, a sequence of nodes and the function returns a sequence of elements. In the main part of the query, the `document` constructor is used to indicate that its content is to be the document element of the constructed tree.

Query 4 can be expressed in XQuery as follows:

```
<bookdata> {
  let $a := doc("http://example.org/books")//author
```

```
  for $name in distinct-values($a/name)
  return
    <person>
      <name> { $name } </name>
      <authored
      {
          for $b in doc("http://example.org/books")//book
          where some $ba in $b/author
                satisfies $ba/name = $name
          return
            <book> { $b/@*, $b/* except $b/author } </book>
      }
      </authored>
    </person>
  }
</bookdata>
```

This implementation is in fact similar to the implementation of use case XMP-Q4 in [79] and exhibits two noteworthy functionalities: (1) The use of `distinct-value` in line 3 to avoid duplication in the result, if an author occurs multiple times in the document. (2) The use of an existentially quantified condition in lines 10–11, to find books where some (read: at least one) of the authors have the same name as the currently considered author.

Using aggregation expressions (see lines 8 and 10), Query 6 can be expressed in XQuery as follows:

```
<results> {
  let $doc := doc("http://example.org/books")/bookdata
  for $category in $doc//category[@id="Essay"]//category
  return
    <category>
      { $category/@id }
      <average-number-of-authors>{
        fn:avg(for $book in $doc//book
               where @type = $category/@id
               return fn:count($book/author))
      }
      </average-number-of-authors>
    </category>
  }
</results>
```

Combining data can be expressed in a very compact manner in XQuery, as the following expression of Query 7 shows:

```
<book>
  { for $book in doc("http://example.org/books")//book
    where title="Bellum Civile" and author/name="Julius Caesar"
    return ($book/@*, $book/*)
  }
```

```
  {
    for $book in doc("http://example.org/books")//book
    where @id="bellum_civile"
    return ($book/@*, $book/*)
  }
</book>
```

Query 9 can be expressed in XQuery as follows:

```
<results>
  { let $doc := doc("http://example.org/books")
    for $book in doc("http://example.org/books")//book
      for $author in $book/author
        for $co-author in $book/author
        where $author << $co-author
        return
          <co-authors>
            <name> { $author/name } </name>
            <name> { $co-author/name } </name>
          </co-authors>
  }
</results>
```

This implementation does not treat the case where two authors co-authored multiple books. In this case, duplicates are created by the above solution. To avoid this the following refinement uses the before operator << in combination with a negated condition, for specifying that only such pairs of authors should be considered, where there is no book that occurs prior to the currently considered one and which is also co-authored by the current pair of authors:

```
<results>
  { let $doc := doc("http://example.org/books")
    for $book in doc("http://example.org/books")//book
      for $author in $book/author
        for $co-author in $book/author
        where $author << $co-author and not(
          some $pb in doc("http://example.org/books")//book
          satisfies ($pb << $book and
                     $pb//author/name = $author/name and
                     $pb//author/name = $co-author/name))
        return
          <co-authors>
            <name> { $author/name } </name>
            <name> { $co-author/name } </name>
          </co-authors>
  }
</results>
```

XQuery in Industry and Research. From the very start, XQuery's development has been followed by industry and research with equal interest (for reports on the challenges and decisions during this process see, e.g., [106, 109]). Even before the development has finished, initial practical introductions to XQuery have been published, e.g., [53, 163]. Industry interest is also visible in the simultaneous development of standardized XQuery APIs, e.g., for Java [107], and numerous implementations, both open source (e.g., Galax [112]) and commercial (BEA [118], IPSI-XQ [110]). Aside from these main-memory implementations, one can also find streamed implementations of XQuery (e.g., [22, 173]) where the data flows by as the query is evaluated. First results on implementing XQuery on top of standard relational databases (e.g., [97, 139]) indicate that this approach leads to very efficient query evaluation if a suitable relational encoding of the XML data is used. For more implementations, see the XQuery project page at the W3C and the proceedings of the first XIME-P workshop on "XQuery Implementation, Experience and Perspectives"[6].

It is intuitively clear that XQuery is Turing complete since it provides recursive functions and conditional expressions. A formal proof of the Turing-completeness of XQuery is given in [169]. Efficient processing and (algebraic) optimization of XQuery, although acknowledged as crucial topics, have not yet been sufficiently investigated. First results are presented, e.g., in [80, 81, 101, 202, 268, 287, 288]. Moreover, techniques for efficient XPath evaluation, as discussed above, can be a foundation for XQuery optimization.

Beyond querying XML data, it has also been suggested to use XQuery for data mining [278], for web service implementation [228], for querying heterogeneous *relational* databases [281], for access control and policy descriptions [216], for synopsis generation [92], and as the foundation of a visual XML query language (XQBE) [10], of a XML query language with full-text capabilities [6, 7], and of an update [54, 76, 243] and reactive [46] language for XML.

Project page:
   http://www.w3.org/XML/Query
Implementations:
   widely implementated (more than 30 implementations), a list of implementations is available at the project page
Online demonstrations:
   several, e.g.: http://www.oakleaf.ws/xquery/xquerydemo.aspx
   http://oasys.ipsi.fhg.de/xquerydemo/
   http://131.107.228.20/xquerydemo/demo.aspx

3.2   Research Prototypes: The Positional Approach to XML Querying

Characteristics of the Positional Approach. The languages discussed in the following all take the *positional approach* for locating data in an XML document. This approach is often derived from logic or functional programming where patterns are used to specify the position of interesting data inside larger structures.

---

[6] http://www-rocq.inria.fr/gemo/Gemo/Projects/XIME-P/

Essentially, positional languages use expressions that mimic the data to be queried. This allows tree- or graph-shaped *queries* to be expressed very similar to tree- or graph-shaped *data* (as "examples" of the data to be queried, cf. [290]), whereas navigational languages do not provide this close correspondence. However, many languages in this sections (e.g., UnQL, TQL, and Xcerpt) do actually use path expressions mostly as convenient shorthands for parts of queries that are shaped like a single path.

Languages using this "query-by-example" style for queries mostly fall into two categories: (a) query languages influenced by logic or functional programming (UnQL, XML-QL, XMAS, XML-RL, TQL) and (b) visual query languages or visual interfaces for textual query languages (XML-GL, BBQ, and X^2's visual query interface).

UnQL. UnQL [64, 65, 66] (the *Unstructured Query Language*) is a query language originally developed for querying semistructured data and nested relational data-bases with cyclic structures. It has later been adopted to querying XML, but the origins are still apparent in many language properties (for example, UnQL has a non-XML syntax that is very similar to OEM's syntax and does not support querying or construction of ordered data).

The evaluation model and core language of UnQL is based upon structural recursion over labeled trees. It provides both a functional-style language for expressing recursions over trees, cf. [65] and a more approachable surface syntax.[7]

The following expression uses functional style pattern matching for selecting all books in a tree.

```
fun f1(T1 ∪ T2)    = f1(T1) ∪ f1(T2)
 | f1({ L ⇒ T })  = if L = book then {result ⇒ book ⇒ T} else f1(T)
 | f1({})          = {}
 | f1(V)           = {}
```

UnQL's *surface syntax* uses *query patterns* and *construction patterns* and a query consists of a single **select** ... **where** ... or **traverse** rule that separate construction from querying. Queries may be nested, in which case the separation of querying and construction is abandoned.

Query 1 can be expressed in UnQL as

```
select { results ⇒ {
  select { result ⇒ { Book,
    select { author ⇒ {
               author ⇒ Author,
               authorName ⇒ Name
             } }
    where { author ⇒ \Author } ← Book,
          { name ⇒ \Name } ← Author
  where { book ⇒ \Book } ← Bib
where bookdata ⇒ Bib ← DB
```

---

[7] The syntax from [64, 65] is used and not the slightly differing syntax in [66].

The ← scopes a query pattern, i.e., it specifies that the left-hand query pattern is to be found in bindings for the right-hand variable. The ⇒ operator is the direct edge traversal operator. E.g., book ⇒ author specifies that author is a direct child of book in the XML document. Recursive traversals can be specified using regular path expressions including regular expressions over labels. E.g., _* traverses over arbitrary many elements with any label, [^book]* over arbitrary many elements with any label except book.

UnQL also provides traverse clauses for reduction and restructuring queries like Query 3:

```
traverse DB given X
   case translator ⇒ _ then X := {}
   case category ⇒ _    then X := {}
   case \L ⇒ _          then X := {l ⇒ X}
```

This query is evaluated by traversing the tree in the database and matching recursively each element against the three case expressions. All elements except translators and categories are copied to the newly constructed tree, structured as in the input data.

UnQL is probably the first language to propose a pattern-based querying (albeit with subqueries instead of rule chaining) for semistructured data (including XML).

Evaluation and optimization of UnQL has been investigated in [64, 66]. UnQL's evaluation is founded in graph simulation, see [66]. [64] shows that all queries expressible in UnQL can be evaluated in PTIME. This is true even for queries against cyclic graph data (e.g. XML documents using cyclic ID/IDREF references). This efficiency is reflected by UnQL's expressiveness: on trees encoding relational or nested relational databases, UnQL is exactly as expressive as relational or nested relational algebra, resp.

Project page:
    http://www.research.att.com/~suciu/unql-home.html[8]
Implementation:
    available from the project page
Online demonstration:
    none

XML-QL. XML-QL [99, 100] is a pattern- and rule-based query language for XML developed specifically to address the W3C's call for an XML query language (that resulted in the development of XQuery). Like UnQL, it uses *query patterns* (called *element patterns* in [99]) in a WHERE clause. Such patterns can be augmented by variables for selecting data. The result of a query is specified as a *construction patterns* in the CONSTRUCT clause. An XML-QL query always consists of a single WHERE-CONSTRUCT rule, which may be divided into several (nested) subqueries.

---

[8] Not accessible at the time of writing.

Query 1 can be expressed in XML-QL as follows:

```
WHERE
  <bookdata>
    <book>
    </> ELEMENT_AS $b
  </>
CONSTRUCT
  <results>
    <result>
      $b
      WHERE <author>
              <name> $n </>
            </> ELEMENT_AS $a
      CONSTRUCT $a
                $n
    </>
  </>
```

Variables are preceded in XML-QL by $. Note how the grouping of authors with their books is expressed using a nested query. Also note the tag minimization (end tags abbreviated by </> as in SGML), e.g., in line 4 and 5. In line 4, the variable $b is restricted to data matching the pattern in lines 3 and 4. Such "pattern restrictions" are indicated in XML-QL using the ELEMENT_AS keyword.

One of the main characteristics of XML-QL is that it uses query patterns containing multiple variables that may select several data items at a time instead of path selections that may only select one data item at a time. Furthermore, variables are similar to the variables of logic programming, i.e. "joins" can be evaluated over variable name equality. Since XML-QL does not allow one to use more than one separate rule, it is often necessary to employ subqueries to perform complex queries.

Query 6 cannot be expressed in XML-QL due to lack of aggregation, in particular structural aggregation (e.g., counting the number of children of an element). The following query returns all books classified in a sub-category of "Novel":

```
WHERE
  <book type=$Sub>
  </> ELEMENT_AS $b,
  <category id='Novel'>
    <category* id=$Sub>
    </>
  </>
CONSTRUCT $b
```

As discussed, above joins are simply expressed by repeated occurrences of the same variable (lines 2 and 5). In line 5 a further feature of XML-QL is shown: instead of element labels one can use regular path expressions in patterns.

Transformation queries such as Query 2, where the output closely resembles the input except for some rather localized changes (e.g., omission of elements or changing labels), cannot in general be expressed in XML-QL.

Also XML-QL does not provide any means for testing the non-existence of elements and therefore cannot express queries such as "Return all books that have no translator.".

No results on complexity or expressiveness of XML-QL have been published.

Project page:
    http://www.research.att.com/~mff/xmlql/doc/
Implementation:
    available from the project page
Online demonstration:
    none

XMAS. XMAS [189], the *XML Matching And Structuring language* is an XML query language developed as part of MIX [18] and builds upon XML-QL. Like XML-QL, XMAS uses *query patterns* and *construction patterns*, and rules of the form CONSTRUCT ...WHERE .... However, XMAS extends XML-QL in that it provides a powerful *grouping construct*, instead of relying on subqueries for grouping data items within an element.

Query 1 can be expressed in XMAS as follows:

```
WHERE
  <bookdata>
    $B: <book>
          $A: <author>
                <name> $N </name>
              </>
        </>
  </>
CONSTRUCT
  <results>
    <result>
      $B
      <book-author>
        $A
        <name> $N </name>
      </> {$A,$N}
    </> {$B}
  </>
```

Here, one can observe the two main syntactic differences to XML-QL: (1) In XMAS, grouping is expressed by enclosing the variables on whose bindings the grouping is performed in curly braces and attaching them to the end of the subpattern that specifies the structure of the resulting instances. In the above example, a result element is created for every instance of $B (indicated by {$B} after the closing tag of the element result). Within every such result element, all authors of a book (indicated by {$A}) are collected nested in `book-author` elements (the `book-author` element is necessary for grouping variables are allowed only after closing tags or single variables in XMAS).

(2) XMAS also provides a more compact syntax for *pattern restrictions* that allow one to restrict the admissible bindings of a variable as seen in line 3 ($B in front of the subpattern instead of XML-QL's `ELEMENT_AS` $B at the end).

Grouping queries can be specified even more concisely by using "implicit collection labels": instead of specifying the grouping variables explicitly, all variables nested inside square brackets are considered grouping variables for that grouping, unless there is another grouping (i.e., block enclosed by square brackets) closer to the variable occurrence. Using implicit collection labels, Query 1 can be expressed as:

```
WHERE
  <bookdata>
    $B: <book>
          $A: <author>
                <name> $N </name>
              </>
        </>
  </>
CONSTRUCT
  <results>
    [<result>
      $B
      [<book-author>
        $A
        <name> $N </name>
      </book-author>]
    </>]
  </>
```

No results on complexity or expressiveness of XMAS have been published.

BBQ [215] is a visual interface for XMAS that allows browsing of XML data as well as authoring of XMAS queries based on a DTD of the data to be queried. Figure 4 shows the two-pane query editor with a query pattern on the left and an (empty) construct pattern at the right.

Project page:
    http://www.db.ucsd.edu/projects/MIX/
Implementation:
    publicly available only as part of the BBQ online demonstration
Online demonstration:
    using BBQ http://www.db.ucsd.edu/Projects/MIX/BBQ_User_Interface.
    html

XML-RL. XML-RL [187] is a a pattern-based query language based on logic programming. Patterns are expressed by terms that may contain logic variables

Fig. 4. Screenshot of BBQ's query editor (Munroe and Papakonstantinou [215], © Kluwer, B.V.)

and may be partly abbreviated with a path syntax similar to abbreviated XPath. An XML-RL query program consists of one or more rules denoted by $A \Leftarrow L_1, \ldots, L_n$ where A is used for construction and $L_1, \ldots, L_n$ are query pattern. Rules may interact via rule chaining and it is possible to use recursion.

Query 1 can be expressed in XML-RL as follows:

```
/results/result: (book:$b, {author: $a}, {authorName: $n})
⇐
(file:bib.xml)
/bookdata/book: $b(author: $a(name:$n))
```

The URL in line 3 defines the input data for the query. Analogously it is also possible to give an URL in the construct part of the query (line 1). Notice the curly brackets in line 1. They specify, that authors and author names are to be grouped by book.

XML-RL does not provide specific support for transformation queries such as Query 3, but they can be solved using recursive rules.

Query 6 can be expressed in XML-RL.

```
/results/result: ($i, avg-number-of-authors: $avg)
⇐
(file:bib.xml)
/bookdata/category: (@id: Writing, category//category/@id: $i),
(file:bib.xml)
/bookdata/book: #b (@type: $i, author: #a),
$avg = count(#a) ÷ count(#b) ;
```

```
/bookdata/category: (@id: Writing, category/@id: $i),
(file:bib.xml)
/bookdata/book: #b (@type: $i, author: #a),
$avg = count(#a) ÷ count(#b)
```

This rule has two alternative query expressions (separated as in Prolog by ;) but only a single head. The first alternative covers the case of indirect subcategories of "Writing", the second the case of direct ones. In both cases, the id attribute of a category is selected and joined with the type attribute of books. The books are collected in the *list* variable #b, all their authors in the list variable #a. Finally, the average number of authors per publication in that sub-category is computed by dividing the number of elements in the two lists.

No results on complexity or expressiveness of XML-RL have been published.

Project page:
    none
Implementation:
    not publicly available
Online demonstration:
    none

TQL. TQL [70, 93] is an XML query language based upon ambient logic [71], a modal logic conceived for describing the structural and computational properties of distributed and mobile computation. Ambient logic uses, for the structural descriptions at least, a logic of labeled trees and is thus a reasonable foundation for an XML query language.

[70] describes a representation of XML documents in ambient logic, called "information trees": XML is considered an edge-labeled graph. No distinction between attributes and elements is considered. Also the order of elements in an XML document is not preserved.

Based upon this data structure, TQL queries are specified as from ...select rules. Query and construction are separated (except for grouping queries that are, as in XML-QL and UnQL, expressed using nested queries), the query is specified in the from clause, the construction in the select clause. TQL programs consist of a single such rule. Instead of chaining rules, recursion is provided by a special recursion operator rec similar to the minimal and maximal fix point operators in modal logic. The following expression (taken from [70]) can be used as a condition in from clauses and test, recursively, whether a tree is binary:

```
rec $Binary. 0 Or (%[$Binary] | %[$Binary])
```

Variables are indicated in TQL using $. The expression %[$Binary] matches elements with arbitrary label (indicated by the wild card %) and satisfying the condition specified in square brackets, viz. to be binary trees.

Query 1 can be expressed in TQL as follows (assuming $Bib is bound to the sample data from Section 2.2:

```
from $Bib |= .bookdata[ .book [ $Book ] ]
select
    results [ result [
                book [ $Book ]
              | from $Book |= .author [
                                    $Author And .name [$Name] ]
                  select
                      author-and-name [ author [ $Author ], name [ $Name
                      ] ]
            ]
        ]
```

As stated above, grouping queries are expressed using nested queries. Notice, how in line 1 (and in line 6) the $Book ($Author) variables are bound to the sub-tree reached by a matching book (author) edge.

TQL provides a rich path syntax for abbreviating path-shaped queries. E.g., the expression

```
from $Bib |= .bookdata.%*.category[!.id[Writing] | .category*.label[$Label]
select $Label
```

returns the value of all labels reachable over arbitrary many category edges (.category*) from a category that may occur at any depth (.%*) and has no id with value "Writing".

In [70], it is claimed that TQL is particularly well suited for testing integrity constraints or schema validation, as it provides full boolean expressions including negation, existential, universal quantification, and (structural) recursion with the rec operator.

Project page:
    http://www.di.unipi.it/~ghelli/tql/
Implementation:
    available from the project page
Online demonstration:
    none

Xcerpt. Xcerpt [30, 56, 58, 247, 248] is a query language designed after principles given in [63] for querying both data on the "standard Web" (e.g., XML and HTML data) and data on the Semantic Web (e.g., RDF, Topic Maps, etc. data). This Section addresses using Xcerpt on the "standard Web", Section 4.6, on the Semantic Web.

Xcerpt is "data versatile", i.e. the same Xcerpt query can access and generate, as answers, data in different Web formats. Xcerpt is "strongly answer-closed", i.e. it not only allows one to construct answers in the same data formats as the data queries like, e.g., XQuery [78], but also allows further processing of the data generated by this same query program. Xcerpt's queries are pattern-based and allow to incompletely specify the data to retrieve, by (1) not explicitly specifying all children of an element, (2) specifying descendant elements at indefinite

depths (restrictions in the form of regular path expressions being possible), and
(3) specifying optional query parts. Xcerpt's evaluation of incomplete queries is
based on a novel unification algorithm called "simulation unification" [57, 62].
Xcerpt's processing of XML documents is graph-oriented, i.e., Xcerpt is aware of
the reference mechanisms (e.g., ID/IDREF attributes and links) of XML. Xcerpt
is rule-based. An Xcerpt rule expresses how data queried can be re-assembled
into new data items. One might say that an Xcerpt rule corresponds to an SQL
view. Xcerpt allows both traversal of cyclic documents and recursive rules, termination being ensured by so-called memoing, or tabling, techniques. Xcerpt rules
can be chained forward or backward, backward chaining being the processing of
choice for the Web. Indeed, if rules can, like Xcerpt's rules, query any Web site,
then a forward processing of rule-based programs could require starting a program's evaluation at all Web sites. Xcerpt is inspired from Logic Programming.
However, since it does not offer backtracking as a programming concept, Xcerpt
can also be seen "set-oriented functional".

All of the queries from Section 2.3 can be expressed in Xcerpt. In the following, solutions for Query 2, 5, 7, and 8 are omitted as they are similar to other
solutions shown.

Query 1 can be expressed in Xcerpt as follows:

```
GOAL
results [
  all result [
    var Book,
    all var Author,
    all var AuthorName
  ]
]
FROM
bookdata {{
  var Book → book {{
    var Author → author {{
      name [ var AuthorName ] }}
  }}
}}
END
```

As stated above, Xcerpt rules allow a separation of construction and querying. In the query part (enclosed by FROM and END), a pattern of the requested
data is specified: a bookdata element with a book child (associated with the
variable Book using the "pattern restriction" operator →) that in turn has an
author child (bound to the variable Author) with a name child whose content
is bound to the Variable AuthorName. Notice the use of double curly braces in
line 10, indicating an incomplete, unordered pattern. A matching bookdata element may have additional children not specified in the query and the order
among the children is irrelevant for the query. Square brackets as in line 13 and
in the construct part (between GOAL and FROM) specify that the order of the

children matters. Single brackets specify that the pattern is complete. Note that incomplete query patterns might result in several alternative variable bindings.

Similar to XMAS, Xcerpt allows to group answers using the constructs `all` and `some`. Intuitively, `all t` collects all possible different instances of the subexpression `t` that might result from alternative variable bindings. As shown in the example above, grouping constructs may also be nested. In the example above, the construct term creates a `result` subterm for each alternative binding of `Book`, and within each such `result` subterm, it groups all authors and authornames associated with that particular book.

In general, an Xcerpt program may contain multiple rules, as shown in the following solution for Query 3:

```
GOAL
var Result
FROM
transform [ bookdata {{ }}, result [ var Result ] ]
END

CONSTRUCT
transform [ var Element, result [ ] ]
FROM
  desc var Element → /translator|category/
END

CONSTRUCT
transform [ var Element, result [ var Label [ all var Child ] ] ]
FROM
and {
  desc var Element → var Label [[ var Child ]]
  where {
          and { var Label != "translator", var Label != "category }
       },
  transform [ var Child, result [ var ChildTransformed ] ]
}
END
```

Xcerpt rules come in two flavors: GOAL ... FROM ... END and CONSTRUCT ... FROM ... END. The first may only occur once in a program, specifies the ultimate result of the entire program similar to Prolog goals, and does not participate in rule chaining. The latter form is used for all other rules.

Here, the two lower rules transform (recursively) an input element as specified in the query: if it is a translator or a category the result of the transformation is empty, otherwise the children of the element are recursively transformed and the result of these transformations is used to reconstruct the structure of the input data.

Notice the use of the `desc` operator in lines 10 and 17 indicating a pattern that is incomplete in depth. Also notice the use of a `where` clause in line 18 to restrict matches to elements that are neither translators nor categories. In line

17, a *label variable* is used: whereas the variable `Element` is bound to the entire element matched by the pattern, `Label` is bound to the label of the element, i.e., a string such as "book".

Query 4 can be expressed in Xcerpt as follows:

```
GOAL
bookdata [
  all person [
    name [ var Name ],
    authored [
      all book [
        all var NonAuthorChildren
      ] group by { var Book }
    ]
  ]
]
FROM
bookdata {{
  desc var Book → book [[
    author {{ name [ var Name ] }},
    var NonAuthorChildren → !/author/ {{ }}
  ]]
}}
END
```

In the query part all books (at any depth) are selected together with the names of their authors and non-author children (notice the use of a negated regular expression on the label for the non-author children). For each name of an author, a `person` element is constructed (note the position of the `all` in line 3) containing the name and an `authored` element. In the author element all books for that author are nested again using `all` with a `group by` clause for explicitly naming the grouping variable.

Query 6 can be expressed in Xcerpt as follows:

```
GOAL
results [
  all category [
    attributes [ id [ var ID ] ],
    average-number-of-authors [
      div( count( all var Author ), count( all var Book ) )
    ]
  ]
]
FROM
bookdata {{
  desc category {{ attributes {{ id [ var ID ] }} }},
  desc var Book → book {{
    attributes {{ type [ var ID ] }},
    desc var Author → author {{ }}
```

```
  }}
}}
END
```

The average number of authors is calculated in line 6 using the structural aggregation function count over all books and authors for a category. In typical logic-programming style, the join between the id attribute of categories and the type attribute of books is expressed by repeating the same variable.

Query 9 can be expressed in Xcerpt as follows:

```
GOAL
results [
  all co-authors [
    name [ var Author ],
    name [ var CoAuthor ]
  ]
]
FROM
bookdata {{
  desc book {{
    author {{ name {{ var Author }} }},
    author {{ name {{ var CoAuthor }} }}
}}
END
```

This query profits from two features of Xcerpt: (1) Xcerpt's simulation unification is injective. This ensures that the two children of the book element in line 10 are different without requiring the query author to explicit state that the author and the co-author must be different. (2) Xcerpt's grouping is set based and uses unification for equality, i.e., two terms with same structure and values are considered equal even if they represent distinct elements in the input. Therefore the above program does not generate duplicates (as, e.g, the first XQuery solution for Query 9 in Section 3.1x).

A visual language, called *visXcerpt* [28, 29], has been conceived as a visual rendering of textual Xcerpt programs, making it possible to freely switch during programming between the visual and textual view, or rendering, of a program (cf. Figure 5 showing a textual and visual representation of an Xcerpt query).

Static type checking methods have been developed for Xcerpt [59, 283] that are based on seeing tree grammars in their various disguises, e.g., DTD, XML Schema, RelaxNG, as definitions of abstract data type.

A declarative semantics for Xcerpt has been proposed in [62, 247]. A formal procedural semantics for Xcerpt has been proposed in [62] in the form of a a proof procedure. An implementation of this semantic in Haskell has been realized using Constraint Programming techniques [247]. The XQuery use case [79] has been worked out in Xcerpt (cf. [174] (in German) and [45]). Based on Xcerpt and extending it, a reactive language called XChange [55, 61] for updates and events on the Web is currently being developed.

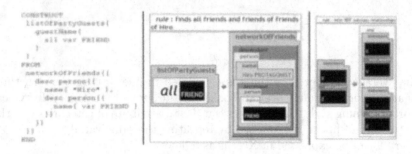

Fig. 5. Xcerpt and visXcerpt representation of a query

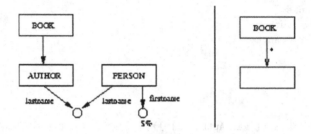

Fig. 6. Graph representation of an XML-GL query(Ceri et al. [75], © Elsevier, Inc.)

Project page:
  http://www.xcerpt.org/
Implementation:
  available from the project page
Online demonstration:
  http://demo.xcerpt.org and, using visXcerpt, http://visxcerpt.xcerpt.
  org/

XML-GL. XML-GL [74, 75, 91] is a visual, rule-based query language for XML. Queries are specified as rules with a clear separation between query and construction. Queries are specified on the left-hand of a rule, construction on the right-hand. Figure 6 shows an XML-GL rule. Both sides of a rule are essentially (visual) patterns of the graph structure to be matched or constructed, but enriched with visual representations of a number of additional operators and functions (such as arithmetic operators, wildcards, predicates, negation, ordering, etc.). Connections between the two sides indicate where matched data occurs in the result.

Although XML-GL programs contain only a single rule, complex queries may contain multiple left-hand and right-hand sides for expressing set queries, such as unions, differences, cartesian product, and even heterogeneous unions. The original proposal of XML-GL does not allow recursive rules, but in [222] an extension of XML-GL in this direction is proposed.

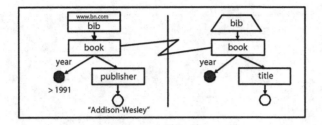

Fig. 7. XQBE Query(Braga et al. [47], © Elsevier, Inc.)

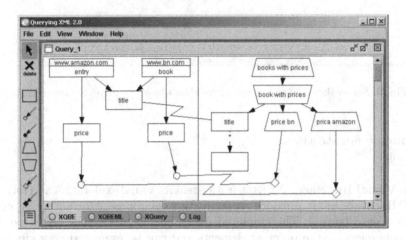

Fig. 8. Screenshot of XQBE's query editor(Braga et al. [47], © Elsevier, Inc.)

Recently, a visual interface for XQuery, called XQBE [10, 47], based on XML-GL has been developed. Figure 7 shows the XQBE representation of the following XQuery expression (Query XMP-Q1 in [79]):

```
<bib>
{
  for $b in document("www.bn.com/bib.xml")/bib/book
  where $b/publisher="Addison-Wesley" and $b/@year>1991
  return <book year="{$b/@year}"> {$b/title} </book>
}
</bib>
```

Based on this visualization of XQuery expressions, an interactive editor for XQuery expressions is described in [47] (cf. Figure 8).

Project page:
    XQBE: http://dbgroup.elet.polimi.it/xquery/XQBE.html
Implementation:
    XQBE: available from the project page

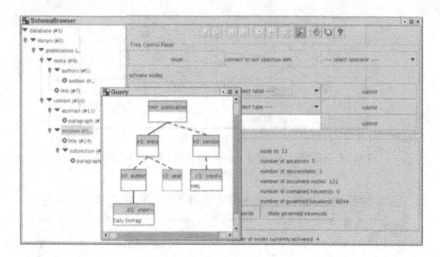

Fig. 9. Screenshot of X^2's query editor(Meuss et al. [209], © Springer-Verlag)

Online demonstration:
    none

X^2's Visual Interface. X^2 [209] is a system for visual exploration and retrieval of XML databases. It provides an interactive environment for authoring visual queries, see Figure 9. The employed query language is rather restricted, but supports querying the order of elements and can be evaluated very efficiently (see [207]). Instead of constructing new data based on the results of a query, the system gathers all matched data in a novel data structure called "Complete Answer Aggregates" [207, 208] and allows the user to browse this structure, thereby exploring the data contained in the database. While browsing, the user can refine and reissue the query.

Project page:
    http://www.cis.uni-muenchen.de/people/Meuss/caa.html and
    http://www.cis.uni-muenchen.de/~weigel/Projekte/X2.html
Implementation:
    not publicly available
Online demonstration:
    none

4   RDF Query Languages

RDF Query Languages can be grouped into several families that differ in aspects like data model, expressivity, support for schema information, and kind of queries. As a "family", we consider languages that build upon each other, are heavily influenced by each other, or share a large part of their properties. In the following, we shall consider the six families *SPARQL, RQL, XPath-, XSLT-, and XQuery-based Languages, Metalog, Reactive Languages*, and *Deductive Languages*. In addition, we briefly introduce a number of additional languages that don't fall into one of the above-mentioned families.

4.1   The SPARQL Family

The SPARQL family consists of the four query languages *SquishQL, RDQL, SPARQL*, and *TriQL*. Common to all four languages in this family is that they "regard RDF as triple data without schema or ontology information unless explicitly included in the RDF source".

Basic RDF Access: SquishQL and RDQL. The main objectives of SquishQL [212, 213] are ease-of-use and similarity to SQL. SquishQL relies on a query model for RDF influenced by [141]. SquishQL offers so-called "triple patterns" and conjunctions between triple patterns for specifying parts of RDF graphs to retrieved. *"This results in quite a weak pattern language but it does ensure that in a result all variables are bound."* [213]. SquishQL queries have the following form:

SELECT variables (identifies the variables whose bindings are returned)
FROM   model URI
WHERE   list of triple patterns
AND   boolean expression (the filter to be applied to the result)
USING   name FOR URI, ...

In SquishQL, Query 1 can be expressed as follows:

```
SELECT ?essay, ?author, ?authorName
FROM   http://example.org/books
WHERE  (?essay, <rdf:type>, <books:Essay>),
       (?essay, <books:author>, ?author),
       (?author, <books:name>, ?authorName)
USING  books FOR http://example.org/books#,
       rdf FOR http://www.w3.org/1999/02/22-rdf-syntax-ns#
```

In SquishQL, Query 2 can (almost) be expressed as follows:

```
SELECT ?property, ?propertyValue
FROM   http://example.org/books
WHERE  (?essay, <books:book-title>, "Bellum Civile")
       (?essay, ?property, ?propertyValue),
USING  books FOR http://example.org/books#
```

A property value can be a node with other properties, that an answer to Query 2 should return. Since SquishQL has no means to express recursion, such indirect properties cannot be returned by the above query if the schema of the data is unknown or recursive.

Other queries from Section 2.3 cannot be expressed in SquishQL.

In a SquishQL query, the AND clause serves to express constraints on variable values so as filter the bindings returned. The following query returns the URIs of persons that have authored a book with title "Bellum Civile".

```
SELECT ?person
FROM    http://example.org/books
WHERE   (?book, <books:author>, ?person)
        (?book, <books:title>, ?title)
AND     ?title = 'Bellum Civile'
```

An answer to an SquishQL query is a set of bindings for the variables occurring in the query. SquishQL does not support RDFS concepts.

Project page:
   Inkling: http://swordfish.rdfweb.org/rdfquery/
Implementation:
   Inkling [212]

RDQL, a "RDF Data Query Language", is an evolution of the SquishQL versions SquishQL [213], and Inkling [212] influenced by rdfDB [140]. RDQL has been recently submitted to the W3C for standardisation [213, 251, 252, 253]. RDQL queries have the same form as SquishQL queries. As with SquishQL, an answer to an RDQL query is a set of bindings for the variables occurring in the query. Like SquishQL, RDQL supports only selection and extraction queries.

RDQL is intentionally kept simple, operating only on the data level of RDF, with the goal to make RDQL amenable to standardisation as a "low-level RDF language". RDQL's authors see inferencing as a possible feature of an "RDF implementation", not of the query language RDQL: *"if a graph implementation provides inferencing to appear as 'virtual triples' (i.e. triples that appear in the graph but are not in the ground facts), then an RDQL query will include those triples as possible matches in triple patterns."* [253]. As a consequence, queries referring to RDFS relations such as type, set or class are cumbersome and/or complex.

The RDQLPlus (http://rdqlplus.sourceforge.net/) implementation of RDQL provides a language extension, called RIDIQL [284]. RIDIQL supports updates and a transparent use of the inference abilities of the Jena Toolkit [136].

Project pages:
   http://www.hpl.hp.com/semweb/rdql.htm
   RDFStore: http://rdfstore.sourceforge.net/
Implementations:
   Jena Toolkit [136, 251, 252, 253], RAP (RDF API for PHP) [221], PHP XML
   Classes (http://phpxmlclasses.sourceforge.net/), RDFStore [240],
   Rasqal (http://www.redland.opensource.ac.uk/rasqal/),
   Sesame (http://www.openrdf.org/index.jsp),
   RDQLPlus (http://rdqlplus.sourceforge.net/),
   3store (http://sourceforge.net/projects/threestore/) [146].

Online demonstrations:

Sesame: http://www.openrdf.org/demo.jsp

RAP: http://www3.wiwiss.fu-berlin.de/rdfapi-php/test/custom_
rdql_test.php

RDFStore: http://demo.asemantics.com/rdfstore/www2003/

SquishQL and RDQL queries cannot be composed. Negation can be used in filters, or AND clauses, as in the previous query, but not in WHERE clauses, i.e. triple patterns can only occur positively. Disjunctions and optional matching cannot be expressed. Although a variable in SquishQL and RDQL queries can be bound to blank nodes, there is no way to specify blank nodes in SquishQL's and RDQL's triple patterns. As a consequence, a query returning the blank nodes of a graph cannot be expressed in SquishQL and RDQL. SquishQL and RDQL have no form of recursion or iteration: By conjunction of triple patterns, one can express in SquishQL and RDQL only paths of a given length. Only selection and extraction queries can be expressed in SquishQL and RDQL, i.e., of the queries of Section 2.3, only Query 1 and (an approximation of) Query 2. Like SquishQL, RDQL does not support RDFS concepts, although at least one of its implementations, that given in the Jena Toolkit [136], supports the transitive closures of the RDFS relations rdfs:subClassOf and rdfs:subPropertyOf. No formal semantics has been defined for SquishQL or RDQL. The complexity of SquishQL and RDQL has not been investigated so far.

SPARQL. SPARQL [239], a "Query Language for RDF" formerly called BrQL [238], has been developed by members of the W3C "RDF Data Access" Working Group. SPARQL is an extension of RDQL [253] designed according to requirements and use cases [87] and is still under development. SPARQL extends RDQL with facilities to:

- Extract RDF subgraphs.
- Construct, using CONSTRUCT clauses, one new RDF graph with data from the RDF graph queried. Like RDQL queries, the new graph can be specified with triple, or graph, patterns.
- Return, using DESCRIBE clauses, "descriptions" of the resources matching the query part. The exact meaning of "description" is not yet defined, cf. [267] for a proposal.
- Specify OPTIONAL triple or graph query patterns, i.e., data that should contribute to an answer if present in the data queried, but whose absence does not prevent to return an answer.
- Testing the absence, or non-existence, of tuples.

SPARQL queries have the following form:

PREFIX   Specification of a name for a URI (like RDQL's USING)

SELECT   Returns all or some of the variables bound in the WHERE clause.

CONSTRUCT Returns a RDF graph with all or some of the variable bindings.

DESCRIBE   Returns a "description" of the resources found.

```
ASK        Returns whether a query pattern matches or not
WHERE      list, i.e., conjunction of query (triple or graph) patterns
OPTIONAL   list, i.e., conjunction of optional (triple or graph) patterns
AND        boolean expression (the filter to be applied to the result)
```

An extension of Query 1 returning the translators of a book, if there are some, can be expressed in SPARQL as follows:

```
PREFIX    books: http://example.org/books#
PREFIX    rdf: http://www.w3.org/1999/02/22-rdf-syntax-ns#
SELECT    ?essay, ?author, ?authorName, ?translator
FROM      http://example.org/books
WHERE     (?essay  books:author     ?author),
          (?author books:authorName ?authorName)
OPTIONAL (?essay  books:translator ?translator)
```

Using the CONSTRUCT clause, restructuring and non-recursive inference queries can be expressed in SPARQL. Query 4 can be expressed in SPARQL as follows:

```
PREFIX     books: http://example.org/books#
CONSTRUCT (?y books:authored ?x)
FROM       http://example.org/books
WHERE      (?x books:author ?y)
```

and Query 9 by

```
PREFIX     books: http://example.org/books#
CONSTRUCT (?x books:co-author ?y)
FROM       http://example.org/books
WHERE      (?book books:author ?x)
           (?book books:author ?y)
AND        (?x neq ?y)
```

Project page:
    http://www.w3.org/2001/sw/DataAccess/
Implementation:
    none
Online demonstration:
    none

TriQL. TriQL extends RDQL by constructs supporting querying of named graphs [72], as introduced in TriG [40] by the authors of TriQL. Named graphs allow one to filter RDF statements after their sources or authors, like in the following query: *"Return the books with rating above a threshold of 5, using only information asserted by Marcus Tullius Cicero."* This can be expressed in TriQL as follows:

```
SELECT ?books
WHERE  ?graph ( ?books books:rating ?rating )
```

```
          (?graph    swp:assertedBy ?warrant)
          (?warrant swp:authority <http://people.net/cicero>)
USING   books FOR http://example.org/books#,
          swp    FOR <http://www.w3.org/2004/03/trix/swp-1/>
```

Project page:
   http://www.wiwiss.fu-berlin.de/suhl/bizer/TriQL/
Implementation:
   none
Online demonstration:
   none

4.2   The RQL Family

Under "RQL family", we group the three languages *RQL*, *SeRQL*, and *eRQL*.
Common to these languages is that they support combining data and schema
querying. Furthermore, the RDF data model they rely on slightly deviates from
the standard data model for RDF and RDFS: (1) cycles in the subsumption hierarchy are forbidden, and (2) for each property, both a domain and a range must
be defined. These restrictions ensure a clear separation of the three abstraction
layers of RDF and RDFS: (1) data, i.e. description of resources such as persons,
XML documents, etc., (2) schemas, i.e. classifications for such resources, and
(3) meta-schemas specifying meta-classes such as `rdfs:Class`, the class of all
classes, and `rdfs:Property` the class of all of properties. They make possible a
flexible type system tailored to the specificities of RDF and RDFS.

RQL. RQL, the "RDF Query Language", is developed at ICS-FORTH [84, 158,
159, 160, 161], and the base for the two other members of the RQL family, SeRQL
and eRQL.

Basic Schema Queries. A salient feature of RQL is the use of the types from
RDFS schemas. The query `subClassOf(books:Writing)` returns the sub-classes
of the class `books:Writing`[9]. A similar query, using `subPropertyOf` instead of
`subClassOf`, returns the the sub-properties of a property . The following query
returns the domain ($C1) and range ($C2) of the property `author` defined at the
URI named `book` (The prefix $ indicates "class variable", i.e., a variable ranging
on schema classes). It can be expressed in RQL in three different manners:

1. using class variables:
   ```
   SELECT $C1, $C2  FROM {$C1}books:author{$C2}
   USING  NAMESPACE books = &http://example.org/books#
   ```

2. using a *type constraint*:
   ```
   SELECT C1, C2  FROM Class{C1}, Class{C2}, {;C1}books:author{;C2}
   USING  NAMESPACE books = &http://example.org/books#
   ```

3. without class variables or type constraints:

---

[9] Assuming: `USING NAMESPACE books = &http://example.org/books-rdfs#`

```
SELECT C1, C2  FROM subClassOf(domain(book:author)){C1},
                    subClassOf(range(books:author)){C2}
USING  NAMESPACE books = &http://example.org/books#
```

The query `topclass(books:Historical_Essay)` returns the top of the subsumption hierarchy, i.e., `books:Writing`, cf. Figure 2. A similar query returns leaves of the subsumption hierarchy. The query `nca(books:Historical_Essay, books:Historical_Novel)` returns the nearest common ancestor of the classes of 'historical essays' and 'historical novels', i.e., the class `books:Essay` of 'essays'. RQL has "property variables" prefixed by @ using which RDF properties can be queried (like classes using class variables). The following query, with property variables prefixed by @, similar to the formerly introduced class variables, returns the properties, together with their actual ranges, that can be assigned to resources classified as `books:Writing`:

```
SELECT @P, $V  FROM {;books:Writing}@P{$V}
USING  NAMESPACE books = &http://example.org/books#
```

Combining these facilities, Query 8 is expressible in RQL as follows:
`SELECT X, Y  FROM Class{X}, subClassOf(X){Y}`.

Data Queries. With RQL, data can be retrieved by its types, by navigating to the appropriate position in the RDF graph. Restrictions can be expressed using filters. Classes, as well as properties, can be queried for their (direct and indirect[10]) extent. The query `books:Writing` returns the resources classified `books:Writing` or one of its sub-classes. This query can also be expressed as follows: `SELECT X FROM books:Writing{X}`. Prefixing the variable X in the previous queries, yields queries returning only resources directly classified as `books:Writing`, i.e., for which a statement $(X, \text{rdf:type}, \text{books:Writing})$ exists. The extent of a property can be similarly retrieved. The query `^books:author` returns the pairs of resources X, Y that stand in the `books:author` relation, i.e., for which a statement $(X, \text{books:author}, Y)$ exists. RQL offers extended dot notation as used in OQL [73], for navigation in data and schema graphs. This is convenient for expressing Query 1:

```
SELECT X, Y, Z FROM {X;books:Essay}books:author{Y}.books:authorName{Z}
USING  NAMESPACE books = &http://example.org/books#
```

The data selected by an RDF query can be restricted with a `WHERE` clause:

```
SELECT X, Y FROM {X;books:Essay}books:author.books:authorName{Y},
          ?           {X}books:title{T}
WHERE  T = "Bellum Civile"
USING  NAMESPACE books = &http://example.org/books#
```

---

[10] i.e. deduceable by inference.

Mixed Schema and Data Queries. With RQL, access to data and schema can be combined in all manners, e.g., the expression X;books:Essay restricts bindings for variable X to resources with type books:Essay. Types are often useful for filtering, but type information can also be interesting on their own, e.g., to return a "description" of a resource understood as its schema:

```
SELECT $C, ( SELECT @P, Y  FROM {Z ; ^$D} ^@P {Y}
              WHERE  Z = X and $D = $C )
FROM   ^$C {X}, {X}books:title{T}  WHERE T = "Bellum Civile"
USING  NAMESPACE books = &http://example.org/books#
```

This query returns the classes under which the resource with title "Bellum Civile" is directly classified; ^$C{X} selects the values in the direct extent of any class.

Further features of RQL are not discussed here, e.g., support for containers, aggregation, and schema discovery. Although RQL has no concept of "view", extension RVL [191] of RQL gives a facility for specifying views. In RVL the inverse relation of books:author can be defined as a view as follows:

```
CREATE NAMESPACE mybooks = &http://example.org/books-rdfs-extension#
VIEW    authored(Y, X)  FROM {X}books:author{Y}
USING  NAMESPACE books = &http://example.org/books#
```

RQL has been criticised for its large number of features and choice of syntactic constructs (like the prefixes ^ for calls and @ for property variables), which resulted in the simplifications SeRQL and eRQL of RDF. RQL is far more expressive than most other RDF query languages, especially those of the SquishQL family. Most queries of Section 2.3, except those queries referring to the transitive closures of arbitrary relations, can be expressed in RQL: RDF supports only the transitive closures of rdfs:subClassOf and rdfs:subPropertyOf.

Query 1 is already given in RQL above. Query 2 cannot be expressed in RQL exactly, since RQL has no means to select "everything related to some resource". However, a modified version of this query, where a resource is described by its schema, is also given above. Reduction queries, e.g. Query 3, can often be concisely expressed in RQL, in particular if types are available:

```
SELECT S, @P, 0
FROM   (Resources minus (SELECT T FROM {B}books:translator{T})){S},
       (Resources minus (SELECT T FROM {B}books:translator{T})){0},
       {S}@P{0}
USING  NAMESPACE books = &http://example.org/books#
```

An implementation of the restructuring Query 4 is given above in the extension RVL of RQL. RQL is convenient for expressing aggregation queries, e.g., Query 5:

```
max(SELECT Y
    FROM   {B;books:Writing}books:author.books:authorName{A},
           {B}books:pubYear{Y}
    WHERE  A = "Julius Caesar")
```

Inference queries that do not need recursion, e.g., Query 9, can be expressed in RQL as follows:

```
SELECT A1, A2  FROM {Z}books:author{A1}, {Z}books:author{A2}
WHERE   A1 != A2
USING  NAMESPACE books = &http://example.org/books#
```

In RVL, an expression of Query 9 can actually create new statements as follows:

```
CREATE NAMESPACE mybooks = &http://example.org/books-rdfs-extension#
VIEW    mybooks:co-author(A1, A2)
FROM    {Z}books:author{A1}, {Z}books:author{A2}  WHERE A1 != A2
USING  NAMESPACE books = &http://example.org/books#
```

Both typing rules and a formal semantics for RQL have been specified [161]. No formal complexity study of RDF has been published yet. An implementation of RDF is given with the so-called "ICS-FORTH RDFSuite". RQL has influenced several later proposals for RDF query languages, e.g., BrQL and SPARQL, cf. Section 4.1.

Project page:
  http://139.91.183.30:9090/RDF/RQL/
Implementation:
  RDFSuite (http://139.91.183.30:9090/RDF/index.html)
Online demonstration:
  http://139.91.183.30:8999/RQLdemo/

SeRQL. SeRQL [52, 67] is derived from RQL and differs from the latter as follows:

- SeRQL does not support RDF and RDFS types, except literal types.
- SeRQL modifies and extends RQL's path expressions. SeRQL compound path expressions instead use an "empty node", {}, for path concatenation. SeRQL provides a shorthand notation for retrieving several values of a property in a single path expression, simplifying, e.g., Query 9: In SeRQL, one can write FROM {Book} <books:author> {X, Y} instead of FROM {Book} <books:author> {X}, {Book} <books:author> {Y}. Furthermore, SeRQL supports optional path expressions (using square brackets), e.g.: SELECT * FROM {Book} <books:title> {Title};
  [<books:translator> {Translator} [<books:age> {Age}]].
- SeRQL provides a shorthand notation for expressing several properties of a resource in a FROM clause. The following SeRQL query returns the authors of books entitled "Bellum Civile" having a translator named "J.M. Carter" (note the ';' separating the different properties):
```
SELECT Author  FROM {Book} <books:title> {"Bellum Gallicum"};
          <books:translator>{}<books:translatorName>{"J.M. Carter"};
          <books:author> {Author}
USING NAMESPACE books = <!http://example.org/books#>
```

– SeRQL eases querying a reified statement by enclosing the non-reified version
  of the statement in curly brackets.

SeRQL cannot express all queries of Section 2.3. Selection and extraction queries
can be expressed in SeRQL (with the same limitation as with RQL, cf. above).
In contrast to RQL, SeRQL has neither set operations, nor existential or universal quantification. As a consequence, Query 3 cannot be expressed in SeRQL.
Thanks to the CONSTRUCT clause, SeRQL, like RQL, can express restructuring
and simple inference queries, e.g., Query 4 can be expressed as:

```
CONSTRUCT        {Author} <mybooks:authored> {Book}
FROM             {Book} <books:author> {Author}
USING NAMESPACE books   = <!http://example.org/books#>
                 mybooks = <!http://example.org/books-rdfs-extension#>
```

Aggregation queries cannot be expressed in SeQL (according to [67], adding
aggregation to to SeRQL is planned). The transitive closure of rdfs:subClassOf
is provided in SeRQL's implementation by means of the RDFS-aware storage of
Sesame. However, neither the transitive closures of arbitrary relations nor general
recursion can be expressed in SerQL.

Project page:
    Sesame http://www.openrdf.org/
Implementation:
    Implementation in Prolog[11]: http://gollem.swi.psy.uva.nl/twiki/pl/
    bin/view/Library/SeRQL
Online demonstrations:
    http://www.openrdf.org/demo.jsp

eRQL. eRQL [271] proposes a radical simplification of RQL based mostly on
a keyword-based interface. It is the expressed goal of the authors of eRQL to
provide with a *"Google-like query language but also with the capacity to profit
of the additional information given by the RDF data"*.[12] eRQL has only three
query constructs:
One-word queries. Single words are valid eRQL queries, e.g., the query CAESAR
returns all statements in which the string "CAESAR" occurs in any manner.
Surprisingly, "phrase queries" like "Bellum civile" do not seem to be expressible
in eRQL.
Neighbourhood queries. Neighbourhood queries are expressed by varying numbers
of curly braces indicating the level of neighbourhood. They return not only the
statements containing a word, as one-word queries, but also the statements related to ("in the neighbourhood of") a statement. For instance, the {{CAESAR}}
returns the following statements (cf. Figure 2):

---

[11] Using the Semantic Web library of SWI Prolog http://www.swi-prolog.org/.
[12] http://www.dbis.informatik.uni-frankfurt.de/~tolle/RDF/eRQL/

```
_:1 books:author _:2.                    _:1 books:title "Bellum Civile".
_:1 books:authorName "Julius Caesar".    _:1 books:translator _:4.
_:1 books:author _:3.
```

{{{CAESAR}}} extends the "neighbourhood" one step further, etc.

Conjunctive and disjunctive queries. Both, neighbourhood and one-word queries can be combined using the boolean operators AND and OR. No negation is provided, however.

Many queries of Section 2.3 cannot be expressed in eRQL. The extraction query Query 2 can be *approximated* in eRQL as: {{"Bellum" AND "Civile"}}. eRQL does not allow the selection of a neighbourhood of unknown size around a resource, e.g., for obtaining a "concise-bounded descriptions" [267]. Indeed, in contrast to the claims of eRQL's authors, this requires knowledge of the schema of the data queried. Nevertheless, the need for a language like eRQL is evident for exploiting RDF data with search engines.

Project page:
    http://www.dbis.informatik.uni-frankfurt.de/~tolle/RDF/eRQL/
Implementation(s):
    eRQLEngine cf. project page
Online demonstration:
    none

4.3   Query Languages Inspired from XPath, XSLT or XQuery

This section is devoted to languages inspired from, or extending XML query languages. Some of them (viz. [246, 266, 277]) can be implemented with a few additional functions and/or by normalising the data before querying.

XQuery for RDF: The "Syntactic Web Approach". [242, 246] propose to rely on the XML Query Language *XQuery* (cf. Section 3.1) for querying RDF data. The approach, called "Syntactic Web", consists of (1) a preliminary "normalisation" of the RDF data being queried essentially by (a) serialising RDF data in XML as collections of statements, and (b) grouping the statements by their subjects, and (2) defining in XQuery, functions conveying the semantics of RDFS, e.g., a function rdf:instance-of-class returning the (sequence of the) resources (represented by their description element) that are (direct or indirect) instances of a class:

```
define function rdf:instance-of-class($t as element(description)*,
                                      $base-name as xs:string)
    as element(description)*
{
    $t[rdf:type = $base-name]
    ,
    for $i in $t[rdfs:subClassOf = $base-name]
    return rdf:instance-of-class($t, string($i/@rdf:about))
}
```

Using the function defined above, and assuming a convenient normalisation of the RDF data queried, Query 1 can be expressed as follows:

```
let $t := document("http://example.org/books")//description
for $essay in rdf:instance-of-class($t, "books:Essay"),
    $author in $t[rdf:about = $essay/books:author]
return  <result>  {$essay, $author}  </result>
```

The "Syntactic Web" approach also proposes a normalisation of Topic Maps and specific XQuery functions for querying Topic Maps data. This approach has several advantages. It makes it possible to return answers in any possible XML format and to query both, standard Web and Semantic Web data with the same query language, providing the uniformity advocated in [231]. [257] suggests a similar approach.

Project page:
    none
Implementation(s):
    not publicly available
Online demonstration:
    none

XSLT for RDF: TreeHugger and RDF Twig. Similar in spirit to the Syntactic Web Approach [242, 246], TreeHugger [266] proposes to rely on XSLT for querying and transforming RDF data. Due to limitations of XSTL 1.0, the normalisation of RDF data is not performed by an XSLT program, but by "extension functions". The normalisation of RDF is based on the "striped syntax" [50], with properties represented both as elements and attributes (causing problems with multi-valued properties). Three extension functions are provided: (1) for loading an RDF document, (2) for loading an RDF document and handling the vocabulary of RDFS, and (3) for loading an RDF document and handling the vocabulary of both RDFS and OWL. XPath, upon which XSLT relies, is extended with a prefix inv for querying the inverse of an RDF property.

Query 1 can be expressed as follows in TreeHugger:

```
<results xmlns:xsl="http://www.w3.org/1999/XSL/Transform"
  xmlns:books="http://example.org/books#"
  xmlns:th="http://rootdev.net/net.rootdev.treehugger.TreeHugger"
  xmlns:rdfs="http://www.w3.org/2000/01/rdf-schema#"
  xmlns:rdf="http://www.w3.org/1999/02/22-rdf-syntax-ns#"
  xsl:version="1.0">

<!-- Load RDF document -->
<xsl:variable name="doc"
  select="th:documentRDFS('http://example.org/books')" />
<xsl:for-each select="$doc/books:Essay">
  <xsl:for-each select="books:author/*">
    <result>
```

```
            <xsl:value-of select="inv:books:author" />
            <xsl:value-of select="." />
            <authorName>
                <xsl:value-of select="books:authorName/*" />
            </authorName>
        </result>
    </xsl:for-each>
  </xsl:for-each>
</results>
```

Project page:
    http://rdfweb.org/people/damian/treehugger/
Implementation(s):
    Cf. project page
Online demonstration:
    http://swordfish.rdfweb.org/discovery/2003/09/treehugger/

RDF Twig [277] is another extension of XSLT 1.0, with functions for querying RDF. It is based on "redundant" or "non-redundant" depth or breadth first traversals of the RDF graph, , i.e., traversals that repeat or do not repeat elements in the XML-based representation of RDF that are reachable from by various paths. Two query mechanisms are provided: A small set of logical operations on the RDF graph, and an interface to RDQL cf. Section 4.1.

Query 1 can be expressed as follows in RDF Twig:

```
<xsl:stylesheet xmlns:xsl="http://www.w3.org/1999/XSL/Transform"
    version="1.0"
    xmlns:rt="http://nwalsh.com/xslt/ext/com.nwalsh.xslt.saxon.RDFTwig"
    xmlns:twig="http://nwalsh.com/xmlns/rdftwig#"
    xmlns:books="http://example.org/books#"
    xmlns:rdf="http://www.w3.org/1999/02/22-rdf-syntax-ns#">
  <xsl:template match="/">
    <xsl:variable name="model"
        select="rt:load('http://example.org/books')"/>
    <!-- this is used as default model from now on-->
    <xsl:variable name="pType"
        select="rt:property('http://www.w3.org/1999/02/22-rdf-syntax-ns#',
                            'type')"/>
    <xsl:variable name="essays"
        select="rt:find($label, 'books:Essay')"/>
    <xsl:variable name="tree"
        select="rt:twig($essays)/twig:result"/>
    <results>
        <xsl:for-each select="rt:find($label, 'books:Essay')">
            <result>
                <xsl:value-of select="rt:twig(.)" />
                <xsl:value-of select="rt:twig(.)/twig:result/books:author" />
            </result>
        </xsl:for-each>
```

```
   </results>
 </xsl:template>
```

Project page:
   http://rdftwig.sourceforge.net/
Implementation:
   Cf. project page
Online demonstration:
   none

Versa. Developed as part of the Python-based *4Suite* XML and RDF toolkit[13], Versa [219, 220, 223] is a query language for RDF inspired from, but significantly different to, XPath. Versa can be used in lieu of XPath in the XSLT version of 4Suite. Like the Syntactic Web Approach, TreeHugger, and RDF Twig, Versa is aligned with XML. Like XPath, Versa can be extended by externally defined functions. Versa's authors claim that Versa is easier to learn than RDF query languages inspired from SQL.

Versa has constructs for a *forward traversal* of one or more RDF properties, e.g., all() - books:author -> * selects those resources that are author of other resources. Instead of the wildcard *, string-based restrictions can be expressed. Using Versa's forward traversal operators, Query 1 can be expressed as follows:

```
distribute(type(books:Essay), ".",
    "distribute(.-books:author->*, ".", ".-books:authorName->*)")
```

The function distribute() returns a list of lists containing the result of the second, third, ... argument valuated starting from each of the resources selected by the first argument. As in XPath, . denotes the current node.

Versa has a *Forward filter* for selecting the subject of a statement, e.g., type(books:Essay) |- books:title -> eq("Bellum Civile") returns the essays entitled "Bellum Civile". Versa has also constructs for a *backward traversal* (but no backward filter), e.g., the essays entitled "Bellum Civile" can also be returned by (books:Essay <- rdf:type - *) |- books:title -> eq("Bellum Gallicum"). Versa's function traverse serves to traverse paths of arbitrary length, e.g., the following query returns all sub-classes of books:Writing:

```
traverse(books:Writing, rdf:subClassOf, vtrav:inverse, vtrav:transitive)
```

Similarly, Versa's function filter provides a general filter, e.g., all essays entitled "Bellum Gallicum" having a translator named "J. M. Carter" are returned by the following query:

```
filter(books:Essay <- rdf:type - *,
   ". - books:title -> eq('Bellum Gallicum')",
      ". - books:translator -> books:translatorName -> eq('J. M. Carter')"
```

---

[13] http://4suite.org/

Selection and extraction queries can be easily implemented in Versa, although the selection of related items is not very convenient, as the above implementation of Query 1 demonstrates. In contrast to most RDF query languages, Versa allows the extraction of RDF subgraphs of arbitrary sizes, as required by Query 2. Reduction queries can be expressed in Versa, e.g., using negation or set difference. Query 3 can be implemented in Versa as follows:

```
difference(all(),
    union(type(rdfs:Class),
        union(type(rdfs:Property,
            all() <- books:translator - *))
        )
    )
```

Restructuring, combination, and inference queries cannot be expressed in Versa, as the result of a Versa query is always a list (possibly a list of lists). However, Query 4 and 9 can be approximated in Versa as follows:

```
distribute(all(), ". - books:author -> *", ". - books:author -> *")
```

Answers to this query include "Julius Caesar" (as if he would be a co-author of himself !). This does not seem to be avoidable with Versa. Versa also provides several aggregation functions. Query 5 can be expressed as follows in Versa:

```
max(filter(all(),
    ". - books:author -> books:authorName -> eq('Julius Caesar')"
    )
    - books:year -> *)
```

Query 6 can be implemented in Versa using the function `length` as follows:

```
distribute(traverse(books:Writing, rdf:subClassOf,
                vtrav:inverse,vtrav:transitive),
        ".",
        "max(length((. <- rdf:type *) - books:author -> *))"
        )
```

Neither a formal semantics, nor the language complexity have been investigated so far.

Project page:
    http://uche.ogbuji.net/tech/rdf/versa/
Implementation(s):
    available as part of 4Suite from http://4suite.org/
Online demonstration:
    none

Path-Based Access to RDF: RDF Path, RPath, RxPath, RxSLT, and RxUpdate. [229] sketches a language called RDF Path. RDF Path's syntax is similar to that of XPath. Node-tests for RDF data are added, e.g., arc() and subj(), and constructs of XPath not relevant for RDF are dropped. Functions and value tests are not considered in depth in this early draft. The fact that, in contrast to XML trees, RDF graphs do not have roots is not considered. As a consequence, finding a starting point for an RDF Path expression is an open issue.

Query 1 is not expressible, since related information cannot be selected. A variation of Query 2, *"Return the names of all authors of historical essays entitled 'Bellum Civile'."* can be expressed as follows:

```
*[rdf:type/books:Historical_Essay books:title/"Bellum Civile"]/
     books:author/*/books:authorName
```

Project page:
    http://infomesh.net/2003/rdfpath/
Implementation(s):
    none
Online demonstration:
    none

RPath [201] is another adaption of XPath to RDF, though focused on two RDF applications, CC/PP, a formalism for expressing device profiles, and UAProf, a formalism for expressing characteristics of (mobile) computers such as screen resolution and colour depth. RPath has location steps, *vertex-edge-tests* corresponding to node-tests in XPath, and predicates. RPath differences from XPath reflect the differences between the data models of XML and RDF, e.g., RPath's axes can follow a path along vertices (RDF predicates) and edges (RDF subjects and objects). As with RDF Path, the fact that RDF graphs are not rooted is not considered. Thus, it is not clear where an RPath expression should start from. This might not be too serious a problem, for the CC/PP and UAProf yield RDF graphs that are rooted two-level trees.

The variation of Query 2 considered above, *"Return the names of all authors of historical essays entitled 'Bellum Civile'."* can be expressed as follows:

```
/@vertex()[
   rdf:type/@books:Historical_Essay and
   books:title/@vertex()[equals('Bellum Civile')]
 ]/books:author/books:authorName
```

In contrast to most RDF query languages inspired from XPath, RPath does not require specifying paths where expressions match vertices, i.e., RDF classes, and edges (properties), alternate (like in striped RDF [50]). Thus, the previous query can also be expressed as follows:

```
outerVertex::vertex()[
   outEdge::rdf:type/outVertex::books:Historical_Essay and
```

```
    outEdge::books:title/outVertex::vertex()[equals('Bellum Civile')]
  ]/outEdge::books:author/outEdge::books:authorName
```

Project page:
    none
Implementation(s):
    prototype in Java, based on a CC/PP engine from Sun
Online demonstration:
    none

RxPath is another adaption of XPath to RDF, defined within the project Rx4RDF[14], aiming at improving the accessibility of RDF for non-experts. In contrast to RDF Path and RPath, and similarly to TreeHugger and RDF Twig, RxPath is essentially *"a mapping between the RDF Abstract Syntax to the XPath Data Model"* [263]. This mapping is performed in four steps:

1. A top-level XML element is created for every RDF resource where the tag is the type of the resource,
2. "Each root element has a child element for each statement the resource is the subject of. The name of each child is [the] name of the property in the statement" [262],
3. "Each of these children have [a] child text node if the object of the statement is a literal or a child element if the object is a resource." [262], and
4. "Object elements have the same name and children as the equivalent root element for the resource, thus defining a potentially infinitely recursive tree." [262].

Since this mapping might lead to infinite trees, RxPath relies on a circularity-test for the evaluation of such axes ensuring that elements previously encountered are skipped (as a consequence, blank nodes have to be assigned a unique URI.) Furthermore, RxPath changes the semantics of the closure axes to only consider elements representing RDF properties in the original RDF model (this is easy as the mapping from RDF into an XML document discussed above uses a striped representation of RDF statements [50]). Finally, an expression such as descendant::rdf:type only matches an element representing an rdf:type property if all elements on the path to that property that represent any RDF property actually represent an rdf:type property. Thus, descendant::rdf:type is actually closer to the regular tree expression (rdf:type._)* than to the XPath expression descendant::rdf:type.

The variation of Query 2 considered above, *"Return the names of all authors of historical essays with the title 'Bellum Civile'."* can be expressed as follows (assuming the prefix books denotes http://example.org/books-rdfs#):

```
/books:Historical_Essay[books:title = 'Bellum Civile']/
    books:author/*/books:authorName
```

---

[14] Phttp://rx4rdf.liminalzone.org/rx4rdf

Based on RxPath, two languages have been defined, RxSLT [264] and Rx-Update [265]. RxSLT is *"syntactically identical to XSLT 1.0"* [264], but uses RxPath instead of XPath 1.0. RxUpdate is syntactically very similar to XUp-date [185], but again uses RxPath instead of XPath to update RDF models. Note that RxSLT, like XSLT, is only capable of producing XML. Thus, new RDF data can only be created by using the XML serialisation of RDF.

Project page:
    http://rx4rdf.liminalzone.org/rx4rdf
Implementation(s):
    Cf. project page (prototype in Python)
Online demonstration:
    none

RDFT and the Query Language of Nexus: XSLT-Style RDF Query Languages. RDFT [95] is a draft proposal closely related to XSLT 1.0. Like XSLT 1.0., RDFT uses templates that are matched recursively against the data structure. Since the structural recursion is performed against an RDF graph which can be cyclic, termination must be ensured. This issue has not yet been addressed. RDFT uses an adaption of XPath, called NodePath, for querying RDF graphs expressed in XML as "striped" [50]. Querying RDFS or OWL data has not yet been addressed.

RDFT only supports a subset of XSLT. A macro mechanism is introduced, as illustrated in lines 3–7 and 10 of the following implementation of Query 1 (for simplicity, only books and their authors are returned without considering the author's names):

```
<rt:stylesheet rt:version="1.0"
                xmlns:rt="http://purl.org/vocab/2003/rdft/">
  <rt:macro-set rt:prefix="rdf">
    <rt:macro name="type"
        value="resource(
      'http://www.w3.org/1999/02/22-rdf-syntax-ns#type')/resource()"/>
  </rt:macro-set>
  <rt:root-template>
    <rt:apply-templates
        rt:select="/resource()[rdf:type =
                        resource("http://example.org/books#Essay")/>
  </rt:root-template>
  <!-- Template for the Essay
  <rt:template pattern="resource()[rdf:type =
    resource('http://example.org/books#Essay')" />
    <xsl:value-of select="." />
    <rt:apply-templates
        rt:select="resource('http://example.org/books#author')/resource()/>
  </rt:template>
  <!-- Template for the author -->
  <rt:template
```

```
    pattern="resource('http://example.org/books#author')/resource()">
      <xsl:value-of select="." />
  </rt:template>
</rdft:stylesheet>
```

The [95] specification is not clear about the result of such a query: An XML tree or some form of an RDF graph? The description of rt:element seems to indicate the former, the description of rt:value-of the latter.

Project page:
   http://www.semanticplanet.com/2003/08/rdft/spec
Implementation(s):
   none
Online demonstration:
   none

[1] sketches another approach to querying RDF, and some form of XML, using an XSLT-like language. The basic idea is to translate RDF (expressed in XML) and also some non-RDF XML documents into a hierarchy of (attribute carrying) elements, based on the relations between the elements. The result of a query is some (hierarchical) view over this element tree. [1] does not address cyclic relations among elements but the language used seems to indicate that only proper hierarchies can be queried. RDF statements are mapped to nodes of an XML document as follows: Nodes represent RDF properties, an RDF statement (S, P, O) is represented by edges from all nodes representing some property with the value S to a node representing the property P with value O. A resource that never occurs as an object is assigned as value to a special property called query:seed. [1] seems to indicate that there can be only one such query:seed node, an assumption that does not hold for general RDF graphs. The query language provides a means for matching such property nodes based on the identifier (represented as URI or XML QName) of the property and the type (as determined by an rdf:type statement) of the value of the property.

Query 1 can be expressed as follows:

```
<query:plan>
  <query:template match="query:seed" type="books:Essay">
    <query:call name="query:insert" rename="book">
      <query:call name="query:format" rename="title"
                  value="book:title" />
      <query:call name="query:traverse" />
    </query:call>
  </query:template>
  <query:template match="book:author">
    <query:call name="query:insert" rename="author">
      <query:call name="query:format" rename="name"
                  value="book:authorName" />
    </query:call>
  </query:template>
</query:plan>
```

An excerpt of the result of this query on the sample data from Figure 2 would be:

```
...
<book title="Bellum Civile">
  <author name="Julius Caesar" />
  <author name="Aulus Hirtius" />
</book>
...
```

Project page:
  none
Implementation(s):
  not publicly available, no report on any implementation
Online demonstration:
  none

XsRQL: An XQuery-Style RDF Query Language. XsRQL [162], an XQuery-style RDF Query Language, is inspired from XQuery 1.0 [41], aiming at simplicity and flexibility. XsRQL departs from XQuery as follows: (1) The data model is adapted from RDF ([162] is rather vague on this point), (2) the path language considered is adapted to RDF and has only the axis child, (3) RDF properties are distinguished (from subjects and objects) by using @.[15]

Query 1 can be approximated in XsRQL as follows:

```
declare prefix books:  = <http://example.org/books#>;
declare prefix rdf:    = <http://www.w3.org/1999/02/22-rdf-syntax-ns#>;

for $essay in
        datasource(<http://example.org/books>)//*[@rdf:type/books:Essay],
    $author in $essay/@books:author/*
return
  $essay, $author, $author/@books:authorName/*
```

XsRQL neither supports closure, nor a descendant-like axis, nor some other means of traversing an arbitrary-length path in the data structure. Therefore, it is not possible to also return resources classified by any sub-class of *books:Essay*.

Project page:
  http://www.fatdog.com/xsrql.html
Implementation(s):
  none
Online demonstration:
  none

---

[15] In XPath, @ indicate (flat) XML attributes. Since RDF properties are structured, in XsRQL a path expression may follow a @ step.

4.4   Metalog: Querying in Controlled English

Metalog [195, 196, 197] is a system for querying and reasoning with Semantic Web data. Its early proposal has led to the claim that *"Metalog has been the first semantic web system to be designed, introducing reasoning within the Semantic Web infrastructure by adding the query/logical layer on top of RDF"* cf. http://www.w3.org/RDF/Metalog/. Metalog notably differs from other RDF query languages for two reasons: (1) Metalog combines querying with *reasoning*, and (2) the language syntax is a controlled natural language (English), i.e., a non-ambiguous language reminding of natural language.

Query 1 can be expressed in Metalog as follows:

```
comment: some definitions of variables (or representations)
ESSAY   represents the term "Essay"
        from the ontology "http://example.org/books#".
AUTHORED-BY represents the verb "author"
        from the ontology "http://example.org/books#".
IS      represents the verb "rdf:type"
        from RDF "http://www.w3.org/1999/02/22-rdf-syntax-ns#".
BELLUM_CIVILE represents the book "Bellum_Civile"
        from the collection of books "http://example.org/books#".

comment: RDF triples written as Metalog statements.
BELLUM_CIVILE IS an ESSAY.
BELLUM_CIVILE is AUTHORED-BY "Julius Caesar".
BELLUM_CIVILE is AUTHORED-BY "Aulus Hirtius".

comment: a Metalog query
do you know SOMETHING that IS an ESSAY and that is AUTHORED-BY SOMEONE?
```

Project page:
    http://www.w3.org/RDF/Metalog/
Implementation(s):
    Cf. project page
Online demonstration:
    none

4.5   Query Languages with Reactive Rules

Algae. Algae[16] is an RDF query language developed as part of the W3C Annotea project (http://www.w3.org/2001/Annotea/) aiming at enhancing Web pages with semantic annotations, expressed in RDF and collected from 'annotation servers', as Web pages are browsed. Algae is based on two concepts: (1) "Actions" are the directives ask, assert, and fwrule that determine whether an expression is used to query the RDF data, insert data into the graph, or to specify ECA-like rules. (2) Answers to Algae queries are bindings for query variables

---

[16] Also called "Algae2". This survey follows [237] and retains the name "Algae".

Table 1. Answer to Query 1

?title	?translator	Proof
"Bellum Civile"	"J. M. Carter"	_:1 rdf:type <http://exam...ks-rdfs#Essay>. _:1 books:author _:2. _:2 books:authorName ''Julius Caesar''. _:1 books:title ''Bellum Civile''. _:1 books:translator ''J. M. Carter''.

as well as triples from the RDF graph as "proofs" of the answer. Algae queries can be composed. Syntactically, Algae is based on the RDF syntax N-triples [133]. Algae extends the N-triple syntax with the above mentioned "actions" and with so-called "constraints", written between curly brackets, that specify further arithmetic or string comparisons to be fulfilled by the data retrieved.

Query 1 can be expressed as follows:

```
ns rdf   = <http://www.w3.org/1999/02/22-rdf-syntax-ns#>
ns books = <http://example.org/books#>
read <http://example.org/books> ()
ask (   ?essay   rdf:type          <http://example.org/books#Essay> .
        ?essay   books:author      ?author .
        ?author books:authorName ?authorName )
collect( ?essay, ?author, ?authorName )
```

This query becomes more interesting if we are not only interested in the titles of essays written by "Julius Caesar" but also want the translators of such books returned, if there are any:

```
ns rdf   = <http://www.w3.org/1999/02/22-rdf-syntax-ns#>
ns books = <http://example.org/books#>
read <http://example.org/books> ()
ask (   ?essay rdf:type            <http://example.org/books#Essay> .
        ?essay books:author        ?author .
        ?author books:authorName   ''Julius Caesar'' .
        ?essay books:title         ?title .
        ~?essay books:translator ?translator .
    )
collect( ?title, ?translatorName )
```

Note ~ used to declare 'translator' an optional. This query returns the answer given in Table 1.

Query 2 and Query 4 cannot be expressed in Algae due to the lack of closure, recursion, and negation. Queries 5 and 6 cannot be expressed in Algae due to the lack of aggregation operators. All other queries can be expressed in Algae, most of them requiring 'extended action directives' [236].

No formal semantics has been published for Algae.

Project page:

http://www.w3.org/2004/05/06-Algae/ and for the Annotea project
http://www.w3.org/2001/Annotea/

Implementation(s):

W3C Annotation Server http://annotest.w3.org/annotations

Online demonstration:

Query interface to the W3C Annotation Server using Algae as query language: http://annotest.w3.org/annotations?explain=false

iTQL. iTQL, a query and update language, has been defined for Kowari Metastore, an open source database for the storage of RDF data. iTQL offers commands for querying, `select`, updating, `delete` and `insert`, and transaction management, `commit` and `rollback`. The syntax of iTQL is reminiscent of SQL, and therefore also of RDQL. The querying capabilities of iTQL are limited like those of RDQL: iTQL supports only simple selections. iTQL allows nested queries.

Query 1 can be expressed as follows in iTQL:

```
alias <http://example.org/books#> as books;
alias <http://www.w3.org/2000/01/rdf-schema#> as rdfs;
alias <http://www.w3.org/1999/02/22-rdf-syntax-ns#> as rdf;

select $essay, $author, $authorName
where $essay          <books:author>      $author
  and $author         <books:authorName>  $authorName
  and $essay          <rdf:type>          $type
  and (trans($type    <rdfs:subClassOf>   <books:Essay>)
  or  $type           <tks:is>            <books:Essay>)
```

iTQL's function `trans` computes the transitive closure of a relation, in the example of `rdfs:subClassOf`. Paths of arbitrary length in an RDF graph can be traversed using iTQL's function `walk`. Like SQL, iTQL allows sorted answers and accessing answers in a paged mode using `limit` and `offset`.

Project page:

http://www.kowari.org

Implementations:

Kowari Metastor
Tucana Knowledge Server

Online demonstration:

WQL. WQL, Wilbur Query Language, is the name given in [182] to query primitives of Ivanhoe [180], a frame-based API inspired from [153, 178] for the Nokia Wilbur Toolkit [183], a collection of APIs for XML, RDF, and DAML written in CLOS, Common Lisp Object System [181].

In WQL, like in Ivanhoe, a RDF or DAML resource is represented as a frame with a slot for each property. The (possibly multiple) values of a slot correspond to objects of RDF statements, with the resources represented by the frame as subjects. Three WQL variants are discussed and compared in [144]:

- a basic query language, WQL proper, with constructs value and all-values for a path-based selection of one or all resources, and relatedp for testing resource relations.
- an embedding, called WQL+CL, of the above-mentioned basic language in Common Lisp.[17]
- WQL+CL+inference, an extension of WQL+CL, with a data store providing inferencing based upon the "transparent" (or "hidden") inference extensions described in [179].

In the following, WQL proper and, where appropriate, the "transparent inferencing" of WQL+CL+inference are considered. WQL+CL is not considered, for it is more akin to a programming language than a query language.

The following query returns the labels of all classes the book identified by http://example.org/books\#Bellum_Civile belongs to:

```
(setf *db* (make-instance 'db))
(load-db (make-url "http://example.org/books")
         :locator "http://example.org/books")
(add-namespace "books" "http://example.org/books#")
(all-values !"http://example.org/books#Bellum_Civile"
           '(:seq !rdf:type (:seq (:rep* !rdfs:subClassOf) !rdfs:label)))
```

Note :seq constructing a sequence of slots, i.e., RDF relations, to be traversed by the query and :rep* traversing the transitive closure of a slot/relation. all-values returns all resources, (represented as frames, reachable on the specified path from the source frame, i.e., the frame with identifier http://example.org/books\#Bellum_Civile.

Project page:
Wilbur Toolkit: http://wilbur-rdf.sourceforge.net/
Implementation:
Cf. project page
Online demonstration:
none

4.6   Deductive Query Languages

N3QL. N3QL, sketched in [35], is derived from the rule fragment of Notation 3 [34] (shorthand N3), a syntax for and extension of RDF with variables, rules, and quoting for easy expression of statements about statements. N3QL differs from the rule fragment of N3 in that its syntax has "query language style" clauses such as select and where.

---

[17] It is unclear whether WQL+CL restricts Common Lisp.

An N3QL query is an N3 expression and all N3QL reserved words are the RDF properties of an RDF (usually, but not necessarily) blank node representing the query.

Query 1 can be expressed as follows in N3QL:

```
@prefix books: <http://example.org/books#>.
@prefix n3ql: <http://www.w3.org/2004/ql#>.
@prefix rdf:  <http://www.w3.org/1999/02/22-rdf-syntax-ns#>.
[] n3ql:select { n3ql:result n3ql:is (?book ?author ?authorName) };
   n3ql:where  { ?book    rdf:type          books:Essay;
                  ?book    books:author      ?author;
                  ?author  books:authorName  ?authorName }.
```

The answer to this query is the RDF graph specified in the `n3ql:select` clause, a set of RDF collections (indicated by the collection constructor `()`) of bindings for the three variables.

[35] seems to indicate that a N3QL query is equivalent to a N3 rule, the **where** part of the N3QL query being the rule's premise, and the **select** part, the rule's consequence. However, whereas N3 rules can express transitive closures, this is not the case of N3QL queries. The following N3 rule specifies the transitive closure of a RDF property:

```
@prefix rdfs: <http://www.w3.org/2000/01/rdf-schema#>.
{?x rdfs:subClassOf ?z; ?z rdfs:subClassOf ?y}
                    => {?x rdfs:subClassOf ?y}
```

Note that the description of N3QL does not clearly specify which of the syntactic constructs of N3 can be used in N3QL. [35] states that N3QL is a restricted form of N3 where formulae cannot be nested and literals cannot be subjects of statements. The N3 syntax for anonymous nodes, for navigating in the RDF graph using path expressions, and for quantified variables gives rise to concise expressions of of queries such as *"Return the books written by the author named 'Julius Caesar'."*:

```
@prefix books: <http://example.org/books#>.
@prefix n3ql: <http://www.w3.org/2004/ql#>.
[] n3ql:select { n3ql:result n3ql:is (?book) };
   n3ql:where  { ?book!books:author!books:authorName ''Julius Caesar'' }.
```

Project page:
    http://www.w3.org/DesignIssues/N3QL.html
Implementations:
    CWM http://www.w3.org/2000/10/swap/doc/cwm.html
    EulerSharp http://eulersharp.sourceforge.net/2003/03swap/
Online demonstration:
    none

R-DEVICE. R-DEVICE [19] is a *"deductive object-oriented knowledge-base system for querying and reasoning about RDF metadata."*[18] It is a reimplementation of the X-DEVICE language [20] in the C Language Integrated Production System, or CLIPS, cf. http://www.ghg.net/clips/CLIPS.html, using the CLIPS Object-Oriented Language, COOL. RDF triples are mapped to objects as follows:

- RDF resources are represented as objects, the types of which are the resource's RDF types, i.e., the values of the rdf:type properties. For resources that are classified in multiple classes, a 'dummy class' is introduced which represents a common subclass of all the classes the resource is classified in.
- RDF properties are realized as multi-slots, i.e., slots with multiple values, in the class which is the domain of the property. If no domain is given, i.e., if the property can be applied to any resources, a slot is added to the class representing rdfs:Resource, the top of the RDF resource hierarchy.

Assertions generated, e.g., through rules, can require dynamic class and/or object re-definitions.

Query 1 can be expressed as follows:

```
(deductiverule q1
  ?book <- (? (rdf:type books:Essay) (books:author ?author))
  ?author <- (? (books:authorName ?authorName))
 =>
  (result (book ?book) (author ?author) (authorName ?authorName))
)
```

Note the production-rule like syntax of R-DEVICE.

R-DEVICE provides constructs for traversing arbitrary length paths of slots and objects, properties and resources, both with and without restriction on the type of slot that may be traversed. This allows one to implement both Query 2 and Query 8. Query 2 can be expressed as follows:

```
(deductive rule q2
  ?book <- (? (rdf:type books:Essay) (books:title ''Bellum  Civile''))
  (($?p) ?related)
 =>
  (result (book ?book) (related ?related))
)
```

Project page:
    http://lpis.csd.auth.gr/systems/r-device.html
Implementation:
    Cf. project page
Online demonstration:
    none

---

[18] http://lpis.csd.auth.gr/systems/r-device.html

TRIPLE. TRIPLE [147, 259, 260] is a rule-based query, inference, and transformation language for RDF. TRIPLE is based upon ideas published in [96]. TRIPLE's syntax is close to F-Logic [170]. F-Logic is convenient for querying semi-structured data, e.g., XML and RDF, as it facilitates describing schemaless or irregular data [188]. Other approaches to querying XML and/or RDF are XPathLog and the ontology management platform Ontobroker[19]. TRIPLE has been designed to address two weaknesses of previous approaches to querying RDF: (1) Predefined constructs expressing RDFS' semantics that restrain a query language's extensibility, and (2) lack of formal semantics.

Instead of predefined RDFS-related language constructs, TRIPLE offers Horn logic rules (in F-Logic syntax) [170]. Using TRIPLE rules, one can implement features of, e.g., RDFS. Where Horn logic is not sufficient, as is the case of OWL, TRIPLE is designed to be extended by external modules implementing, e.g., an OWL reasoner. Thanks to its foundations in Horn logic, TRIPLE can inherit much of Logic Programming's formal semantics. Referring to, e.g., a representation of UML in RDF [176, 177], the authors of TRIPLE claim in [260] that TRIPLE is well-suited to query non-RDF meta-data. This can be questioned, especially if, in spite of [126], one considers the rather awkward mappings of Topic Maps into RDF proposed so far.

TRIPLE differs from Horn logic and Logic Programming as follows [260]:

- TRIPLE supports resources identified by URIs.
- RDF statements are represented in TRIPLE by slots, allowing the grouping and nesting of statements; like in F-Logic, Path expressions inspired from [119] can be used for traversing several properties.
- TRIPLE provides concise support for reified statements. Reified statements are expressed in TRIPLE enclosed angle brackets, e.g.:

  `Julius_Caesar[believes-><Junius_Brutus[friend-of -> Julius_Caesar]>]`
- TRIPLE has a notion of module allowing specification of the 'model' in which a statement, or an atom, is true. 'Models' are identified by URIs that can prefix statement or atom using @.
- TRIPLE requires an explicit quantification of all variables.

Query 1 can be approximated as follows:

```
rdf    := 'http://www.w3.org/1999/02/22-rdf-syntax-ns#'.
books := 'http://example.org/books#'.
booksModel := 'http://example.org/books'.
FORALL B, A, AN  result(B, A, AN) <-
    B[rdf:type -> books:Essay;
      books:author -> A[books:authorName -> AN]]@booksModel.
```

This query selects only resources directly classified as `books:Essay`. Query 1 is properly expressed below.

TRIPLE's rules give rise to specify properties of RDF. [260] gives the following implementation of a part of RDFS's semantics:

---
[19] `http://www.ontoprise.de/products/ontobroker`

```
rdf        := 'http://www.w3.org/1999/02/22-rdf-syntax-ns#'.
rdfs       := 'http://www.w3.org/2000/01/rdf-schema#'.
type       := rdf:type.
subPropertyOf := rdfs:subPropertyOf.
subClassOf    := rdfs:subClassOf.

FORALL Mdl @rdfschema(Mdl) {
  transitive(subPropertyOf).
  transitive(subClassOf).
  FORALL O,P,V O[P->V] <-
               O[P->V]@Mdl.
  FORALL O,P,V O[P->V] <-
               EXISTS S S[subPropertyOf->P] AND O[S->V].
  FORALL O,P,V O[P->V] <-
               transitive(P) AND EXISTS W (O[P->W] AND W[P->V]).
  FORALL O,T   O[type->T] <-
               EXISTS S (S[subClassOf->T] AND O[type->S]).
}
```

Inference from range and domain restrictions of properties are not implemented by the rule given above. This is not limitation of TRIPLE, though, for the following rules provides them:

```
  FORALL S,T  S[type-$>$T] <-
              EXISTS P, O (S[P-$>$O] AND P[rdfs:domain-$>$T]).
  FORALL O,T  O[type->T] <-
              EXISTS P, S (S[P-$>$O] AND P[rdfs:range-$>$T]).
```

With the rules given above, the approximation of Query 1 given above only needs to be modified so as to express the 'model' it is evaluated against: instead of @booksModel, @rdfschema(booksModel) should be used, i.e., the original 'model' should be extended with the above-mentioned implementing RDFS' semantics. Most queries of Section 2.3 can be expressed in TRIPLE. Aggregation queries cannot be expressed in TRIPLE, for the language does not support aggregation.

[260] specifies an RDF, and therefore XML, syntax for a fragment of TRIPLE. By relying on translations to RDF, one can query data in different formalisms with TRIPLE, e.g., RDF, Topic Maps, and UML. This, however, might lead to rather awkward queries. Some aspects of RDF, viz. containers, collections, and anonymous nodes, are not supported by TRIPLE. The complexity of TRIPLE has not been investigated so far.

Project page:
    http://triple.semanticweb.org/
Implementation:
    Cf. project page

Online demonstration:
Cf. project page
`http://ontoagents.stanford.edu:8080/triple/`[20]

Xcerpt. Xcerpt [30, 56, 58, 248], cf. `http://xcerpt.org`, is a language for querying both data on the "standard Web" (e.g., XML and HTML data) and data on the Semantic Web (e.g., RDF, Topic Maps, etc. data). Using Xcerpt for querying XML data is addressed in Section 7. This Section is devoted to applying Xcerpt to querying RDF data.

Three features of Xcerpt are particularly convenient for querying RDF data. (1) Xcerpt's pattern-based incomplete queries are convenient for collecting related resources in the neighbourhood of some given resources and to express traversals of RDF graphs of indefinite lengths. (2) Xcerpt chaining of (possibly recursive rules) is convenient for expressing RDFS's semantics, e.g., the transitive closure of the `subClassOf` relation, as well as all kinds of graph traversals. (3) Xcerpt's optional construct is convenient for collecting properties of resources.

All nine queries from Section 2.3 can be expressed in Xcerpt's both on the XML serialization (cf. Section 3.2) and on the RDF serialization of the sample data from Section 2.2. The following Xcerpt programs show solutions for the queries against the RDF serialization.

[44] proposes two views on RDF data: as in most other RDF query languages as plain triples with explicit joins for structure traversal and as a proper graph.

On the plain triple view, Query 1 can be expressed in Xcerpt as follows:

```
DECLARE ns-prefix rdf = "http://www.w3.org/1999/02/22-rdf-syntax-ns#"
DECLARE ns-prefix books = "http://example.org/books#"

GOAL
  result [
    all essay [
      id [ var Essay ],
      all author [
        id [ var Author ],
        all name [ var AuthorName ]
      ]
    ]
  ]
FROM
  and{
    RDFS-TRIPLE [
      var Essay:uri{}, "rdf:type":uri{}, "books:Essay":uri{}
    ],
    RDF-TRIPLE [
      var Essay:uri{}, "books:author":uri{}, var Author:uri{}
    ],
```

---

[20] Not functioning at the time of writing.

```
RDF-TRIPLE [
  var Author:uri{}, "books:authorName":uri{}, var AuthorName
]
}
END
```

Using the prefixes declared in line 1 and 2, the query pattern (between
FROM and END) is a conjunction of tree queries against the RDF triples represented in the predicate RDF-TRIPLE. Notice that the first conjunct actually
uses RDFS-TRIPLE. This view of the RDF data contains all basic triples plus the
ones entailed by the RDFS semantics [148] (cf. [44] for a detailed description).
Using RDFS-TRIPLE instead of RDF-TRIPLE ensures that also resources actually
classified in a sub-class of books:Essay are returned.

Xcerpt's approach to RDF querying shares with [242] and a few other approaches in Section 4.3 the ability to construct arbitrary XML as in this rule.

On Xcerpt's graph view of RDF, the same query can be expressed as follows:

```
DECLARE ns-prefix rdf = "http://www.w3.org/1999/02/22-rdf-syntax-ns#"
DECLARE ns-prefix books = "http://example.org/books#"

GOAL
  result [
    all essay [
      id [ var Essay ],
      all author [
        id [ var Author ],
        all name [ var AuthorName ]
      ]
    ]
  ]
FROM
  RDFS-GRAPH {{
    var Essay:uri {{
      rdf:type {{ "books:Essay":uri {{ }} }},
      books:author {{
        var Author:uri {{
          books:name {{ var AuthorName }}
        }}
      }}
    }}
  }}
END
```

The RDF graph view is represented in the RDF-GRAPH predicate. Here, the
RDFS-GRAPH view is used that extends RDF-GRAPH as RDFS-TRIPLE extends
RDF-TRIPLE. Triples are represented similar to striped RDF/XML: each resource
is a direct child element in RDF-GRAPH with a sub-element for each statement
with that resource as object. The sub-element is labeled with the URI of the
predicate and contains the object of the statement. As Xcerpt's data model is a
rooted *graph* this can be represented without duplication of resources.

In contrast to the previous query no conjunction is used but rather a nested pattern that naturally reflects the structure of the RDF graph with the exception that labeled edges are represented as nodes with edges to the elements representing their source and sink.

To illustrate this graph view, consider the following rule showing how to generate the graph view from the triple view introduced above:

```
CONSTRUCT
  RDF-GRAPH {
    all var Subject @ var Subject:var SubjectType {
      all optional var Predicate {
        ^var Object
      },
      all optional var Predicate {
        var Literal
      }
    } }
FROM
  or{
    RDF-TRIPLE[
      var Subject:var SubjectType{},
      var Predicate:uri{},
      optional var Literal as literal{{}},
      optional var Object:/uri|blank/{{}}
    ],
    RDF-TRIPLE[
      /.*/:/.*/{{}},
      /.*/:/.*/{{}},
      var Subject:var SubjectType{{}}
    ]  }
END
```

Notice the use of the `optional` keyword in lines 16 and 17. This indicates that the contained part of the pattern does not have to occur in the data, but if it does occur the contained variables are bound appropriately. `Optional` allows queries with alternatives to be expressed very concisely and is therefore crucial for RDF where all properties are optional by default.

In lines 3 and 5 the construction of a graph is shown: by using the operators @ and ^ a (possibly cyclic) link can be constructed.

Xcerpt rules are convenient for making the language "RDF serialisation transparent". For each RDF serialisation, a set of rules expresses a translation from or into that serialisation. However, the rules for parsing RDF/XML [25], the official XML serialisation, are very complex and lengthy due to the high degree of flexibility RDF/XML allows. They can be found in [44], similar functions for parsing RDF/XML in XQuery are described in [246]. The following rules parse RDF data serialised in the RXR (Regular XML RDF) format [11], a far simpler and more regular RDF serialisation.

The following rule extracts all triples from an RXR document. Since different types (such as URI, blank node, or literal) of subjects and objects of RDF triples are represented differently in RXR, the conversion of the RXR representation into the plain triples is performed in separate rules, see [44].

```
DECLARE ns-prefix rxr = "http://ilrt.org/discovery/2004/03/rxr/"

CONSTRUCT
  RDF-TRIPLE[
    var Subject, var Predicate:uri{}, var Object
  ]
FROM
  and[
    rxr:graph {{
      rxr:triple {
        var S → rxr:subject{{}},
        rxr:predicate{ attributes{ rxr:uri{ var Predicate } } },
        var O → rxr:object{{}}
      }
    }},
    RXR-RDFNODE[ var S, var Subject ],
    RXR-RDFNODE[ var O, var Object ]
  ]
END
```

Querying RDF data with Xcerpt is the subject of ongoing investigation [44].

4.7   Other RDF Query Languages

RDF-QBE [241] is inspired from QBE [289, 290], the database query language that introduced the celebrated "Query by Example" paradigm. An RDF graph, expressed in the syntax of Notation 3 [34]), is used to describe query patterns, variables are expressed as blank nodes that, according to [172] doe not have explicit identifiers. The representation of variables as blank nodes leads to a major restriction of RDF-QBE : Query patterns can only be tree-shaped.[21] RDF-QBE is especially convenient for expressing selection and extraction queries. However, the expressive power of RDF-QBE is limited: Not all queries of Section 2.3 can be expressed.

Project page:
    none
Implementation:
    described in [241] but not publicly available
Online demonstration:
    none

RDFQL. RDFQL is the query language of RDF Gateway [154], a platform for developing and deploying Semantic Web applications combining a "native"

---

[21] [241] (wrongly) suggests that this restriction reduces query-answering to tree matching because the data queried is not necessarily tree-shaped.

RDF database engine, a Web server, and a server-side scripting language. The RDF database engine allows for the integration of standard and Semantic Web using so-called "virtual tables" and inference rules for deductive reasoning (so far, libraries for OWL and RDFS are provided). RDF Gateway supports several serialisations of RDF, viz. RDF/XML, N3, and NTriples. Although similar to RDQL, cf. Section 4.1, RDFQL differs from RDQL as follows: (1) RDFQL includes database commands for transaction management, e.g., commit and rollback, (2) RDFQL includes SQL-like update commands, (3) RDFQL allows accessing data from disk-based, in-memory, or external[22] "data sources", and (4) RDFQL's command INFER allows specification of deduction rules to be used when querying.

With RDFQL's rules, the semantics of RDFS can be expressed as follows:

```
RULEBASE rdfs
{
   INFER {[rdf:type] ?a [rdf:Property]} from {?a ?x ?y};
   INFER {[rdf:type] ?x ?z} from {[rdfs:domain] ?a ?z} and {?a ?x ?y};
   INFER {[rdf:type] ?u ?z} from {[rdfs:range] ?a ?z}
         and {?a ?x ?u} and uri(?u)=?u;
   INFER {[rdf:type] ?x [rdfs:Resource]} from {?a ?x ?y};
   INFER {[rdf:type] ?u [rdfs:Resource]} from {?a ?x ?u} and uri(?u)=?u
   INFER {[rdfs:subPropertyOf] ?a ?c}
         from {[rdfs:subPropertyOf] ?a ?b} and {[rdfs:subPropertyOf] ?b ?c}
   INFER {?b ?x ?y} from {[rdfs:subPropertyOf] ?a ?b}
         and {?a ?x ?y}
   INFER {[rdfs:subClassOf] ?x [rdfs:Resource]}
         from {[rdf:type] ?x [rdfs:Class]}
   INFER {[rdfs:subClassOf] ?x ?z} from {[rdfs:subClassOf] ?x ?y}
         and {[rdfs:subClassOf] ?y ?z}
   INFER {[rdf:type] ?a ?y} from {[rdfs:subClassOf] ?x ?y}
         and {[rdf:type] ?a ?x}
}
```

{?P ?S ?O} denotes in RDFQL an RDF statement with subject S, property P, and object O, i.e., RDFQL uses a prefix notation for RDF statements. uri(?u)=?u serves to detect whether the object of an RDF statement is a resource (in which case it has an URI and this URI is equal to the "value" of the resource itself) or a literal.

Query 1 can be implemented as follows:

```
session.namespaces["books"] = "http://example.org/books#";
var booksdata = new DataSource("http://example.org/books");
SELECT ?essay, ?author, ?authorName USING booksdata WHERE
      {[rdf:type] ?essay [books:Essay]}
  and {[books:author] ?essay ?author}
  and {[books:authorName] ?author ?authorName}
ORDER BY ?authorName DESC;
```

---

[22] I.e., identified, e.g., by an URI.

Project page:
    http://www.intellidimension.com/
Implementations:
    RDF Gateway
    Cf. project page for a limited, non-commercial use
Online demonstration:
    none[23]

5   Topic Maps Query Languages

5.1   tolog: Logic Programming for Topic Maps

tolog [122, 123, 124, 125] is the query language of the Ontopia Knowledge Suite[24]. tolog has also been selected in April 2004 as an initial straw-man for the ISO Topic Maps Query Language. tolog is inspired from Logic Programming and has SQL-style constructs. tolog provides a means for identifying a topic by its (internal) identifier and its subject indicator, e.g., the topic (type) "Novel" of the sample data can be accessed either by its identifier Novel, or its subject indicator i"http://example.org/books#Novel".[25] URI prefixes can be used, e.g., using books for i"http://example.org/books#" gives rise to the short form books:Novel for the above-mentioned subject indicator. Note that tolog URI prefixes contain indicators and therefore differ from XML namespaces. In tolog, all occurrences of variables must be prefixed with $.

The original version of tolog [123]) has two kinds of Prolog-like "predicates", "built-in" and "dynamic association predicates". tolog has a "dynamic association predicate" for querying the extent of each association type, e.g., authors-for-book(b1, $AUTHOR: author) selects the authors of book b1 (note the association role identifying the topic 'author'). tolog has only two "dynamic association predicates" similar to "dynamic occurrence predicates". The original version of tolog has only two "built-in predicates", instance-of($INSTANCE, $CLASS) and direct-instance-of($INSTANCE, $CLASS), conveying the semantics of the subsumption hierarchy.

The current version of tolog [122, 124] has further built-in predicates, e.g., role-player and association-role, for enumerating the associations, association roles, occurrences, and topics. These allow querying arbitrary topic maps without a-priori knowledge of the types used in the topic maps. Query 2 can only be implemented only using these predicates:

```
select $RELATED from
  title($BOOK, "Bellum Civile"),
  related($BOOK, $RELATED)?
related($X, $Y) :- {
```

---

[23] However, the project page implemented in RDF Gateway is a show case.
[24] http://www.ontopia.net/solutions/products.html
[25] The prefix i serves to distinguish different identifiers.

```
    role-player($R1, $X), association-role($A, $R1),
    association-role($A, $R2), role-player($R2, $Y) |
    related($X, $Z), related($Z, $Y)
}.
```

Conjunctions are expressed, as in Prolog, by commas. Disjunctions are in curly braces the disjuncts being separated by |.

The built-in predicates `instance-of` and `direct-instance-of` can indeed be implemented using tolog rules as follows [123]:

```
direct-instance-of($INSTANCE, $CLASS) :-
   i"http://psi.topicmaps.org/sam/1.0/#type-instance"(
      $INSTANCE : i"http://psi.topicmaps.org/sam/1.0/#instance",
      $CLASS : i"http://psi.topicmaps.org/sam/1.0/#class").
super-sub($SUB, $SUPER) :-
   i"http://www.topicmaps.org/xtm/1.0/core.xtm#superclass-subclass"(
      $SUB    : i"http://www.topicmaps.org/xtm/1.0/core.xtm#subclass",
      $SUPER : i"http://www.topicmaps.org/xtm/1.0/core.xtm#superclass").
descendant-of($DESC, $ANC) :- {
   super-sub($DESC, $ANC) |
   super-sub($DESC, $INT), descendant-of($INT, $ANC)
}.
instance-of($INSTANCE, $CLASS) :- {
   direct-instance-of($INSTANCE, $CLASS) |
   direct-instance-of($INSTANCE, $DCLASS), descendant-of($DCLASS, $CLASS)
}.
```

Negation is available, however its semantics in tolog is not yet specified [124]. tolog has constructs for aggregation and sorting (although deemed insufficient [124]), paged queries using `limit` and `offset` as in SQL, and a module concept. Thanks to tolog's (possibly recursive) rules, Queries 7 and 8 can be implemented in tolog.

Neither the formal semantics, nor the complexity of tolog have been investigated yet.

Project page:
    http://www.ontopia.net/omnigator/docs/query/tutorial.html[26]
Implementations:
    Ontopia Knowledge Suite: http://www.ontopia.net/solutions/products.html
    Topic Maps toolkit TM4J: http://tm4j.org/
Online demonstrations:
    Omnigator: http://www.ontopia.net/
    http://www.ontopia.net/omnigator/models/index.jsp[27]

---

[26] Tutorial.
[27] The demonstrator does not seem to support testing tolog queries.

5.2   AsTMA?: Functional Style Querying of Topic Maps

AsTMa? [14, 15] is a functional query language in the style of XQuery [41]. AsTMa? offers several path languages for accessing data in topic maps. With AsTMa?, answers can be re-structured, yielding new XML documents.

Query 1 can be implemented as follows:

```
<books>
{ forall [$book (Writing)] in http://example.org/books
    return
    <book>
      {$book,
      forall $author in ($book -> author / author-for-book) return
      <author>
        {$author}
        <name>{$author/bn}</name>
      </author>
    </book>  }
</books>
```

Query 1 can also be implemented as follows, using path expressions for accessing topics and associations:

```
<books>
{ forall [$book (Writing)] in http://example.org/books
    return
    <book>
      {$book,
      forall [ (author-for-book)
              Writing : $book
              author:   $author ]
           in http://example.org/books return
      <author>
        {$author}
        <name>{$author/bn}</name>
      </author>
    </book>  }
</books>
```

Project page:
    http://astma.it.bond.edu.au/querying.xsp
Implementation):
    As part of the Perl XTM module, available via CPAN
Online demonstration:
    http://astma.it.bond.edu.au/query/

5.3   Toma: Querying Topic Maps Inspired from SQL

Toma [175, 234] combines SQL syntax and path expressions for querying Topic Maps, i.e., the following query selects all books, specified as topics classified as Writing, with their authors:

```
select  topic[book], topic[author]
from    topic-type["Writing"].topic[book],
        topic[book]..assoc[a]..topic[author],
        assoc-type["author-for-book"].assoc[a]
```

Toma provides access to all Topic Maps concepts, including the subsumption hierarchy. Information about a topic such as topic identifier, basename, and subject identifier are accessed using the long name, or . notation, common in object-oriented languages, e.g., $topic.bn = 'Julius Caesar' compares the base-name, short bn, of topics, short by $topic, with the string "Julius Caesar". Associations can be traversed using ->, predefined associations with special semantics, such as the instance-of and superclass-subclass associations, can be traversed transitively when traversing the subsumption hierarchy. $start.super(1..*) selects all super-classes of the current class. Instead of 1..*, an interval, or a single number, can indicate how many superclass-subclass associations should be traversed. A similar notation is available for instance-of associations.

Query 1 can be expressed as follows:

```
select  $book, $author, $author.bn
where   $book.type(1..*).id = 'Writing'
   and  author-for-book%a->Writing = $book
   and  author-for-book%a->author = $author
```

Query 3 can be expressed as follows:

```
select  $topic
where   $topic.type(1..*).si.sir != 'http://example.org/books#Translator'
   and  not exists ($t.type(1) = $topic)
   and  not exists ($t.type(1..*) = $x and $topic.super(1..*) = $x)
```

This query selects all topics that are neither used as type of another topic, nor typed Translator. All topics are selected that neither (a) have the subject identifier http://example.org/books#Translator, nor (b) are the type of some topic, nor (c) are a sub-class of some topic that is some topic's type.

Project page:
    http://www.spaceapplications.com/toma/
Implementation:
    Not freely available
Online demonstration:
    none

5.4   Path-Based Access to Topic Maps: XTMPath and TMPath

Following the success of XPath, a number of path-based query languages have been proposed for Topic Maps, cf. [16] for an overview of a plea for the inclusion of path navigation in the upcoming ISO Topic Maps query language.

XTMPath [17] is a path-based query language relying on the XTM [232] serialisation of topic maps in XML. The following path selects all topics that are

(directly) typed
`Historical_Novel`:

```
topic[instanceOf/topicRef/@href = "\#Historical\_Novel"]}
```

This path expression reflects the XTM serialisation:

```
<topic id="b1">
  <instanceOf> <topicRef xlink:href="#Historical_Novel"/> </instanceOf>
</topic>
```

Note that (1) Only a limited subset of the XPath constructs is supported by XTMPath, mostly the child and descendant axis and some simple predicates (in XPath's abbreviated syntax), and (2) XTMPath operates on data conforming to a single DTD[28], viz., the DTD of XTM DTD [17], leading to treating the axis "child" like the axis "descendant" with a few exceptions, e.g., `instanceOf`.

Project page:
   http://cpan.uwinnipeg.ca/htdocs/XTM/XTM/Path.html
Implementation:
   Available from CPAN as part of the XTM toolkit
Online demonstration:
   none

6   Conclusion: Salient Aspects of the Query Languages Considered

This article is an attempt to give a survey of both query languages proposed for the "standard Web" (i.e., basically XML data), and query languages for the Semantic Web (i.e. mostly RDF and Topic Maps). Query languages targeting OWL have not been considered in this survey, because as of writing (March 2005), they still are in their infancy and the few languages proposed so far can only query meta-data.

Inspite of the exclusions described in Section 1 (programming languages tools for XML, reactive languages for the Web, rules languages, and OWL query languages) a considerable number of languages have been considered in this article. Indeed, we are not aware of any other effort to survey Web and/or Semantic Web query languages at the same level of depth and breadth.

Even though the field is moving extremely fast and new proposals are always emerging, it is already possible and worthwhile to stress some of the salient aspects of Web and Semantic Web query languages:

Path vs. Logic or Navigational vs. Positional. Web and Semantic Web query languages express basic queries using one of two paradigms, paths à la XPath, or

---

[28] Document Type Definition, cf. [48].

Logic, à la Logic Programming. These two paradigms can also be named "navigational" and "positional", respectively, stressing that (path-oriented) navigations inherently conflict with referential transparency. One might expect that both kinds of languages will continue to be investigated, yielding interesting opportunities for further comparison and research.

Logical Variables. When Web and Semantic Web query languages have variables, they almost always are logical variables, i.e., Logic Programming or Functional Programming variables, as opposed to variables in imperative programming languages that are amenable to explicit assignments.

Referential Transparency and (Weak or Strong) Answer-Closure. Referential Transparency (i.e., within the same scope, an expression always means the same), *the* trait of declarative languages, is, if not fully achieved, obviously striven for by both positional and logic, query languages, especially in Semantic Web query languages. Some query languages are "weakly answer-closed" or "answer-closed" in the sense of [79], i.e., they deliver answers in the formalism of the data queried. A few query languages are "strongly answer-closed", i.e., they make query programs possible that can further process data generated by these very programs. Arguably, strong answer-closure is important for structuring programs and sustaining the so-called "separation of concerns" in programming. One might expect that positional Web and Semantic Web query languages will mature into well-designed, referentially transparent and strongly answer-closed languages.

Backtracking-Free Logic Programming or Set-Oriented Functional Query Evaluation. Positional, or logic query languages that offer construct similar to rules or views, are, with a few exceptions or unclear cases, backtracking-free. Equivalently, they can be called set-oriented functional. This convergence of two programming paradigms in Web query languages seems promising for further research.

Incomplete Queries and Answers. Many query languages offer means for incomplete specifications of queries, paying tribute to the "semi-structured" [3] nature of data on the Web, i.e., that data on the Web either has no schemas or does not fully respect its schema. Incomplete query specifications are extremely useful on the Semantic Web, too. In querying an RDF graph or topic maps, incomplete queries are very useful for easily accessing the neighbourhood of resources. Indeed such incomplete specifications considerably simplify and ease programming.

Versatile vs. Data Format Specific Query Languages. Most RDF query languages are RDF-specific, and even specifically designed for one serialisation. The authors are convinced that an evolution towards data format "versatile" languages that are capable of easily accommodating XML, RDF, Topic Maps, OWL, etc. without requiring "serialisation consciousness" from the programmer, should be striven for.

Reasoning Capabilities. Interestingly, but not surprisingly, not all XML query languages have views, rules, or similar concepts allowing the specification of other forms of reasoning. Surprisingly, the same holds true of RDF query languages.

Many authors of RDF query languages see deduction and reasoning to be a feature of an underlying RDF store offering materialisation, i.e., completion of RDF data with derivable data prior to query evaluation. This is surprising, because one might expect many Semantic Web applications to access not only one RDF data store at one Web site, but instead many RDF data stores at different Web sites and to draw conclusions combining data from different stores. Such an RDF query scenario requires, on the decentralised and open Web, deduction at query time, i.e., when queries are evaluated.[29]

Language Engineering. Language engineering issues, e.g., abstract data types and static type checking, modules, polymorphism, and abstract machines, have clearly not yet made their way in the Web query languages, as they did not in database query languages. This situation opens avenues for promising research of great practical, as well as theoretical relevance.

Acknowledgements

The authors are thankful to Renzo Orsini, Ian Horrocks, Michael Kraus, and Oliver Bolzer for stimulating discussions and useful suggestions during the production of the report [60], that has been an important input for this overview.

This research has been funded by the European Commission and by the Swiss Federal Office for Education and Science within the 6th Framework Programme project REWERSE number 506779 (cf. http://rewerse.net).

References

[1] Langdale Consultants . Nexus Query Language. Online only, 2000.
[2] S. Abiteboul, D. Quass, J. McHugh, J. Widom, and J. Wiener. The Lorel Query Language for Semistructured Data. *International Journal on Digital Libraries1(1):68-88, April 1997.*, 1(1):68–88, 1997.
[3] S. Abiteboul, P. Buneman, and D. Suciu. *Data on the Web: From Relations to Semistructured Data and XML.* Morgan Kaufmann, 1999.
[4] J. Alferes, W. May, and P. Patranjan. *State of the Art on Evolution and Reactivity*, 2004.
[5] S. Amer-Yahia, M. F. Fernandez, D. Srivastava, and Y. Xu. PIX: Exact and Approximate Phrase Matching in XML. In *Proc. ACM SIGMOD Conf.*, 2003.
[6] S. Amer-Yahia, C. Botev, S. Buxton, P. Case, J. Doerre, D. McBeath, M. Rys, and J. Shanmugasundaram. *XQuery and XPath Full-Text.* W3C, 2004. URL http://www.w3.org/TR/xquery-full-text-requirements/.
[7] S. Amer-Yahia, C. Botev, and J. Shanmugasundaram. TeXQuery: A Full-Text Search Extension to XQuery. In *Proc. Int. World Wide Web Conf.*, 2004.
[8] S. Amer-Yahia, L. V. S. Lakshmanan, and S. Pandit. FleXPath: Flexible Structure and Full-Text Querying for XML. In *Proc. ACM SIGMOD Conf.*, 2004.

---

[29] Indeed, materialising conclusions from all possible combinations of Web sites is infeasible.

[9] V. Apparao, S. Byrne, M. Champion, S. Isaacs, I. Jacobs, A. L. Hors, G. Nicol, J. Robie, R. Sutor, C. Wilson, and L. Wood. Document Object Model (DOM) Level 1 Specification. Recommendation, W3C, 10 1998.

[10] E. Augurusa, D. Braga, A. Campi, and S. Ceri. Design and Implementation of a Graphical Interface to XQuery. In *Proc. Symposium of Applied Computing*, pages 1163–1167. ACM Press, 2003. ISBN 1-58113-624-2. doi: http://doi.acm.org/10.1145/952532.952759.

[11] D. Backett. Modernising Semantic Web Markup. In *Proc. XML Europe*, April 2004.

[12] E. Bae and J. Bailey. CodeX: an approach for debugging XSLT transformations. In *Web Information Systems Engineering, 2003. WISE 2003. Proceedings of the Fourth International Conference on*, 2003.

[13] J. Bailey. Transformation and Reaction Rules for Data on the Web. In *Proc. Australasian Database Conference*, 2005.

[14] R. Barta. AsTMa? Tutorial. Technical report, Bond University, 2003.

[15] R. Barta. AsTMa= Language Definition. Online only, 2007.

[16] R. Barta. Path Language for Topic Maps: Full speed ahead? Online only, 2004.

[17] R. Barta and J. Gylta. *XTM::Path*, 2002.

[18] C. Baru, A. Gupta, B. Ludäscher, R. Marciano, Y. Papakonstantinou, and P. Velikhov. XML-Based Information Mediation with MIX. In *Proc. ACM SIGMOD International Conference on Management of Data*, 1999.

[19] N. Bassiliades and I. Vlahavas. Capturing RDF Descriptive Semantics in an Object Oriented Knowledge Base System. In *Proc. International Word Wide Web Conference*, May 2003.

[20] N. Bassiliades and I. Vlahavas. Intelligent Querying of Web Documents Using a Deductive XML Repository. In *Proc. Hellenic Conference on Artificial Intelligence*, April 2002.

[21] R. Baumgartner, S. Flesca, and G. Gottlob. The Elog Web Extraction Language. In *Proc. International Conference on Logic for Programming, Artificial Intelligence, and Reasoning*, December 2001.

[22] R. J. Bayardo, D. Gruhl, V. Josifovski, and J. Myllymaki. An Evaluation of Binary XML Encoding Optimizations for fast Stream based XML Processing. In *Proc. Int. World Wide Web Conf.*, pages 345–354. ACM Press, 2004. ISBN 1-58113-844-X. doi: http://doi.acm.org/10.1145/988672.988719.

[23] S. Bechhofer, F. van Harmelen, J. Hendler, I. Horrocks, D. McGuinness, P. Patel-Schneider, and L. Stein. *OWL Web Ontology Language—Reference*. W3C, 2004. URL http://www.w3.org/TR/owl-ref/.

[24] D. Beckett. *Turtle - Terse RDF Triple Language*, February 2004.

[25] D. Beckett and B. McBride. *RDF/XML Syntax Specification (Revised)*. W3C, 2004. URL http://www.w3.org/TR/rdf-syntax-grammar/.

[26] M. Benedikt, W. Fan, and G. Kuper. Structural Properties of XPath Fragments. In *Proc. International Conference on Database Theory*, 2003.

[27] V. Benzaken, G. Castagna, and A. Frisch. CDuce: An XML-Centric General-Purpose Language. In *Proc. International Conference on Functional Programming*, 2003.

[28] S. Berger, F. Bry, and S. Schaffert. A Visual Language for Web Querying and Reasoning. In *Proc. Workshop on Principles and Practice of Semantic Web Reasoning*, LNCS 2901. Springer-Verlag, December 2003.

[29] S. Berger, F. Bry, S. Schaffert, and C. Wieser. Xcerpt and visXcerpt: From Pattern-Based to Visual Querying of XML and Semistructured Data. In *Proc. Int. Conf. on Very Large Databases*, 2003.

[30] S. Berger, F. Bry, O. Bolzer, T. Furche, S. Schaffert, and C. Wieser. Xcerpt and
visXcerpt: Twin Query Languages for the Semantic Web. In *Proc. Int. Semantic
Web Conf.*, 11 2004. I4 I3.

[31] A. Berglund, S. Boag, D. Chamberlin, M. Fernandez, M. Kay, J. Robie, and
J. Simeon. *XML Path Language (XPath) 2.0*. W3C, 2005.

[32] A. Berlea and H. Seidl. Binary Queries for Document Trees. *Nordic Journal of
Computing*, 11(1):41–71, 2004.

[33] A. Berlea and H. Seidl. fxt—A Transformation Language for XML Documents.
*Journal of Computing and Information Technology, Special Issue on Domain-
Specific Languages*, 2001.

[34] T. Berners-Lee. Notation 3, an RDF language for the Semantic Web. Online
only, 2004.

[35] T. Berners-Lee. N3QL—RDF Data Query Language. Online only, 2004.

[36] T. Berners-Lee. Semantic Web Road Map. Online only, 2004.

[37] T. Berners-Lee, J. Hendler, and O. Lassila. The Semantic Web—A new form of
Web content that is meaningful to computers will unleash a revolution of new
possibilities. *Scientific American*, 2001.

[38] G. J. Bex, S. Maneth, and F. Neven. A Formal Model for an Expressive Fragment
of XSLT. *Information Systems*, 27(1):21–39, 2002. ISSN 0306-4379. doi: http:
//dx.doi.org/10.1016/S0306-4379(01)00033-3.

[39] P. Biron and A. Malhotra. *XML Schema Part 2: Datatypes*. W3C, 2001. URL
http://www.w3.org/TR/xmlschema-2/.

[40] C. Bizer. The TriG Syntax. Online only, April 2004.

[41] S. Boag, D. Chamberlin, M. Fernandez, D. Florescu, J. Robie, and J. Simeon.
XQuery 1.0: An XML Query Language. W3C, 2005.

[42] S. Boag, D. Chamberlin, M. F. Fernndez, D. Florescu, J. Robie, and J. Simon.
XQuery 1.0: An XML Query Language. Working draft, W3C, 2 2005.

[43] H. Boley, B. Grosof, M. Sintek, S. Tabet, and G. Wagner. RuleML Design. Online
only, 2002.

[44] O. Bolzer. Towards Data-Integration on the Semantic Web: Querying RDF with
Xcerpt. Diplomarbeit/Master thesis, University of Munich, 2 2005.

[45] O. Bolzer, F. Bry, T. Furche, S. Kraus, and S. Schaffert. Development of Use
Cases, Part I: Illustrating the Functionality of a Versatile Web Query Language.
Deliverable I4-D3, REWERSE, 3 2005. I4.

[46] A. Bonifati, D. Braga, A. Campi, and S. Ceri. Active XQuery. In *Proc. Int.
Conf. on Data Engineering*, page 403. IEEE Computer Society, 2002.

[47] D. Braga, A. Campi, S. Ceri, and E. Augurusa. XQuery by Example. In *Proc.
Int. World Wide Web Conf.*, 2003.

[48] T. Bray, J. Paoli, C. M. Sperberg-McQueen, E. Maler, and F. Yergeau. *Extensible Markup Language (XML) 1.0 (Third Edition)*. W3C, 2004. URL
http://www.w3.org/TR/REC-xml/.

[49] J.-M. Bremer and M. Gertz. XQuery/IR: Integrating XML Document and Data
Retrieval. In *Int. Workshop on the Web and Databases*, 2002.

[50] D. Brickley. RDF: Understanding the Striped RDF/XML Syntax. Online only,
October 2001.

[51] D. Brickley, R. Guha, and B. McBride. *RDF Vocabulary Description Language
1.0: RDF Schema*. W3C, 2004. URL http://www.w3.org/TR/rdf-schema/.

[52] J. Broekstra and A. Kampman. SeRQL: A Second Generation RDF Query Language. In *Proc. SWAD-Europe Workshop on Semantic Web Storage and Retrieval*, 2003.

[53] M. Brundage. *XQuery: The XML Query Language*. Addison-Wesley, 2004.

[54] E. Bruno, J. L. Maitre, and E. Murisasco. Extending XQuery with Transformation Operators. In *Proc. ACM symposium on Document Engineering*, pages 1–8. ACM Press, 2003. ISBN 1-58113-724-9. doi: http://doi.acm.org/10.1145/958220.958223.

[55] F. Bry and P.-L. Pătrânjan. Reactivity on the Web: Paradigms and Applications of the Language XChange. In *Proc. Symposium of Applied Computing*. ACM, 3 2005. I4 I5.

[56] F. Bry and S. Schaffert. A Gentle Introduction into Xcerpt, a Rule-based Query and Transformation Language for XML. In *Proc. Int. Workshop on Rule Markup Languages for Business Rules on the Semantic Web*, 2002.

[57] F. Bry and S. Schaffert. Towards a Declarative Query and Transformation Language for XML and Semistructured Data: Simulation Unification. In *Proc. Int. Conf. on Logic Programming*, volume 2401 of *LNCS*. Springer-Verlag, 7 2002.

[58] F. Bry and S. Schaffert. The XML Query Language Xcerpt: Design Principles, Examples, and Semantics. In *Proc. Int. Workshop on Web and Databases*, volume 2593 of *LNCS*. Springer-Verlag, 2002.

[59] F. Bry, W. Drabent, and J. Maluszynski. On Subtyping of Tree-structured Data A Polynomial Approach. In *Proc. Workshop on Principles and Practice of Semantic Web Reasoning, St. Malo, France*, volume 3208 of *LNCS*. REWERSE, Springer-Verlag, 9 2004. I4 I3.

[60] F. Bry, T. Furche, L. Badea, C. Koch, S. Schaffert, and S. Berger. Identification of Design Principles for a (Semantic) Web Query Language. Deliverable I4-D1, REWERSE, 2004.

[61] F. Bry, P.-L. Pătrânjan, and S. Schaffert. Xcerpt and XChange: Logic Programming Languages for Querying and Evolution on the Web. In *Proc. Int. Conf. on Logic Programming*, LNCS, 2004.

[62] F. Bry, S. Schaffert, and A. Schröder. A contribution to the Semantics of Xcerpt, a Web Query and Transformation Language. In *Proc. Workshop Logische Programmierung*, March 2004.

[63] F. Bry, T. Furche, L. Badea, C. Koch, S. Schaffert, and S. Berger. Querying the Web Reconsidered: Design Principles for Versatile Web Query Languages. *Journal of Semantic Web and Information Systems*, 1(2), 2005. I4.

[64] P. Buneman, S. Davidson, G. Hillebrand, and D. Suciu. A Query Language and Optimization Techniques for Unstructured Data. In *Proc. ACM SIGMOD Conf.*, pages 505–516. ACM Press, 1996. ISBN 0-89791-794-4. doi: http://doi.acm.org/10.1145/233269.233368.

[65] P. Buneman, S. B. Davidson, and D. Suciu. Programming Constructs for Unstructured Data. In *Proc. Int. Workshop on Database Programming Languages*, page 12. Springer-Verlag, 1996. ISBN 3-540-76086-5.

[66] P. Buneman, M. Fernandez, and D. Suciu. UnQL: A Query Language and Algebra for Semistructured Data Based on Structural Recursion. *VLDB Journal*, 9(1): 76–110, 2000.

[67] A. b.v. and S. A. Ltd. *The SeRQL query language*, chapter 5. Aduna b.v., Sirma AI Ltd., 2002.

[68] D. Calvanese, G. D. Giacomo, M. Lenzerini, and M. Y. Vardi. Containment of Conjunctive Regular Path Queries with Inverse. In *Proc. Int. Conf. on the Principles of Knowledge Representation and Reasoning*, pages 176–185, 2000.

[69] D. Calvanese, G. D. Giacomo, M. Lenzerini, and M. Y. Vardi. Query Processing using Views for Regular Path Queries with Inverse. In *Proc. ACM Symposium on Principles of Database Systems*, pages 58–66, 2000.

[70] L. Cardelli and G. Ghelli. TQL: a Query Language for Semistructured Data based on the Ambient Logic. *Mathematical Structures in Computer Science*, 14(3):285–327, 2004. ISSN 0960-1295. doi: http://dx.doi.org/10.1017/S0960129504004141.

[71] L. Cardelli and A. D. Gordon. Anytime, Anywhere: Modal Logics for Mobile Ambients. In *Proc. Symposium on Principles of Programming Languages*, pages 365–377. ACM Press, 2000. ISBN 1-58113-125-9. doi: http://doi.acm.org/10.1145/325694.325742.

[72] J. Carroll, C. Bizer, P. Hayes, and P. Stickler. Named Graphs, Provenance and Trust. Technical Report HPL-2004-57, HP Labs, 2004.

[73] R. G. G. Cattell, D. K. Barry, M. Berler, J. Eastman, D. Jordan, C. Russell, O. Schadow, T. Stanienda, and F. Velez, editors. *Object Data Standard: ODMG 3.0*. Morgan Kaufmann, 2000.

[74] S. Ceri, S. Comai, E. Damiani, P. Fraternali, S. Paraboschi, and L. Tanca:. XML-GL: A Graphical Language for Querying and Reshaping XML Documents. In *Proc. W3C QL'98 – Query Languages*, 1998.

[75] S. Ceri, S. Comai, E. Damiani, P. Fraternali, S. Paraboschi, and L. Tanca. XML-GL: a Graphical Language for Querying and Restructuring XML Documents. In *Proc. Int. World Wide Web Conf.*, 1999.

[76] D. Chamberlin and J. Robie. XQuery Update Facility Requirements. Working draft, W3C, 2005.

[77] D. Chamberlin, J. Robie, and D. Florescu. Quilt: An XML Query Language for Heterogeneous Data Sources. In *Proc. Workshop on Web and Databases*, 2000.

[78] D. Chamberlin, P. Fankhauser, M. Marchiori, and J. Robie. *XML Query (XQuery) Requirements*. W3C, 2003.

[79] D. Chamberlin, P. Fankhauser, D. Florescu, M. Marchiori, and J. Robie. *XML Query Use Cases*. W3C, 2005.

[80] L. Chen and E. A. Rundensteiner. ACE-XQ: A CachE-aware XQuery Answering System. In *Proc. Workshop on the Web and Databases*, 2002.

[81] Z. Chen, H. V. Jagadish, L. V. Lakshmanan, and S. Paparizos. From Tree Patterns to Generalized Tree Patterns: On Efficient Evaluation of XQuery. In *Proc. Int. Conf. on Very Large Databases*, 2003.

[82] T. T. Chinenyanga and N. Kushmerick. An Expressive and Efficient Language for XML Information Retrieval. *Journal of the American Society for Information Science and Technology*, 53(6):438–453, 2002.

[83] V. Christophides, S. Cluet, and G. Moerkotte. Evaluating Queries with Generalized Path Expressions. In *Proc. ACM SIGMOD International Conference on Management of Data*, pages 413–422, 1996.

[84] V. Christophides, D. Plexousakis, G. Karvounarakis, and S. Alexaki. Declarative Languages for Querying Portal Catalogs. In *Proc. DELOS Workshop: Information Seeking, Searching and Querying in Digital Libraries*, 2000.

[85] J. Clark. *XSL Transformations (XSLT) Version 1.0*. W3C, 1999.

[86] J. Clark and S. DeRose. *XML Path Language (XPath) Version 1.0*. W3C, 1999.

[87] K. Clark. *RDF Data Access Use Cases and Requirements*. W3C, 2004.

[88] J. Coelho and M. Florido. CLP(Flex): Constraint Logic Programming Applied to XML Processing. In *Proc. Int. Conf. on Ontologies, Databases, and Applications of Semantics for Large Scale Information Systems*, volume 3291 of *LNCS*. Springer-Verlag, 2004.

[89] S. Cohen, Y. Kanza, Y. Kogan, Y. Sagiv, W. Nutt, and A. Serebrenik. EquiX—a search and query language for XML. *Journal of the American Society for Information Science and Technology*, 53(6):454–466, 2002. ISSN 1532-2882. doi: http://dx.doi.org/10.1002/asi.10058.

[90] S. Cohen, J. Mamou, Y. Kanza, and Y. Sagiv. XSEarch: A Semantic Search Engine for XML. In *Proc. Int. Conf. on Very Large Databases*, 2003.

[91] S. Comai, E. Damiani, and P. Fraternali. Computing Graphical Queries over XML Data. *ACM Transactions on Information Systems*, 19(4):371–430, 2001. ISSN 1046-8188. doi: http://doi.acm.org/10.1145/502795.502797.

[92] S. Comai, S. Marrara, and L. Tanca. XML Document Summarization: Using XQuery for Synopsis Creation. In *Proc. Int. Workshop on Database and Expert Systems Applications*, 2004.

[93] G. Conforti, G. Ghelli, A. Albano, D. Colazzo, P. Manghi, and C. Sartiani. The Query Language TQL. In *Proc. Int. Workshop on the Web and Databases*, 2002.

[94] J. Cowan and R. Tobin. *XML Information Set (Second Edition)*. W3C, 2004. URL http://www.w3.org/TR/2004/REC-xml-infoset-20040204/.

[95] I. Davis. RDF Template Language 1.0. Online only, September 2003.

[96] S. Decker, D. Brickley, J. Saarela, and J. Angele. A Query and Inference Service for RDF. In *Proc. W3C QL'98 – Query Languages 1998*, December 1998.

[97] D. DeHaan, D. Toman, M. P. Consens, and M. T. zsu. A Comprehensive XQuery to SQL Translation using Dynamic Interval Encoding. In *Proc. ACM SIGMOD Conf.*, pages 623–634. ACM Press, 2003. ISBN 1-58113-634-X. doi: http://doi.acm.org/10.1145/872757.872832.

[98] A. Deutsch and V. Tannen. Containment and Integrity Constraints for XPath Fragments. In *Proc. Int. Workshop on Knowledge Representation meets Databases*, 2001.

[99] A. Deutsch, M. Fernandez, D. Florescu, A. Levy, and D. Suciu. XML-QL: A Query Language for XML. In *Proc. W3C QL'98 – Query Languages 1998*. W3C, 1998.

[100] A. Deutsch, M. Fernandez, D. Florescu, A. Levy, and D. Suciu. A Query Language for XML. In *Proc. Int. World Wide Web Conf.*, 1999.

[101] A. Deutsch, Y. Papakonstantinou, and Y. Xu. The NEXT Logical Framework for XQuery. In *Proc. Int. Conf. on Very Large Databases*, 2004.

[102] C. Dong and J. Bailey. Optimization of XML Transformations Using Template Specialization. In *Proc. Int. Conf. on Web Information Systems Engineering*, 2004.

[103] C. Dong and J. Bailey. Static Analysis of XSLT Programs. In *Proc. Australasian Database Conf.*, pages 151–160. Australian Computer Society, Inc., 2004. ISBN 1-111-11111-1.

[104] D. Draper, P. Frankhauser, M. Fernndez, A. Malhotra, K. Rose, M. Rys, J. Simon, and P. Wadler. XQuery 1.0 and XPath 2.0 Formal Semantics. Working draft, W3C, 2 2005.

[105] D. Eastlake and A. Panitz. Reserved Top Level DNS Names. RFC 2606, IETF, 1999.

[106] A. Eisenberg and J. Melton. An early Look at XQuery. *SIGMOD Record*, 31 (4):113–120, 2002. ISSN 0163-5808. doi: http://doi.acm.org/10.1145/637411. 637433.

[107] A. Eisenberg and J. Melton. An early Look at XQuery API for Java^{TM}(XQJ). *SIGMOD Record*, 33(2):105–111, 2004. ISSN 0163-5808. doi: http://doi.acm. org/10.1145/1024694.1024717.

[108] D. Fallside. *XML Schema Part 0: Primer*. W3C, 2001. URL http://www. w3.org/TR/xmlschema-0/.

[109] P. Fankhauser. XQuery Formal Semantics: State and Challenges. *SIGMOD Record*, 30(3):14–19, 2001. ISSN 0163-5808. doi: http://doi.acm.org/10.1145/ 603867.603870.

[110] P. Fankhauser and P. Lehti. XQuery by the book: The IPSI XQuery Demonstrator. In *XML Conference & Exhibition*, 2002.

[111] M. Fernandez, A. Malhotra, J. Marsh, M. Nagy, and N. Walsh. *XQuery 1.0 and XPath 2.0 Data Model*. W3C, 2004.

[112] M. Fernndez, J. Simon, B. Choi, A. Marian, and G. Sur. Implementing XQuery 1.0 : The Galax Experience. In *Proc. Int. Conf. on Very Large Databases*, 2003.

[113] R. Fikes, P. Hayes, and I. Horrocks. OWL-QL – A Language for Deductive Query Answering on the Semantic Web. *Journal of Web Semantics*, To appear.

[114] D. Florescu, M. Fernandez, A. Levy, and D. Suciu. A Query Language and Processor for a Web-site Management System. In *Proc. Workshop on Management of Semi-structured Data*, 1997.

[115] D. Florescu, A. Levy, M. Fernandez, and D. Suciu. A Query Language for a Web-site Management System. *SIGMOD Record*, 26(3):4–11, 1997.

[116] D. Florescu, A. Grnhagen, and D. Kossmann. XL: An XML Programming Language for Web Service Specification and Composition. In *Proc. International World Wide Web Conference*, May 2002.

[117] D. Florescu, A. Grnhagen, and D. Kossmann. XL: An XML Programming Language for Web Service Specification and Composition. *Computer Networks*, 42 (5), 2003.

[118] D. Florescu, C. Hillery, D. Kossmann, P. Lucas, F. Riccardi, T. Westmann, M. J. Carey, and A. Sundararajan. The BEA Streaming XQuery Processor. *VLDB Journal*, 13(3):294–315, 2004. ISSN 1066-8888. doi: http://dx.doi.org/10.1007/s00778-004-0137-1.

[119] J. Frohn, G. Lausen, and H. Uphoff. Access to Objects by Path Expressions and Rules. In *Proc. International Conference on Very Large Databases*, 1994.

[120] N. Fuhr and K. Gross. XIRQL: a Query Language for Information Retrieval in XML Documents. In *Proc. ACM Conference on Research and Development in Information Retrieval*, 2001.

[121] L. Garshol. The Linear Topic Map Notation. Online only, 2007.

[122] L. Garshol. tolog–Language tutorial. Online only, 2004.

[123] L. Garshol. tolog 0.1. Technical report, Ontopia, 2003.

[124] L. Garshol. Extending tolog—Proposal for tolog 1.0. In *Proc. Extreme Markup Languages*, 2003.

[125] L. Garshol. tolog—A topic map query language. In *Proc. XML Europe*, 2001.

[126] L. M. Garshol. Living with Topic Maps and RDF. Online only, 2003.

[127] R. Goldman, S. Chawathe, A. Crespo, and J. McHugh. A Standard Textual Interchange Format for the Object Exchange Model (OEM). Technical report, Database Group, Stanford University, 1996.

[128] G. Gottlob and C. Koch. Monadic Datalog and the Expressive Power of Languages for Web Information Extraction. In 51, editor, *Journal of the ACM*, volume 1, pages 74–113, 2004.

[129] G. Gottlob and C. Koch. Monadic Queries over Tree-Structured Data. In *Proc. Annual IEEE Symposium on Logic in Computer Science*, pages 189–202. IEEE Computer Society, 2002. ISBN 0-7695-1483-9.

[130] G. Gottlob, C. Koch, and R. Pichler. Efficient Algorithms for Processing XPath Queries. In *Proc. International Conference on Very Large Databases*, 2002.

[131] G. Gottlob, C. Koch, and R. Pichler. XPath Query Evaluation: Improving Time and Space Efficiency. In *Proc. International Conference on Data Engineering*, 2003.

[132] G. Gottlob, C. Koch, and R. Pichler. The Complexity of XPath Query Evaluation. In *Proc. ACM Symposium on Principles of Database Systems*, 2003.

[133] J. Grant and D. Backett. *RDF Test Cases*. W3C, February 2004.

[134] S. Groppe and S. Bttcher. XPath Query Transformation based on XSLT Stylesheets. In *Proc. Int. Workshop on Web Information and Data Management*, pages 106–110. ACM Press, 2003. ISBN 1-58113-725-7. doi: http://doi.acm.org/10.1145/956699.956723.

[135] P. Grosso, E. Maier, J. Marsh, and N. Walsh. *XPointer Framework*. W3C, 2003. URL http://www.w3.org/TR/xptr-framework/.

[136] H. L. S. W. R. Group. Jena – A Semantic Web Framework for Java. Online only, 2004.

[137] T. Grust. Accelerating XPath Location Steps. In *Proc. ACM SIGMOD Conf.*, 2002.

[138] T. Grust, M. V. Keulen, and J. Teubner. Accelerating XPath Evaluation in any RDBMS. *ACM Transactions on Database Systems*, 29(1):91–131, 2004. ISSN 0362-5915. doi: http://doi.acm.org/10.1145/974750.974754.

[139] T. Grust, S. Sakr, and J. Teubner. XQuery on SQL Hosts. In *Proc. Int. Conf. on Very Large Databases*, 2004.

[140] R. Guha. rdfDB Query Language. Online only, 2000.

[141] R. Guha, O. Lassila, E. Miller, and D. Brickley. Enabling Inferencing. In *Proc. W3C QL'98 – Query Languages 1998*, December 1998.

[142] L. Guo, F. Shao, C. Botev, and J. Shanmugasundaram. XRANK: Ranked Keyword Search over XML Documents. In *Proc. ACM SIGMOD Conf.*, 2003.

[143] Z. Guo, M. Li, X. Wang, and A. Zhou. Scalable XSLT Evaluation. In *Proc. Asia Pacific Web Conference*, 2004.

[144] P. Haase, J. Broekstra, A. Eberhart, and R. Volz. A Comparison of RDF Query Languages. In *Proc. International Semantic Web Conference*, 2004.

[145] M. Harren, M. Raghavachari, O. Shmueli, M. Burke, V. Sarkar, and R. Bordawekar. XJ: Integration of XML Processing into Java. In *Proc. International World Wide Web Conference*, 2004.

[146] S. Harris and N. Gibbins. 3store: Efficient Bulk RDF Storage. In *Proc. International Workshop on Practical and Scalable Semantic Systems*, 2003.

[147] A. Harth. Triple Tutorial. Online only, 2004.

[148] P. Hayes and B. McBride. *RDF Semantics*. W3C, 2004. URL http://www.w3.org/TR/rdf-mt/.

[149] J. Hidders. Satisfiability of XPath Expressions. In *Int. Workshop on Databse Programming Languages*, 2003.

[150] I. Horrocks, F. van Harmelen, and P. Patel-Schneider. *DAML+OIL*. Joint US/EU ad hoc Agent Markup Language Committee, 2001. URL http://www.daml.org/2001/03/daml+oil-index.html.

[151] I. Horrocks, P. Patel-Schneider, H. Boley, S. Tabet, B. Grosof, and M. Dean. *SWRL: A Semantic Web Rule Language—Combining OWL and RuleML*. W3C, 2004. URL http://www.w3.org/Submission/2004/SUBM-SWRL-20040521/.

[152] H. Hosoya and B. Pierce. XDuce: A Typed XML Processing Language. *ACM Transactions on Internet Technology*, 3(2):117–148, 2003.

[153] J. Hynynen and O. Lassila. On the Use of Object-Oriented Paradigm in a Distributed Problem Solver. *AI Communications*, 2(3):142–151, 1989.

[154] Intellidimension. RDF Gateway. Online only, 2004.

[155] *ISO/IEC 13250 Topic Maps*. International Organization for Standardization, 1999. URL http://www.y12.doe.gov/sgml/sc34/document/0322_files/iso13250-2nd-ed-v2.pdf.

[156] S. Jain, R. Mahajan, and D. Suciu. Translating XSLT Programs to Efficient SQL Queries. In *Proc. Int. World Wide Web Conf.*, pages 616–626. ACM Press, 2002. ISBN 1-58113-449-5. doi: http://doi.acm.org/10.1145/511446.511526.

[157] B. Johnson and B. Shneiderman. Tree-maps: a Space-Filling Approach to the Visualization of Hierarchical Information Structures. In *Proc. Int. Conf. on Visualization*, pages 284–291, 1991.

[158] G. Karvounarakis, V. Christophides, D. Plexousakis, and S. Alexaki. Querying RDF Descriptions for Community Web Portals. In *Proc. Journees Bases de Donnees Avancees*, 2001.

[159] G. Karvounarakis, S. Alexaki, V. Christophides, D. Plexousakis, and M. Scholl. RQL: A Declarative Query Language for RDF. In *Proc. International World Wide Web Conference*, May 2002.

[160] G. Karvounarakis, A. Magkanaraki, S. Alexaki, V. Christophides, D. Plexousakis, M. Scholl, and K. Tolle. Querying the Semantic Web with RQL. *Computer Networks and ISDN Systems Journal*, 42(5):617–640, August 2003.

[161] G. Karvounarakis, A. Magkanaraki, S. Alexaki, V. Christophides, D. Plexousakis, M. Scholl, and K. Tolle. RQL: A Functional Query Language for RDF. In P. Gray, P. King, and A. Poulovassilis, editors, *The Functional Approach to Data Management*, chapter 18, pages 435–465. Springer-Verlag, 2004. ISBN 3-540-00375-4.

[162] H. Katz. XsRQL: an XQuery-style Query Language for RDF. Online only, 2004.

[163] H. Katz, D. Chamberlin, D. Draper, M. Fernandez, M. Kay, J. Robie, M. Rys, J. Simeon, J. Tivy, and P. Wadler. *XQuery from the Experts: A Guide to the W3C XML Query Language*. Addison-Wesley, 1st edition, 8 2003.

[164] M. Kay. *XPath2.0 Programmer's Reference*. John Wiley, 8 2004.

[165] M. Kay. *XSLT 2.0 Programmer's Reference*. John Wiley, 3rd edition, 8 2004.

[166] M. Kay. XSLT and XPath Optimization. In *XML Europe*, 2004.

[167] M. Kay. *XSL Transformations (XSLT) Version 2.0*. W3C, 2005.

[168] M. Kay, N. Walsh, H. Zongaro, S. Boag, and J. Tong. XSLT 2.0 and XQuery 1.0 Serialization. Working draft, W3C, 2 2005.

[169] S. Kepser. A Simple Proof of the Turing-Completeness of XSLT and XQuery. In *Proc. Extreme Markup Languages*, 2004.

[170] M. Kifer, G. Lausen, and J. Wu. Logical Foundations of Object Oriented and Frame Based Languages. *Journal of ACM*, 42:741–843, 1995.

[171] C. Kirchner, Z. Oian, P. Singh, and J. Stuber. Xemantics: a Rewriting Calculus-Based Semantics of XSLT. Technical Report A01-R-386, LORIA, 2002.

[172] G. Klyne, J. Carroll, and B. McBride. *Resource Description Framework (RDF): Concepts and Abstract Syntax*. W3C, 2004. URL http://www.w3.org/TR/rdf-concepts/.

[173] C. Koch, S. Scherzinger, N. Schweikardt, and B. Stegmaier. FluXQuery: An Optimizing XQuery Processor for Streaming XML Data. In *Proc. Int. Conf. on Very Large Databases*, 2004.

[174] S. Kraus. Use Cases für Xcerpt: Eine positionelle Anfrage- und Transformationssprache für das Web. Diplomarbeit/Master thesis, University of Munich, 2004.

[175] R. Ksiezyk. Answer is just a question [of matching Topic Maps]. In *Proc. XML Europe*, 2000.

[176] M. Lacher and S. Decker. On the Integration of Topic Maps and RDF Data. In *Proc. Extreme Markup Languages*, 2001.

[177] M. Lacher and S. Decker. RDF, Topic Maps, and the Semantic Web. *Markup Languages: Theory and Practice*, 3(3):313–331, December 2001.

[178] O. Lassila. BEEF Reference Manual—A Programmer's Guide to the BEEF Frame System, Second Version. Technical Report HTKK-TKO-C46, Department of Computer Science, Helsinki University of Technology, 1991.

[179] O. Lassila. Taking the RDF Model Theory Out for a Spin. In *Proc. Semantic Web Working Symposium*, June 2002.

[180] O. Lassila. Ivanhoe: an RDF-Based Frame System. Online only, 2004.

[181] O. Lassila. Enabling Semantic Web Programming by Integrating RDF and Common Lisp. In *Proc. Semantic Web Working Symposium*, july 2001.

[182] O. Lassila. Wilbur Query Language Comparison. Online only, 2004.

[183] O. Lassila. Wilbur Semantic Web Toolkit. Online only, 2004.

[184] O. Lassila and R. Swick. *Resource Description Framework (RDF) Model and Syntax Specification*. W3C, 1999. URL http://www.w3.org/TR/1999/REC-rdf-syntax-19990222/.

[185] A. Laux and L. Martin. *XUpdate—XML Update Language*. XML:DB Initiative, 2000. URL http://xmldb-org.sourceforge.net/xupdate/xupdate-wd.html.

[186] J. Liu and M. Vincent. Query translation from XSLT to SQL. In *Proc. Int. Database Engineering and Applications Symposium*, 2003.

[187] M. Liu. A Logical Foundation for XML. In *Proc. International Conference on Advanced Information Systems Engineering*. Springer-Verlag, 2002.

[188] B. Ludäscher, R. Himmeroeder, G. Lausen, W. May, and C. Schlepphorst. Managing Semistructured Data with FLORID: A Deductive Object-oriented Perspective. *Information Systems*, 23(8):1–25, 1998.

[189] B. Ludäscher, Y. Papakonstantinou, and P. Velikhov. *A Brief Introduction to XMAs*. Database Group, University of California, San Diego, 1999.

[190] A. Magkanaraki, G. Karvounarakis, V. Christophides, D. Plexousakis, and T. Anh. Ontology Storage and Querying. Technical Report 308, Foundation for Research and Technology Hellas, April 2002.

[191] A. Magkanaraki, V. Tannen, V. Christophides, and D. Plexousakis. Viewing the Semantic Web Through RVL Lenses. In *Proc. International Semantic Web Conference*, October 2003.

[192] D. Maier. Database Desiderata for an XML Query Language. In *Proc. W3C QL'98 – Query Languages 1998*, December 1998.

[193] A. Malhotra, J. Melton, and N. Walsh. XQuery 1.0 and XPath 2.0 Functions and Operators. Working draft, W3C, 2 2005.

[194] F. Manola, E. Miller, and B. McBride. *RDF Primer*. W3C, 2004. URL http://www.w3.org/TR/rdf-primer/.

[195] M. Marchiori and J. Saarela. Towards the Semantic Web: Metalog. Online only, 1999.

[196] M. Marchiori and J. Saarela. Query + Metadata + Logic = Metalog. In *Proc. W3C QL'98 – Query Languages 1998*, December 1998.

[197] M. Marchiori, A. Epifani, and S. Trevisan. Metalog v2.0: Quick User Guide. Technical report, W3C, 2004.

[198] W. Martens and F. Neven. Frontiers of tractability for typechecking simple XML transformations. In *Proceedings of the ACM Symposium on Principles of Database Systems (PODS)*, pages 23–34, 2004.

[199] M. Marx. Conditional XPath, the First Order Complete XPath Dialect. In *Proc. ACM Symposium on Principles of Database Systems*, pages 13–22. ACM, 6 2004.

[200] M. Marx. XPath with Conditional Axis Relations. In *Proc. Extending Database Technology*, 2004.

[201] K. Matsuyama, M. Kraus, K. Kitagawa, and N. Saito. A Path-Based RDF Query Language for CC/PP and UAProf. In *Proc. IEEE Conference on Pervasive Computing and Communications Workshops*, 2004.

[202] N. May, S. Helmer, and G. Moerkotte. Quantifiers in XQuery. In *Proc. Int. Conf. on Web Information Systems Engineering*, 2003.

[203] W. May. XPath-Logic and XPathLog: A Logic-Programming Style XML Data Manipulation Language. *Theory and Practice of Logic Programming*, 3(4):499–526, 2004.

[204] D. McGuinness and F. van Harmelen. *OWL Web Ontology Language—Overview*. W3C, 2004. URL http://www.w3.org/TR/owl-features/.

[205] E. Meijer and M. Shields. XMLambda: A functional language for constructing and manipulating XML documents. Online only, 1999.

[206] E. Meijer, W. Schulte, and G. Bierman. Programming with Circles, Triangles and Rectangles. In *Proc. XML Conference and Exhibition*, 2003.

[207] H. Meuss and K. U. Schulz. Complete Answer Aggregates for Treelike Databases: a novel Approach to combine querying and navigation. *ACM Transactions on Information Systems*, 19(2):161–215, 2001. ISSN 1046-8188. doi: http://doi.acm.org/10.1145/382979.383042.

[208] H. Meuss, K. U. Schulz, and F. Bry. Towards Aggregated Answers for Semistructured Data. In *Proc. Int. Conf. on Database Theory*, pages 346–360. Springer-Verlag, 2001. ISBN 3-540-41456-8.

[209] H. Meuss, K. U. Schulz, F. Weigel, S. Leonardi, and F. Bry. Visual Exploration and Retrieval of XML Document Collections with the Generic System X2. *Journal on Digital Libraries*, 2005.

[210] H. Meyer, I. Bruder, A. Heuer, and G. Weber. The Xircus Search Engine. In *INEX Workshop*, pages 119–124, 2002.

[211] G. Miklau and D. Suciu. Containment and Equivalence for an XPath Fragment. In *Proc. ACM Symposium on Principles of Database Systems*, pages 65–76. ACM Press, 2002. ISBN 1-58113-507-6. doi: http://doi.acm.org/10.1145/543613.543623.

[212] L. Miller. Inkling: RDF query using SquishQL. Online only, 2004.

[213] L. Miller, A. Seaborne, and A. Reggiori. Three Implementations of SquishQL, a Simple RDF Query Language. In *Proc. International Semantic Web Conference*, June 2002.

[214] T. Milo, D. Suciu, and V. Vianu. Typechecking for XML transformers. In *Proceedings of the Nineteenth ACM SIGMOD-SIGACT-SIGART Symposium on Principles of Database Systems, May 15-17, 2000, Dallas, Texas, USA*, pages 11–22. ACM, 2000. ISBN 1-58113-214-X.

[215] K. D. Munroe and Y. Papakonstantinou. BBQ: A Visual Interface for Integrated Browsing and Querying of XML. In *Proc. Conf. on Visual Database Systems*, pages 277–296. Kluwer, B.V., 2000. ISBN 0-7923-7835-0.

[216] M. Murata, A. Tozawa, M. Kudo, and S. Hada. XML Access Control using Static Analysis. In *Proc. ACM Conf. on Computer and Communications Security*, pages 73–84. ACM Press, 2003. ISBN 1-58113-738-9. doi: http://doi.acm.org/10.1145/948109.948122.

[217] M. Nilsson, W. Siberski, and J. Tane. Edutella Retrieval Service: Concepts and RDF Syntax. Online only, June 2004.

[218] M. Odersky. Report on the Programming Language Scala. Technical report, Ecole Polytechnique Federale de Lausanne, 2002.

[219] U. Ogbuji. Versa by example. Online only, 2004.

[220] U. Ogbuji. Thinking XML: Basic XML and RDF techniques for knowledge management: Part 6: RDF Query using Versa. Online only, April 2002.

[221] R. Oldakowski and C. Bizer. RAP: RDF API for PHP. In *Proc. International Workshop on Interpreted Languages*, 2004.

[222] B. Oliboni and L. Tanca. A Visual Language should be easy to use: a Step Forward for XML-GL. *Information Systems*, 27(7):459–486, 2002. ISSN 0306-4379. doi: http://dx.doi.org/10.1016/S0306-4379(02)00007-8.

[223] M. Olson and U. Ogbuji. Versa Specification. Online only, 2003.

[224] D. Olteanu. *Evaluation of XPath Queries against XML Streams*. Dissertation/Ph.D. thesis, University of Munich, 1 2005.

[225] D. Olteanu, H. Meuss, T. Furche, and F. Bry. XPath: Looking Forward. In *Proc. EDBT Workshop on XML-Based Data Management*, volume 2490 of *LNCS*. Springer-Verlag, 3 2002.

[226] P. O'Neil, E. O'Neil, S. Pal, I. Cseri, G. Schaller, and N. Westbury. ORDPATHs: Insert-friendly XML Node Labels. In *Proc. ACM SIGMOD Conf.*, pages 903–908. ACM Press, 2004. ISBN 1-58113-859-8. doi: http://doi.acm.org/10.1145/1007568.1007686.

[227] K. Ono, T. Koyanagi, M. Abe, and M. Hori. XSLT Stylesheet Generation by Example with WYSIWYG Editing. In *Proc. Symposium on Applications and the Internet*, 2002.

[228] N. Onose and J. Simeon. XQuery at your Web Service. In *Proc. Int. World Wide Web Conf.*, pages 603–611. ACM Press, 2004. ISBN 1-58113-844-X. doi: http://doi.acm.org/10.1145/988672.988754.

[229] S. Palmer. Pondering RDF Path. Online only, 2003.

[230] Y. Papakonstantinou, H. Garcia-Molina, and J. Widom. Object Exchange across Heterogeneous Information Sources. In *Proc. International Conference on Data Engineering*, pages 251–260, 1995.

[231] P. Patel-Schneider and J. Simeon. The Yin/Yang Web: XML Syntax and RDF Semantics. In *Proc. International World Wide Web Conference*, May 2002.

[232] S. Pepper and G. Moore. *XML Topic Maps (XTM) 1.0*. TopicMaps.org, 2001. URL http://www.topicmaps.org/xtm/index.html.

[233] E. Pietriga, J.-Y. Vion-Dury, and V. Quint. VXT: a Visual Approach to XML Transformations. In *Proc. ACM Symposium on Document Engineering*, pages 1–10. ACM Press, 2001. ISBN 1-58113-432-0. doi: http://doi.acm.org/10.1145/502187.502189.

[234] R. Pinchuk. Toma - Topic Map Query Language. Online only, 2004.

[235] M. Plusch. *Water: Simplified Web Services and XML Programming*. Wiley, 2002. ISBN 0764525360.

[236] E. Prud'hommeaux. Algae Extension for Rules. Online only, 2004.

[237] E. Prud'hommeaux. Algae RDF Query Language. Online only, 2004.

[238] E. Prud'hommeaux and A. Seaborne. BRQL – A Query Language for RDF. Online only, 2004.

[239] E. Prud'hommeaux and A. Seaborne. SPARQL Query Language for RDF, February 2005.

[240] A. Reggiori and D.-W. van Gulik. RDFStore—Perl API for RDF Storage. Online only, 2004.

[241] D. Reynolds. RDF-QBE: a Semantic Web Building Block. Technical Report HPL-2002-327, HP Labs, 2002.

[242] J. Robie. The Syntactic Web: Syntax and Semantics on the Web. In *Proc. XML Conference and Exposition*, December 2001.

[243] J. Robie. Updates in XQuery. In *XML Conference & Exhibiton*, 2001.

[244] J. Robie, J. Lapp, and D. Schach. XML Query Language (XQL). In *Proc. W3C QL'98 – Query Languages 1998*, December 1998.

[245] J. Robie, E. Derksen, P. Frankhauser, E. Howland, G. Huck, I. Macherius, M. Murata, M. Resnick, and H. Schning. XQL (XML Query Language). Online only, 1999.

[246] J. Robie, L. M. Garshol, S. Newcomb, M. Fuchs, L. Miller, D. Brickley, V. Christophides, and G. Karvounarakis. The Syntactic Web: Syntax and Semantics on the Web. *Markup Languages: Theory and Practice*, 3(4):411–440, 2001.

[247] S. Schaffert. *Xcerpt: A Rule-Based Query and Transformation Language for the Web*. Dissertation/Ph.D. thesis, University of Munich, 2004.

[248] S. Schaffert and F. Bry. Querying the Web Reconsidered: A Practical Introduction to Xcerpt. In *Proc. Extreme Markup Languages*, August 2004.

[249] S. Schott and M. L. Noga. Lazy XSL Transformations. In *Proc. ACM Symposium on Document Engineering*, pages 9–18. ACM Press, 2003. ISBN 1-58113-724-9. doi: http://doi.acm.org/10.1145/958220.958224.

[250] T. Schwentick. XPath Query Containment. *SIGMOD Record*, 2004.

[251] A. Seaborne. RDQL – RDF Data Query Language. Online only, 2004.

[252] A. Seaborne. A Programmer's Introduction to RDQL. Online only, 2002 April.

[253] A. Seaborne. RDQL – A Query Language for RDF. Online only, January 2004.

[254] D. Seipel. Processing XML-Documents in Prolog. In *Workshop on Logic Programming*, 2002.

[255] D. Seipel and J. Baumeister. Declarative Methods for the Evaluation of Ontologies. *KI–Knstliche Intelligenz*, 4:51–57, 2004.

[256] D. Seipel, J. Baumeister, and M. Hopfner. Declaratively Querying and Visualizing Knowledge Bases in XML. In *Proc. Int. Conf. on Applications of Declarative Programming and Knowledge Management*, 2004.

[257] R. Shearer. REX evaluation. Online only, 2004.

[258] J. E. Simpson. *XPath and XPointer*. O'Reilly, 1st edition, 9 2002.

[259] M. Sintek and S. Decker. TRIPLE—An RDF Query, Inference, and Transformation Language. In *Proc. Deductive Database and Knowledge Management*, October 2001.

[260] M. Sintek and S. Decker. TRIPLE—A Query, Inference, and Transformation Language for the Semantic Web. In *Proc. International Semantic Web Conference*, June 2002.

[261] M. Smith, C. Welty, and D. McGuinness. *OWL Web Ontology Language—Guide*. W3C, 2004. URL http://www.w3.org/TR/owl-guide/.

[262] A. Souzis. RxPath. Online only, 2004.

[263] A. Souzis. RxPath Specification Proposal. Online only, 2004.

[264] A. Souzis. RxSLT. Online only, 2004.

[265] A. Souzis. RxUpdate. Online only, 2004.

[266] D. Steer. TreeHugger 1.0 Introduction. Online only, 2003.

[267] P. Stickler. CBD—Concise Bounded Description. Online only, 2004.

[268] I. Tatarinov and A. Halevy. Efficient Query Reformulation in peer Data Management Systems. In *Proc. ACM SIGMOD Conf.*, pages 539–550. ACM Press, 2004. ISBN 1-58113-859-8. doi: http://doi.acm.org/10.1145/1007568.1007629.

[269] J. Tennison. *XSLT and XPath On The Edge*. John Wiley, 10 2001.

[270] A. Theobald and G. Weikum. The XXL Search Engine: Ranked Retrieval of XML Data using Indexes and Ontologies. In *Proc. ACM SIGMOD Conf.*, pages 615–615. ACM Press, 2002. ISBN 1-58113-497-5. doi: http://doi.acm.org/10.1145/564691.564768.

[271] K. Tolle and F. Wleklinski. easy RDF Query Language (eRQL). Online only, 2004. URL http://www.dbis.informatik.uni-frankfurt.de/~tolle/RDF/eRQL/.

[272] A. Tozawa. Towards Static Type Checking for XSLT. In *Proc. ACM Symposium on Document Engineering*, pages 18–27. ACM Press, 2001. ISBN 1-58113-432-0. doi: http://doi.acm.org/10.1145/502187.502191.

[273] A. Trombetta and D. Montesi. Equivalences and Optimizations in an Expressive XSLT Fragment. In *Proc. Int. Database Engineering and Applications Symposium*, 2004.

[274] L. Villard and N. Layada. An Incremental XSLT Transformation Processor for XML Document Manipulation. In *Proc. Int. World Wide Web Conf.*, pages 474–485. ACM Press, 2002. ISBN 1-58113-449-5. doi: http://doi.acm.org/10.1145/511446.511508.

[275] P. Wadler. Two semantics for XPath. Online only, 2000.

[276] M. Wallace and C. Runciman. Haskell and XML: Generic Combinators or Type-Based Translation. In *Proc. International Conference on Functional Programming*, 1999.

[277] N. Walsh. RDF Twig: accessing RDF graphs in XSLT. In *Proc. Extreme Markup Languages*, 2003.

[278] J. W. W. Wan and G. Dobbie. Mining Association Rules from XML data using XQuery. In *Proc. Workshop on Australasian Information Security, Data Mining Web Intelligence, and Software Internationalisation*, pages 169–174. Australian Computer Society, Inc., 2004.

[279] S. Waworuntu and J. Bailey. XSLTGen: A System for Automatically Generating XML Transformations via Semantic Mappings. In *Proc. Int. Conf. on Conceptual Modeling*, 2004.

[280] F. Weigel. A Survey of Indexing Techniques for Semistructured Documents. Master's thesis, Institute for Informatics, University of Munich, http://www.pms.ifi.lmu.de/index.html\#PA_Felix.Weigel, 2002.

[281] N. Wiegand. Investigating XQuery for Querying across Database Object Types. *SIGMOD Record*, 31(2):28–33, 2002. ISSN 0163-5808. doi: http://doi.acm.org/10.1145/565117.565122.

[282] U. Wiger. XMErl—Interfacing XML and Erlang. In *Proc. International Erlang User Conference*, 2000.

[283] A. Wilk and W. Drabent. On Types for XML Query Language Xcerpt. In *Proc. Workshop on Principles and Practice of Semantic Web Reasoning*, LNCS 2901. Springer-Verlag, 2003.

[284] C. Wilper. RIDIQL Reference. Online only, 2004.

[285] P. T. Wood. On the Equivalence of XML Patterns. In *Proc. Int. Conf. on Computational Logic*, pages 1152–1166. Springer-Verlag, 2000. ISBN 3-540-67797-6.

[286] C. Zaniolo. The Database Language GEM. In *Proc. ACM SIGMOD Conf.*, 1983.

[287] X. Zhang, B. Pielech, and E. A. Rundesnteiner. Honey, I shrunk the XQuery!: an XML Algebra Optimization Approach. In *Proc. International Workshop on Web Information and Data Management*, pages 15–22. ACM Press, 2002. ISBN 1-58113-593-9. doi: http://doi.acm.org/10.1145/584931.584936.

[288] X. Zhang, K. Dimitrova, L. Wang, M. E. Sayed, B. Murphy, B. Pielech, M. Mulchandani, L. Ding, and E. A. Rundensteiner. Rainbow: multi-XQuery Optimization using Materialized XML Views. In *Proc. ACM SIGMOD Conf.*, pages 671–671. ACM Press, 2003. ISBN 1-58113-634-X. doi: http://doi.acm.org/10.1145/872757.872861.

[289] M. Zoof. Query By Example. In *Proc. AFIPS National Computer Conference*, 1975.

[290] M. Zoof. Query By Example: A Data Base Language. *IBM Systems Journal*, 16 (4):324–343, 1977.

Evolution and Reactivity for the Web

José Júlio Alferes[1] and Wolfgang May[2]

[1] Centro de Inteligência Artificial - CENTRIA, Universidade Nova de Lisboa,
2829-516 Caparica, Portugal
jja@di.fct.unl.pt
[2] Institut für Informatik, Universität Göttingen, 37083 Göttingen, Germany
may@informatik.uni-goettingen.de

Abstract. The Web and the Semantic Web, as we see it, can be understood as a "living organism" combining autonomously evolving data
sources, each of them possibly reacting to events it perceives. Rather
than a Web of data sources, we envisage a Web of Information Systems,
where each such system, besides being capable of gathering information
(querying persistent data, as well as "listening" to volatile data such as
occurring events), is capable of updating persistent data, communicating
the changes, requesting changes of persistent data in other systems, and
being able to react to requests from other systems. The dynamic character of such a Web requires declarative languages and mechanisms for
specifying the evolution of the data.

In this course we will talk about foundations of evolution and reactive
languages in general, and will then concentrate on some specific issues
posed by evolution and reactivity in the Web and in the Semantic Web.

1   Introduction

Use of the *Web* today –commonly known as the "World Wide Web"– mostly
focuses on the page-oriented perspective: most of the Web consists of browsable
HTML pages only. From this point of view, the Web can be seen as a graph
that consists of the resources as nodes, and the *hyperlinks* form the edges. Here,
queries are stated against individual nodes, or against several nodes. As such, the
Web is mainly seen from its static perspective of autonomous *sources*, whereas
the *behavior* of the sources, including active interaction of resources does not
play any important role here.

But there is more on the Web of today than HTML pages. Leaving the su-
perficial point of view of HTML pages, the Web can be seen as a set of *data
sources*, some of which are still browsing-oriented, but there are also database-
like resources that can actually be queried. Moreover, there are specialized information sources like Web Services and Portals.

With these representations, the perspective may shift more to the idea of a
Web consisting of (a graph of) *information systems*. In these information systems, data extraction may be thought not only in terms of local queries, but also
in terms of global queries that are stated against the Web, or against a group

N. Eisinger and J. Małuszyński (Eds.): Reasoning Web 2005, LNCS 3564, pp. 134–172, 2005.

(or community) of nodes on the Web. Given the highly heterogeneous and autonomous characteristics of the Web, this requires appropriate query languages, and a way to deal with the integration of data from the various sources.

But such an infrastructure of autonomous sources should allow for more than querying. Consider a set of sources of travel agencies and airline companies. It is important to be capable of querying such a set for, e.g. timetables of flights, availability of flight tickets, etc. But a Web consisting of information systems should allow for more. For example: it should allow for drawing conclusions based on knowledge (e.g. in the form of derivation rules) available on each node; it should allow for making reservations via a travel agency, and automatically make the corresponding airline company (and also other travel agencies) aware of that; it should allow airline companies to change their selling policies, and have travel agencies automatically aware of those changes; etc. The Web, as we see it, with such capabilities can be seen as forming an active, "living" infrastructure of autonomous systems, where reactivity, evolution and its propagation plays a central role.

In this course, we discuss issues related to this question. The focus and the message of the course is on the *concepts* – specific formalisms are given as examples and illustrations. Section 2 classifies different kinds of evolution and reactivity in the (Semantic) Web and motivates the use of rules, especially ECA rules as the target formalism. Section 3 discusses foundations for modeling and reasoning about temporal issues, i.e., formalizing temporal structures, specification of actions and processes, and events. These concepts are then combined in Section 4 where existing rule-based approaches to evolution and reactivity are discussed. The application of these concepts to the Semantic Web is then discussed in Section 5. A proposal how such a framework could look like is sketched in Section 6.

2   Concepts in Evolution and Reactivity in the Web

2.1   Local and Global Reactivity and Evolution

In contrast to the conventional (Hypertext) Web, the Semantic Web consists of *active* nodes that are able to answer queries, to evolve and to communicate. Evolution of the Web is a twofold aspect: on today's Web, evolution means mainly evolution of individual Web sites that are updated locally. In contrast, considering the Web as a "living organism" that *consists* of autonomous data sources, but that will *show* a global "behavior" leads to a notion of evolution of the Web as *cooperative evolution* of (the state of) its individual resources.[1]

Below, we incrementally introduce such behavior and sketch the concepts that arise: simple reactive behavior (non-state-changing), local evolution of nodes (i.e. state-changing), and collaboration of nodes, both non-state-changing and state-changing.

---

[1] For further details on the global behavior, and its relation to querying and evolution aspects see [42].

Pure Reactivity Without Evolution. The most basic and primitive activity on the Web is query answering. From the point of view of the user, querying is a static issue: there is no actual dynamic aspect in it (except possibly a delay). Nevertheless, from the point of view of the resources, there comes reactivity into play: when answering queries, the resources must answer in reaction to a query message, and in case that the query is answered with cooperation of several resources, the resources do also exchange messages.

Local Updates and Evolution. The state of such a Web node can be classified into three conceptual levels: facts (e.g. in XML, RDF or OWL; divided into data and metadata); a knowledge base given by derivation rules; and behavior (e.g., reaction patterns), e.g. of a Web Service.

When updating the Conventional Web, the update is expressed as a specific update operation on a specific Web site, using e.g. an XML update language. For the Semantic Web data formats, RDF and OWL, also update languages are available. Here, simple data updates and ontology evolution has to be distinguished.

Global Evolution. The power of the Semantic Web raises from the combination of the knowledge and behavior of sets of data sources. Especially, as an *intelligent Web*, a *cooperative evolution* of (the state of) its individual nodes is required.

Thus, having data flow and dependencies between Web sites, besides a plain communication mechanism, mechanisms to maintain consistency between Web sites by update propagation are required. Update propagation consists of (i) propagating an update, and (ii) processing/materializing the update at another Web resource. The latter, as we have just seen, is solved by local update languages. So, the remaining problem turns out to be how to communicate changes on the (Semantic) Web. Often a change is not propagated as an explicit update, but there must be "evolution" of "the Web" as a consequence of a change to some information.

For this, it is clear that we need a "global" language for communicating changes, and communication strategies for how to propagate pieces of information through the Semantic Web, seeing it globally as the union of *all* information throughout the Web. In it, the *Semantic*-property of the Web is crucial for automatically mediating between several actual schemata.

In this setting, evolution on the Web takes place by: either local changes in data sources via updates; or local evolution of Web Services by reaction to events on the Web due to their own, specified, behavior.

2.2   Event-Condition-Action (Reactive) Rules for Evolution

Following a well-known and successful paradigm, we propose to use rules, more specifically, *reactive rules* according to the *Event-Condition-Action* (ECA) paradigm for the specification of reactivity. An important advantage of them is that the *content* of the communication can be separated from the *generic semantics* of the rules themselves. Cooperative and reactive behavior is then based on events (e.g., an update at a data source where possibly others depend on). The depending resources detect events (either they are delivered explicitly to them, or they poll them via the communication means of the Web; see next section) Then, conditions are checked (either simple data conditions, or e.g. tests if the event is relevant, trustable etc.), which are queries to one or several nodes and are to be expressed in the proposed query framework. Finally, an appropriate action is taken (e.g., updating own information accordingly). The action part can also be formulated as a transaction whose ACID properties ensure that either all actions in a transaction are performed, or nothing of is done; this also allows to check postconditions. In the literature, ECA rules are also referred to as triggers, active rules, or reactive rules.

The language for the ECA rules must comprise a language for describing events (in the "Event" part; there are atomic events, such as simple data updates or incoming messages, and *composite events* such as "if first A happens and then B"), the language for queries (in the "Condition" part), and a language for actions (including updates) and transactions (in the "Action" part). An important requirement here is that event specification and detection be as much declarative and application-level as possible. This point calls for modular design of the sublanguages and the ECA language, and the respective processors.

Usually, ECA rules are *patterns* that contain variables to be bound in the event part that are communicated to the condition and action parts.
A well-known example for simple ECA rules are e.g. the SQL triggers:

```
ON database-update WHEN condition BEGIN pl/sql-fragment END
```

where the values of the updated tuple are accessible as old and new.

These triggers react on local events in the database. For cooperative evolution and reactivity on the Web, events and other information must be *communicated*.

2.3   Communication Structure and Propagation of Knowledge

Communication on the Web as a living organism consisting of autonomous sources takes place as *peer-to-peer communication*. In this setting, evolution takes place if a resource (or its knowledge) evolves locally, and another resource that depends upon it also evolves (as a reaction). The communication can be classified by *communication strategies*.

– Push: an information source informs a client of the updates. A directed, targeted propagation of changes by the *push* strategy is only possible along registered communication paths. It takes place by explicit *messages*, that can be update messages, or just information about what happened. In this case, control flow and data flow are in parallel and synchronous.
– Pull: resources that obtain information from a source can *pull* updates by either explicitly asking whether it executed some updates recently, or can regularly update themselves based on queries against the source. Communication is based on queries and answers (that are in fact again sent as messages).

In this case, control flow and data flow are antiparallel, which has obvious drawbacks.

The above basic forms describe direct communication. Advanced communication strategies are then based on these, providing more efficient data and control flow:

- *broadcast:* general *push* to all peers.
- *blackboard:* separates the data source from answering of *pull*-queries and allows for a pre-filtering by a short *push* (to the blackboard) from where clients *pull*.
- *publish-and-subscribe* services (see e.g. [60]) receive messages from publishers and notify subscribers if the messages match the subscriptions. Here, the communication follows a pure *push* pattern, i.e., information (published items) are pushed from their originators to the pub/sub service, and derived information (notification about changes) is pushed from the pub/sub service to its subscribers.
- *continuous query systems* (see e.g., NiagaraCQ [14]) allow users to "register" queries at the service that then continuously evaluates the query (together with other queries) against the source, and informs the user about the answer (or when the answer changes). Here, communication combines *pull* and *push*: the CQ system *pulls* information from sources, and *pushes* derived information to the end user.

Note that both in the case of push and pull strategies, the actual reactivity, i.e., how the instance that is informed reacts on an *event*, can be expressed by ECA rules as described in the previous section:

- push: on an event (update), send a message (control flow + data flow).
- pull: regularly send a query (control flow) and, on a query, send an answer (data flow).
- The behavior of pub/sub and continuous query systems can also be expressed by simple ECA rules.

3   Foundations of Evolution and Reactivity

In the previous section we described the concepts that enable evolution and reactivity on the Semantic Web. In this section, we describe the theoretical background and formal means for analyzing and describing these concepts[2].

For dealing with evolution, be it in the Web or in any other context, a formal understanding of how the knowledge evolves and how to represent such evolution is needed. We start this section by describing foundational work on *models* for (temporal) knowledge evolution, that considers sequences of *states*. We then proceed by presenting temporal logics, that allow to *reason* about evolution in these models. When considering evolving sequences of states, the *actions* that

---

[2] A more complete survey on these foundational issues can be found at [1].

cause transitions of states are also relevant. For this, in Sections 3.3 and 3.4, we show logics for dealing with transition systems and formalisms for defining (complex) actions, respectively. Finally, we focus our attention on events, which in general are manifestations (i.e. visible consequences) of action execution, that may trigger evolution.

All these concepts are combined in Section 4, where existing rule-based approaches for evolution and reactivity are exposed.

3.1   Models of Dynamics and Temporal Structures

Kripke structures serve as a *generic* model-theoretic framework for multi-state structures: the semantics of the individual states is given by some single-state interpretations, and the Kripke structure provides the "infrastructure" that connects the states. Some (arbitrary) logic is used for the single-state interpretations, and this logic is extended, in a modular way, with additional concepts for handling the multi-state aspects. This can be done by modalities (in our situation, temporal modalities, but modalities of knowledge and belief are also often used).

Many approaches to multi-state reasoning use Kripke structures explicitly; here, temporal logics will be described. Other, often specialized, formalisms extend single-state formalisms with a notion of state (in which Kripke structures are –more or less explicitly– the model of choice).

Yet other formalisms –although basically mappable to Kripke semantics– put emphasis on the dynamic aspects, whereas the individual states and their properties become less important (Transaction Logic, and, even much stronger, process calculi).

Kripke Structures. Assume some logic (e.g., first-order logic) to describe individual states. A (first-order) *Kripke structure* is a triple $\mathcal{K} = (\mathcal{G}, \mathcal{R}, \mathcal{M})$ where $\mathcal{G}$ is a set of states (to be interpreted as states or possible worlds), $\mathcal{R} \subseteq \mathcal{G} \times \mathcal{G}$ is an *accessibility relation*, and M is a function which maps every state $g \in \mathcal{G}$ to a (first-order) structure $\mathcal{M}(g) = (M(g), \mathcal{U}(g))$ over Σ with universe $\mathcal{U}(g)$. $\mathcal{G}$ and $\mathcal{R}$ are called the *frame* of $\mathcal{K}$. A *path* p in a Kripke structure $\mathcal{K} = (\mathcal{G}, \mathcal{R}, \mathcal{M})$ is a sequence $p = (g_0, g_1, g_2, \ldots)$, $g_i \in \mathcal{G}$ with $\mathcal{R}(g_i, g_{i+1})$ holding for all i.

As mentioned above, Kripke structures provide just a multi-state "infrastructure": a suitable single-state-logic must then be chosen for an application, which is then extended to Kripke structures. *Temporal extensions*, where the Kripke structure is interpreted as a temporal structure, are suitable for our project. Even in the area of temporal applications, there are different interpretations of Kripke structures.

Labeled Transition Systems/Path Structures. Labeled transition systems are one of the fundamental concepts for modeling processes (cf. [51], [61]). We present LTSs here (semantically equivalent to the original literature) as an extension of the above Kripke Structures. A *labeled transition system (LTS)* consists of a set $\mathcal{G}$ of states/configurations, a set $\mathcal{A}$ of actions/labels (elementary actions, or programs), and, for every $a \in \mathcal{A}$, $\mathcal{R}(a) \subseteq \mathcal{G} \times \mathcal{G}$ is a binary relation that provides the interpretation of actions (i.e., the *labeled* accessibility relation).

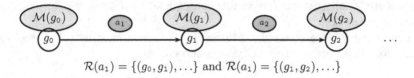

$$\mathcal{R}(a_1) = \{(g_0, g_1), \ldots\} \text{ and } \mathcal{R}(a_1) = \{(g_1, g_2), \ldots\}$$

Fig. 1. Excerpt of a Kripke Structure as an LTS

Another view of the same thing are *path structures*. The idea goes back to propositional *Dynamic Logic* [32], the term *path model* came up with *Process Logic* [34], where especially extended, derived accessibility relations for composite actions/programs/processes are defined (see Section 3.3).

3.2   Temporal Logics

Temporal –and other– model logics provide modal operators for modalizing the semantics of formulas of an underlying single-state logic. Due to the historical development of modal logics, the modal operators $\Box$ and $\Diamond$ were introduced. $\Box F$ stands for "F is necessary true", resp. "F holds in all possible worlds", and $\Diamond F$ for "F is possibly true", resp. "there is some possible world where F holds". Translated to modal logic of time (temporal logic), the operators are interpreted as: $\Box F$ – "always" (F holds in all subsequent states), and $\Diamond F$ – "sometimes" (F eventually holds). For reasoning in temporal Kripke structures, there are two alternatives: *linear time* considers a single path, whereas *branching time* considers a whole tree-like structure.

Linear Time Temporal Logics. The most intuitive idea for interpreting temporal logic is a sequence of states. Here, the basic operators of temporal modal logic are others, having a pure temporal semantics: $\circ$ ("nexttime") and until:

- $\circ F$: in the next state, F holds.
- F until G: there is a subsequent state where G holds, and in all states between now and this state, F holds.

The semantics of the temporal modal operators $\Diamond$ and $\Box$, is equivalently defined via until (note that there is a also an inductive definition based on $\circ$ which is typically used for model checking-like approaches):

- $\Diamond P :=$ true until P and $\Box P := \neg \Diamond \neg P$.

The Logics PLTL and FOTL. Linear Temporal Logic LTL (as propositional PLTL or as first-order FOTL) extends propositional logic with the above temporal operators: each state is a propositional or first-order interpretation, and the states are connected as a *linear* Kripke structure (or, a single path in a branching Kripke structure is considered).

The language of LTL formulas is defined as follows:

- Every (propositional or first-order) formula is an LTL formula.
- With F and G LTL formulas, $\circ F$, $\Box F$, $\Diamond F$ and (F until G) are LTL formulas.

The satisfaction relation $\models_{LTL}$ (for short also denoted by $\models$) is defined according to the inductive definition of the syntax with respect to a propositional or first-order (infinite) linear Kripke structure $\mathcal{K} = (\mathcal{G} = \{g_1, g_2, \ldots\}, \{(n, n+1) \mid n \in \mathbb{N}\}, \mathcal{M})$, based on the propositional satisfaction relation $\models_{PL}$ or $\models_{FOL}$:

Let $g = g_i$ a state in $\mathcal{K}$, A an atomic formula, F and G LTL formulas and, in the first-order case, χ a variable assignment. Then,

$$(g, \chi) \models A \quad :\Leftrightarrow \quad (M(g), \chi) \models_{PL/FOL} A \,,$$

$$(g, \chi) \models \neg F \quad :\Leftrightarrow \quad \text{not } (g, \chi) \models F \,,$$

$$(g, \chi) \models F \wedge G \quad :\Leftrightarrow \quad (g, \chi) \models F \text{ and } (g, \chi) \models G \,,$$

$$(g_i, \chi) \models \circ F \quad :\Leftrightarrow \quad (g_{i+1}, \chi) \models F \,,$$

$$(g_i, \chi) \models F \text{ until } G \quad :\Leftrightarrow \quad \text{there is a } j \geq i \text{ s.t. } (g_j, \chi) \models G$$
$$\text{and for all } k : i \leq k < j, (g_k, \chi) \models F \,.$$

Branching Time Temporal Logics. Applying the classical temporal modalities $\Diamond$ and $\Box$ (without $\circ$ and until) in a *branching* structure leads to surprising interpretations: Whereas in linear time logic, $g \models \Diamond F$ means that F will eventually hold in the possible future ("sometimes"), the same formula for branching time means that there *is a future*, where F will eventually hold ("not never"). For this aspect and the (dis)advantages of linear vs. branching time logic, see [37] (L. Lamport: "'Sometimes' is Sometimes 'Not Never'") and [20] (E. A. Emerson and C.-L. Lei: "Modalities for Model Checking: Branching Time Strikes Back") and several other papers.

The Logic CTL. For combining the expressiveness of both linear and branching time logic, the logics UB (*unified branching time*) [5] and CTL (*Computation Tree Logic*) [16] have been introduced:

- temporal modal operators $\circ$, $\Diamond$, $\Box$ and until (although $\Diamond$ and $\Box$ can be expressed by until, they are used here as "basic" operators to obtain the syntax definition described below),
- an existential path quantifier E ("there exists a path such that ...") and a universal path quantifier A ("on all paths").

CTL distinguishes between two different types of formulas: state formulas that hold *in* a state (all first-order formulas are state-formulas), and path formulas, that hold on paths, i.e., on *sequences* of states.

The language of CTL-formulas does not allow arbitrary combinations, but is defined as follows:

- Every first-order formula is a CTL-state formula.
- With F and G CTL-state formulas, $\neg F$, $F \wedge G$ and $F \vee G$ are CTL-state formulas.
- With F a CTL-state formula and x a variable, $\forall x : F$ and $\exists x : F$ are CTL-state formulas.
- With F and G CTL-state formulas, $\circ F$, $\square F$, $\diamond F$ and $(F\ \text{until}\ G)$ are CTL-path formulas.
- With P a CTL-path formula, $\neg P$ is a CTL-path formula.
- With P a CTL-path formula, $\mathsf{A}P$ and $\mathsf{E}P$ are CTL-state formulas.
- Every CTL-state formula is a CTL-formula.

With the above definition, in CTL every (possibly negated) modal operator is immediately preceded by a path quantifier.

The satisfaction relation $\models_{\mathrm{CTL}}$ (for short also denoted by $\models$) is defined according to the inductive definition of the syntax with respect to a first-order Kripke structure $\mathcal{K} = (\mathcal{G}, \mathcal{R}, \mathcal{M})$, based on the first-order satisfaction relation:

Let $g \in \mathcal{G}$ be a state, $p = (g_0, g_1, \ldots)$ a path in $\mathcal{K}$, A an atomic first-order formula, F and G CTL-state formulas, P a CTL-path formula and χ a variable assignment. Then,

$$
\begin{aligned}
(g, \chi) &\models A & :&\Leftrightarrow\ (M(g), \chi) \models_{PL/FOL} A\ , \\
(g, \chi) &\models \neg F & :&\Leftrightarrow\ \text{not}\ (g, \chi) \models F\ , \\
(g, \chi) &\models F \wedge G & :&\Leftrightarrow\ (g, \chi) \models F\ \text{and}\ (g, \chi) \models G\ , \\
(p, \chi) &\models \circ F & :&\Leftrightarrow\ (g_1, \chi) \models F\ , \\
(p, \chi) &\models F\ \text{until}\ G & :&\Leftrightarrow\ \text{there is an}\ i \geq 0\ \text{s.t.}\ (g_i, \chi) \models G\ \text{and} \\
& & & \quad \text{for all}\ j : 0 \leq j < i,\ (g_i, \chi) \models F\ , \\
(p, \chi) &\models \neg P & :&\Leftrightarrow\ \text{not}\ (p, \chi) \models P\ , \\
(g, \chi) &\models \mathsf{E}P & :&\Leftrightarrow\ \text{there is a path}\ p = (g = g_0, g_1, \ldots)\ \text{in}\ \mathcal{K}\ \text{s.t.}\ (p, \chi) \models P.
\end{aligned}
$$

The semantics of the modal operators $\diamond$, $\square$, and of the path quantifier A is defined via until and E:

$$
\diamond P := \text{true until}\ P\ , \quad \square P := \neg \diamond \neg P\ , \quad \mathsf{A}P := \neg \mathsf{E}\neg P\ .
$$

Extensions. There exist multiple extensions of CTL in different directions. The CTL family itself provides even more expressiveness,

- CTL$^+$ and CTL* extend to arbitrary combinations of temporal operators to path formulas; especially, "fairness" requirements cannot be expressed in CTL, but need more complex path formulas:
  - "Justice" requires that an action that is executable continuously ("waiting") from a certain state on, is eventually executed:
    CTL*: $\mathsf{A}((\diamond\square(\text{Action waiting})) \rightarrow \diamond(\text{Action is executed}))$
    (carefully note the implication semantics $A \rightarrow B \Leftrightarrow \neg A \vee B$ of this formula)

- "Compassion (strong Fairness)" is the (stronger) requirement that every action that is executable/asked for infinitely often, is also eventually executed: CTL*: $A(($□◇(Action waiting)$) \rightarrow$ ◇(Action is executed)$)$
- The semantics of the accessibility relation wrt. execution of actions is considered e.g., in *Dynamic Logic* and *Hennessy-Milner-Logic* (see subsequent sections).
- Past Tense Logics add past-time temporal operators: • (previous state), ♦ (sometimes in the past), ■ (always in the past), and since (e.g., A since B), symmetrical to the future tense operators.

  In [22], it is shown that in the propositional case, past-tense connectives do not increase the expressiveness of temporal logic. The use of modal temporal logic for executable process specifications is described in [23], quite similar to Transaction Logic (see Section 4.3).

3.3 Logics for Labeled Transition Systems and Path Structures

The above approaches formalize a sequence of states without any special semantics for the transition. When considering evolving sequences of states, the transition is also relevant. In approaches taking this into account, in general there is a set $\mathcal{A}$ of (atomic) actions with which the transitions are labeled. The labeled transition relation leads straightforwardly to *polymodal* logics (i.e., each modality is also labeled with actions).

The following logics use not only *atomic* actions in their formulas, but define also restricted languages for *composite actions* or *programs* based on these actions.

Dynamic Logic. Dynamic Logic [32, 33, 52] provides a logic for labeled transition systems. The main difference between CTL and Dynamic Logic lies in the scope of the modalities: There, the modal operators ◇ and □ are interpreted in their historical sense as "possibly" and "necessarily", i.e., they do not apply to paths here, but only to single transitions. The modal operators are labeled with *programs* given by the algebra $\langle \mathcal{A}, \{ ; , \cup, ^* \} \rangle$, (";" denotes sequential composition, $\cup$ denotes alternative composition ("choice"), and * denotes iteration). With every program a, a binary transition relation $\mathcal{R}(a) \subset \mathcal{G} \times \mathcal{G}$ is assigned.

- any (propositional or) first order formula is a DL formula, and
- for any DL formula F and any action or program a, $\langle a \rangle_{DL} F$ is a DL formula with the semantics

$$g \models \langle a \rangle_{DL} F \Leftrightarrow \text{there is a state } h \text{ such that } (g, h) \in \mathcal{R}(a) \text{ and } h \models F .$$

In agreement with the tradition, $\square_{DL} F := \neg \diamond_{DL} \neg F$ is defined to be the dual of $\diamond_{DL}$.

Here, the difference between the interpretation of the modal operators between CTL and Dynamic Logic becomes visible: In CTL, the modal operators reach into the future along a *single* path and the path quantifiers range orthogonally over all possible futures, speaking about paths not about states. In

Dynamic Logic, the modal operators look ahead one step on every path (i.e., they correspond to CTL's path quantifiers, not to CTL's modal operators). Thus, the *eventually*, *always*, and *until*-operators can not be expressed in DL without resorting to a fixpoint logic. Instead, "if now, a is executed, F will definitely/probably hold" can be expressed.

Hennessy-Milner Logic. In [58] and [48], Hennessy-Milner-Logic, $\mathcal{HML}$, a modal logic interpretation of the CCS calculus (see Section 3.4) is given whose modalities are very similar to those of Dynamic Logic. The set of formulas of Hennessy-Milner-Logic, $\mathsf{Fml}_{\mathcal{HML}}$, is defined inductively as

- $\mathsf{T} \in \mathsf{Fml}_{\mathcal{HML}}$,
- $F \in \mathsf{Fml}_{\mathcal{HML}} \Rightarrow \neg F \in \mathsf{Fml}_{\mathcal{HML}}$,
- $F, G \in \mathsf{Fml}_{\mathcal{HML}} \Rightarrow F \wedge G \in \mathsf{Fml}_{\mathcal{HML}}$,
- $F \in \mathsf{Fml}_{\mathcal{HML}}$ and $a \in \mathcal{A} \Rightarrow \Diamond_{\mathcal{HML}} F \in \mathsf{Fml}_{\mathcal{HML}}$.

(instead of $\Diamond_{\mathcal{HML}}$, also $\langle a \rangle_{\mathcal{HML}}$ can be written).
CCS (see Section 3.4) does not use a notion of propositional or first-order states, but is based on the notion of *processes* as nodes of its LTS structures. The satisfaction relation $\models_{\mathcal{HML}}$ (for short also denoted by $\models$) between processes and $\mathcal{HML}$-formulas is defined similar to Dynamic Logic by

1. $P \models \mathsf{T}$ for all processes P ,
2. $P \models \neg F$ $:\Leftrightarrow$ not $P \models F$,
3. $P \models F \wedge G$ $:\Leftrightarrow$ $P \models F$ and $P \models G$,
4. $P \models \Diamond_{\mathcal{HML}} F$ $:\Leftrightarrow$ there is a process P' s.t. $P \xrightarrow{a} P'$ and $P' \models F$.

Additionally, derived expressions in $\mathcal{HML}$ are defined:
- $\mathsf{F} \equiv \neg \mathsf{T}$,
- $F \vee G \equiv \neg(\neg F \wedge \neg G)$,
- $\Diamond_{\mathcal{HML}} F \equiv \langle a_1 \rangle_{\mathcal{HML}} \dots \langle a_n \rangle_{\mathcal{HML}} F$ for $a = a_1 \cdot \dots \cdot a_n$,
- $\boxed{a}_{\mathcal{HML}} F \equiv \neg \Diamond_{\mathcal{HML}} \neg F$.

Similar to the discussion about CTL and Dynamic Logic above, it is not possible in $\mathcal{HML}$ to express properties like "P will eventually execute a" or "in the next step, P will execute a". Instead, "if now, a is executed, F will definitely/probably hold" can be expressed.

Process Logic. In contrast to Dynamic Logic and Hennessy-Milner Logic, where all formulas apply to states, the syntax of logics for path structures focusses on the notion of path formulas: their $\models$-relation relates paths to formulas. Nevertheless, in those logics, paths consisting of exactly one state actually take the role of states.

   Process Logic [34] is a (propositional) logic for describing activities, based on path structures. It uses **path structures** with a slightly different focus of the semantics of formulas: $\mathcal{P}$ is a relation assigning sets of paths to *programs*, i.e., it extends $\mathcal{R}$ to compound programs (thereby defining a restricted language of compound programs or transactions):

– if α and β are programs, then so are $\alpha\beta$, $\alpha \cup \beta$, and α^*.

Note that Process Logic does not have a notion of "parallel" actions. The accessibility relation is in the same way extended to these programs:

$$\begin{aligned}
\mathcal{P}_\alpha &= \mathcal{R}_\alpha \text{ for actions/primitive programs } \alpha, \\
\mathcal{P}_{\alpha\beta} &= \mathcal{P}_\alpha \mathcal{P}_\beta = \{pq \mid p \in \mathcal{P}_\alpha \text{ and } q \in \mathcal{P}_\beta\}, \\
\mathcal{P}_{\alpha \cup \beta} &= \mathcal{P}_\alpha \cup \mathcal{P}_\beta, \\
\mathcal{P}_{\alpha^*} &= \bigcup_{i < \omega} \mathcal{P}_{\alpha^i}.
\end{aligned}$$

In Process Logic, all formulas are *path formulas*, i.e., evaluated against paths. Its syntax extends Dynamic Logic with the following connectives:

– if X and Y are formulas, then so are $\mathbf{f}X$, and X **suf** Y.

– if α is a program and X is a formula, then $\diamondsuit_{PR} X$ is a formula.

The satisfaction relation $\models$ is extended to a relation between paths and state formulas. Let $p = (s_o, s_1, \ldots)$ be a path.

$p \models X \qquad \Leftrightarrow \quad s_0 \models X$ for primitive (propositional or first-order) formulas X. (not explicit, but see [34–Def.4.1, p.155])

$p \models \mathbf{f}X \qquad \Leftrightarrow \quad s_0 \models X$.

$p \models X$ **suf** $Y \quad \Leftrightarrow \quad$ there is a $q \in \mathcal{P}_\alpha$ s.t.
        (i) q is a proper suffix of p and $q \models Y$, and
        (ii) for all r, if r is a proper suffix of p and q is a proper suffix of r, then $r \models X$.

$p \models \diamondsuit_{PR} X \quad \Leftrightarrow \quad$ there is a $q \in \mathcal{P}_\alpha$ s.t. $pq \models X$.

Note that the semantics of $\diamondsuit_{PR}$ is different from the usual semantics of $\diamondsuit$: $p \models \diamondsuit_{PR} X$ states that from the *endpoint* of path p, there is a path q executing α s.t. then the whole path pq satisfies X.

Transaction Logic (cf. Section 4.3) is another logic which is based on path structures; using *temporal connectives* instead of temporal *modal operators*.

Summary and Examples. While the static aspects (i.e., the states) use the same formalism (except in Hennessy-Milner Logic), i.e., propositional or first-order logic (where special approaches exist that use predicates only (Datalog) or functions only (Evolving Algebras) [30, 31]), the dynamic aspects are described differently in the above approaches as shown below:

Example 1. *Consider two persons, Alice and Bob who have bank accounts with a given balance given by a function, balance(name). Actions are debit(name, amount) and deposit(name, amount).*
Considering the excerpt of a Kripke Structure given in Figure 1, e.g.,

$$\mathcal{M}(g_0) = \{balance(Alice) = 200, balance(Bob) = 100\},$$
$$(g_0, g_1) \in \mathcal{R}(debit(Alice, 20)), \quad (g_1, g_2) \in \mathcal{R}(deposit(Bob, 20)).$$

Obviously,

$$\mathcal{M}(g_1) = \{balance(Alice) = 180, balance(Bob) = 100\} \ and$$
$$\mathcal{M}(g_2) = \{balance(Alice) = 180, balance(Bob) = 120\} \ .$$

The semantics of debit can be specified in Hennessy-Milner Logic and Dynamic Logic by

$\forall Acc, Am_1, Am_2 :$
$balance(Acc_1) = Am \rightarrow [debit(Acc_1, Am_2)]balance(Acc_1) = Am_1 - Am_2$
(where [a] denotes the "always" modality $\boxed{a}$ *).*

Both logics allow now for reasoning about sequences, e.g., expressing a simple integrity constraint that any sequence of actions debit(Acc_1, Am) and deposit(Acc_2, Am) keeps the sum of the overall balances unchanged.
Hennessy-Milner Logic can express this by

$\forall Acc_1, Acc_2, Am, B_1, B_2, Sum :$
$Sum = balance(Acc_1) + balance(Acc_2) \rightarrow$
$\quad [debit(Acc_1, Am) \cdot deposit(Acc_2, Am)]Sum = balance(Acc_1) + balance(Acc_2).$

Analogous for Dynamic Logic (with ";" as sequential concatenation).
Process Logic's transition relation $\mathcal{P}$ for programs will e.g. contain

$$(g_0, g_2) \in \mathcal{P}_{debit(Alice,20) \ deposit(Bob,20)} \ ,$$

making the above "transition by a composite action" explicit in the model. We also have

$(g_0, g_1) \models \mathbf{f}(balance(Alice) = 200 \wedge balance(Bob) = 100) \wedge$
$\quad \langle deposit(Bob, 20) \rangle \mathbf{last}(balance(Alice) = 180 \wedge balance(Bob) = 120)$
$\quad with \ \mathbf{last} \ as \ formally \ defined \ in \ [34] \ .$

The above example shows that modal logics are useful for *reasoning about* temporal structures, especially proving correctness. Up to here, "actions" occurred only for the definition of paths that then satisfy formulas – i.e., to check if something "is true" after executing some actions. Also, the notions of actions and events are not really distinguishable, because both notions are identified with the labels of the transitions. So far, one can see an action as an action from the point of view of generating the next state, and as an event from the point of view of looking at the transition afterwards.

For *specifying* pure *evolution*, the notions of *actions, transactions* (that have to satisfy several requirements), and *processes* are used to describe what sequences of transitions are actually executed. When coming to *reactivity*, we want to express implications (rules) that under certain circumstances, something must be done. These circumstances can not only be static conditions, but also dynamic occurrences of *events*. The goal of these rules is to check *if something happened*, and then *to make something happen*.

3.4   Actions, Transactions, and Processes

Some of the above languages already define restricted mechanisms for (reasoning about the effects of) actions and composite actions. Other, rule-based formalisms will be discussed in Section 4.1. There are also several frameworks and formalisms for the definition of composite actions as *programs*, *processes*, or *transactions* (which is essentially the same from different points of view and with different consequences regarding parallelism and interference). Simple "programs" have been discussed above for *Dynamic Logic*. More complex specifications of activities and interaction, e.g. between different Web nodes, can be given in terms of *Process Algebras* that are discussed just below. *Transaction Logic* is another, rule based formalism for defining, executing, and even a restricted amount of planning that will be discussed later in Section 4.3.

Process Algebras. Process Algebras describe the semantics of processes in an algebraic way, i.e., by a set of elementary processes (carrier set) and a set of constructors. The semantics can either be given as *denotational semantics*, i.e., by specifying the denotation of every element of the algebra (e.g., CSP – Communicating Sequential Processes, [35]), or as an *operational semantics* by specifying the behavior of every element of the algebra (e.g., CCS – Calculus of Communicating Systems, [45, 46]). Processes defined by Process Algebras can e.g. be used for the specification of *communication*, i.e., for basic protocols, or for defining the behavior of interacting (Semantic) Web Services (note that process algebras provide concepts for defining infinite processes), or in the action part of ECA rules.

Basic Process Algebra (BPA). For a given set $\mathcal{A}$ of atomic actions,

$$BPA_{\mathcal{A}} = \langle \mathcal{A}, \{\perp, +, \cdot\} \rangle$$

is the basic algebra – i.e., containing the least reasonable set of operators – for constructing processes over $\mathcal{A}$. $\perp$ is a constant denoting a deadlock, $+$ denotes alternative composition, and $\cdot$ denotes sequential composition: if x and y are processes, then $x+y$ and $x \cdot y$ are processes (syntax and semantics are formally introduced later on with CCS). These are essentially the processes that have also been presented above in Dynamic Logic and Hennessy-Milner-Logic.

Calculus of Communicating Systems (CCS). CCS extends BPA by more expressive operators. The carrier set of a CCS [45, 46, 47] algebra is given by a set $\mathcal{A}$ of action names from which processes are built by using several connectives. Every element of the algebra is called a *process*. By carrying out an action, a process changes into another process. Considering the modeling as an LTS, a process can be regarded as a state or a configuration. Action names become labels and the transition relation is given by the rules specifying the execution of actions. A CCS algebra with a carrier set $\mathcal{A}$ is defined as follows:

1. With X a (process) variable, X is a process expression.
2. Every $a \in \mathcal{A}$ is a process expression.

3. With $a \in \mathcal{A}$ and P a process expression, $a : P$ is a process expression (pre-fixing; sequential composition).

4. With P and Q process expressions, $P \times Q$ is a process expression (parallel composition).

5. With I a set of indices, $P_i : i \in I$ process expressions, $\sum_{i \in I} P_i$ is a process expression (alternative composition).

6. With $A \subseteq \mathcal{A}$ a set of actions and P a process expression, $P \upharpoonright A$ is a process expression (restriction to a set of visible actions).

7. With I a set of indices, X_i variables, P_i process expressions, $\text{fix}_j \boldsymbol{X} \boldsymbol{P}$ is a process expression (definition of a communicating system of processes). The fix operator binds the variables X_i, and fix_j is one of the $|I|$ processes which are defined by this expression.

The fix operator can be omitted if defining equations of the form $Q := P$ are allowed, where Q is a new process identifier and P is a process expression. Process expressions not containing any free variables are *processes*.

The (operational) semantics of a CCS algebra is given by transition rules:

$$a : P \xrightarrow{a} P \quad , \quad \frac{P_i \xrightarrow{a} P}{\sum_{i \in I} P_i \xrightarrow{a} P} \text{ (for } i \in I) \quad , \quad \frac{P \xrightarrow{a} P' \quad Q \xrightarrow{b} Q'}{P \times Q \xrightarrow{ab} P' \times Q'} \quad ,$$

$$, \quad \frac{P \xrightarrow{a} P'}{P \upharpoonright A \xrightarrow{a} P' \upharpoonright A} \text{ (for } a \in A) \quad , \quad \frac{P_i\{\text{fix } \boldsymbol{X}\boldsymbol{P}/\boldsymbol{X}\} \xrightarrow{a} P'}{\text{fix}_i \boldsymbol{X}\boldsymbol{P} \xrightarrow{a} P'} \quad .$$

Additionally, there are some derived operators and constants

$$\boldsymbol{0} := \sum_{\emptyset} P_i \quad , \quad P_1 + P_2 := \sum_{i \in \{1,2\}} P_i \quad ,$$

and, for asynchronous communication and delays,

$$\partial P \quad := \text{fix } X(1 : X + P) \quad , \quad X \text{ not free in } P, \text{ and}$$
$$P_1 | P_2 := P \times \partial Q + \partial P \times Q$$

with the corresponding transition rules

$$\frac{P \xrightarrow{a} P'}{P + Q \xrightarrow{a} P'} \quad , \quad \frac{Q \xrightarrow{a} Q'}{P + Q \xrightarrow{a} P'} \quad , \quad \partial P \xrightarrow{1} \partial P \quad , \quad \frac{P \xrightarrow{a} P'}{\partial P \xrightarrow{a} P'}$$

$$\frac{P \xrightarrow{a} P'}{P | Q \xrightarrow{a} P' | Q} \quad , \quad \frac{Q \xrightarrow{a} Q'}{P | Q \xrightarrow{a} P | Q'} \quad , \quad \frac{P \xrightarrow{a} P' \quad Q \xrightarrow{b} Q'}{P | Q \xrightarrow{ab} P' | Q'}$$

In CCS and related concepts, such as CSP [35] and ACP [6], there is no explicit notion of states, the properties of a state are given by the (sequences of) actions which can be executed.

Example 2. *Consider again the scenario of Example 1. There, it has been described how to reason about a structure. Having now a notion of processes, we can describe how transitions belong together:*

- *a common money transfer is already a simple process:*

$$transfer(Am, Acc_1, Acc_2) := debit(Acc_1, Am) : deposit(Acc_2, Am) .$$

- *a standing order (i.e., a banking order that has to be executed regularly) is defined as a fixpoint process. The following process transfers a given amount from one account to another every first of a month:*

fix $X(rec\_msg(first\_of\_month) : debit(Acc_1, Am) : deposit(Acc_2, Am) : \partial X)$

(assuming the receipt of a message as a communicating action).
- *A more detailed view could e.g. communicate with the repository for checking if the balance will stay positive:*

fix $X(\ rec\_msg(first\_of\_month) : send\_msg(query\_(Acc_1 > Am?))$:
$(\partial : rec\_msg(yes) : debit(Acc_1, Am) : deposit(Acc_2, Am)+$
$(\partial : rec\_msg(no) : send\_msg(error))) : \partial X)$

In this example, the fact that it is the 1st of a month is communicated explicitly by sending (issued e.g. by a timer process) and receiving actions.

Another way would be to consider "1st of a month" as an event and, instead of a fixpoint process, have a rule that states "if this event occurs, then do ...".
Also, for querying the account, this model uses active waiting (∂) – here it would also be possible to have a rule that reacts on the incoming message.

3.5   Event Languages and Event Algebras

The main difference between actions and events is roughly that an event is the visible consequence of an action. E.g., the action is to "debit of 200 E from Alice's bank account", and visible events are "a change of Alice's bank account" (that is immediately detectable from an update), or "the balance of Alice's bank account becomes below zero" (which has to be derived from an update). Additionally, there are system events and external events like temporal events ("1st of a month") and incoming messages. Obviously, actions and events are correlated, but an action can raise several events, raising the problem how events are *detected*. In this section we focus on languages for event specification and on event detection.

In the context of the Web, an (atomic) event is in general any detectable occurrence, i.e., local events (updates, temporal events, and transactional events), incoming messages including queries and answers, updates of data anywhere in the Web, or any occurrences somewhere in an application, that are (possibly) represented in explicit data, or signaled events.

Reactivity is in general not based on atomic events only, but uses the notion of *composite events*, e.g., "when E_1 happened and then E_2 and E_3, but not E_4 after at least 10 minutes, then do A". Composite events are usually defined in terms of an *event algebra*.

So, there is the need for several integrated languages: a language for atomic events and their metadata, and (application-specific) languages for expressing the contents of different types of events, and a declarative language for describing complex events, together with algorithms for handling complex events. The latter languages are not concerned with what the information contained in the event might be, but only with types of events.

Complex Events, Event Algebras

Event Algebras. The term "algebra" describes a very generic (mathematical) concept that has many applications in Computer Science: Boolean Algebra, Relational Algebra, or natural numbers (with only an operator succ(.), or with operators "+" and "*") are algebras. An algebra consists of a "domain" (i.e., a set of "things"), and a set of operators (with a given arity). Operators map elements of the domain to other elements of the domain. Algebra *terms* are formed by nesting operators. Each of the operators has a "semantics", that is, a definition how the result of applying it to some input should look like. **Algebra expressions** are built over basic constants and operators (inductive definition).

For an event algebra, the constants are the atomic events, and the operators serve for combining composite events, e.g.: "A and B", "A or B", or "A and then B". Event algebras contain not only the aforementioned straightforward conjunctive, disjunctive and sequential connectives, but also additional operators. A bunch of event algebras have been defined that provide also e.g. "negative events" in the style that "when E_1 happened, and then E_3 but not E_2 in between, then do something", "periodic" and "cumulative" events, e.g., [13, 55].

An Example. In [13], an event algebra which is used for event detection in the context of ECA-rules ("on ⟨event⟩ if ⟨condition⟩ do ⟨action⟩") in active databases is proposed. Semantically, an event is a predicate $E : T \rightarrow \{\text{true}, \text{false}\}$ where T denotes a set of time instances (or, in embedding into the model of Kripke structures, transitions where the event could be detected). For a given set of elementary events, the set of events is defined inductively:

- If E and F are events, then $E\nabla F$ and $E\triangle F$ are events.
- If $E_1, \ldots, E_n$ are events and $m < n \in \mathbb{N}$, then $\text{ANY}(m, E_1, \ldots, E_n)$ is an event.
- If E and F are events, then $E; F$ is an event.
- If E_1, E_2 and E_3 are events, then $A(E_1, E_2, E_3)$ and $A^*(E_1, E_2, E_3)$ are events.
- If E_1, E_2 and E_3 are events, then $\neg(E_1)[E_2, E_3]$ is an event.

The semantics of composite events is defined as follows, where detection of a complex event means that its "final" atomic subevent is detected:

(1) $(E\nabla F)(t)$ $:\Leftrightarrow$ $E_1(t) \vee E_2(t)$,
(2) $(E\triangle F)(t)$ $:\Leftrightarrow$ $E_1(t) \wedge E_2(t)$,
(3) $(E_1; E_2)(t)$ $:\Leftrightarrow$ $\exists t_1 \leq t : E_1(t_1) \wedge E_2(t)$,

(4) $\mathsf{ANY}(m, E_1, \ldots, E_n)(t)$ $\;:\Leftrightarrow\; \exists t_1 \leq \ldots \leq t_{m-1} \leq t,\; 1 \leq i_1, \ldots, i_m \leq n$ pairwise
distinct s.t. $E_{i_j}(t_j)$ for $1 \leq j < m$ and $E_{i_m}(t)$,

(5) $\neg(E_2)[E_1, E_3](t)$ $\;:\Leftrightarrow\; E_3(t) \wedge (\exists t_1 : E_1(t_1) \wedge$
$\wedge\, (\forall t_2 : t_1 \leq t_2 < t : \neg(E_2(t_2) \vee E_3(t_2)))) \,,$

(6) $A(E_1, E_2, E_3)(t)$ $\;:\Leftrightarrow\; E_2(t) \wedge (\exists t_1 : E_1(t_1) \wedge (\forall t_2 : t_1 \leq t_2 < t : \neg E_3(t_2))),$

(7) $A^*(E_1, E_2, E_3)(t)$ $\;:\Leftrightarrow\; \exists t_1 \leq t : E_1(t_1) \wedge E_3(t) \,,$
when this event occurs, a specified action for every occurrence of E_2 has to be executed in t.

The constructs ∇ ("or") and $\triangle$ ("and") are standard and straightforward. "$(E_1; E_2)$" denotes the successive occurrence of E_1 and E_2, where in case that E_2 is a complex event, it is possible that subevents of E_2 occur *before* E_1 occurs. ANY denotes the occurrence of m events out of n in arbitrary order, which is also expressible by a special ∇-$\triangle$-;-schema. (5) is a complex event which detects the non-occurrence of E_2 in the interval between E_1 and the next E_3. (6) is an "aperiodic" event which is signaled whenever E_2 occurs after E_1 without E_3 occurring in-between. Note that $\neg(E_2)[E_1, E_3]$ occurs with the *terminating* event E_3 whereas $A(E_1, E_2, E_3)$ occurs with *every* E_2 in the interval (if E_3 never occurs, the interval is endless). The "cumulative aperiodic event" (7) occurs with E_3 and then requires the execution of a given set of actions corresponding to the occurrences of E_2 in the meantime. Thus, it is not a simple event, but more an active rule, stating a temporal implication of the form "if E_1 occurs, then for each occurrence of an instance of E_2, collect its parameters, and when E_3 occurs, report all collected parameters (in order to do something)".

In general, events are parameterized, and event specifications contain free variables that are bound in the event detection.

Example 3. *Consider again the scenario of Example 1. Events in this scenario are e.g. "1st of a month", "a deposit to account x" (in this case, the event directly corresponds to an action), or "the balance of account x goes below zero" (due to a debit action). Composite events are e.g., "there were no deposits to an account for 100 days" which can be expressed in the above event language as*

$E_1(Acct) :=$
$(\neg(\exists X : deposit(Acct, X)))[deposit(Acct, Am) \wedge t = date, date = t{+}100 days] \,.$

An aperiodic event is e.g. "the balance of account x goes below zero and there is another debit without any deposit in-between" which is expressed in the above event language as

$$E_2(Acct) := A(\, debit(Acct, Am_1) \wedge balance(Acct) < 0,$$
$$debit(Acct, Am_2), deposit(Acct, Am_3)) \,.$$

A cumulative periodic event is e.g. used for "after the end of a month, send an account statement with all entries of this month:

$E_3(Acct, list) :=$
$A^*(first\_of\_month, (debit(Acct, Am)\nabla deposit(Acct, Am)), first\_of\_next\_month)$

where the event occurs with $first\_of\_next\_month$ and carries a list of the debit and deposit actions.

Event Detection. As described above, an event algebra mainly consists of the definition of event combinators and their semantics (given in general in terms of sequences that "satisfy" the composite event). For practical issues, it is necessary to *detect* the event. Since events are *volatile* data (and for efficiency reasons), it is not possible to do this by querying, but event detection must be done incrementally *on-the-fly.*

Work on complex events does not only define the semantics of events and complex events, but in general also describes algorithms for efficient detection and tracing of events. Incremental *residuation* has been used in [55] in an approach that uses an event-style algebra for *scheduling* of tasks, which is similar to the reduction steps in the operational semantics given in Section 3.4 for CCS.

Past tense modalities with incremental bookkeeping have been employed for checking temporal constraints and temporal conditions in ECA-style rules, e.g. in [15, 56]. [15] uses full first-order past temporal logic, with $\exists$ and $\forall$ quantifiers. [56] replaces the quantifiers by a functional assignment $[X \leftarrow t]\varphi(X)$ that binds a variable X to the value of a term t in a given state. This ensures safety of formulas, but the full expressiveness of using a universal quantifier is not provided.

From the theoretical point of view, the used techniques amount to the same principles, although formalized differently by *residuation, automata, graph techniques* and *rewriting.*

They are in general restricted to the area of distributed/active databases where the location and communication of events is fixed.

Example 4. *Consider again the scenario of Example 3.*

Detection of the first event means to start event detection of $E_1(Acct)$ (with internal parameter t_0) for Acct whenever a deposit occurs at timepoint t_0. The detection ends when either another deposit to Acct occurs, or the date t_0+100 days is reached, and the event actually occurs.

Detection of the second event means to start event detection of $E_2(Acct)$ whenever a debit occurs and the resulting balance is below zero. The detection ends when either a deposit to Acct occurs (then, the event is not reported), or another debit happens (then, the event is actually detected and reported).

Detection of the third event means to start event detection of $E_3(Acct)$ at the first day of a month. Internal bookkeeping is done for every debit or deposit (action/event), and the event finally occurs at the first day of the next month.

Considering an event "(if) balance of Account changes (then immediately phone me)", the detection means to translate it as "either a debit or a deposit occurs".

In the (Semantic) Web, event detection requires to solve two issues:

– translating (atomic) event specifications into underlying actions (as the final one in the above example), and

− detecting remote events. Up to now, events were always considered to be local, or at least communicated explicitly by messages.

3.6   Combining Static and Dynamic Aspects

It is desirable that event sequences can be combined with requirements on the state of resources at given intermediate timepoints, e.g. "when at timepoint t_1, a cancelation comes in and somewhere in the past, a reservation request came in at a timepoint when all seats were booked, then, the cancelation is charged with an additional fee". In this case, the event detecting engine has to state a query at the moment when a given (sub)event is detected. For being capable of describing these situations, a formalism (and system) that deals with sequences of events and queries is required. This is not covered by the above approaches (except in some extent [15]).

A language that covers these issues will be presented in Section 4.3: Transaction Logic.

4   Rule-Based Languages for Evolution and Reactivity

Rule-based languages for evolution and reactivity can mainly be grouped into two aspects:

− languages defining individual actions directly in terms of their effects on a structure. These languages can immediately be used for "programming" and reasoning.
− languages defining the higher-level interplay of actions, i.e., when and how a certain sequence of actions has to be executed. Here also *transaction* models have to be considered.

4.1   Action Languages

Action languages are formal models that are used for representing actions and for reasoning about the effects of actions [53, 4, 24, 25, 27, 28, 29, 18] that have been mainly developed in the Knowledge Representation and Reasoning community.

Central to this method of formalizing actions is the concept of a labeled transition system (LTS). Usually, the states are first-order structures, where the predicates are divided into static and dynamic ones, the latter called *fluents* (cf. [54]). Action programs (in languages such as language $\mathcal{B}$ and $\mathcal{C}$, below) are sets of sentences that describe the transitions by specifying which dynamic predicates change in the environment after the execution of an action. Evolving Algebras/Abstract State Machines, also described below, are a special kind of action programs.

Usual problems here are to predict the consequences of the execution of a sequence of (sets of) actions, or to determine a set of actions implying a desired conclusion in the future (planning). Several action query languages exist that allow for querying such a transition system, going beyond the simple queries of knowing what is true after a given sequence of actions has been executed (allowing e.g. to reason about which sets of actions lead to a state where some goal is true, i.e. planning as in [18]).

Situation Calculus. The first, and most prominent concept here is the situation calculus (originally in [44], reprinted in [43], see also [53]).

States (or situations) are elements of the domain, occurring as an argument for distinguished predicates $\mathsf{holds}(p(x), s)$ and $\mathsf{occurs}(a(x), s)$ where p is a predicate of the application domain and a is an action. Events (mainly equivalent to actions) in a situation produce new situations: $\mathsf{do}\ a(s)$ denotes the situation which is obtained by executing an action a in a situation s. A situation is a first order functional term $\mathsf{do}\ a_n(\mathsf{do}\ a_{n-1}(\ldots(\mathsf{do}\ a_1(s_0))))$, where a_i are actions and s_0 is a constant denoting the initial situation; the values of fluents in s_0 are specified by formulas of the form $\mathsf{holds}(p(x), s_0)$.

Actions are characterized by *preconditions*, e.g.

$$\mathsf{occurs}(a(x), S) \rightarrow \mathsf{holds}(p(x), S)$$

and their *normal effect*, e.g.

$$\mathsf{holds}(p(x), S) \wedge \mathsf{occurs}(a(x), S) \rightarrow \mathsf{holds}(q(y), do\ a(x)(S))$$

describing how an action changes some fluents. The frame problem is solved by adding axioms for assuming that fluents which are not explicitly changed, remain unchanged.

There exist different versions of the situation calculus, e.g., the one used in GOLOG [40], a logic programming language. There, the predicate holds is omitted and the preconditions are characterized by a distinguished predicate, i.e. $\mathsf{Poss}(a(x), s) \equiv \mathsf{holds}(p(x), S)$. In GOLOG, frame axioms are stated explicitly.

Statelog. Statelog [38] provides a logical framework for active rules which precisely and unambiguously defines the meaning of rules. Moreover, it allows to study fundamental properties of active rules like termination, confluence and expressive power.

A *Statelog rule r* is an expression of the form

$$[S+k_0]\ H \leftarrow [S+k_1]\ B_1,\ \ldots\ ,[S+k_n]\ B_n$$

where the head H is a Datalog atom, B_i are Datalog literals (atoms A or negated atoms $\neg A$), and $k_i \in \mathbb{N}_0$. Access to different database states is accomplished via *state terms* of the form $[S+k]$, where $S+k$ denotes the k-fold application of the unary function symbol "+1" to the *state variable* S. A rule r is called *local* it $k_0 = k_i$ for all $i = 1, \ldots, n$, *progressive*, if $k_0 \geq k_i$ for all $i = 1, \ldots, n$, and *1-progressive*, if $k_0 = k_i + 1$ for all $i = 1, \ldots, n$. A *Statelog program* is a finite set of progressive Statelog rules. In general, the rules of a Statelog program define a sequence of (intermediate) *transitions*. A Statelog activity (raised by an external event that makes some progressive rule applicable) ends when no more progressive rules are applicable. Then the system is idle until the next external event occurs.

Logic Programming notions (e.g., *local stratification*) and declarative semantics (e.g., *perfect model*) developed for deductive rules can be applied directly to Statelog. It uses a notion of *state-stratified semantics* as the canonical model of a Statelog program wrt. a given database state: P is called state-stratified, if there are no negative cyclic rule dependencies *within a single state*. This notion is closely related to *XY-stratification* [65] and *ELS-stratification* [36].

Language $\mathcal{B}$. The $\mathcal{B}$ language [27, 25] is a generalization of the so-called language $\mathcal{A}$ [24](which itself represents the propositional fragment of the ADL formalism [50]). It allows conditional and non-deterministic actions and, unlike $\mathcal{A}$, also for the representation of actions with indirect effects. A program in $\mathcal{B}$ is a set of static and dynamic laws, of the forms, respectively:

$$L \textbf{ if } F, \quad \text{and}$$
$$A \textbf{ causes } L \textbf{ if } F$$

where L is a fluent literal, F a conjunction of literals, and A an action name. Intuitively a static law states that every possible state satisfying the conjunction F must also satisfy L, and a dynamic law states that if F is satisfied when action A occurs then L is true in the subsequent state. Given a set of static and dynamic laws, a labeled transition system is defined. Basically, states are all interpretations closed under the static laws, and there is an arc from a state s to a state s' with label a iff all Ls of dynamic rules of the form a **causes** L **if** F, where F holds in s, belong to s', and nothing else differs from s to s'.

A program in $\mathcal{A}$ is as in $\mathcal{B}$ but without static laws. Besides the above briefly described language $\mathcal{B}$, several other extension of the language $\mathcal{A}$ exist. Language $\mathcal{AR}$ [26], as for $\mathcal{B}$, also allows for modeling indirect effects of actions but in this case, instead of static laws, constraints of the form **always** F, where F is a propositional formula, are used. Language $\mathcal{A}_K$ [57] further extends $\mathcal{AR}$ for formalizing sensing actions (i.e. actions for determining the truth value of fluents). Another extension of $\mathcal{A}$ is the language $\mathcal{PDL}$ [41] which is particularly tailored for specifying policies. A survey and comparisons on extensions of $\mathcal{A}$ can be found in [19].

Language $\mathcal{C}$. As in language $\mathcal{B}$, also in $\mathcal{C}$ [29, 28] statements of the language are divided into static and dynamic laws. The main distinction between $\mathcal{C}$ and $\mathcal{B}$, besides the fact that $\mathcal{C}$ allows for arbitrary formulas to be caused by actions (rather than simply literals as in $\mathcal{B}$) and arbitrary formulas as conditions (rather than conjunction only), is that $\mathcal{C}$ distinguishes between asserting that a fluent "holds" and making the stronger assertion that "it is caused", or "has a causal explanation".

A program in $\mathcal{C}$ is a set of static and dynamic laws of the forms, respectively:

$$\textbf{caused } F \textbf{ if } G, \quad \text{and}$$
$$\textbf{caused } F \textbf{ if } G \textbf{ after } U$$

where F and G are formulas over fluent literals, and U is a formula with both fluent literals and action names.

Intuitively, a static law states that the formula G causes the truth of the formula F, and a dynamic rule states that after U, the static rule "**caused** F **if** G" is in force. The definition of a transition system for $\mathcal{C}$ is based on *causal theories* [28]. The idea behind causal theories is that something is true iff it is caused by something else. Every state s is now characterized by a set $M(s)$ and a causal theory $T(s)$ (consisting of the static rules from P and possibly additional ones). Given a causal theory T and a set M of fluents, the causal theory T_M of formulae is defined as follows:

$$T_M = \{F|\ \text{"\textbf{caused} } F \text{ \textbf{if} } G\text{"} \in T \text{ and } M \models G\}$$

We say M is a *causal model* of T iff M is the unique model of T_M. For all states s in the LTS, the interpretation $M(s)$ must be a causal model of $T(s)$.

Given a state s with $T(s)$, $M(s)$ and a set of actions K (executed in a transition), the resulting causal theory $T(s, K)$ is given by the static laws of P and the static laws enforced by the dynamic laws whose preconditions are true in $M(s) \cup K$. Then there is an arc with label K between s and a state s' iff $T(s') = T(s, K)$ and $M(s')$ is a causal model of $T(s, k)$. It is worth noting that in $\mathcal{C}$, contrary to $\mathcal{B}$, fluent inertia is not assumed by default.

Various extensions to $\mathcal{C}$ have recently appeared in the literature. Most prominently, the language $\mathcal{C}$++ [28] and the language $\mathcal{K}$ [18]. $\mathcal{C}$++ further allows for multi-valued, additive fluents which can be used to encode resources and allows for a more compact representation of several practical problems. The language $\mathcal{K}$ allows for representing and reasoning about incomplete states, and for solving planning problems.

For more details on these languages, as well on the implementation of fragments of them in logic programming, see [19, 25, 28].

Evolving Algebras/Abstract State Machines. The concept of "Evolving Algebras" has been introduced for specifying the operational semantics of processes in [30, 31]. Evolving Algebras have originally not been introduced from the logical point of view, but for describing the operational semantics of processes in the sense of Turing's Thesis: "Every algorithm can be described by a suitable Evolving Algebra". Thus, for any given algorithm, on any level of abstraction an Evolving Algebra can be given.

In universal algebra, a first-order structure over a signature where the equality symbol is the only relation symbol (i.e., everything is represented by functions), is called an *algebra*.

The *signature* Σ of an Evolving Algebra is a finite set of function symbols, each of them with a fixed arity, including 0-ary constants. Note that every relation can be represented by its characteristic function. The names in Σ are divided into two groups: static and dynamic functions (i.e., *fluents* as in e.g., Situation Calculus [53], GOLOG [40], also [54]). A state of an Evolving Algebra over Σ is then an interpretation of Σ, inducing an evaluation of terms.

An Evolving Algebra EA is given by an initial state $Z(EA)$ (which also determines the interpretation of the static function symbols for all states) and a program $P(EA)$ (a set of transition rules and rule schemata) describing the change of the interpretation of state-dependent function symbols in a Pascal-like syntax.

An *elementary update rule* is an update of the interpretation of a function symbol at one location: $f(t_1, \ldots, t_n) := t_0$, where f is an n-ary function symbol and t_i are terms.

The set of rules is defined by structural induction by defining blocks and conditionals (if-then); also rule schemata that contain free variables are allowed. A program $P(EA)$ of an Evolving Algebra EA is a finite set of rules and rule schemata. A program is then executed by applying rules, inducing again a Kripke structure.

4.2 Event-Condition-Action Rules in Databases

Event-Condition-Action rules have already been motivated in Section 2.2 as a common means to express system behavior. They are intuitively easy to understand, and provide a well-understood formal semantics: when an event occurs, evaluate a condition, and if the condition is satisfied then execute an action. Above, we have discussed several approaches for the event and action parts. Additionally, several execution models can be chosen that specify how the rule is applied (before or after or deferred, statement-oriented or set-oriented, its transactional embedding etc.), modified by further policies of the ECA engine (e.g. for conflict resolution).

Depending on the choice of the above sublanguages and semantics, a broad range of behaviors can be designed. ECA languages based on atomic events are e.g. used for maintaining consistency (as in the well-known SQL triggers) in course of execution of a surrounding process. On the other end of the range, ECA languages that allow for complex events can themselves be used for *specifying* the behavior of a system in a rule-based way.

Types of ECA rules. Mainly, two kinds of ECA rules can be distinguished:

- low-level: rules that react directly on changes of the underlying data. These are provided as triggers in most database systems, e.g., SQL, of the form

  ```
  ON database-update WHEN condition BEGIN pl/sql-fragment END
  ```

  where the values of the updated tuple are accessible as old and new.
- application-level: ECA engines that react on application-level events that are raised by updates of underlying data, messages etc.

4.3 Transaction Logic

Transaction Logic $\mathcal{TR}$ [8] is another comprehensive rule-based formalism that does not have a strict ECA distinction, but follows the Logic Programming style. In $\mathcal{TR}$, in contrast to modal logic where states are given as first-order structures, states are given as abstract *theories* over a signature $\mathcal{L}$ – that can e.g. be first-order theories, or OWL-based worlds. The evaluation of formulas wrt. states is provided by an abstract *state data oracle* $\mathcal{O}^d$ that answers queries (possibly with free variables) for every individual state. Transitions are given by the *state transition oracle* $\mathcal{O}^t$ which maps pairs of database states to sets of ground formulas (over a set $\mathcal{A}$ of action names, corresponding to the labels of the elementary transitions). Thus, with $\mathcal{G}$ denoting the set of state identifiers, $(\mathcal{G}, \mathcal{O}^t, \mathcal{O}^d)$ gives the same information as a labeled Kripke structure, an LTS, or a path model for Process Logic.

Since in Transaction Logic, the internal representation and model of states is not predetermined, structures of any type are allowed as a basis. For example, a pure functional signature (e.g. static algebras), a pure relational signature (Datalog), first-order, or even object-oriented (F-Logic) or OWL models can be used in the data oracle.

Formally, the semantics of $\mathcal{TR}$ formulas is based on a version of *path structures*, i.e., the satisfaction of formulas is defined on paths, not on states: A *path* of length $k \geq 1$ is a finite sequence $\pi = \langle \mathcal{D}_1, \mathcal{D}_2, \dots, \mathcal{D}_k \rangle$ of state identifiers; $\pi_1 \circ \pi_2 = \langle \mathcal{D}_1, \dots, \mathcal{D}_i \rangle \circ \langle \mathcal{D}_i, \dots, \mathcal{D}_k \rangle$ is a *split* of π.
A path structure (here: over a first-order $\mathcal{L}$) $\mathcal{M}$ is a triple $\langle \mathcal{U}, \mathcal{I}_{\mathcal{F}}, \mathcal{I}_{path} \rangle$ where

- $\mathcal{U}$ is the *domain* of $\mathcal{M}$,
- $\mathcal{I}_{\mathcal{F}}$ is a (state-independent) interpretation of the function symbols in $\mathcal{L}$,
- $\mathcal{I}_{path}$ assigns to every path $\pi = \langle \mathcal{D}_1, \dots, \mathcal{D}_n \rangle$ a semantic structure $\langle \mathcal{U}, \mathcal{I}_{\mathcal{F}}, \mathcal{I}_{\mathcal{P}} \rangle$ where $\mathcal{I}_{\mathcal{P}}$ is an interpretation of the predicate symbols in $\mathcal{L} \cup \mathcal{A}$.

$\mathcal{I}_{path}$ is subject to two restrictions:

- Compliance with the data oracle: $\mathcal{I}_{path}(\langle \mathcal{D} \rangle) \models \phi$ for every $\phi \in \mathcal{O}^d(\mathcal{D})$,
- Compliance with the transition oracle: $\mathcal{I}_{path}(\langle \mathcal{D}_1, \mathcal{D}_2 \rangle) \models a$ whenever $a \in \mathcal{O}^t(\mathcal{D}_1, \mathcal{D}_2)$.

Transaction formulas are built by the connectives $\neg, \vee, \wedge, \oplus, \otimes$, and the quantifiers $\exists$ and $\forall$. Let π be a path and β a variable assignment. Then,

for formulas of the state language $\mathcal{L}$:
$$(\mathcal{M}, \langle \mathcal{D} \rangle, \beta) \models_{\mathcal{TR}} s\text{-}fml \quad \Leftrightarrow \quad (\mathcal{I}_{path}(\langle \mathcal{D} \rangle), \beta) \models_{(\mathcal{O}^d, \mathcal{O}^t)} s\text{-}fml$$
$$\Leftrightarrow \quad s\text{-}fml \in \mathcal{O}^d(\mathcal{D}) ,$$
for formulas of the transition language $\mathcal{A}$:
$$(\mathcal{M}, \langle \mathcal{D}_1, \mathcal{D}_2 \rangle, \beta) \models_{\mathcal{TR}} t\text{-}fml \quad \Leftrightarrow \quad (\mathcal{I}_{path}(\langle \mathcal{D}_1, \mathcal{D}_2 \rangle), \beta) \models_{(\mathcal{O}^d, \mathcal{O}^t)} t\text{-}fml$$
$$\Leftrightarrow \quad t\text{-}fml \in \mathcal{O}^t(\mathcal{D}_1, \mathcal{D}_2) ,$$
$$(\mathcal{M}, \pi, \beta) \models_{\mathcal{TR}} \phi \otimes \psi \quad \Leftrightarrow \quad (\mathcal{M}, \pi_1, \beta) \models_{\mathcal{TR}} \phi \text{ and } (\mathcal{M}, \pi_2, \beta) \models_{\mathcal{TR}} \psi$$
$$\text{for some split } \pi = \pi_1 \circ \pi_2 \text{ of } \pi , \text{ and}$$
$$(\mathcal{M}, \pi, \beta) \models_{\mathcal{TR}} \phi \oplus \psi \quad \Leftrightarrow \quad (\mathcal{M}, \pi_1, \beta) \models_{\mathcal{TR}} \phi \text{ or } (\mathcal{M}, \pi_2, \beta) \models_{\mathcal{TR}} \psi$$
$$\text{for } every \text{ split } \pi = \pi_1 \circ \pi_2 \text{ of } \pi .$$

Due to the restriction of $\mathcal{O}^t$ to elementary actions, parallel composition of actions in a single transition is not possible. In [9], an interleaving semantics for parallelism is given.

Example 5. *Consider again the states from Example 1 (note that the function balance is interpreted state-dependently), consider the path $\pi := \langle g_0, g_1, g_2 \rangle$. For* *each state g_i, $\mathcal{O}^d(g_i)$ is the theory induced by $\mathcal{M}(g_i)$. The transition oracle $\mathcal{O}^t$ represents the transition relation $\mathcal{R}$, i.e., $\phi \in \mathcal{O}^t(g, g')$ if and only if $(g, g') \in \mathcal{R}(\phi)$ for action literals ϕ:*

$$\mathcal{O}^t(g_0, g_1) = \{debit(Alice, 20)\} \quad and \quad \mathcal{O}^t(g_1, g_2) = \{deposit(Bob, 20)\} \ .$$

We have $(\mathcal{M}, \pi) \models debit(Alice, 20) \otimes deposit(Bob, 20)$ and also – mixing state and transition queries
$$(\mathcal{M}, \pi) \models (balance(Alice)+balance(Bob) = 300) \otimes debit(Alice, 20) \otimes$$
$$deposit(Bob, 20) \otimes (balance(Alice)+balance(Bob) = 300) \ .$$

ECA Semantics by Serial Implication. In the same way as standard implication is derived from disjunction as $A \to B \Leftrightarrow \neg A \lor B$, *(right) serial implication* is defined as $A \Rightarrow B \Leftrightarrow \neg A \oplus B$ (which is the main application of the serial disjunction). With this, temporal constraints in the style of ECA rules can be defined.

Example 6. *Consider again Examples 1 and 5. The rule "if there is a debit and the resulting balance is below zero, then send a message" is specified by*

$$debit(Acct, Am) \otimes balance(Am) < 0 \Rightarrow sendmsg(...) \ .$$

Analogously, *left serial implication* allows for stating preconditions.

Transaction Bases and the Serial Horn Fragment. A *transaction base* is a set of formulas of the form $a_0 \leftarrow a_1 \otimes \ldots \otimes a_n$, which play a special role for *Transaction Logic* programming, providing a top-down SLD-style proof procedure. With such rules, *transactions* can be defined, providing a declarative specification of the database evolution. To execute a_0 (in LP terminology: to prove a_0) in a state $\mathcal{D}$ means to execute or prove $a_0 \leftarrow a_1 \otimes \ldots \otimes a_n$ by generating intermediate states; thus, the final state $a_0(\mathcal{D})$ is "specified" as $a_1 \otimes \ldots \otimes a_n(\mathcal{D})$. Note that depending on the "nature" of the a_i they can denote events (that cannot be forced, but whose presence constrains the ways to make the body true), conditions on states (also acting as constraints), or actions (which are then to be executed/proven as heads of other rules).

Example 7. *Consider again Examples 1 and 5. The "money transfer" transaction is defined as*

$$transfer(Am, Acc_1, Acc_2) \leftarrow debit(Acc_1, Am) \otimes deposit(Acc_2, Am) \ .$$

Consider now the case that debit and deposit are not atomic actions, but instead there is an underlying (relational) database with a table balance(Acct, Amount), manipulated by delete and insert actions. Then, debit and deposit actions can be specified by their effect on balance:

$debit(Acc, Am) \leftarrow$
$\quad balance(Acc) = N \otimes balance.delete(Acc, N) \otimes balance.insert(Acc, N{-}Am)$
$deposit(Acc, Am) \leftarrow$
$\quad balance(Acc) = N \otimes balance.delete(Acc_1, N) \otimes balance.insert(Acc, N{+}Am) \ .$

The combination of the above mechanisms for expressing and enforcing constraints, expressing ECA rules, defining transactions, planning with SLD resolution and further features of Transaction Logic provides a very expressive framework.

4.4   Transactional Requirements

In general, evolution consists not of arbitrary execution of independent actions, but of execution of certain processes (e.g. defined as a process algebra in Section 3.4). The interaction between these processes can be more or less close:

- each of them runs mainly on independent data, doing only some communication as provided by CCS, or
- processes run on shared data.

In both cases, besides communication/cooperation there are certain additional requirements. Here, the database community uses the notion of *transactions* for guaranteeing correct behavior. Usually, transactions adhere to the ACID paradigm:

Atomicity: A transaction is (logically) a unit that cannot be further decomposed: its effect is *atomic*, i.e., all updates are executed completely, or nothing at all ("all-or-nothing").

Concistency: A transaction is a correct transition from one state to another. The final state is not allowed to violate any integrity condition (otherwise the transaction is undone and rejected).

Isolation: Databases are multi-user systems. Although transactions are running *concurrently*, this is hidden against the user (i.e., after starting a transaction, the user does not see changes by other transactions until finishing his transaction, *simulated* single-user).

Durability: If a transaction completes successfully, all its effects are durable (=persistent).

In the Web environment, not only "simple" transactions, but also *long transactions* and *hierarchical transactions* are used.

Summary. The previous sections – especially those on Kripke Structures and Modal Logics, ECA rules and Transaction Logics – also illustrate the duality between seeing evolution as a rule-driven process, and describing it declaratively via constraints: Modal Logics are primarily used for *describing* structures via their constraints and *reasoning* about them. The semantics of ECA rules is targeted to *generate* such a structure (or even more, to generate one possible path and proceed along it, moving and forgetting from one state to the next). Transaction Logic can be interpreted as both ways: reasoning about possible paths, and, as *Transaction Logic Programming*, running an evolving system. Moreover, temporal logics etc. allow also to reason about systems of ECA rules (correctness, termination etc.).

5   Evolution and Reactivity on the Web

The previous two sections have introduced the abstract concepts and some sample formalisms for handling evolution and reactivity. In this section, we present the current basis and prerequisites for extending and applying these concepts to the Web and to the Semantic Web. The high-level concepts like Kripke structures, modal logics, rules, ECA rules, event algebras with event detection mechanisms, and transactions apply with slight adaptations to the Semantic Web. They have to be *instantiated* for this environment: What are the *actions* and *events* in this setting? What syntactical and semantical frameworks are used for the high-level concepts?

In today's Web environment, XML (as a format for storing and exchanging data), RDF (as an abstract data model for states), OWL (as an additional framework for state theories), and communication issues (Web Services, SOAP, WSDL) provide the natural underlying concepts.

5.1   States and Nodes in the Semantic Web

In the Semantic Web as a network of autonomous nodes, there is not a single "state", but the notion of "current state" has to deal with different data models, incompleteness, and inconsistency (which is dealt with in another chapter of this volume on *querying*). Thus, every node has its own current view of the global state. The same holds for events: only events that are somehow known to the node can be considered.

The knowledge of a node in the Semantic Web is represented in RDF, RDFS, and/or OWL. OWL provides a model theory, thus, instead of first-order structures and first-order logic used in classical approaches, Kripke structures and logics for OWL are a prospective basis.

In the Semantic Web, the state of a node in this setting consists of the common notion of "state wrt. an application", and additionally derivation rules and behavioral rules. In a wider sense also the state of event detection algorithms belongs of the state of a node. Preferably, all this is expressed in RDF/OWL; larger internal databases are actually stored in plain XML, but mapped to an RDF/OWL ontology.

Thus, actions have to be able to change this state: XML updates, RDF updates, ontology updates, and service calls.

5.2   Existing Languages for Updates

XML Updates. There are several proposals for languages that provide update capabilities for XML data. Usually, update languages are designed as an extension of a query language with update capabilities. At least, an addressing mechanism for selecting parts of XML documents that are to be modified is needed.

XML:DB's XUpdate. XUpdate [64] is an update language developed by the XML:DB group, its latest language specification was released in late 2000 as a working draft. Note that, at that time, the query languages XPath, XQL, and XML-QL and the transformation language XSLT were already defined, but XQuery did not yet exist. Thus, also the name "XUpdate" is not related to XQuery. Similar to XSLT, XUpdate is written in XML syntax and makes use of XPath [62] expressions for selecting nodes to be processed afterwards. Simple atomic update operations to XML documents are possible with XUpdate. Several XML database systems implement this language, e.g. eXist [21].

XQuery Update extensions. A proposal to extend XQuery [63] with update capabilities is presented in [59]. XQuery is extended with a FOR ... LET ... WHERE ... UPDATE ... structure. The UPDATE part contains specifications of update operations (i.e. delete, insert, rename, replace) that are to be executed in sequence. For ordered XML documents, two insertion operations are considered: insertion before a child element, and insertion after a child element. Using a nested FOR...WHERE clause in the UPDATE part, one might specify an iterative execution of updates for nodes selected by an XPath expression. Moreover, by nesting update operations, updates can be expressed at multiple levels within an XML structure. Update operations very similar to those described in [59] have been specified and implemented in [39], extended e.g. by means to specify conditional updates. The solution has been incorporated into Software AG's Tamino[1] product.

XChange. XChange [11] is a declarative language for specifying evolution of data on the (Semantic) Web. XChange builds upon Xcerpt [10, 12], a declarative query and transformation language for the (Semantic) Web. The XChange update language uses rules to specify *intensional updates*, i.e. a description of updates in terms of queries.

RDF Updates. Basically, languages for RDF updates are built in the same way as for XML and SQL updates by extending a query language. There is not yet a definitive decision about an RDF query+update language.

5.3   Atomic Events in the Semantic Web

In the context of the (Semantic) Web, the *global handling* of events must also be investigated. In addition to local events, there are remote and "global" events. Similar to the classical case, there are (local) data level events and rules, and (local, remote, and global) application-level ones. The notion of composite events is then defined as usual.

Local Events. Local events are comparable with those discussed before for the classical case: temporal events, receipts of messages, local data level events and local application level events. Data level events are e.g. updates of underlying XML or RDF repositories (we discuss the concrete syntax and semantics later).

---

[1] http://www.tamino.com

Application-level events in the Semantic Web are also described or translatable to RDF (a special case are e.g. SOAP calls).

Remote Events. As illustrated above, detection of, and reaction upon, remote events is an important feature for the Semantic Web. An event detection engine must also be able to detect/discover remote events that are not explicitly communicated. This is especially the case when working with complex events (see below). It can be done by using remote event bases (when the location of an event is known, and it is known that it is traced in an event base), or by regularly polling remote data (e.g. fuel prices at my favorite petrol station, or stock courses). In this case, again, publish/subscribe systems or continuous-query services can be applied (especially, when they maintain a history).

For concrete *atomic events*, it must also be distinguished between the event itself (carrying application-specific information), and its metadata, like the type of event (update, temporal event, receipt of message, ...), time of occurrence, the time of detection/receipt (e.g., to refuse it, when it had been received too late) and the event origin or its generator (if applicable; e.g. in terms of its URI).

Implicit Events. Most of the events *can* be expressed alternatively as detection of updates of a given database (communicated via publish/subscribe systems), or by queries but, especially in the *Semantic* Web, a declarative specification from the point of view of an application-level *event* is intended. The reduction of the detection to an actual update is then left to the semantic component.

Example 8 (Events). *Consider the situation when Oracle bought the Retek company on 22.3.2005; 11.25 $ per share, 631 million Dollar total. Firstly, this is an application-level real world event. It is noted by the (Semantic) Web e.g. as a (local, low-level) database event at New York Stock Exchange as a database update at 09:00 h AST.*

Stock tickers and agents will immediately be informed by push *propagation. An agent in Europe receives a message (raising a local incoming message event) sent at 9:01h AST, received at 14:02h MET, coming from NYSE (trustable), with RDF body, containing the above facts. Analyzing the message body, the agent detects the application level event that Oracle bought Retek together with the detailed financial facts.*

Possible other events that are "detected" in turn by this agent that is probably running investment rules are e.g., that "Oracle bought some company", "an IT company has been bought", "SAP did not succeed in buying Retek", etc., possibly contributing to the detection of composite events.

The original message is also posted to a "Semantic Web Newspaper" service, where smaller clients poll messages e.g. in the evening. For such a client, the incoming event consists e.g. of the information that "at 20:32 PST, I became aware that at 9:00 AST, ...". It can now process the pure facts (that probably explain why the oracle stocks raised/fell during the day), or incorporate the awareness time, e.g., when processing a rule "if I become aware of a large acquisition less than 3 hours after the fact, do something ...".

5.4   ECA Rules in the Semantic Web

There are several abstraction levels on which active rules can be defined:

- programming language level: triggers as built-in constructs of a given database model, like SQL triggers. Usually they are implemented inside the database. This level can e.g. directly be based on the *DOM Level 2/3 Events* [17] or on the triggers of relational storage of RDF data.
- logical level – XML. Here ECA rules consist of distinguished event-condition-action parts that are also marked up in XML/RuleML; one of the results of the research in I5 (jointly with I1) should be an ECA-ML language.

  This requires a definition of atomic update events on XML data; probably on the same level and granularity as updates in XUpdate located by XSL patterns or by using an update language like XChange.
- semantic level: RDF. Here, several aspects can (also independently) be lifted from XML:
  - use XML-ECA rules on underlying RDF/OWL data,
  - use RDF/OWL descriptions of events, conditions, and actions in the XML-ECA framework,
  - use an RDF/OWL ontology even on the rule level. (Conversely, rules in this ontology can themselves use event/condition/action parts in XML, and even data in XML).

Updates and Actions. There are different ways how to express the actions to be taken.

- Explicit updates: In this case the action is an explicit update statement e.g. described in XUpdate, XQuery+Updates, XChange, or in an RDF Update language. This requires knowledge of the underlying schema.
- Explicit actions: In this case by calling a procedure/method (SOAP),
- Semantic/Intensional: This requires the declarative specification of what has to be changed, using an RDF/OWL ontology of changes (to RDF data).

5.5   Trigger-Like Local ECA Rules

Trigger-like local ECA rules have to react directly on the changes of the database, which is assumed to be in XML or RDF format. While triggers in relational databases/SQL were only able to react on changes of a given tuple or an attribute of a tuple, the XML and RDF models call for more expressive event specifications according to the (tree or graph) structure.

XML. Work on triggers for XQuery has e.g. been described in [7] with **Active XQuery** and in [3], emulating the trigger definition and execution model of the SQL3 standard that specifies a syntax and execution model for ECA rules in relational databases. *Active XQuery* uses the same syntax and switches as SQL's `CREATE TRIGGER`.

The following proposal has been developed in [2]: For modifications of an XML tree, the following atomic events could be considered:

- ON DELETE OF *xsl-pattern*: if a node matching the *xsl-pattern* is deleted,
- ON INSERT OF *xsl-pattern*: if a node matching the *xsl-pattern* is inserted,
- ON MODIFICATION OF *xsl-pattern*: if anything in the subtree is modified,
- ON UPDATE OF *xsl-pattern*: the value (text or attribute) of a node matching the *xsl-pattern* is modified,
- ON INSERT INTO *xsl-pattern*: if a node is inserted (directly) into a node matching the *xsl-pattern*,
- ON INSERT [IMMEDIATELY] BEFORE|AFTER *xsl-pattern*: if a node is inserted (immediately) before or after a node matching the *xsl-pattern*.

All triggers should make relevant values accessible, e.g., OLD AS ... and NEW AS ... (like in SQL), both referencing the complete node to which the event happened, additionally INSERTED AS, DELETED AS referencing the inserted or deleted node.

Similar to the SQL STATEMENT and ROW triggers, the granularity has to be specified for each trigger; the following granularities are proposed here:

- FOR EACH STATEMENT (as in SQL),
- FOR EACH NODE: for each node in the *xsl-pattern*, the rule is triggered only at most once (cumulative, if the node is actually concerned by several matching events) per transaction,
- FOR EACH MODIFICATION: each individual modification (possibly for some nodes in the *xsl-pattern* more than one) triggers the rule.

For data-dependent information propagation, mainly FOR EACH NODE and FOR EACH MODIFICATION are adequate.

The implementation of such triggers in XML repositories is probably to be based on the *DOM Level 2/3 Events* [17].

RDF. RDF triples, describing properties/values of a resource are much more similar to SQL. In contrast to XML, there is no assignment of data with subtrees (which makes it impossible to express "deep" modifications in a simple event; such things have then to be expressed in the condition part). A proposal can e.g. be found in [49]. The following proposal has been developed in [2]:

- ON DELETE OF *property* [OF *class*],
- ON INSERT OF *property* [OF *class*],
- ON UPDATE OF *property* [OF *class*].

If a property is removed from/added to/updated of a resource of a given class, then the event is raised.

Additionally,

 – ON CREATE OF *class* is raised if a new resource of a given class is created.

Probably, also metadata changes have to be detected:

 – ON NEW CLASS is raised if a new class is introduced,
 – ON NEW PROPERTY [OF CLASS *class*] is raised, if a new property (optionally: to a specified class) is introduced.

All triggers should make relevant values accessible, e.g., OLD AS ... and NEW AS ... (like in SQL), both referencing the original/new value of the property, RESOURCE AS ... and PROPERTY AS ... refer to the modified resource and the property (as URIs), respectively.
Trigger granularity is FOR EACH STATEMENT or FOR EACH TRIPLE.

5.6   Local and Global ECA Rules

While "triggers" are restricted, programming-language concepts, general ECA rules provide an abstract concept using an own language. Especially in our setting, they are usually separated from the database. Thus, they do not react on "physical" events in the database, but on *logical* events (that nevertheless are actually raised by events in a database).

Local ECA Rules. Local ECA rules are more general than triggers. They still react on local events only, but they use an own event language that is based on a set of atomic events (that are not necessarily simple update operations) and that usually also allows for composite events. Their event detection mechanism is not necessarily located in the database. Detection of atomic logical events can be based on

 – database triggers that generate events that are visible/detectable outside the database, or
 – they have to poll the database regularly if such an event occurred.

Global ECA Rules. Global ECA rules have to be used if a composite event consists of subevents at different locations (or if the source of an event is not able to process local rules). When considering global rules in the Web and in the Semantic Web, the local ECA concept has to be extended stepwise:

 – "distributed" variants of the above local ECA rules, with events that explicitly mention a database/node where the event is located (e.g., "change of *xpath-expr* at *url*"),
 – rules that react on events in a set of known databases (e.g., "when a new researcher is added at one of the participants nodes" (which itself is a dynamic set)),
 – high-level rules of an application, that are not based on schema knowledge of individual databases, often even not explicitly on a given database (e.g.,

"when a publication p becomes known that deals with ...". Here, Semantic Web reasoning comes heavily into play even for detecting atomic events "somewhere in the Web". Such rules will probably be used in the "Travel Planning Scenario".

Requirements. The target of development and definition of languages for (ECA) rules, events, and actions in the Semantic Web should be a semantic approach, i.e., based on an (extendible) ontology for rules, events, and actions that also allows for reasoning about these concepts.

6   A Framework Proposal, Conclusions and Further Issues

Languages. For developing an ECA proposal for the Semantic Web, several languages with well-defined interfaces are needed. In [2], a preliminary framework for expressing ECA rules for the Semantic Web has been proposed.

ECA rules are marked up in the language that we will probably call ECA-ML (XML), or even formulated more abstractly in RDF, using an OWL ECA ontology. In general, the rules use sublanguages for describing *events* (metadata, including a contents part that contains the actual event), according to an *event ontology* (EventML), conditions (allowing to embed XQuery), and (trans)actions (embedding SOAP for service calls as atomic actions). A language for actual messages (XML, to be exchanged) is also needed.

An important principle here is to provide a *framework* that covers the *concepts* described above, not specific *languages* – there are multiple possible event, condition (query), and (trans)action languages. Thus, we propose a metamodel with a (basic) set of languages embedded in a modular concept of languages:

Rule Language. The rule language ECA-ML (namespace eca), provides rule elements with event, condition, and action subelements. These in turn contain subelements of event, condition, and action markup languages. The concrete language can be indicated as a language attribute (e.g., as a commonly known name, or as a URI where further information can be found).

Example 9. *Consider the* REWERSE *Personalized Portal scenario as described in [2]. The scenario consists of participants' nodes, working group nodes, and a central project node.*

The following rule propagates the change of a person's phone number from a participant's node to the information server of a working group. It reacts on a change of a phone number in the local database. If the person whose number changes, belongs to the working group (checked by an XPath query against the WG's database), the change is propagated to a remote server (by an explicit XQuery+Update statement against the WG's database):

```
<eca:rule>
  <variable name="WGUrl">http://...</variable>
  <eca:event>
    <evt:atomic>
      <change-of select="person//phone">
        <variable name="phone" select="."/>
        <variable name="person" select="$phone/ancestor::person"/>
      </change-of>
    </evt:atomic>
  </eca:event>
  <eca:condition language="XPath">
    $WGUrl//person[matches(name,$person/name)]
  </eca:condition>
  <eca:action language="XQuery+Updates">
    update $WGUrl
    set //person[matches(name,$person/name)]/phone := $phone
  </eca:action>
</eca:rule>
```

Event Language. The proposal contains a simple event language that allows to express terms in an event algebra. The basis are atomic events that can again be given in several languages. The generic approach proposes an XSL-style language for detecting changes in the local database (syntactic XML sugar to the trigger events in Section 5.5). The event language comprises constructs like <seq>, <disj>, <conj>, <forany> and <forall> with <variable> subelements, <cumulative> with appropriate switches, etc.

Condition Language. For condition languages, we propose to use existing languages like XPath, XQuery, RDQL, Xcerpt etc.

Action Language. The proposal contains a simple action language that allows to express composite actions. The basis are atomic actions that can again be given in several languages (e.g., XUpdate, XQuery+Update, XChange, or SOAP calls). The action language comprises constructs like <seq>, <conj>, <if test="..."> and <while test="..."> with appropriate switches, and <forall> with <variable> subelements, providing similar constructs as for CCS process specifications.

Implementation Issues. The modular design of the languages must be mirrored in a modular design of the architecture. For providing composability, the modules must adhere to standardized interfaces. The overall architecture must provide addressing and coupling mechanisms for addressing modules and services that implement concrete languages over the Web.

Conclusion. Research in Evolution and Reactivity for the Semantic Web requires a profound knowledge of existing concepts, logics, and formal methods in the areas of (active and distributed) databases, software engineering, and Web technology such as semistructured data and communication mechanisms.

Further Issues. Due to the restricted space (and time), a lot of issues has not been discussed here: evolution at the level of RDF/OWL, evolution of rules of knowledge bases and behavioral rules, evolution in communities of peers, and super-peers and concepts from agent and multi-agent systems.

References

1. J. J. Alferes, J. Bailey, M. Berndtsson, F. Bry, J. Dietrich, A. Kozlenkov, W. May, P. L. Pătrânjan, A. Pinto, M. Schroeder, and G. Wagner. State-of-the-art on evolution and reactivity. Technical Report IST506779/Lisbon/I5-D1/D/PU/a1, REWERSE, September 2004.
2. J. J. Alferes, M. Berndtsson, F. Bry, M. Eckert, N. Henze, W. May, P. L. Pătrânjan, and M. Schroeder. Use-cases on evolution. Technical Report IST506779/Lisbon/I5-D2/D/PU/a1, REWERSE, September 2004.
3. James Bailey, Alexandra Poulovassilis, and Peter T. Wood. An event-condition-action language for XML. In *Int. WWW Conference*, 2002.
4. C. Baral, M. Gelfond, and Alessandro Provetti. Representing actions: Laws, observations and hypotheses. *Journal of Logic Programming*, 31(1–3):201–243, April–June 1997.
5. M. Ben-Ari, Z. Manna, and A. Pnueli. The temporal logic of branching time. In *8th Annual ACM Symp. on Principles of Programming Languages*, 1981.
6. J. A. Bergstra and J. W. Klop. Algebra of communicating processes with abstraction. *Theoretical Computer Science*, 1(37):77–121, 1985.
7. Angela Bonifati, Daniele Braga, Alessandro Campi, and Stefano Ceri. Active XQuery. In *Intl. Conference on Data Engineering (ICDE)*, pages 403–418, San Jose, California, 2002.
8. A. J. Bonner and M. Kifer. An overview of transaction logic. *Theoretical Computer Science*, 133(2):205–265, 1994.
9. A. J. Bonner and M. Kifer. Concurrency and communication in transaction logic. In *ICDT'95: Advances in Logic-Based Languages*, 1995.
10. François Bry and Sebastian Schaffert. Towards a declarative query and transformation language for XML and semistructured data: Simulation unification. In *Intl. Conf. on Logic Programming (ICLP)*, number 2401 in LNCS, pages 255–270, 2002.
11. François Bry, Paula Lavinia Pătrânjan, and Sebastian Schaffert. Xcerpt and XChange: Deductive Languages for Data Retrieval and Evolution on the Web. In *Proc. of Workshop on Semantic Web Services and Dynamic Networks, Ulm, Germany, (22nd – 24th September 2004)*. GI, 2004.
12. François Bry and Sebastian Schaffert. Querying the Web Reconsidered: A Practical Introduction to Xcerpt. In *Proc. of Extreme Markup Languages 2004, Montreal, Quebec, Canada, (2nd – 6th August 2004)*, 2004.
13. S. Chakravarthy, V. Krishnaprasad, E. Anwar, and S.-K. Kim. Composite events for active databases: Semantics, contexts and detection. In *Proceedings of the 20th VLDB*, pages 606–617, 1994.
14. Jianjun Chen, David J. deWitt, Feng Tian, and Yuang Wang. NiagaraCQ: A scalable continuous query system for internet databases. In *ACM Intl. Conference on Management of Data (SIGMOD)*, pages 379–390, 2000.

15. Jan Chomicki. Efficient checking of temporal integrity constraints using bounded history encoding. *ACM Transactions on Database Systems (TODS)*, 20(2):149–186, 1995.

16. E. M. Clarke and E. A. Emerson. Design and synthesis of synchronization skeletons using branching time temporal logic. In *Proc. of the IBM Workshop on Logics of Programs*, number 131 in Lecture Notes in Computer Science, 1981.

17. Document object model (DOM). http://www.w3.org/DOM/, 1998.

18. Thomas Eiter, Wolfgang Faber, Nicola Leone, Gerald Pfeifer, and Axel Polleres. A Logic Programming Approach to Knowledge-State Planning: Semantics and Complexity. *ACM Transactions on Computational Logic*, 5(2):206–263, 2004.

19. Thomas Eiter, Wolfgang Faber, Gerald Pfeifer, and Axel Polleres. Declarative planning and knowledge representation in an action language. In Ioannis Vlahavas and Dimitris Vrakas, editors, *Intelligent Techniques for Planning*. Idea Group, Inc., 2004.

20. E. A. Emerson and C.-L. Lei. Modalities for model checking: Branching time strikes back. In *12th Annual ACM Symp. on Principles of Programming Languages*, 1985.

21. eXist: an Open Source Native XML Database. http://exist-db.org/.

22. D. Gabbay, A. Pnueli, S. Shelah, and J. Stavi. On the temporal analysis of fairness. In *ACM Symposium on Principles of Programming Languages*, pages 163–173, 1980.

23. Dov Gabbay. The declarative past, and imperative future: Executable temporal logic for interactive systems. In B. Banieqbal, B. Barringer, and A. Pnueli, editors, *Temporal Logic in Specification*, number 398 in Lecture Notes in Computer Science, pages 409–448. Springer, 1989.

24. M. Gelfond and V. Lifschitz. Representing actions and change by logic programs. *Journal of Logic Programming*, 17:301–322, 1993.

25. M. Gelfond and V. Lifschitz. Action languages. *Electronic Transactions on Artificial Intelligence*, 2(3-4):193–210, 1998.

26. E. Giunchiglia, G. Kartha, and V. Lifschitz. Representing actions: Indeterminacy and ramifications. *Artificial Intelligence*, 95:409–443, 1997.

27. E. Giunchiglia, J. Lee, V. Lifschitz, N. Mc Cain, and H. Turner. Representing actions in logic programs and default theories: a situation calculus approach. *Journal of Logic Programming*, 31:245–298, 1997.

28. E. Giunchiglia, J. Lee, V. Lifschitz, N. McCain, and H. Turner. Nonmonotonic causal theories. *Artificial Intelligence*, 153:49–104, 2004.

29. E. Giunchiglia and V. Lifschitz. An action language based on causal explanation: Preliminary report. In *AAAI'98*, pages 623–630, 1998.

30. Y. Gurevich. Logic and the challenge of computer science. In *Current Trends in Theoretical Computer Science*, pages 1–57. Computer Science Press, 1988.

31. Y. Gurevich. Evolving algebras 1993: Lipari guide. In E. Börger, editor, *Specification and Validation Methods*, pages 9–36. Oxford University Press, 1995.

32. D. Harel. *First-Order Dynamic Logic*. Number 68 in Lecture Notes in Computer Science. Springer, 1979.

33. D. Harel. Dynamic Logic. In D. Gabbay and F. Guenther, editors, *Handbook of Philosophical Logic, Volume II - Extensions of Classical Logic*, pages 497–604. Reidel Publishing Company, 1984.

34. D. Harel, D. Kozen, and R. Parikh. Process Logic: Expressiveness, decidability, completeness. *Journal of Computer and System Sciences*, 25(2):144–170, 1982.

35. C.A.R. Hoare. *Communicating Sequential Processes*. Prentice Hall, 1985.

36. David B. Kemp, Kotagiri Ramamohanarao, and Peter J. Stuckey. ELS Programs and the Efficient Evaluation of Non-Stratified Programs by Transformation to ELS. In Tok Wang Ling, Alberto O. Mendelzon, and Laurent Vieille, editors, *Intl. Conference on Deductive and Object-Oriented Databases (DOOD)*, number 1013 in Lecture Notes in Computer Science, pages 91–108, Singapore, 1995. Springer.

37. L. Lamport. 'sometimes' is sometimes 'not never'. In *7th Annual ACM Symp. on Principles of Programming Languages*, 1980.

38. Georg Lausen, Bertram Ludäscher, and Wolfgang May. On logical foundations of active databases. In Jan Chomicki and Gunter Saake, editors, *Logics for Databases and Information Systems*, chapter 12, pages 389–422. Kluwer Academic Publishers, 1998.

39. Patrick Lehti. Design and Implementation of a Data Manipulation Processor for an XML Query Language (diploma thesis), August 2001. Technische Universität Darmstadt.

40. H.J. Levesque, R. Reiter, Y. Lesprance, F. Lin, and R. Scherl. Golog: A logic programming language for dynamic domains. *Journal of Logic Programming*, 31:59–83, 1997.

41. J. Lobo, R. Bhatia, and S.Naqvi. A policy description language. In *National Conference on Artificial Intelligence (AAAI)*, 1999.

42. Wolfgang May, José Júlio Alferes, and François Bry. Towards generic query, update, and event languages for the Semantic Web. In *Principles and Practice of Semantic Web Reasoning (PPSWR)*, number 3208 in Lecture Notes in Computer Science, pages 19–33. Springer, 2004.

43. John McCarthy. *Formalizing Common Sense*. Ablex, Norwood, 1990.

44. John McCarthy and P. J. Hayes. Some philosophical problems from the standpoint of artificial intelligence. *Machine Intelligence*, 4, 1969.

45. R. Milner. Calculi for synchrony and asynchrony. *Theoretical Computer Science*, 25:267–310, 1983.

46. R. Milner. *Communication and Concurrency*. Prentice-Hall, 1989.

47. R. Milner. Operational and algebraic semantics of concurrent processes. In J. v. Leeuwen, editor, *Handbook of Theoretical Computer Science*, volume B: Formal Models and Semantics, chapter 19, pages 1201–1242. Elsevier, 1990.

48. R. Milner, J. Parrow, and D. Walker. A calculus of mobile processes. *Information and Computation*, 1(100):1–77, 1992.

49. George Papamarkos, Alexandra Poulovassilis, and Peter T. Wood. Event-condition-action rule languages for the semantic web. In *Workshop on Semantic Web and Databases (SWDB'03)*, 2003.

50. E. Pednault. Exploring the middle ground between STRIPS and the Situation Calculus. In *Proc. of the 1st International Conference on Principles of Knowledge Representation and Reasoning (KR'89)*, pages 324–332. Morgan Kaufmann Publishers Inc., 1989.

51. G. Plotkin. A structured approach to operational semantics. Technical Report DAIMI FN-19, Aarhus University, 1981.

52. V. R. Pratt. Semantical considerations on Floyd-Hoare Logic. In *17.th IEEE Symp. on Foundations of Computer Science*, pages 109–121, 1976.

53. R. Reiter. Proving properties of states in the situation calculus. *Artificial Intelligence*, 64(2):337–351, 1993.

54. E. Sandewall. *Features and Fluents: A Systematic Approach to the Representation of Knowledge about Dynamical Systems*. Oxford University Press, 1994.

55. Munindar P. Singh. Semantical considerations on workflows: An algebra for intertask dependencies. In *Intl. Workshop on Database Programming Languages*, electronic Workshops in Computing, Gubbio, Italy, 1995. Springer.

56. A. Prasad Sistla and Ouri Wolfson. Temporal Conditions and Integrity Constraints in Active Database Systems. In *Proceedings ACM SIGMOD International Conference on Management of Data (SIGMOD 1995)*, pages 269–280, 1995.

57. T. Son and C. Baral. Formalizing sensing actions - a transition function based approach. *Artificial Intelligence*, 125(1-2):19–91, 2001.

58. C. Stirling. Temporal logics for CCS. In *Linear Time, Branching Time and Partial Order in Logics and Models of Concurrency*, number 354 in Lecture Notes in Computer Science, pages 660–672. Springer, 1989.

59. Igor Tatarinov, Zachary G. Ives, Alon Halevy, and Daniel Weld. Updating XML. In *ACM Intl. Conference on Management of Data (SIGMOD)*, pages 133–154, 2001.

60. Feng Tian, Berthold Reinwald, Hamid Pirahesh, Tobias Mayr, and Jussi Myllymaki. Implementing a scalable XML publish/subscribe system using relational database systems. In *ACM Intl. Conference on Management of Data (SIGMOD)*, 2004.

61. J. van Benthem and J. Bergstra. Logic of transition systems. *Journal of Logic, Language, and Information*, 3:247–283, 1995.

62. World Wide Web Consortium, http://www.w3.org/TR/xpath. *XML Path Language (XPath)*, Nov 1999.

63. World Wide Web Consortium, http://www.w3.org/TR/xquery/. *XQuery: A Query Language for XML*, Feb 2001.

64. XML:DB Initiative, http://xmldb-org.sourceforge.net/. *XUpdate - XML Update Language*, September 2000.

65. Carlo Zaniolo. A unified semantics for active and deductive databases. In N. W. Paton and M. W. Williams, editors, *Proceedings of the 1st International Workshop on Rules in Database Systems*, Workshops in Computing, pages 271–287. Springer-Verlag, 1994. ISBN 3-540-19846-6.

Personalization for the Semantic Web[*]

Matteo Baldoni[1], Cristina Baroglio[1], and Nicola Henze[2]

[1] Dipartimento di Informatica, Università degli Studi di Torino,
c.so Svizzera 185, I-10149, Torino, Italy
{baldoni, baroglio}@di.unito.it
[2] ISI - Semantic Web Group, University of Hannover,
Appelstr. 4, D-30167 Hannover, Germany
henze@kbs.uni-hannover.de

Abstract. Searching for the meaning of the word "personalization" on a popular search engine, one finds twenty-three different answers, including *"the process of matching categorized content with different end users based on business rules ... upon page request to a Webserver"*, *"using continually adjusted user profiles to match content or services to individuals"*, and also *"real-time tailoring of displays, particularly Web pages, to a specific customer's known preferences, such as previous purchases"*. A little more generally, personalization is a process by which it is possible to give the user optimal support in accessing, retrieving, and storing information, where solutions are built so as to fit the preferences, the characteristics and the taste of the individual. This result can be achieved only by exploiting machine-interpretable semantic information, e.g. about the possible resources, about the user him/herself, about the context, about the goal of the interaction. Personalization is realized by an inferencing process applied to the semantic information, which can be carried out in many different ways depending on the specific task. The objective of this paper is to provide a coherent introduction into issues and methods for realizing personalization in the Semantic Web.

1   Introduction

Personalized information systems aim at giving the individual user optimal support in accessing, retrieving, and storing information. The individual requirements of the user are to be taken into account in such different dimensions like the current task, the goal of the user, the context in which the user is requesting the information, the previous information requests or interactions, the working process s/he is involved in, the level of expertise, the device s/he is using to

---

[*] This research has partially been funded by the European Commission and by the Swiss Federal Office for Education and Science within the 6th Framework Programme project REWERSE number 506779 (cf. http://rewerse.net). Matteo Baldoni and Cristina Baroglio have also been supported by MIUR Cofin 2003 "Logic-based development and verification of multi-agent systems (MASSiVE)" national project.

N. Eisinger and J. Małuszyński (Eds.): Reasoning Web 2005, LNCS 3564, pp. 173–212, 2005.

display the information, the bandwidth and availability of the communication channel, the abilities (disabilities or handicaps) of the user, his/her time constraints, and many, many more. Different research disciplines have contributed to explore personalization techniques and to evaluate their usefulness within various application areas: E.g. hypertext research has studied personalization in the area of so-called adaptive hypertext systems, collaborative filtering research has investigated recommender systems, artificial intelligence techniques have been widely used to cluster Web data, usage data, and user data, reasoning and uncertainty management has been adopted to draw conclusions on appropriate system behavior, and so forth.

Many attempts have been done to apply personalization techniques to the *World Wide Web* as a natural extension of work on hypertext and hypermedia, however, the Web is an information space thought for human to human communication, while personalization requires software systems (broadly speaking "machines") to take part to the interaction and help. Such systems require *knowledge* to be expressed in a machine-interpretable format, which in the Web is not available. The development of languages for expressing information in a machine-processable form is characteristic of the *Semantic Web* initiative, as Tim Berners-Lee pointed out since 1998. Over this knowledge layer, the use of *inferencing mechanisms* is envisioned as a fundamental means for performing a content-aware navigation, producing an overall behavior that is closer to the user's intuition and desire. This is the reason why the Semantic Web is the most appropriate environment for realizing personalization. In other words, the Semantic Web is *deeply connected* to the idea of personalization in its very nature.

In the following we will see how the notion of personalization applies to the Semantic Web, overview the expectations, the mechanisms, the languages and tools, and set the state of the art. The paper is organized as follows. Section 2 introduces personalization as the key feature of the Semantic Web. Section 3 reports the state of the art in personalized Web systems, mainly based on the concept of "user model". Section 4 explains how WWW adaptive systems can take advantage of the Semantic Web. Conclusions follow.

2   Demands of Personalization in the (Semantic) Web

The objective of the Semantic Web is a content-aware navigation and fruition of the resources. This means being able, by means of proper mechanisms, to identify those resources that better satisfy the requests not only on the basis of descriptive keywords but also on the basis of *knowledge*. There is, in fact, a general agreement that the use of knowledge increases the precision of the answers. Such a knowledge, as we will see, represents different things, information about the user, the user's intentions, the context. One of the key features that characterize the Semantic Web is that its answers are always personalized or adapted so to meet specific requirements. It will not be the case that the answer to a query about "book" will contain links to bookshops and links to travel agencies. This Web of knowledge is currently being built on top of the more traditional World Wide Web and requires the definition of proper languages and mechanisms. Let us now introduce a few basic concepts.

The first key concept is that of *user model*, that is a machine-interpretable representation of knowledge about the user. The user model, however, may contain different kinds of information; depending on what the user model contains, different reasoning technique might be necessary. Often the user model contains general information, e.g. age and education. In this case, in the tradition of works on personalization, the adaptation occurs at the level of information selection and, especially, presentation. Different users better understand different ways of explaining things. Choosing the best possible communication pattern is fundamental in application systems that supply a kind of information which, because of its nature, might be difficult to understand but that it is important for the user to comprehend. Think, for example, to health-care systems, where medical information is supplied to persons of different age and education. In order for this kind of task to be executed, it is necessary to enrich the data sources and the data itself with semantic information. To this aim, one of the greatest difficulties is to define adequate ontologies.

More and more frequently, however, the Semantic Web is not seen as an information provider but as a *service provider*. This is actually in the line with the latest view of the World Wide Web as a platform for sharing resources and services. We can divide services in two families: "world services" and "web services". A world service is, for instance, a shop, a museum, a restaurant, whose address, type and description is accessible over the Web. A Web service, instead, is a resource, typically a software device, that can be automatically retrieved and invoked over the Web, possibly by another service.

To begin with, let us consider services of the former kind, world services. The scenarios in which these services are considered adopt user models, in which a different kind of information is considered: the location of the user, which is supposed to vary along time. Typically this information is *not* supplied by the user but it is obtained by the system in a way that is transparent to him/her. In the simplest case, the user (a tourist or a person who is abroad for work) describes in a qualitative way a service of interest, as done with the regular Web browsers. The answer, however, contains only information about world services that are located nearby. The scenario can be made more complex if one adds the time dimension. In this case the user is not necessarily interested in a service that is available now, the system is requested to store the user's desire and alert the user whenever a matching event occurs, that refers to a service that is nearby. As an example, consider a user who loves classical ballet. He is traveling, and has just arrived at Moscow. After a couple of days he receives an SMS informing him that in the weekend Romeo and Juliet is going to be held at the Boljsoi Theater and that tickets are available. Notice that besides a different kind of information contained in the user model, also the mechanism by which personalization is obtained is very different from the previous case: here the answer changes according to the *context*, in this case given by the position of the user in space and time, and the answer is not always immediately subsequent the query. As we have seen, in fact, a *triggering mechanism* is envisioned that alerts the user whenever an event that satisfies the description occurs. The word "triggering mechanism" makes one think of a sort of reactive system, nevertheless, many alternatives might be explored and, in particular, inference mechanisms. Moreover, this approach is suitable also to a very different application domain, such as *ambient intelligence*, where appliances are the world services to be handled.

Strongly related to these topics, the recent success of decentralized applications has caused a growing attention towards decentralized approaches to user modeling. In this framework, the target applications include personal guides for navigation or ambient devices, integrated Web-sites (e.g. newspapers), portals (e.g. Yahoo), e-commerce Web-sites (e.g. Amazon), or recommender sites (e.g. MovieLens). In ubiquitous environments distributed sensors follow a user's moves and, based on the tasks typically performed by him/her, on preferences induced from history and on the specific characteristics of the given context, perform adaptation steps to the ambient-dependent features of the supported functionalities.

As a last observation, when the answer is time-delayed, as described, the descriptions of the services (or more in general, of the events) of interest are sometimes considered as part of the user model. In this case the user model does not contain general information about the user but a more specific kind of information. Alternatively, this can be seen as a configuration problem: I configure a personalized assistant that will warn me when necessary. It is interesting to observe that no-one considers these as queries. An example application is a personalized agenda: the idea is to use an automatic configuration system for filling the agenda of a tourist, taking into account his/her preferences and the advertisements of cultural events in the visited area as they are published. Indeed, filling the agenda could be considered as the topmost level of a system that also retrieves services triggered by events and biased by the user's location. This kind of systems should perform also personalization w.r.t. the device by which the user interacts with the system (mobile, laptop).

Many scenarios that refer to world services could naturally be extended so as to include *Web services*. In this case, the meaning of localization should be revised, if at all applicable, while the idea of combining services, as proposed in the case of the tourist agenda, should be explored with greater attention; Web service automatic composition is, actually, quite a hot topic as research in the field proves [20, 5]. Both, Web-service-based and ubiquitous computing, applications can be considered as conglomerates of independent, autonomous services developed by independent parties. Such components are not integrated at design time, they are integrated dynamically at run-time, according to the current needs. A frequently used metaphor is a free-market of services where the user buys a complex service, that is composed dynamically on the basis of the available (smaller) services. For example, an e-learning course can be assembled dynamically by composing learning objects stored in independent repositories. The composition is performed so as to satisfy the specific characteristics of the student. For instance, a vision-impaired student will be returned audio materials.

Another, orthogonal, case is the one in which the user model contains (or is accompanied by) the description of what the user would like to *achieve*. There are situations in which this description cannot be directly related to specific resources or services, but it is possible to identify (or compose) a set of resources so as to satisfy the user's *desires*. In this case a planning process is to be enacted. Sometimes besides the planning process other reasoning techniques are envisioned in order to supply a more complete support to the user. An application domain in which the goal-driven approach seems particularly promising is, once again, *e-learning*. In this case the goal is the learning goal of the user, that is to say a high-level description of the knowledge that s/he would like to acquire, and the plan contains the learning resources that the user should use for acquiring the desired expertise. The whole interaction with the user is supposed to be carried on through a browser. It is important to remark that students are not the only kind of users of this sort of systems. Also teachers should access them but with a different aim. For instance, a teacher might look for learning resources for a new course that s/he will teach. A new notion is, then, introduced, that of *role*. Not only user models contain general or specific information about the users' interests but they also contain the role that the user plays. Depending on the role, different views might be supplied by the system (personalization at the level of presentation) and different actions might be allowed. Rather than being just one of the many features from a user model, the role could, actually, be considered as orthogonal to it (the role is independent from the specific user). Beyond e-learning, the concept of role is useful in many application domains. In health care, there are patients and there are doctors and nurses. In tourism, there are tourists and there are travel agencies.

Another basic concept is that of *domain knowledge*. For understanding the meaning of this word, let us consider the intuitive application case of e-learning. Here the system needs to be supplied with a body of knowledge that not only contains the semantic description of the single learning resources, but it also contains definitions of *more abstract* concepts, not directly related to the courses and defined on the basis of other concepts. This knowledge is used to bias the construction of solutions that make sense from a *pedagogical* point of view. The use of a knowledge of this kind might be exported also to other application domains, whenever similar reasoning techniques are adopted.

Summarizing, the goal of personalization in the Semantic Web is to make easier the access to the right resources. This task entails two orthogonal processes: *retrieval* and *presentation*. Retrieval consists in finding or constructing the right resources when they are needed, either on demand or (as by the use of automatic updates) when the information arises in the network. Once the resources have been defined they are presented in the most suitable way to the user, taking into account his/her own characteristics and preferences. To these aims it is necessary to have a model of the user, that is, a representation of those characteristics according to which personalization will occur. It is also necessary to apply inferencing techniques which, depending on the task, might range from the basic ontology reasoning mechanisms supplied by Description Logics (like subsumption and classification) to the most various reasoning techniques developed in Artificial Intelligence.

3   Personalization in the World Wide Web

Personalization in the World Wide Web can be compared to creating individual views on Web data according to the special interests, needs, requirements, goals, access-context, etc. of the current beholder. The ideas and solutions for creating these individual views are manifold and require interdisciplinary engagement: human computer interaction specialists, e.g. for creating meaningful user interfaces with good usability rankings; artificial intelligence experts, e.g. for mining Web data, or for creating dynamic and accurate models of users; and software engineers for creating generic infrastructure for maintaining personalized views on Web data, and for sufficient user interaction support.

In this article, we focus on those aspects of personalization which aim at improving the selection, access and retrieval of Web resources. The creation of appropriate user interfaces and user awareness is out of scope of this article.

Definition 1 (Personalizing the access to Web data). *Personalizing the access to Web data defines the process of supporting the individual user in finding, selecting, accessing, and retrieving Web resources (or meaningful sub-sets of this process).*

With this definition, we can more precisely say that the process of personalization is a process of *filtering the access* to Web content *according to the individual needs and requirements of each particular user*. We can distinguish two different classes of filters: those filter which have been created for a certain *hypermedia system*, and those, which have been created for a *network of Web resources*. The difference between these filters is in the way how they treat the underlying document space: if they have precise information on the structure and relations between the documents (this means the hypertext system), or whether they use dynamics and networking effects in the Web in order to provide individual views on Web data.

The first class of filters has been investigated since the beginnings of the nineties of the last century under the topic of *Adaptive Hypermedia Systems*. The second belongs to *Web Mining* techniques, both Web usage and Web content mining. The personalized systems based on Web mining are often called *recommender systems*, which are in focus of research since the mid-nineties of the last century.

In the following, we describe techniques and methods for personalization in the field of adaptive hypermedia (see Section 3.1), and Web mining (see Section 3.2). Afterwards, we will summarize approaches to user modeling.

3.1   Adaptive Hypermedia Systems

An *adaptive hypermedia system* enlarges the functionality of a hypermedia system. It *personalizes* a hypermedia systems for the individual users: Each user has her or his individual view and individual navigational possibilities for working with the hypermedia system. A general definition of hypertext / hypermedia is given in [58]:

Definition 2 (Hypertext). *A set of nodes of text which are connected by links. Each node contains some amount of information (text) and a number of links to other nodes.*

Definition 3 (Hypermedia). *Extension of hypertext which makes use of multiple forms of media, such as text, video, audio, graphics, etc.*

Discussions on the definitions of hypertext can be found for example in [24, 47]. The terms hypertext and hypermedia are often synonymous [47]. Throughout this text, we use the term *hypermedia*. For a general, functionality-oriented definition of adaptive hypermedia systems, we follow the proposal of P. Brusilovsky [17].

Definition 4 (Adaptive hypermedia system). *"By adaptive hypermedia systems we mean all hypertext and hypermedia systems which reflect some features of the user in the user model and apply this model to adapt various visible aspects of the system to the user."*

The support of adaptive methods in hypermedia systems is advantageous if there is *one* common system which serves *many* users with *different* goals, knowledge, and experience, *and* if the underlying hyperspace is relatively *large* [17]. Adaptation of hypermedia systems is also an attempt to overcome the "lost in hyperspace problem" (for a discussion, see for example [47]). The user's goals and knowledge can be used for limiting the number of available links in a hypermedia system.

Techniques in Adaptive Hypermedia. As we have explained, a hypermedia system consists of documents which are connected by links. Thus, there are generally two aspects which can be adapted to the users: the *content* and the links. Let us begin with *content level adaptation*.

By adapting the content to a user, the document is tailored to the needs of the user, for example by hiding too specialized information or by inserting some additional explanations. According to [17], we can identify the following methods for content level adaptation:

- *Additional explanations*: Only those parts of a document are displayed to a user which fit to his goals, interest, tasks, knowledge, etc.
- *Prerequisite explanations*: Here the user model checks the prerequisites necessary to understand the content of the page. If the user lacks to know some prerequisites, the corresponding information is integrated in the page.

- *Comparative explanations*: The idea of comparative explanations is to explain new topics by stressing their relations to known topics.
- *Explanation variants*: By providing different explanations for some parts of a document, those explanations can be selected which are most suited for the user. This extends the method of prerequisite explanations.
- *Sorting*: The different parts of a document are sorted according to their relevance for the user.

The following techniques are used for implementing the above stated adaptation methods [17]:

- *Conditional text*: Every kind of information about a knowledge concept is broken into text parts. For each of these text parts, the required knowledge for displaying it to the user is defined.
- *Stretch text*: Some keywords of a document can be replaced by longer descriptions if the user's actual knowledge requires that.
- *Page or page fragment variants*: Here, different variants of whole pages or parts of them are stored.
- *Frame based technique*: This technique stores page and fragment variants into concept frames. Each frame has some slots which present the page or page fragments in a special order. Certain rules decide which slot is presented to the user.

Content level adaptation requires sophisticated techniques for improved presentation. The current systems using content level adaptation do so by enriching their documents with meta information about prerequisite or required knowledge, outcome, etc. The documents or fragments contained in these systems have to be written more than once in order to obtain the different explanations.

Link Level Adaptation. By using link level adaptation, the user's possibilities to navigate through the hypermedia system are personalized. The following methods show examples for adaptive navigation support:

- *Direct guidance*: Guide the user sequentially through the hypermedia system. Two methods can be distinguished, "next best" and "page sequencing" (or "trails"). The former provides a next-button to navigate through the hypertext. The latter generates a reading sequence through the entire hypermedia or through some part of it.
- *Adaptive sorting*: Sort the links of a document due to their "relevance" to the user. The relevance of a link to the user is based on the system's assumptions about him/her. Some systems sort links depending on their similarity to the present page. Or by ordering them according to the required prerequisite knowledge. These methods are known as "similarity sorting" and "prerequisite knowledge sorting".
- *Adaptive hiding*: Limit the navigational possibilities by hiding links to irrelevant information. Hiding of links can be realized by making them unavailable or invisible.

- *Link annotation*: Annotate the links to give the user hints about the content of the pages they point to. The annotation might be text, coloring, an icon, or dimming. The most popular method for link annotation (in the educational area) is the so called "traffic light metaphor". Here the educational state of a link is estimated by the system with respect to the user's actual knowledge state. The link pointing to the page is then annotated by a colored ball. A *red* ball in front of a link indicates that the user lacks some knowledge for understanding the pages; thus the page is not recommended for reading. A *yellow* ball indicates links to pages that are not recommended for reading; this recommendation is less strict than in case of a red ball. A *green* ball is in front of links which lead to recommended pages. *Grey* balls give the hint that the content of the corresponding page is already known to the user. Variants in the coloring exist. A mix of traffic light metaphor and adaptive hiding is also used in some systems. For an evaluation about adaptive hiding and adaptive navigation we refer to [67].
- *Map annotation*: Here, graphical overviews or maps are adapted with some of the above mentioned methods.

Techniques for link level adaptation depend on the specific system and are, for example, discussed in [17]. Here the assumptions that the system makes about the user play an important role to decide what and how to adapt. Link level adaptation restricts the number of links and thus the number of navigational possibilities. It is useful to prevent the user from "getting lost in hyperspace". As in the case of content level adaptation, a description of the content of the documents is required for implementing the adaptation tasks.

Case Study: Adaptive Educational Hypermedia Systems. Adaptive educational hypermedia systems (AEHS) have been developed and tested in various disciplines and have proven their usefulness for improved and goal-oriented learning and teaching. In this section, we propose a component-based logical description of AEHS, in contrast to the functionality-oriented definition 4. This component-based definition is motivated by Reiter's theory of diagnosis [62] which settles on characterizing systems, observations, and diagnosis in first-order logic (FOL). We decompose adaptive educational hypermedia systems into basic components, according to their different roles: Each adaptive (educational) hypermedia system is obviously a hypermedia system, therefore it makes assumptions about documents and their relations in a *document space*. It uses a *user model* to model various characteristics of individual users or user groups. During runtime, it collects *observations* about the user's interactions. Based on the organization of the underlying document space, the information from the user model and from the system's observation, the *adaptive functionality* is provided.

In this section, we will give a logic-based definition for AEHS. We have chosen first order logic (FOL) as it allows us to provide an abstract, generalized formalization. The notation chosen in this paper refers to [64]. The aim of this logic-based definition is to accentuate the main characteristics and aspects of adaptive educational hypermedia.

Definition 5 (Adaptive Educational Hypermedia System (AEHS)). *An Adaptive Educational Hypermedia System (AEHS) is a Quadruple*

$$(DOCS, \ UM, \ OBS, \ AC)$$

with

DOCS: Document Space: *A finite set of first order logic (FOL) sentences with constants for describing documents (and knowledge topics), and predicates for defining relations between these constants.*

UM: User Model: *A finite set of FOL sentences with constants for describing individual users (user groups), and user characteristics, as well as predicates and rules for expressing whether a characteristic applies to a user.*

OBS: Observations: *A finite set of FOL sentences with constants for describing observations and predicates for relating users, documents/topics, and observations.*

AC: Adaptation Component: *A finite set of FOL sentences with rules for describing adaptive functionality.*

The components "document space" and "observations" describe basic data (DOCS) and run-time data (OBS). The user model and adaptation components process this data, e.g. for estimating a user's preferences (UM), or for deciding about beneficial adaptive functionalities for a user (AC). A collection of existing AEHS, described according to this logic-based formalism, is reported in [36, 35]. In these works a characterization is given of the systems belonging to the first generation of AEHS (e.g. Interbook [18]), to the second generation of adaptive educational hypermedia systems (e.g. NetCoach [71] and KBS Hyperbook [34]), as well as of a recent system, which is also an authoring framework for adaptive educational hypermedia (AHA!2.0 [15]).

To make an example, let us then describe by the above formalism an AEHS, called Simple, having the following functionality. Simple can annotate hypertext-links by using the traffic light metaphor with two colors: red for non recommended, green for recommended pages. Later, we will extend this system to demonstrate the use (and the usefulness) of a domain model in an AEHS. Simple can be modeled by a quadruple $(DOCS_s, UM_s, OBS_s, AC_s)$, whose elements are defined as follows:

– $DOCS_s$: This component is made of a set of n constants and a finite set of predicates. Each of the constants represents a document in the document space (the documents are denoted by $D_1, D_2, \ldots, D_n$). The predicates define pre-requisite conditions, i.e. they state which documents need to be studied before a document can be learned, e.g. $preq(D_i, D_j)$ for certain $D_i \neq D_j$ means that D_j is a prerequisite for D_i. N.B.: This AEHS does not employ an additional knowledge model.

– UM_s: it contains a set of m constants, one for each individual user $U_1, U_2, \ldots, U_m$.

– OBS_s: A special constant ($Visited$) is used within the special predicate obs to denote whether a document has been visited: $obs(D_i, U_j, Visited)$ is the observation that a document D_i has been visited by the user U_j.

– AC_s: This component contains constants and rules. One constant (*Recommended_for_reading*) is used for describing the values of the "learning_state" of the adaptive functionality, two constants (*Green_Icon* and *Red_Icon*) for representing values of the adaptive functionality. The learning state of a document is described by a set of rules of kind:

$$\forall U_i \forall D_j (\forall D_k preq(D_j, D_k) \Longrightarrow$$
$$obs(D_k, U_i, Visited)) \Longrightarrow$$
$$learning\_state(D_j, U_i, Recommended\_for\_reading)$$

This component contains also a set of rules for describing the adaptive link annotation with traffic lights. Such rules are of kind:

$$\forall U_i \forall D_j learning\_state(D_j, U_i, Recommended\_for\_reading)$$
$$\Longrightarrow document\_annotation(D_j, U_i, Green\_icon)$$

or of kind:

$$\forall U_i \forall D_j \neg learning\_state(D_j, U_i, Recommended\_for\_reading)$$
$$\Longrightarrow document\_annotation(D_j, U_i, Green\_icon)$$

We can extend this simple AEHS by using a *knowledge graph* instead of a domain graph. The system, called Simple1, is able to give a more differentiated traffic light annotation to hypertext links than Simple. It is able to recommend pages (green icon), to show which links lead to documents that will become understandable (dark orange icon), which might be understandable (yellow icon), or which are not recommended yet (red icon). As in the previous case, let us represent Simple1 by a quadruple $(DOCS_{s1}, UM_{s1}, OBS_{s1}, AC_{s1})$:

– $DOCS_{s1}$: The document space contains all axioms of the document space of Simple, $DOCS_s$, but it does not contain any of the predicates. In addition, it contains a set of s constants which name the knowledge topics $T_1, T_2, \ldots, T_s$ in the knowledge space. It also contains a finite set of predicates, stating the learning dependencies between these topics: $depends(T_j, T_k)$, with $T_j \neq T_k$, means that topic T_k is required to understand T_j.

The documents are characterized by predicate *keyword* which assigns a nonempty set of topics to each of them, so $\forall D_i \exists T_j keyword(D_i, T_j)$, but keep in mind that more than one keyword might be assigned to a same document.

– UM_{s1}: The user model is the same as in Simple, plus an additional rule which defines that a topic T_i is assumed to be learned whenever the corresponding document has been visited by the user. To this aim, Simple 1 uses the constant *Learned*.

The rule for processing the observation that a topic has been learned by a user is as follows (*p_obs* is the abbreviation for "processing an observation"):

$$\forall U_i \forall T_j (\exists D_k keyword(D_k, T_j) \wedge obs(D_k, U_i, Visited)$$
$$\Longrightarrow p\_obs(T_j, U_i, Learned)$$

- OBS_{s1}: Are the same as in Simple.
- AC_{s1}: The adaptation component of Simple1 contains two further constants (w.r.t. Simple), representing new values for the learning state of a document. Such constants are: *Might_be_understandable* and *Will_become_understandable* (the meaning is intuitive). Two more constants are added for representing new values for adaptive link annotation. They are: *Orange_Icon* and *Yellow_Icon*. Such constants appear in the rules that describe the *educational state* of a document, reported hereafter.

The first rule states that a document is recommended for learning if *all* the prerequisites to the keywords of this document have already been learnt:

$$\forall U_i \forall D_j (\forall T_k keyword(D_j, T_k) \implies$$
$$(\forall T_l depends(T_k, T_l) \implies p\_obs(T_l, U_i, Learned)$$
$$\implies learning\_state(D_j, U_i, Recommended\_for\_reading)))$$

The second rule states that a document might be understandable if at least some of the prerequisites have already been learnt by this user:

$$\forall U_i \forall D_j (\forall T_k keyword(D_j, T_k) \implies$$
$$(\exists T_l depends(T_k, T_l) \implies$$
$$p\_obs(T_l, U_i, Learned)$$
$$\wedge \neg learning\_state(D_j, U_i, Recommended\_for\_reading)$$
$$\implies learning\_state(D_j, U_i, Might\_be\_understandable)))$$

The third rule entails that a document will become understandable if the user has some prerequisite knowledge for at least one of the document's keywords:

$$\forall U_i \forall D_j (\exists T_k keyword(D_j, T_k) \implies$$
$$(\exists T_l depends(T_k, T_l) \implies$$
$$p\_obs(T_l, U_i, Learned)$$
$$\wedge \neg learning\_state(D_j, U_i, Might\_be\_understandable)$$
$$\implies learning\_state(D_j, U_i, Will\_become\_understandable)))$$

Four rules describe the adaptive link annotation:

1) $\forall U_i \forall D_j learning\_state(D_j, U_i, Recommended\_for\_reading)$
   $\implies document\_annotation(D_j, U_i, Green\_Icon)$
2) $\forall U_i \forall D_j learning\_state(D_j, U_i, Will\_become\_understandable)$
   $\implies document\_annotation(D_j, U_i, Orange\_Icon)$
3) $\forall U_i \forall D_j learning\_state(D_j, U_i, Might\_be\_understandable)$
   $\implies document\_annotation(D_j, U_i, Yellow\_Icon)$
4) $\forall U_i \forall D_j \neg learning\_state(D_j, U_i, Recommended\_for\_reading)$
   $\implies document\_annotation(D_j, U_i, Red\_Icon)$

Discussion: Why a logical characterization of adaptive (educational) hypermedia is needed. With Brusilovsky's definition of adaptive hypermedia, we can describe the general functionality of an *adaptive* hypermedia system, and we can compare which kind of adaptive functionality is offered by such a system.

In the literature, we can find reference models for adaptive hypermedia, e.g. the AHAM Reference Model [16], or the Munich Reference Model [43]. Both the AHAM and Munich Reference models extend the Dexter Hypertext Model [31], and provide a framework for describing the different components of adaptive hypermedia systems. In both cases, the focus is posed on process modeling and on the engineering of adaptive hypermedia applications, so we can say that these models are *process-oriented*.

However, a formal description of adaptive educational hypermedia, which allows for a system-independent characterization of the adaptive functionality, is still missing. Currently, we cannot answer a request like the following: "I want to apply the adaptive functionality X in my system. Tell me what information is required with the hypermedia-documents, which interactions at runtime need to be monitored, and what kind of user model information and user modeling is required". At the moment, we can only describe the functionality with respect to a *specific* environment, which means we can describe the functionality only in terms of the system that implements it. We cannot compare different implementations nor can we benchmark adaptive systems. A benchmark of adaptive systems would require at least a comparable initial situation, observations about a user's interactions with the system during some defined interaction period, before the *result* of the system is returned, the *adaptive functionality* as well as the changes in the user model.

The logical definition of adaptive educational hypermedia given here focuses on the components of these systems, and describes which kind of processing information is needed from the underlying hypermedia system (the document space), the runtime information which is required (observations), and the user model characteristics (user model). The adaptive functionality is then described by means of these three components, or more precisely: how the information from these three components, the static data from the document space, the runtime-data from the observations, and the processing-data from the user model, is used to provide the adaptive functionality. The aim of this logical definition of adaptive educational hypermedia is to provide a *language* for describing the adaptive functionality, to allow comparison of adaptive functionality in a well-grounded way, and to enable the re-use of an adaptive functionality in different contexts and systems.

There is, actually, a need for a formalism expressing adaptive functionalities in a system-independent and re-usable manner, which allows their application in various contexts. In the educational context, a typical scenario where re-usable adaptive functionality is required would be: Imagine a learner who wants to learn a specific subject. The learner registers to some learning repository, which stores learning objects. According to his/her current learning progress, some of the learning objects which teach the subject s/he is interested in are useful, some of them require additional knowledge that the learner does not have so far (in accordance to his/her user model), and some might teach the subject only on the surface and are too easy for this learner. This kind of situation has been studied in adaptive educational hypermedia in many applications, and with successful solutions. However, these solutions are specific to certain adaptive hypermedia applications, and are hardly generalizable for re-use in different applications. Another reason why the adaptive functionality is not re-usable today is related to the so-called *open corpus problem* in adaptive (educational) hypermedia [33, 19], which states that currently, adaptive applications work on a fixed set of documents which is defined at the design time of the system, and directly influences the way adaptation is implemented, e.g. that adaptive information like "required prerequisites" is coded on this fixed set of documents.

3.2   Web Mining

In contrast to the approach in adaptive hypermedia, personalization with aid of Web mining does not work on such well-defined corpora like a hypertext system. Instead, it uses effects and dynamics in the network structure in order to detect (virtual) relations between Web resources.

The World Wide Web is seen as the *Web graph*. In this graph, Web resources are the nodes, and links between the Web resources are the edges. NB: as it is practically impossible to create a complete snapshot of the World Wide Web at a certain time point, this Web graph is not a completely known structure. On the contrary, in the case of adaptive hypermedia systems, the underlying hypermedia graph models completely the hypertext.

The approaches in Web Mining-based personalization are centered around detecting relations between Web resources. These relations can be *existing relations*, this means hyperlinks between Web resources, or *virtual relations*, this means that two or more Web resources are related to each other but are not connected via some hyperlink. These existing or virtual relations between Web resources are *mined* on basis of the Web graph. We can distinguish two main approaches for detecting the relations: *Mining based on the content* of the Web resources, or *mining based on the usage* of the Web resources. The two approaches can of course be combined.

Normally, Web Mining-based personalization has no external models like domain or expert models, as those used in adaptive hypermedia, but instead create dynamic models which grow with the number of Web resources integrated into the model.

Recommendation Techniques for Web Mining. In the following, we summarize major recommendation techniques according to Burke [21]. We can distinguish between *content-based, collaborative, demographic, utility-based,* and *knowledge-based* recommendations. Let U and I be respectively a set of users and a set of items, and $\mathcal{U}$ denotes an individual user. Let us outline these techniques:

- *Content-based recommendation:*
  - each user is assumed to operate independently of other users;
  - recommendations can exploit information derived from document contents;

- The system builds user models in the following way: initially, users apply *candidate profiles* against their own preferences. For example, a candidate user profile for the rating of today's news article is presented, the user can accept or reject the ratings for the articles. The profile is maintained by exploiting keywords and content descriptors which contribute to the rating of each article.
- The quality of the learnt knowledge is measured against the classical measures of Information Retrieval, i.e. precision and recall (see e.g. [4]).
- The typical background consists of features of items in I, the typical input to the mining process consists of the user's ratings of some items in I. A learning process is enacted that generates a classifier fitting the user's preferences, expressed by the ratings. The constructed classifier is applied to all the items in I, for finding out which might be of interest.
- limitations:
  * as in all inductive approaches, items must be machine-parsable or with assigned attributes;
  * only recommendations based on what the user has already seen before (and indicated to like) can be taken into account but negative information is as well important;
  * stability vs. plasticity of recommendations;
  * no filtering based on quality, style, or point-of-view (only based on *content*;

- *Collaborative recommendations (social information filtering)*:
  - This technique is basically a process of "word-of-mouth", in fact the items are recommended to a user based upon values assigned by other people with *similar taste*. The underlying hypothesis is that people's tastes are not randomly distributed: there are general trends and patterns within the taste of a person as well as between groups of people. Also in this case a *user model* is to be built. To this aim the users are initially required to explicitly rank some sample objects.
  - The input used for computing the predictions is a set of "Ratings of *similar users*", where the similarity is measured on the basis of the user profile values.
  - The mining process begins with the identification of those users in U that result similar to $\sqcap$, and extrapolates the possible interests and likings of the user at issue from the ratings that similar users gave to items in I.
  - Limitations:
    * a critical mass of users is required before the system can make recommendations;
    * how to get the first rating of a new object?
    * stability vs. plasticity of recommendations.

Demographic recommendation, utility-based recommendation and knowledge-based recommendation are variants which require additional data about the user beyond rating of items:

- *Demographic recommendations*
  In this case, demographic information about all the users in U is exploited: similarly to the previous case, the users that are close to $\mathcal{U}$ are identified, but in this case similarity is computed on the demographic data. Then, the ratings of these users on items in I are used to produce recommendations to the user at issue.
- *Utility-based recommendations*
  In this case the preferences of $\mathcal{U}$ are coded by a *utility function*, which is applied to all the items in I for defining recommendations.
- *Knowledge-based recommendations*
  The knowledge-based approach to recommendation works on a description of the user's needs and on a body of knowledge that describes how items can meet various needs. An inferencing process is used to match the description of the user's needs with the items that can help the user and, thus, are to be recommended.

Case Study: Web Usage Mining in an Online Shop. In this case study, we will see how we can improve selling strategies in an artificial online shop. Our online shop sells a small variety of products. Our goal is to find out which items are commonly purchased together in order to make for example some selected frequent-customers special bundle-offers which are likely to be in their interest.

To detect relations between data items, the concept of *association rules* can be used. Association rules aim at detecting *uncovered relations* between data items, this means relationships which are not inherent in the data like functional dependencies, and normally do not necessarily represent a sort of causality or correlation between the items. A database in which an association rule is to be found is viewed as a set of tuples: each tuple contains a set of items; the items represent the items purchased, and the tuples denote the list of items purchased together. For a definition of association rules, we follow [26]:

Definition 6 (Association Rule). *Given a set of items* $I = \{I_1, I_2, \ldots, I_m\}$ *and a database of transactions* $D = \{t_1, t_2, \ldots, t_n\}$ *where* $t_i = \{I_{i1}, I_{i2}, \ldots I_{ik}\}$ *and* $I_{ij} \in I$, *an* **association rule** *is an implication of the form* $X \Longrightarrow Y$, *where* $X, Y \subset I$ *are sets of items classed* itemsets *and* $X \cap Y = \emptyset$.

To identify the "important" association rules, the two measures *support* and *confidence* are used (see [26]):

Definition 7 (Support). *The* **support** *(s) for an association rule* $X \Longrightarrow Y$ *is the percentage of transactions in the database that contain* $X \cup Y$.

$$\mathbf{support}(X \Longrightarrow Y) = \frac{|\{t_i \in D : X \cup Y \subset t_i\}|}{|D|}$$

Definition 8 (Confidence / Strength). *The* **confidence** *or* **strength** *(α) for an association rule* $X \Longrightarrow Y$ *is the ratio of the number of transactions that contain* $X \cup Y$ *to the number of transactions that contain* X.

$$\mathbf{confidence}(X \Longrightarrow Y) = \frac{|\{t_i \in D : X \cup Y \subset t_i\}|}{|\{t_i \in D : X \subset t_i\}|}$$

The support measures how often the rule occurs in the database, while the confidence measures the strength of a rule. Typically, large confidence values and smaller support values are used, and association rules are mined which satisfy at least a *minimum support* and a *minimum confidence*.

The hard part in the association rule mining process is to detect the high-support (or *frequent*) item-sets. Computationally less costly is then the checking of the confidence. Algorithms for uncovering frequent item-sets exist in the literature [26], most prominent is the Apriori-algorithm [1], which uses the property of frequent itemsets that all subset of a frequent itemset must be frequent, too.

Example: An online Book Shop This (artificial) online book shop sells five different books: Semantic Web, Winnie the Pooh, Data Mining, Faust, and Modern Statistics.

Transaction	Items
t1	Semantic Web, Winnie the Pooh, Data Mining
t2	Semantic Web, Data Mining
t3	Semantic Web, Faust, Data Mining
t4	Modern Statistics, Semantic Web
t5	Modern Statistics, Faust

Customer X is a very good customer, and to tighten the relationship to customer X, we want to make a personal and attractive offer. We see him ordering a book on "Semantic Web". Which bundle offer might be interesting for him? Which book shall we offer to a reduced price: Winnie the Pooh, Data Mining, Faust, or Modern Statistics? We are looking for association rules which have a minimum-support of 30% and a confidence of 50%. The association rules we are interested in are thus :

Semantic Web $\Longrightarrow$ **Data Mining** support: 60%, confidence: 75 %
Semantic Web $\Longrightarrow$ **Faust** support: 20%, confidence: 25%
Semantic Web $\Longrightarrow$ **Winnie the Pooh** support: 20%, confidence: 25 %
Semantic Web $\Longrightarrow$ **Modern Statistics** support: 20%, confidence: 25 %

An often seen pattern is that the books "Semantic Web" and "Data Mining" are bought together, and the association rule "Semantic Web $\Longrightarrow$ Data Mining" satisfies the minimum support of 30%. In 60% of the cases in which customers bought the book "Semantic Web", they also bought the book "Data Mining" (confidence: 60%). Thus, we decide to offer our valuable customer the book "Data Mining" in a personal offer for an attractive price.

NB: The general "association rule problem" is to mine association rules which satisfy a given support and confidence; in the above example, we simplify the approach by asking whether a certain item is obtained in some association rule.

3.3   User Modeling

In a user model, a system's estimations about the preferences, often performed tasks, interests, and so forth of a specific end user (or group of users) are specified (in the following, we will only refer to "the user" wherever a single user a sufficient homogeneous group of users can be meant). We can distinguish between the *user profile* and the *user model*. A *User profile* provides access to certain characteristics of a user. These characteristics are modeled as attributes of the user. Thus, a user profile of user $\mathcal{U}$ gives the instantiations of attributes for $\mathcal{U}$ at a certain timepoint t. Instead, the task of the *user model* is to ascertain the values in the user profile of a user $\mathcal{U}$. Thus, the user model must provide updating and modification policies of the user profile, as well as instructions to detect and evaluate incidents which can lead to update or modification processes. Methods for drawing appropriate conclusions about the incidents must be given, as well as mechanisms for detecting discrepancies in the modeling process. Advanced user modeling approaches also provide mechanisms for dealing with uncertainty in the observations about a user, appropriate error detection mechanisms, and can prioterize the the conclusion on observed incidents.

A very simple user profile identifies all the pages that a user $\mathcal{U}$ has visited, therefore, it is a set of couples:

$$(\mathcal{P}, visited)$$

A simple user model which can create this-like user profiles contains the following rule for interpreting incidents:

"if $\mathcal{U}$ visits page $\mathcal{P}$ then insert $(\mathcal{P}, visited)$ into the user profile of $\mathcal{U}$"

An extension of this simple user model is to recognize the observation that a user $\mathcal{U}$ has bookmarked some page $\mathcal{P}$ and note this in the user profile:

"if $\mathcal{U}$ bookmarks page $\mathcal{P}$ then insert $(\mathcal{P}, important)$ into the user profile of $\mathcal{U}$"

We will not go into detail on user modeling in this article (for more in-depth information refer to [41]). But even from this simple user models above, we can see that interpretation about the user interactions is not at all an easy task. E.g. if we observe a user $\mathcal{U}$ bookmarking a page $\mathcal{P}$: How can we distinguish that $\mathcal{U}$ has stored this page for future reference based on the content of the page from the fact that $\mathcal{U}$ stored this page only because he liked the design of the page? Can we really be sure that bookmarking expresses favor for a page in contrast to denial? Appropriate mechanisms for dealing with uncertainty in the observations about the user, and for continuous affirmation of derived conclusions are essential for good user models (a good reference for studying numerical uncertainty management in user modeling is e.g. given in [38]).

User modeling approaches for *Adaptive Hypermedia* can take advantage of the underlying hypermedia structure or the domain models associated with the hypermedia system. Task models, expert models, or other, external models are used to model the user with respect to this external model. This approach is called *overlay modeling* [30]. As an example, for educational hypermedia systems, the learner's state of knowledge is described as a subset of the expert's knowledge of the domain, hence the term "overlay". Student's lack of knowledge is derived by comparing it to the expert's knowledge.

The critical part of overlay modeling is to find the initial knowledge estimation. The number of observations for estimating the knowledge sufficiently well must be small. In addition, a student's misconceptions of some knowledge concepts can not be modeled. A great variety of approaches for user modeling is available, see e.g. [42, 69]

User Modeling for Web Mining. For Web Mining, the absence of a structured corpus of documents leads to different approaches for user modeling. An interest and/or content-profile of a user is generated (with the aid of classification or clustering techniques from machine learning) based on observations about the user's navigation behavior. A *stereotype user modeling* approach [63] classifies users into *stereotypes*: Users belonging to a certain class are assumed to have the same characteristics. When using stereotype user modeling, the following problem can occur: the stereotypes might be so specialized that they become obsolete (since they consist of at most one user), or a user cannot be classified at all.

Discussion. The user modeling process is the core of each personalization process, because here the system's estimations about the user's needs are specified. If the system identifies the needs not correctly, the personalization algorithms –regardless how good they are– will fail to deliver the expected results for this erroneous modeled user.

3.4   Conclusion: Personalization in the World Wide Web

To develop systems which can filter information according to the requirements of the individual, which can learn the needs of users from observations about previous navigation and interaction behavior, and which can continuously adapt to the dynamic interests and changing requirements is still one of the challenges for building smart and successful Web applications. Although the necessity to "support the users in finding what they need at the time they want" is obvious, building and running personalized Web sites is still a cost-intensive venture which sometimes underachieves [40].

Looking at the techniques in adaptive hypermedia, we can see that re-usability of these techniques is still an unsolved problem. We require a formalism expressing adaptive functionality in a system-independent and re-usable manner, which allows us to apply this adaptive functionality in various contexts, as it has been done e.g. for the adaptive educational hypermedia systems (see Section 3.1). Another reason why adaptive functionality is not re-usable today is related to the so-called *open corpus problem* in adaptive hypermedia, which states that currently, adaptive applications work on a fixed set of documents which is defined at the design time of the system, and directly influences the way adaptation is implemented, e.g. that adaptive information like "required prerequisites" is coded on this fixed set of documents. The introduction of standards for describing such metadata is a step forwards - and is currently undertaken in the Semantic Web.

Looking at the personalization techniques based on Web mining, we can see that the filtering techniques (content-based, collaborative-based, demographic-based, utility-based, knowledge-based, or others) are limited as they require a critical mass of data before the underlying machine learning algorithms produce results of sufficient quality. Explicit, machine-readable information about single Web resources as given in the Semantic Web could be used for improving the quality of the input data for the algorithms.

4   Personalization for the Semantic Web

Functionalities for performing personalization require a machine-processable knowledge layer that is not supplied by the WWW. In the previous section we have studied techniques for developing adaptive systems in the WWW with all the difficulties and limitations brought by working at this level. Let us now see how adaptive systems can evolve benefiting of the Semantic Web. In particular, since the capability of performing some kind of inferencing is fundamental for obtaining personalization, let us see how the introduction of machine-processable semantics makes the use of a wide variety of *reasoning techniques* possible, thus widening the range of the forms that personalization can assume.

4.1   An Overview

The idea of exploiting reasoning techniques for obtaining adaptation derives from the observation that in many (Semantic Web) application domains the goal of the user and the interaction occurring with the user play a fundamental role. Once the goal to be achieved is made clear, the system strives for achieving it, respecting the constraints and the needs of the user and taking into account his/her characteristics. In this context, the ability of performing a semantic-based retrieval of the necessary resources, that of combining the resources in a way that satisfies the user's goals, and, if necessary, of remotely invoking and monitoring the execution of a resource, are fundamental. All these activities can be performed by adopting automated reasoning techniques. To make an example, suppose that, for some reason, a student must learn something about the Semantic Web for a University course. Suppose that the student has access to a repository of educational resources that does not contain any material under the topic "Semantic Web". Let us suppose, however, that the repository contains a lot of information about XML-based languages, knowledge representation, ontologies, and so forth: altogether this information gives knowledge about the Semantic Web, the problem is retrieving it. A classical search engine would not be able to do it, unless the word "Semantic Web" is explicitly contained in the documents. This result can be obtained only by a system that is able to draw as an inference the fact that all these topics are elements of the Semantic Web.

In the Semantic Web every new feature or functionality is built as a new layer that stands on top of the previous ones. Tim Berners-Lee has described this process and structure as the "Semantic Web Tower". In this representation reasoning belongs to the logic and proof layers that lay on the ontology layer. This vision allows the Semantic Web to be developed incrementally.

Data on the Web is basically considered as the set of the available Web resources, each identified by a URI (uniform resource identifier). Such resources are mainly represented by plain XML (eXtensible Markup Language) descriptions. XML stands at the bottom of the tower. It allows a Web document to be written in a structured way, exploiting a user-defined vocabulary. It is perfect as a data interchange format, however, it does not properly supply any semantic information. Sometimes, when the domain is very closed and controlled, the tags can be considered as being associated with a meaning but the solution is risky and the application as such cannot be safely extended.

Semantic annotation of data is done by means of RDF (Resource Description Framework). RDF [59] is the basic Semantic Web (XML-based) language for writing simple statements about Web resources. Each statement is a binary predicate that defines a relation between two resources. These predicates correspond to logical facts. Given semantically-annotated data it is possible to perform some kinds of reasoning. In particular, some query languages have been developed that allow the automatic transformation of RDF-annotated data. Two of the main query languages that are used to transform data encoded in RDF are TRIPLE and RDQL. They are both quite simple in the inferencing that they allow.

TRIPLE [66] is a rule language for the Semantic Web which is based on Horn logic and borrows many basic features from F-Logic but is especially designed for querying and transforming RDF models. In contrast to procedural programming languages, such as C or Java, it is a declarative language which shares some similarities with SQL or Prolog. TRIPLE programs consist of facts and rules, from which it is possible to draw conclusions for answering queries. The language exploits reasoning mechanism about RDF-annotated information resources; translation tools from RDF to TRIPLE and vice versa are provided. An RDF statement, i.e. a "triple", is written as `subject[predicate -> object]`. RDF *models* are explicitly available in TRIPLE: statements that are true in a specific model are written as "@model". Connectives and quantifiers (e.g. `AND`, `OR`, `NOT`, `FORALL`, `EXISTS`) for building logical formulae from statements are allowed as usual.

RDQL [61] is a query language for RDF and is provided as part of the Jena Semantic Web Framework [39] from HP labs, which also includes: an RDF API, facilities for reading and writing RDF in RDF/XML, N3 and N-Triples, an OWL API, and in-memory and persistent storage. RDQL provides a *data-oriented* query model so that there is a more declarative approach to complement the fine-grained, procedural Jena API. It is "data-oriented" in that it only queries the information held in the models; there is no inference being done. Of course, the Jena model may be "smart" in that it provides the impression that certain triples exist by creating them on-demand. However, the RDQL system does not do anything other than take the description of what the application wants, in the form of a query, and returns that information, in the form of a set of bindings.

Going back to *our example*, by using RDF we could semantically annotate the resources that give explanations about XML-based languages, ontologies, knowledge representation, etc. However, the use that we want to do of such resources requires that each of them is explicitly associated to every topic it might have correlations with. This should be done even though some of the topics are related with each other, for instance XML is related to RDF and XML is related to Semantic Web, but also RDF is related to Semantic Web, and ideally we could *exploit such relations* to infer properties of the available resources. What is still missing is the possibility of *expressing knowledge about the domain*.

RDF Schema [60] adds a new layer of functionalities by allowing the representation of *ontologies*. This is done by introducing the notion of "class" of similar resources, i.e. objects showing a set of same characteristics. Resources are then viewed as "individuals" of some class. Classes can be divided in "subclasses", the result is a *hierarchical structure*. From an extensional point of view, every instance of a class is also an instance of its super-class, as such it inherits the properties of that class. It is possible to exploit this mechanism to perform simple inferences about instances and classes w.r.t. the hierarchical structure. A more powerful ontology language is OWL [54] (Web Ontology Language). OWL, the W3C standard for ontology representation, builds on top of RDF and RDF-S and allows the representation of more complex relations, such as transitivity, symmetry, and cardinality constraints.

It is possible to reason about ontologies by means of techniques that are typical of Description Logics. Basically, such techniques are aimed at *classification*, that is, if a resource is an instance of a class, then it will also be an instance of its super-classes. Also, if a resource satisfies a set of properties that define a sufficient condition to belonging to a given class, then the resource is an instance of that class. By means of these techniques we can satisfy the goal of the user of our example: in fact, if we have an ontology in which Semantic Web has as subclasses XML-based languages, knowledge representation, and so on, and we have a set of resources that are individuals of such classes, it is possible to infer that they are also individuals of Semantic Web. The introduction of these inferencing mechanisms is a fundamental step towards personalization, although in order to have real personalization something more is to be done. Indeed, if two different users are both interested in the Semantic Web the system will return as an answer *the same set* of resources because it does not take into account any information about them.

So far, reasoning in the Semantic Web is mostly reasoning about knowledge expressed in some ontology and the ontology layer is the highest layer of the Semantic Web tower that can be considered as quite well assessed. The layers that lie on top of it, in particular the logic layer and the proof layer, are still at a primitive level. The lesson learnt from the analysis that we have done is that for making some personalization we need to represent and reason about *knowledge* and the Semantic Web offers this possibility. Let us, then, see what kinds of knowledge are necessary for performing personalization.

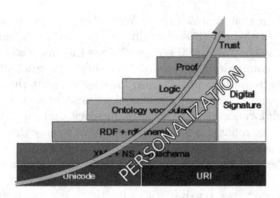

Fig. 1. The Semantic Web tower. Personalization occurs at the ontology layer but mostly at the logic and proof layers

4.2   Knowledge and Reasoning About Knowledge

A system that performs some kind of personalization needs to represent different kinds of *knowledge*: knowledge about the user, knowledge about the user's purpose (sometimes considered as included in the user's description), knowledge about the context, knowledge about the resources that can be queried, retrieved or composed, and domain knowledge that is used by the inferencing mechanism for obtaining personalization.

Knowledge about the user can roughly be viewed as partitioned in generic knowledge about the user's characteristics and preferences and in "state" knowledge. By the word "state knowledge" we hereby mean information that can change and that is relevant w.r.t. a specific application system, such as which exams have been passed in the case of e-learning.

A user's *goal* most of the times is considered as being coincident with a query but there are some distinctive features to take into account. First of all, a query presupposes an answer, and it implies a selection process, that can be performed by means of the most various techniques. The answer is supposed to be returned within a few seconds. In some applications, however, the goal corresponds to a general interest of the user. For example, the user might be a fan of a given music band and whenever the band performs in the user's town, s/he would like to be informed automatically. In this case, we can view the goals as conditions that can are embedded in rules: when some event satisfies a rule condition, the rule is triggered and, typically, the user is warned in a way that can be subject to further personalization (e.g. w.r.t. the physical device that is used –laptop, mobile, hand-held–). In this case, the answer, that depends on location and time, might be returned days or weeks after the rule has been set. Moreover, the same rule might be activated many times by many different events. A third kind of goal, that we have seen, is more abstract and not directly interpretable as a query. It is, for instance, the case of a learning goal: a learning goal is a description of the expertise that a user would like to acquire. The system uses this information to build a solution that contains many Web resources, to be used as learning materials. None of them is (possibly) directly tied with the learning goal; the goal will be reached by the user if s/he will follow the proposed reading path. In other words, the composition of resources is a *means* for reaching the goal.

In performing resource selection, also knowledge about the *context* plays a very important part. In many applications, three kinds of contextual information can be identified: location in time, location in space, and role. *Location in time and space* is used for refining resource selection, that is, only those resources that fit the context description, are shown. The context description is not necessarily expressed by the user, since it might as well be obtained in other ways. In ubiquitous and in ambient computing it could be returned by a sensor network. *Roles* are predefined views, possibly with a limitation of the actions, that the role players can execute. They are used to personalize the selection of information sources, the selection of information and, of course, presentation.

For performing semantic-based processing on the Web it is necessary that the *Web resources* are semantically annotated. This is normally done by means of ontologies. Even though semantic annotation is not so much diffused, the languages for writing such annotations are pretty well assessed. One of the major difficulties is, actually, to retrieve –if any– an ontology that is suitable to the application at hand, avoiding to write a new one unless really necessary.

The last kind of knowledge that is often necessary in personalization tasks, that we called *domain knowledge*, is aimed at giving a structure to the knowledge. Domain knowledge relates the ontological terms in a way that can be exploited by other inferencing mechanisms, and not only to perform ontological reasoning. For instance, planning is a useful reasoning technique for obtaining personalization; there are proposals in the literature that suggest to bias the search of a plan by introducing solution schemas, that correspond to abstract descriptions of solutions that "make sense". For instance, in the e-learning applications when a course is constructed out of a set of available learning materials, the course must "make sense" also from a pedagogical point of view, see [7]. One can then imagine to have a high-level description of the structure of interest, not related to specific materials, which is personalized and filled with contents on demand, in a way that fits the specific user. Moreover, in many scenarios it is useful to express some event-driven behavior (e.g. in the already mentioned touristic application domain). It is especially at this level that rules can play a fundamental role in the construction of personalization systems in the Semantic Web.

Beyond Ontologies: Some Examples. The first scenario that we consider is set in one of the leading application areas for personalization: education. The most typical problem in this framework consists in determining an "optimal reading sequence" through a hyper-space of learning objects (a learning object is a resource with educational purposes). The word optimal does not mean that this is absolutely the best solution, it means that it specifically fits the characteristics and the needs of the given user. It is optimal for that user. So the aim is to support the user in the acquisition of some desired knowledge by identifying a reading path that best fits him/her. Considerable advancements have been yield in this field, with the development of a great number of Web-based systems, like ELM-Art [70], the KBS hyperbook system [34], TANGOW [22], WLog [6] and many others, based on different, adaptive and intelligent technologies.

Different methods have been proposed on how to determine which reading path to select or to generate in order to support in the best possible way the learner's navigation through the hyper-space. All of them require to go *one step beyond* the ontology layer. In fact, pure ontological annotation and ontological reasoning techniques (though necessary) are not sufficient to produce, in an automatic way, the desired sequencing. If in our ontology the class "Semantic Web" is divided in the classes "XML-based languages", "knowledge representation", and "ontologies" we will be able to conclude that each of the individuals that belong to the sub-classes also belong to the super-class. What we cannot do is to impose that the student will be presented resources about *all* such topics, because only the conjunction of the three will let him/her satisfy his/her learning goal. Another thing that we cannot do is to impose that a given topic is presented before another one because only in this way the student will understand them.

If, on the one hand, it is necessary to annotate the actual learning objects, with the ontological terms that represent identifiable pieces of knowledge related to the learning objects themselves, on the other, it is also necessary to structure a domain knowledge in a way that it is possible to perform the personalization task. The desire is to develop an *adaptation component*, that uses such a knowledge, together with a representation of the user's *learning goal* and of knowledge about the user, for producing sequences that fit the user's requirements and characteristics, based on the available learning objects. Such an adaptation component exploits knowledge representations that are not ontologies (though they use ontologies) and it exploits reasoning mechanisms that are not ontological reasoning mechanisms. For instance, in the application domain that has been taken into account, *goal-directed reasoning* techniques seem particularly suitable.

To this purpose, one solution is to interpret the learning resources as atomic actions. In fact, each learning resource has a set of preconditions (competences that are necessary for using it) and a set of effects (the supplied competences). Competences can be connected by causal relationships. Rational agents could use such descriptions and the user's learning goal, expressed as well in terms of competences, for performing the sequencing task. This is, for instance, the solution adopted in the WLog system [6], which exploits techniques taken from the research area of "reasoning about actions and change" (*planning, temporal projection,* and *temporal explanation*) for building personalized solutions.

Another example concerns *Web services*. Generally speaking, a Web service can be seen as any device that can automatically be accessed over the Web. It may alternatively be a software system or a hardware device; a priori no distinction is made. The main difference between a Web service and other devices that are connected to a network stands in the kind of tasks that can be performed: a Web service can be automatically retrieved by searching for the desired functionality (in a way that is analogous to finding Web pages by means of a search engine, given a set of keywords), it can be automatically invoked, composed with other Web services so to accomplish more complex tasks, it must be possible to monitor its execution, and so on. In order to allow the execution of these tasks, it is necessary to enrich the Web service with a machine-processable description, that contains all the necessary information, such as what the service does, which inputs it requires, which results are returned, and so forth. A lot of research is being carried on in this area and none of the problems that we have just enumerated has met its final solution yet. Nevertheless, there are some proposals, especially due to commercial coalitions, of languages that allow the description of the single services, and their interoperation. In this line, the most successful are WSDL [72] and BPEL4WS [14]. This initiative is mainly carried on by the commercial world, with the aim of standardizing registration, look-up mechanisms and interoperability.

Among the other proposals, OWL-S [55] (formerly DAML-S) is more concerned with providing greater expressiveness to service description in a way that can be *reasoned about* [20]. In particular, a service description has three conceptual levels: the *profile*, used for advertising and discovery, the *process model*, that describes how a service works, and the *grounding*, that describes how an agent can access the service. In particular, the process model describes a service as atomic, simple or composite in a way inspired by the language GOLOG and its extensions [45, 50]. In this perspective, a wide variety of agent technologies based upon the *action metaphor* can be used. In fact, we can view a service as an action (atomic or complex) with preconditions and effects, that modifies the state of the world and the state of agents that work in the world. The process model can, then, be viewed as the description of such an action; therefore, it is possible to design agents, which apply techniques for reasoning about actions and change to Web service process models for producing new, composite, and customized services.

Quoting McIlraith [51]: "[...] *Our vision is that agents will exploit user's constraints and preferences to help customize user's requests for automatic Web service discovery, execution, or composition and interoperation* [...]". In different words, personalization is seen as *reasoning* about the user's constraints and preferences and about the *effects*, on the user's knowledge and on the world, of the *action* "interact with a Web service". Techniques for reasoning about actions and change are applied to produce composite and customized services.

A better personalization can be achieved by allowing agents to reason also about the *conversation protocols* followed by Web services. Conversation protocols rule the interactions of a service with its interlocutors: the protocol defines all the possible "conversations" that the service can enact. Roughly speaking, we can consider it as a procedure built upon atomic speech acts. So far, however, no language for Web service specification, e.g. OWL-S, allows the explicit representation of the communicative behavior of Web services at an abstract level, i.e. in a way that can be reasoned about. Let us, however, explain with a simple example how this would be useful: an agent, which is a user's *personal assistant*, is requested to book a ticket at a cinema where they show a certain movie; as a further constraint, the agent does not have to use the user's credit card number along the transaction. While the first is the *user's goal*, the additional request constrains the way in which the agent will *interact* with the service. In this case, in order to personalize the interaction according to the user's request, it is indeed necessary to reason about the service communications. Another possible task of the personal assistant is the organization of a journey: it is necessary to find and make work together (*compose*) services for finding a flight, renting a car, making a reservation at some hotel, maybe the user's personal calendar, etc. All services that have been developed independently and for simpler purposes.

Personalization may involve also other kinds of reasoning, that require knowledge to be represented in other ways. Among them *defeasible reasoning*, which allows taking into account degrees of preference represented as priorities between rules (e.g. DR-DEVICE [11]), *Answer Set Programming* [27], that can deal with incomplete information and default knowledge, *reactivity to events* [48] (the so called ECA rules –event, condition, action–), that allow the propagation of knowledge updates through the Web. All these approaches and techniques conceptually lie at the logic and proof layers of the Semantic Web tower and rely on some kind of rule language.

Rule languages and rule systems are, actually, in the mainstream of research in the Semantic Web area, especially for what regards *exchange of rule sets* between applications. Works in this direction include initiatives for the definition of *rule markup languages*. The aim of introducing rules is to support in a better and wider way the interaction of systems with users as well as of systems with other systems over the Web. Rule markup languages are designed so to allow the expression of rules as modular, stand-alone units in a declarative way, and to allow the publishing and interchange of rules among different systems. Different perspectives can be considered [68]. Rules can be seen as statements that define the terms of the domain, they can be seen as formal statements, which can be directly mapped to executable statements of a software platform, and they can also be considered as statements in a specific executable language.

Two examples of rule markup languages are RuleML [52] and SWRL [37]. The former is a deductive logic language based on XML and RDF. SWRL is a more recent proposal aimed at adding to the OWL language, for defining Web ontologies, the possibility of including Horn-like clauses. The idea is to add the possibility of making deductive inferences that cannot be accomplished by the ontology reasoning techniques. For instance, a consequence of this kind: if X has a brother Y and X has a son Z, then Y is an uncle of Z.

The most important aspect of the standards is its *adoption*, which implies a diffusion of the inference engines that implement them. The hope is that in the near future browsers will support RuleML engines, SWRL engines, and so forth, enabling the use of knowledge over the Web, in the same easy way in which they currently support languages like Java and JavaScript. On the other hand, besides the standards, the way is open for building, on top of the ontology layer, languages that support *heterogeneous* reasoning mechanisms, that fit the requirements of specific personalization problems. This is the reading key of the following section, where a case study is presented together with reasoning techniques for tackling the personalization task. Further examples of personalization problems, reasoning techniques, and prototype systems can be found in [2].

4.3   Case Study: Personalization in an E-Learning Scenario

Let us focus on e-learning and see how reasoning can help personalization in this context. We will begin with the annotation of the learning resources, then, we will introduce some reasoning techniques, all of which exploit a new level of knowledge thus allowing a better personalization.

A learning object can profitably be used if the learner has a given set of prerequisite competences; by using it, the learner will acquire a new set of competences. Therefore, a learning object can be interpreted as an action: in fact, an action can be executed given that a set of conditions holds, and by executing it, a set of conditions will become true. So, the idea is to introduce at the level of the learning objects, some annotation that describes both their *pre-requisites* and their *effects*. Figure 2 shows an example of how this could be done. To make the example realistic, the annotation respects the standard for learning object metadata LOM. LOM allows the annotation of the learning objects by means of an ontology of interest (see for instance [56]), by using the attribute *classification*. A LOM classification consists of a set of ontology elements (*taxons*), with an associated role (the *purpose*). The taxons in the example are taken from the DAML version of the ACM computer classification system ontology [53]. The reference to the ontology is contained in the *source* element. Since the XML-based representation is quite long, for the sake of brevity only two taxons have been reported: the first (relational database) is necessary in order to understand the contents of the learning object, while the other (scientific databases) is a competence that is supplied by the learning object.

The proposed annotation expresses a set of *learning dependencies* between *ontological terms*. Such dependencies can be expressed in a declarative formalism, and can be used by a reasoning system. So, given a set of learning objects each annotated in this way, it is possible to use the standard planners, developed by the Artificial Intelligence community (for instance, the well-known Graphplan [13]), for building the reading sequences. Graphplan is a general-purpose planner that works in STRIPS-like domains; as all planners, the task that it executes is to build a sequence of atomic actions, that allows the transition from an initial state to a state of interest, or goal state. The algorithm is based on ideas used in graph algorithms: it builds a structure called *planning graph*, whose main property is that the information that is useful for constraining the plan search is quickly propagated through the graph as it is built.

General-purpose planners search a sequence of interest in the whole space of possible solutions and allow the construction of learning objects on the basis of any learning goal. This is not always adequate in an educational application framework, where the set of learning goals of interest is fairly limited and the experience of the teachers in structuring the courses and the learning materials is important. For instance, a teacher due to his/her own experience may believe

```
<lom xmlns="http://www.imsglobal.org/xsd/imsmd_v1p2"
xmlns:xsi="http://www.w3.org/2001/XMLSchema-instance"
xsi:schemaLocation="http://www.imsglobal.org/xsd/imsmd_v1p2 imsmd_v1p2p2.xsd">
  <general>
    <title>
      <langstring>module A</langstring>
    </title>
  </general>
  ...
  <classification>
    <purpose>
      ...
      <value><langstring>Prerequisite</langstring></value>
    </purpose>
    <taxonpath>
      <source>
        <langstring>http://daml.umbc.edu/ontologies/classification.daml
        </langstring>
      </source>
      <taxon>
        <entry>
          <langstring xml:lang="en">relational database</langstring>
        </entry>
      </taxon>
    </taxonpath>
  </classification>
  ...
  <classification>
    <purpose>
      ...
      <value><langstring>Educational Objective</langstring></value>
    </purpose>
    <taxonpath>
      <source>
        <langstring>http://daml.umbc.edu/ontologies/classification.daml
        </langstring>
      </source>
      <taxon>
        <entry>
          <langstring xml:lang="en">scientific databases</langstring>
        </entry>
      </taxon>
    </taxonpath>
  </classification>
</lom>
```

Fig. 2. Excerpt from the annotation for the learning object 'module A': "relational database" is an example of prerequisite while "scientific databases" is an example of educational objective

that topic A is to be presented before topic B, although no learning dependence emerges from the descriptions of A and B. This kind of constraint cannot be exploited by a general-purpose planner, being related to the teaching strategy adopted by the teacher.

On the other hand, it is not reasonable to express schemas of this kind in terms of specific learning objects. The ideal solution is to express the aforementioned schemas as *learning strategies*, i.e. a rule (or a set of rules) that specifies the overall structure of the learning object, expressed only in terms of *competences*. The construction of a learning object can, then, be obtained by refining a learning strategy according to specific requirements and, in particular, by choosing those components that best fit the user.

Reasoning About Actions. Reasoning about actions and change is a kind of temporal reasoning where, instead of reasoning about *time* itself, one reasons on *phenomena* that take place in time. Indeed, theories of reasoning about actions and change describe a *dynamic world* changing because of the execution of actions. Properties characterizing the dynamic world are usually specified by propositions which are called *fluents*. The word *fluent* stresses the fact that the truth value of these propositions depends on time and may vary depending on the changes which occur in the world.

The problem of reasoning about the effects of actions in a dynamically changing world is considered one of the central problems in knowledge representation theory. Different approaches in the literature took different assumptions on the temporal ontology and then they developed different abstraction tools to cope with dynamic worlds. However, most of the formal theories for reasoning about action and change (*action theories*) describe dynamic worlds according to the so-called *state-action model*. In the state-action model the world is described in terms of states and *actions* that cause the transition from a state to another. Typically it is assumed that the world persists in its state unless it is modified by an action's execution that causes the transition to a new state (*persistency assumption*).

The main target of action theories is to use a logical framework to describe the effects of actions on a world where *all* changes are caused by the execution of actions. To be precise, in general, a formal theory for representing and reasoning about actions allows us to specify:

1. *causal laws*, i.e. axioms that describe domain's actions in terms of their *precondition* and *effects* on the fluents;
2. action sequences that are executed from the initial state;
3. *observations* describing the value of fluents in the *initial state*;
4. *observations* describing the value of fluents in later states, i.e after some action's execution.

The term *domain description* is used to refer to a set of propositions that express causal laws, observations of the fluents values in a state and possibly other information for formalizing a specific problem. Given a domain description, the principal reasoning tasks are *temporal projection* (or prediction), *temporal explanation* (or postdiction) and *planning*.

Intuitively, the aim of *temporal projection* is to predict an action's future effects based on even partial knowledge about the current state (reasoning from causes to effect). On the contrary, the target of *temporal explanation* is to infer something on the past states of the world by using knowledge about the current situation. The third reasoning task, planning, is aimed at finding an action sequence that, when executed starting from a given state of the world, produces a new state where certain desired properties hold.

Usually, by varying the reasoning task, a domain description may contain different elements that provide a basis for inferring the new facts. For instance, when the task is to formalize the temporal projection problem, a domain description might contain information on (1), (2) and (3), then the logical framework might provide the inference mechanisms for reconstructing information on (4). Otherwise, when the task is to deal with the planning problem, the domain description will contain the information on (1), (3), (4) and we will try to infer (2), i.e. which action sequence has to be executed on the state described in (3) for achieving a state with the properties described in (4).

An important issue in formalization is known as the *persistency problem*. It concerns the characterization of the invariants of an action, i.e. those aspects of the dynamic world that are not changed by an action. If a certain fluent f representing a fact of the world holds in a certain state and it is not involved by the next execution of an action a, then we would like to have an efficient inference mechanism to conclude that f still hold in the state resulting from a's execution.

Various approaches in the literature can be broadly classified in two categories: those choosing classical logics as the knowledge representation language [49, 44] and those addressing the problem by using non-classical logics [57, 23, 65, 29] or computational logics [28, 10, 46, 8]. Among the various logic-based approaches to reasoning about actions one of the most popular is still the situation calculus, introduced by Mc Carthy and Hayes in the sixties [49] to capture change in first order classical logic. The situation calculus represents the world and its change by a sequence of *situations*. Each situation represents a state of the world and it is obtained from a previous situation by executing an action. Later on, Kowalski and Sergot have developed a different calculus to describe change [44], called *event calculus*, in which *events* producing changes are temporally located and they initiate and terminate action effects. Like the situation calculus, the event calculus is a methodology for encoding actions in first-order predicate logic. However, it was originally developed for reasoning about events and time in a logic-programming setting.

Another approach to reasoning about actions is the one based on the use of modal logics. Modal logics adopts essentially the same ontology as the situation calculus by taking the state of the world as primary and by representing actions as state transitions. In particular, actions are represented in a very natural way by modalities whose semantics is a standard Kripke semantics given in terms of accessibility relations between worlds, while states are represented as sequences of modalities.

Both situation calculus and modal logics influenced the design of logic-based languages for agent programming. Recently the research about situation calculus gained a renewed attention thanks to the cognitive robotic project at University of Toronto, that has lead to the development of a high-level agent programming language, called GOLOG, based on a theory of actions in situation calculus [45]. On the other hand, in DyLOG [9], a modal action theory has been used as a basis for specifying and executing agent behavior in a logic programming setting, while the language IMPACT is an example of use of deontic logic for specifying agents: the agent's behavior is specified by means of a set of rules (the agent program) which are suitable to specify, by means of deontic modalities, agent policies, that is which actions an agent is obliged to take in a given state, which actions it is permitted to take, and how it chooses which actions to perform.

Introducing Learning Strategies. Let us now show how the schemas of solution, or *learning strategies*, can be represented by means of rules. In particular, we will use the notation of the language DyLOG.

Learning strategies, as well as learning objects, should be defined on the basis of an ontology of interest. One common need is to express *conjunctions* or *sequences* of learning objects. So for instance, one can say that in his/her view, it is possible to acquire knowledge about *database management* only by getting knowledge about *all* of of a given set of topics, and, among these, *relational databases* must be known before *distributed databases* are introduced.

An example that is particularly meaningful is preparing the material for a basic computer science course: the course may have different contents depending on the kind of student to whom it will be offered (e.g. a Biology student, rather than a Communication Sciences student, rather than a Computer Science student). Hereafter, we consider the case of Biology students and propose a *DyLOG* procedure, named '*strategy('informatics_-for_biologists')*'. This procedure expresses, at an abstract level, a learning strategy for guiding a biology student in a learning path, which includes the basic concepts about how a computer works, together with a specific competence about databases. Notice that no reference to specific learning objects is done.

$strategy('informatics\_for\_biologists')$ **is**
$\quad achieve\_goal(has\_competence('computer\ system\ organization')) \land$
$\quad achieve\_goal(has\_competence('operating\ systems')) \land$
$\quad achieve\_goal(has\_competence('database\ management')).$
$\quad \ldots$

$achieve\_goal(has\_competence('database\ management'))$ **is**
$\quad achieve\_goal(has\_competence('relational\ databases')) \land$
$\quad achieve\_goal(has\_competence('query\ languages')) \land$
$\quad achieve\_goal(has\_competence('distributed\ databases')) \land$
$\quad achieve\_goal(has\_competence('scientific\ databases')).$

strategy is defined as a procedure clause, that expresses the view of the strategy creator on what it means to acquire competence about *computer system organization*, *operating systems*, and *database management*.

Suppose that *module A* is the name of a learning object. Interpreting it as an action, it will have preconditions and effects expressed as in Figure 2. We could represent *module A* and its learning dependencies in DyLOG in the following way:

$access(learningObject('module A'))$ **possible if**
   $has\_competence('distributed\ database')\ \wedge$
   $has\_competence('relational\ database')$.
$access(learningObject('module A'))$ **causes**
   $has\_competence('scientific\ databases')$.

Having a learning strategy and a set of annotated learning objects, it is possible to apply *procedural planning* (supplied by the language) for assembling a reading path that is a sequence of learning resources that are annotated as required by the strategy. Opposite to general-purpose planners, procedural planning searches for a solution in the set of the possible executions of a learning strategy. Notice that, since the strategy is based on competences, rather than on specific resources, the system might need to select between different courses, annotated with the same desired competence, which could equally be selected in building the actual learning path. This choice can be done based on external information, such as a user model, or it may be derive from a further interaction with the user. Decoupling the strategies from the learning objects results in a greater flexibility of the overall system, and simplifies the reuse of the learning objects. As well as learning objects, also learning strategies could be made public and shared across different systems.

Other Approaches to Rule-Based Personalization in an e-Learning Scenario. The above example is just one possible way in which personalization can be realized in the Semantic Web in a practical context. Remaining in the e-learning application domain, many other forms of personalization can be thought of, which require other approaches to rule representation and reasoning. Hereafter, we report another example that is taken from a real system. The personalization rules that we will see realize some of the adaptation methods of adaptive educational hypermedia systems (see Section 3.1). The application scenario is a *Personal Reader*[3] [32, 12] for learning resources. This Personal Reader helps the learner to view the learning resources in a *context*: In this context, more *details* related to the topics of the learning resource, the *general topics* the learner is currently studying, *examples*, *summaries*, *quizzes*, etc. are generated and enriched with personal recommendations according to the learner's current learning state [32, 25]. Let us introduce and comment some of the rules that are used by the Personal Reader for learning resources to determine appropri-

---

[3] http://www.personal-reader.de

ate adaptation strategies. These personalization rules have been realized using
TRIPLE.

Generating links to more detailed learning resources is an adaptive functionality in this example Personal Reader. The adaptation rule takes the *isA* hierarchy
in the domain ontology, in this case the domain ontology for Java programming,
into account to determine domain concepts which are details of the current
concept or concepts that the learner is studying on the learning resource. In particular, more details for the currently used learning resource is determined by
detail_learningobject(LO, LO_DETAIL) where LO and LO_Detail are learning resources, and where LO_DETAIL covers more specialized learning concepts
which are determined with help of the domain ontology.

```
FORALL LO, LO_DETAIL detail_learningobject(LO, LO_DETAIL) <-
    EXISTS C, C_DETAIL(detail_concepts(C, C_DETAIL)
      AND concepts_of_LO(LO, C) AND concepts_of_LO(LO_DETAIL, C_DETAIL))
      AND learning_resource(LO_DETAIL) AND NOT unify(LO,LO_DETAIL).
```

Observe that the rule does neither require that LO_DETAIL covers all specialized learning concepts, nor that it exclusively covers specialized learning concepts. Further refinements of this adaptation rule are of course possible. The
rules for embedding a learning resource into more general aspects with respect
to the current learning progress are similar.

Another example of a *personalization rule* for generating embedding context
is the recommendation of quiz pages. A learning resource Q is recommended as
a quiz for a currently learned learning resource LO if it is a quiz (the rule for
determining this is not displayed) and if it provides questions to at least some
of the concepts learned on LO.

```
FORALL Q quiz(Q) <-
    Q['http://www.w3.org/1999/02/22-rdf-syntax-ns#':type ->
    'http://ltsc.ieee.org/2002/09/lom-educational#':'Quiz']
```

```
FORALL Q, C concepts_of_Quiz(Q,C) <-
    quiz(Q) AND concept(C) AND
    Q['http://purl.org/dc/elements/1.1/':subject -> C].
```

```
FORALL LO, Q quiz(LO, Q) <-
    EXISTS C (concepts_of_LO(LO,C) AND concepts_of_Quiz(Q,C)).
```

Recommendations are personalized according to the current learning progress
of the user, e. g. with respect to the current set of course materials. The following
rule determines that a learning resource LO is **recommended** if the learner studied
at least one more general learning resource (**UpperLevelLO**):

```
FORALL LO1, LO2 upperlevel(LO1,LO2) <-
    LO1['http://purl.org/dc/terms#':isPartOf -> LO2].
```

```
FORALL LO, U learning_state(LO, U, recommended) <-
    EXISTS UpperLevelLO (upperlevel(LO, UpperLevelLO) AND
    p_obs(UpperLevelLO, U, Learned) ).
```

Additional rules deriving stronger recommendations (e. g., if the user has studied *all* general learning resources), less strong recommendations (e.g., if one or two of these haven't been studied so far), etc., are possible, too. Recommendations can also be calculated with respect to the current domain ontology. This is necessary if a user is regarding course materials from different courses at the same time.

```
FORALL C, C_DETAIL detail_concepts(C, C_DETAIL) <-
    C_DETAIL['http://www.w3.org/2000/01/rdf-schema#':subClassOf -> C]
    AND concept(C) AND concept(C_DETAIL).

FORALL LO, U learning_state(LO, U, recommended) <-
    EXISTS C, C_DETAIL (concepts_of_LO(LO, C_DETAIL)
    AND detail_concepts(C, C_DETAIL) AND p_obs(C, U, Learned) ).
```

However, the first recommendation rule, which reasons within one course will be more accurate because it has more fine–grained information about the course and therefore on the learning process of a learner taking part in this course. Thus, a strategy is to prioritize those adaptation rule which take most observations and data into account, and, if these rules cannot provide results, apply less strong rules. This can be realized by defeasible rules [3]: Priorities are used to resolve conflicts, e.g. by giving external priority relations (N.B.: these external priority relations must be acyclic). For example: Rule `r1` determines that the learning state of a learning object is recommended for a particular user if the user has learnt at least one of the general, introductory learning objects in the course, while `r2` says that a learning object is not recommended if the learner has not learnt at least one of the more general concepts. In the following code, `r1 > r2` defines a degree of preference: only when the first rule cannot be applied, the system tries to apply the second.

```
r1: EXISTS UpperLevelLO (upperlevel(LO, UpperLevelLO) AND
        p_obs(UpperLevelLO, U, Learned))
    => learning_state(LO, U, recommended)

r2: FORALL C, C_DETAIL (concepts_of_LO(LO, C_DETAIL)
        AND detail_concepts(C, C_DETAIL) AND NOT p_obs(C, U, Learned)
    => NOT learning_state(LO, U, recommended)
```

and `r1 > r2`.

5   Conclusions

Personalization, which has become one of the major endeavors of research over the Web, has been studied since the mid 90's in fields like Adaptive Hypermedia and Web Mining. In Adaptive Hypermedia each user has a personalized view of the hypermedia system as well as individual navigation alternatives. Personalization is carried out either selecting the proper level of contents, that the user can read, or by modifying the set of links to other documents (for instance by hiding certain connections). Web Mining, on the other hand, is mostly concerned with the identification of relations between Web resources which are not directly connected through links. These new relations can be induced on the basis of resource contents or on the basis of regularities in the behavior of a set of independent users. All these approaches have been applied to the WWW, allowing the realization of adaptive systems even in absence of a universally agreed semantics and of standard languages and tools for representing and dealing with semantics. This heterogeneity entails some limitations. In fact, any technique used to deliberate whether a certain resource or link is to be shown to the user requires a lot of information, about the user, about the reasons for which the user should access that resource, and so on. Actually, most of the early personalization systems either managed "closed-world" resources, as it was the case of many systems for e-learning that handled given repositories of learning materials as well as of e-commerce tools, or they were based on user models refined during the direct interaction with the user.

The birth of the Semantic Web brought along standard models, languages, and tools for representing and dealing with machine-interpretable semantic descriptions of Web resources, giving a strong new impulse to research on personalization. Just as the current Web is inherently heterogeneous in data formats and data semantics, the Semantic Web will be heterogeneous in its reasoning forms and the same will hold for personalization systems developed in the Semantic Web. In this lecture we have analyzed some possible applications of techniques for reasoning about actions and change and of techniques for reasoning about preferences, the so called defeasible logic, but, indeed, the availability of a variety of reasoning techniques, all fully integrated with the Web, opens the way to the design and the development of forms of interaction and of personalization that were unimaginable still a short time ago. To this aim it is necessary to integrate results from many areas, such as Multi-Agent Systems, Security, Trust, Ubiquitous Computing, Ambient Intelligence, Human-Computer Interaction and, of course, Automated Reasoning.

This paper is just an introduction to personalization over the Semantic Web, that presents issues, approaches, and techniques incrementally. We have started from the World Wide Web and, then, moved to more abstract levels step by step towards semantics and reasoning, a pattern that follows the classical view of the Semantic Web as a tower of subsequent layers. More than being exhaustive w.r.t all the different techniques and methods that have been proposed in the literature, we have tried to give a complete overview, that includes historical roots, motivations, interconnections, questions, and examples. In our opinion, personalization plays a fundamental role in the Semantic Web, because what is the Semantic Web but a knowledge-aware Web, able to give each user the answers that s/he expects? Research in this field is at the beginning.

Acknowledgements

The authors are indebted with all the researchers who took part to the stimulating discussions during the meetings of REWERSE and in particular of working group A3 in Munich and Hannover. Special thanks to Viviana Patti and Laura Torasso, who actively contribute to the project.

References

1. R. Agrawal and R. Srikant. Fast algorithms for mining association rules. In *Proc. 20th Int. Conf. Very Large Data Bases (VLDB)*, 1994.
2. G. Antoniou, M. Baldoni, C. Baroglio, R. Baumgartner, F. Bry, T. Eiter, N. Henze, M. Herzog, W. May, V. Patti, S. Schaffert, R. Schidlauer, and H. Tompits. Reasoning methods for personalization on the semantic web. *Annals of Mathematics, Computing & Teleinformatics (AMCT)*, 2(1):1–24, 2004.
3. G. Antoniou and F. van Harmelen. *A Semantic Web Primer.* MIT Press, 2004.
4. R. Baeza-Yates and Berthier Ribeiro-Neto. *Modern Information Retrieval.* ACM Press, 1999.
5. M. Baldoni, C. Baroglio, A. Martelli, and V. Patti. Reasoning about interaction protocols for web service composition. In M. Bravetti and G. Zavattaro, editors, *Proc. of 1st Int. Workshop on Web Services and Formal Methods, WS-FM 2004*, volume 105 of *Electronic Notes in Theoretical Computer Science*, pages 21–36. Elsevier Science Direct, 2004.
6. M. Baldoni, C. Baroglio, and V. Patti. Web-based adaptive tutoring: an approach based on logic agents and reasoning about actions. *Artificial Intelligence Review*, 22(1), September 2004.
7. M. Baldoni, C. Baroglio, V. Patti, and L. Torasso. Reasoning about learning object metadata for adapting scorm courseware. In L. Aroyo and C. Tasso, editors, *Proc. of Int. Workshop on Engineering the Adaptive Web, EAW'04: Methods and Technologies for personalization and Adaptation in the Semantic Web*, pages 4–13, Eindhoven, The Netherlands, August 2004.
8. M. Baldoni, L. Giordano, A. Martelli, and V. Patti. An Abductive Proof Procedure for Reasoning about Actions in Modal Logic Programming. In J. Dix et al., editor, *Proc. of NMELP'96*, volume 1216 of *LNAI*, pages 132–150. Springer-Verlag, 1997.
9. M. Baldoni, L. Giordano, A. Martelli, and V. Patti. Programming Rational Agents in a Modal Action Logic. *Annals of Mathematics and Artificial Intelligence, Special issue on Logic-Based Agent Implementation*, 41(2-4):207–257, 2004.
10. C. Baral and T. C. Son. Formalizing Sensing Actions - A transition function based approach. *Artificial Intelligence*, 125(1-2):19–91, January 2001.
11. N. Bassiliades, G. Antoniou, and I. Vlahavas. A defeasible logic system for the semantic web. In *In Proc. of Principles and Practice of Semantic Web Reasoning (PPSWR04)*, volume 3208 of *LNCS*. Springer, 2004.
12. Robert Baumgartner, Nicola Henze, and Marcus Herzog. The personal publication reader: Illustrating web data extraction, personalization and reasoning for the semantic web. In *Proceedings of 2nd European Semantic Web Conference*, Heraklion, Greece, May 2005.
13. A. Blum and M. Furst. Fast planning through planning graph analysis. *Artificial Intelligence*, 90:281–300, 1997.

14. BPEL4WS. http://www-106.ibm.com/developerworks/library/ws-bpel. 2003.
15. P. De Bra, A. Aerts, D. Smits, and N. Stash. AHA! version 2.0: More adaptation flexibility for authors. In *Proceedings of the AACE ELearn'2002 conference*, October 2002.
16. P. De Bra, G.J. Houben, and H. Wu. AHAM: A dexter-based reference model for adaptive hypermedia. In *ACM Conference on Hypertext and Hypermedia*, pages 147–156, Darmstadt, Germany, 1999.
17. P. Brusilovsky. Methods and techniques of adaptive hypermedia. *User Modeling and User Adapted Interaction*, 6(2-3):87–129, 1996.
18. P. Brusilovsky, J. Eklund, and E. Schwarz. Web-based Educations for All: A Tool for Development Adaptive Courseware. In *Proceedings of the Sevenths International World Wide Web Conference, WWW'98*, 1998.
19. Peter Brusilovsky. Adaptive hypermedia. *User Modeling and User-Adapted Interaction*, 11:87–110, 2001.
20. J. Bryson, D. Martin, S. McIlraith, and L. A. Stein. Agent-based composite services in DAML-S: The behavior-oriented design of an intelligent semantic web. In J. Liu N. Zhong and Y. Yao, editors, *Web Intelligence*. Springer-Verlag, Berlin, 2002. Agent-Based Composite Services in DAML-S: The Behavior-Oriented Design of an Intelligent Semantic Web.
21. R. Burke. Hybrid recommender systems: Survey and experiments. *User Modeling and User-Adapted Interaction*, 12:331–370, 2002.
22. R.M. Carro, E. Pulido, and P. Rodruez. Dynamic generation of adaptive internet-based courses. *Journal of Network and Computer Applications*, 22:249–257, 1999.
23. M. Castilho, O. Gasquet, and A. Herzig. Modal tableaux for reasoning about actions and plans. In S. Steel, editor, *Proc. ECP'97*, LNAI, pages 119–130, 1997.
24. P. de Bra. Hypermedia structures and systems: Online Course at Eindhoven University of Technology, 1997. http://wwwis.win.tue.nl/2L690/.
25. P. Dolog, N. Henze, W. Nejdl, and M. Sintek. The Personal Reader: Personalizing and Enriching Learning Resources using Semantic Web Technologies. In *Proc. of the 3rd International Conference on Adaptive Hypermedia and Adaptive Web-Based Systems (AH 2004)*, Eindhoven, The Netherlands, 2004.
26. M. H. Dunham, editor. *Data Mining*. Prentice Hall, 2003.
27. M. Gelfond and V. Lifschitz. Classical negation in logic programs and disjunctive databases. *New Generation Computing*, 9, 1991.
28. M. Gelfond and V. Lifschitz. Representing action and change by logic programs. *Journal of Logic Programming*, 17:301–321, 1993.
29. L. Giordano, A. Martelli, and C. Schwind. Dealing with concurrent actions in modal action logic. In *Proc. ECAI-98*, pages 537–541, 1998.
30. I.P. Goldstein. The genetic graph: A represenation for the evolution of procedural knowledge. In D. Sleeman and J.S.Brown, editors, *Intelligent Tutoring Systems*. Academic Press, 1982.
31. F. Halasz and M. Schwartz. The Dexter hypertext reference model. *Communications of the ACM*, 37(2):30–39, 1994.
32. N. Henze and M. Kriesell. Personalization Functionality for the Semantic Web: Architectural Outline and First Sample Implementation. In *Proceedings of the 1st International Workshop on Engineering the Adaptive Web (EAW 2004), co-located with AH 2004*, Eindhoven, The Netherlands, 2004.
33. N. Henze and W. Nejdl. Extendible adaptive hypermedia courseware: Integrating different courses and web material. In *Proceedings of the International Conference on Adaptive Hypermedia and Adaptive Web-Based Systems (AH 2000)*, Trento, Italy, 2000.

34. N. Henze and W. Nejdl. Adaptation in open corpus hypermedia. *IJAIED Special Issue on Adaptive and Intelligent Web-Based Systems*, 12, 2001.
35. N. Henze and W. Nejdl. Logically characterizing adaptive educational hypermedia systems. Technical report, University of Hannover, April 2003. http://www.kbs.uni-hannover.de/Arbeiten/Publikationen/2003/ TechReportHenzeNejdl.pdf.
36. N. Henze and W. Nejdl. A logical characterization of adaptive educational hypermedia. *New Review of Hypermedia*, 10(1), 2004.
37. I. Horrocks, P. Patel-Schneider, H. Boley, S. Tabet, and B. Grosof. SWRL: a semantic web rule language combining OWL and RuleML, 2004. http://www.w3.org/Submission/2004/SUBM-SWRL-20040521.
38. A. Jameson. Numerical uncertainty management in user and student modeling: An overview of systems and issues. *User Modeling and User Adapted Interaction*, 5(3/4):193–251, 1996.
39. Jena - A Semantic Web Framework for Java, 2004. http://jena.sourceforge.net/.
40. Jupiter Research Report, October 14th, 2003. http://www.jupitermedia.com/ corporate/releases/03.10.14-newjupresearch.html.
41. A. Kobsa. User modeling: Recent work, prospects and hazards. In M. Schneider-Hufschmidt, T. Kühme, and U. Malinowski, editors, *Adaptive User Interfaces: Principles and Practice*. Elvesier, 1993.
42. A. Kobsa. Generic user modeling systems. *User Modeling and User-Adapted Interaction*, 11:49–63, 2001.
43. N. Koch. *Software Engineering for Adaptive Hypermedia Systems: Reference Model, Modeling Techniques and Development Process*. PhD thesis, Ludwig-Maximilians-Universitt Mnchen, 2001.
44. R. Kowalski and M. Sergot. A Logic-based Calculus of Events. *New Generation of Computing*, 4:67–95, 1986.
45. H. J. Levesque, R. Reiter, Y. Lespérance, F. Lin, and R. B. Scherl. GOLOG: A Logic Programming Language for Dynamic Domains. *J. of Logic Programming*, 31:59–83, 1997.
46. J. Lobo, G. Mendez, and S. R. Taylor. Adding Knowledge to the Action Description Language A. In *Proc. of AAAI'97/IAAI'97*, pages 454–459, Menlo Park, 1997.
47. D. Lowe and W. Hall. *Hypermedia and the Web*. J. Wiley and Sons, 1999.
48. W. May, J.J. Alferes, and F. Bry. Towards generic query, update, and event languages for the semantic web. In *in Proc. of Principles and Practice of Semantic Web Reasoning (PPSWR04)*, volume 3208 of *LNCS*. Springer, 2004.
49. J. McCarthy and P. Hayes. Some, Philosophical Problems from the Standpoint of Artificial Intelligence. *Machine Intelligence*, 4:463–502, 1963.
50. S. McIlraith and T. Son. Adapting Golog for Programming the Semantic Web. In *5th Int. Symp. on Logical Formalization of Commonsense Reasoning*, pages 195–202, 2001.
51. S. A. McIlraith, T. C. Son, and H. Zenf. Semantic Web Services. *IEEE Intelligent Systems*, pages 46–53, March/April 2001.
52. Rule ML. http://www.ruleml.org.
53. Association of Computing Machinery. The ACM computer classification system, 2003. http://www.acm.org/class/1998/.
54. OWL, Web Ontology Language, W3C Recommendation, February 2004. http://www.w3.org/TR/owl-ref/.
55. OWL-S: Web Ontology Language for Services, W3C Submission, November 2004. http://www.org/Submission/2004/07/.

56. W. Nejdl P. Dolog, R. Gavriloaie and J. Brase. Integrating adaptive hypermedia techniques and open rdf-based environments. In *Proc. of The 12th Int. World Wide Web Conference*, Budapest, Hungary, 2003.
57. H. Prendinger and G. Schurz. Reasoning about action and change. a dynamic logic approach. *Journal of Logic, Language, and Information*, 5(2):209–245, 1996.
58. R. Rada. *Interactive Media*. Springer, 1995.
59. RDF. http://www.w3c.org/tr/1999/rec-rdf-syntax-19990222/. 1999.
60. RDFS. http://www.w3.org/tr/rdf-schema/. 2004.
61. RDQL - query language for RDF, Jena, 2005. `http://jena.sourceforge.net/RDQL/`.
62. R. Reiter. A theory of diagnosis from first principles. *Artifical Intelligence*, 32, 1987.
63. E. Rich. User modeling via stereotypes. *Cognitive Science*, 3:329–354, 1978.
64. S. Russell and P. Norvig. *Artificial Intelligence: A Modern Approach*. Prentice Hall, 1995.
65. C. B. Schwind. A logic based framework for action theories. In J. Ginzburg et al., editor, *Language, Logic and Computation*, pages 275–291. CSLI, 1997.
66. M. Sintek and S. Decker. TRIPLE - an RDF Query, Inference, and Transformation Language. In I. Horrocks and J. Hendler, editors, *International Semantic Web Conference (ISWC)*, pages 364–378, Sardinia, Italy, 2002. LNCS 2342.
67. M. Specht. Empirical evaluation of adaptive annotation in hypermedia. In *ED-Media and ED-Telekom*, Freiburg, Germany, 1998.
68. G. Wagner. Ruleml, swrl and rewerse: Towards a general web rule language framework. *SIG SEMIS Semantic Web and Information Systems*, 2004. http://www.sigsemis.org/articles/copy_of_index.html.
69. Geoffrey I. Webb, Michael J. Pazzani, and Daniel Billsus. Machine learning for user modeling. *User Modeling and User-Adapted Interaction*, 11:19–29, 2001.
70. G. Weber and P. Brusilovsky. ELM-ART: An Adaptive Versatile System for Web-based Instruction. *IJAIED Special Issue on Adaptive and Intelligent Web-Based Systems*, 12, 2001.
71. G. Weber, H.C. Kuhl, and S. Weibelzahl. Developing adaptive internet based courses with the authoring system NetCoach. In *Proc. of the Third Workshop on Adaptive Hypermedia, AH2001*, 2001.
72. WSDL. http://www.w3c.org/tr/2003/wd-wsdl12-20030303/. version 1.2, 2003.

Attempto Controlled English:
A Knowledge Representation Language
Readable by Humans and Machines

Norbert E. Fuchs, Stefan Höfler, Kaarel Kaljurand, Fabio Rinaldi,
and Gerold Schneider

Department of Informatics & Institute of Computational Linguistics,
University of Zurich, Switzerland
{fuchs, hoefler, kalju, gschneid, rinaldi}@ifi.unizh.ch
http://www.ifi.unizh.ch/attempto/

Abstract. Attempto Controlled English (ACE) is a knowledge representation language with an English syntax. Thus ACE can be used by anyone, even without being familiar with formal notations. The Attempto Parsing Engine translates ACE texts into discourse representation structures, a variant of first-order logic. Hence, ACE turns out to be a logic language equivalent to full first-order logic. The two views of ACE — natural language and logic language — complement each other, and render ACE both human- and machine-readable. This paper covers both views of ACE. In the first part we present the language ACE in a nutshell, and in the second part we give an overview of the discourse representation structures derived from ACE texts.

1   Introduction

Attempto Controlled English (ACE) is a controlled natural language, i.e. a precisely defined subset of full English that can automatically and unambiguously be translated into full first-order logic. One could say that ACE is a first-order logic language with the syntax of a subset of English. Thus ACE is readable by humans and machines. ACE seems completely natural, but is in fact a formal language that must be learned. Experience shows that one or two days suffice to learn ACE's small number of construction and interpretation rules. More time, though, will be needed to become fluent in ACE.

ACE is based on Discourse Representation Theory [5] whose central concern is to assign meaning to natural language texts and discourses, and to account for the context dependence of meaning. While in general the context of a natural language text is only vaguely defined and can vary, the context of an ACE text is completely fixed. Concretely, an ACE text consists of a sequence of interrelated sentences where each sentence can anaphorically refer to noun phrases occurring in previous sentences. Thus, each sentence is interpreted in the context of the preceding sentences. No further context exists.

N. Eisinger and J. Małuszyński (Eds.): Reasoning Web 2005, LNCS 3564, pp. 213–250, 2005.

Furthermore, the Attempto system is not associated with any specific application domain, or with any particular formal method. By itself it does not contain any knowledge of application domains, of formal methods, or of the world in general. Thus users must explicitly define domain knowledge — definitions, constraints, ontologies — through ACE texts. Words occurring in ACE texts are processed by the Attempto system as uninterpreted syntactic elements, i.e. any interpretation of these words is solely performed by the human writer or reader.

The Attempto Parsing Engine (APE) translates ACE texts unambiguously into discourse representation structures (DRS) the representation language of Discourse Representation Theory. DRSs use a variant of first-order logic, and can be easily translated into any formal language equivalent to first-order logic. For the current version 4 of ACE we developed an extended form of discourse representation structures that allows us to express complex linguistic features, for instance plurals, in first-order logic, and that furthermore supports logical deductions on ACE texts.

A DRS can get a model-theoretic semantics [5], and we can assign the same semantics, i.e. unique meaning, to the ACE text from which the DRS was derived. Thus, the Attempto system treats every ACE sentence as unambiguous, even if people may perceive the same sentence as ambiguous in full English.

2   ACE in a Nutshell

This section is a brief introduction into ACE 4. For a full account readers should consult the ACE documentation found at the Attempto website (see [1]).

Sections 2.1 to 2.6 describe the syntax of ACE 4, sections 2.7 to 2.9 summarize the handling of ambiguity, and section 2.10 explains anaphoric references.

2.1   Vocabulary

The vocabulary of ACE comprises

- predefined function words (e.g. determiners, conjunctions, prepositions),
- content words (nouns, verbs, adjectives, and adverbs).

The Attempto system provides a basic lexicon of content words. Users can define additional, e.g. domain specific, content words with the help of a lexical editor, or can import existing lexica. User-defined words take precedence over words found in the basic lexicon.

2.2   Grammar

The grammar of ACE defines and constrains the form and the meaning of ACE sentences and texts. ACE's grammar is expressed as a small set of construction rules.

2.3   ACE Texts

An ACE text is a sequence of anaphorically interrelated sentences. There are

- simple sentences, and
- composite sentences.

Furthermore, there are query sentences that allow users to interrogate the contents of an ACE text.

2.4   Simple Sentences

A simple sentence describes a situation that can be an event or a state.

> *A customer inserts 2 cards.*
> *A card is valid.*

Simple ACE sentences have the following general structure:

subject + verb + complements + adjuncts

Every sentence has a subject and a verb. Complements (direct and indirect objects) are necessary for transitive verbs (*insert something*) and ditransitive verbs (*give something to somebody*), whereas adjuncts (adverbs, prepositional phrases) are optional.

All elements of a simple sentence can be elaborated upon to describe the situation in more detail. To further specify the nouns *customer* and *card*, we could add adjectives:

> *A new customer inserts 2 valid cards.*

possessive nouns and of-prepositional phrases

> *John's customer inserts a card of Mary.*

or proper nouns and variables as appositions

> *The customer Mr Miller inserts a card A.*

Other modifications of nouns are possible through relative sentences

> *A customer who is new inserts a card that he owns.*

which are described below since they make a sentence composite. We can also detail the insert-event, e.g. by adding an adverb

> *A customer inserts some cards manually.*

or equivalently

> *A customer manually inserts some cards.*

or by adding prepositional phrases, e.g.

> *A customer inserts some cards into a slot.*

We can combine enhancements to arrive at

> *John's customer who is new inserts a valid card of Mary manually into a slot A.*

2.5   Composite Sentences

Composite sentences are recursively built from simpler sentences through coordination, subordination, quantification, and negation.

Coordination by *and* is possible between sentences and between phrases of the same syntactic type.

> *A customer inserts a card and the machine checks the code.*
> *A customer inserts a card and enters a code.*
> *An old and trusted customer enters a card and a code.*

Note that the coordination of the noun phrases *a card and a code* represents a plural object.

Coordination by *or* is possible between sentences, relative clauses and verb phrases.

> *A customer inserts a card or enters a code.*

Coordination by *and* and *or* is governed by the standard binding order of logic, i.e. *and* binds stronger than *or*. Commas can be used to override the standard binding order. Thus the sentence

> *A customer inserts a VisaCard or inserts a MasterCard, and inserts a code.*

means that the customer inserts a VisaCard and a code or, alternatively a MasterCard and a code.

There are two forms of subordination: relative sentences and *if-then* sentences. Relative sentences starting with *who*, *which*, and *that* allow to add detail to nouns, e.g.

A customer who is new inserts a card that he owns.

With the help of if-then sentences we can specify conditional or hypothetical situations, e.g.

If a card is valid then a customer inserts it.

Note the anaphoric reference via the pronoun *it* in the then-part to the noun phrase *a card* in the if-part.

Quantification allows us to speak about all objects of a certain class, or to denote explicitly the existence of at least one object of this class. The textual occurrence of a universal or existential quantifier opens its scope that extends to the end of the sentence, or in coordinations to the end of the respective coordinated sentence.

To express that all involved customers insert cards we can write

Every customer inserts a card.

This sentence means that each customer inserts a card that may, or may not, be the same as the one inserted by another customer. To specify that all customers insert the same card — however unrealistic that situation seems — we can write

There is a card that every customer inserts.

ACE does not know the passive voice. To state that every card is inserted by a customer we write somewhat indirectly

For every card there is a customer who inserts it.

Negation allows us to express that something is not the case, e.g.

A customer does not insert a card.
A card is not valid.

To negate something for all objects of a certain class one uses *no*

No customer inserts more than 2 cards.

or, equivalently, *there is no*

There is no customer who inserts a card.

To negate a complete statement one uses sentence negation

It is not the case that a customer inserts a card.

2.6   Query Sentences

Query sentences permit us to interrogate the contents of an ACE text. There are yes-no queries and wh-queries.

Yes/no-queries establish the existence or non-existence of a specified situation. If we specified

> *A customer inserts a card.*

then we can ask

> *Does a customer insert a card?*

to get a positive answer.

With the help of wh-queries, i.e. queries with query words, we can interrogate a text for details of the specified situation. If we specified

> *A new customer inserts a valid card manually.*

we can ask for each element of the sentence, e.g.

> *Who inserts a card?*
> *Which customer inserts a card?*
> *What does the customer insert?*
> *How does the customer insert a card?*

Note, however, that we cannot ask for the verb itself.

Questions can also be constructed by a sequence of declarative sentences followed by one query sentence. This can be used to temporarily add information to an already existing ACE text before one asks the question. Here is an example.

> *There is John and there is a card that John enters. Does John enter the card?*

2.7   Constraining Ambiguity

To constrain the ambiguity of full natural language ACE employs three simple means

- – some ambiguous constructs are not part of the language; unambiguous alternatives are available in their place,
- – all remaining ambiguous constructs are interpreted deterministically on the basis of a small number of interpretation rules,
- – users can either accept the assigned interpretation, or they must rephrase the input to obtain another one.

2.8   Avoidance of Ambiguity

Here is an example how ACE replaces ambiguous constructs by unambiguous constructs.

In full natural language relative sentences combined with coordinations can introduce ambiguity, e.g.

A customer inserts a card that is valid and opens an account.

In ACE the sentence has the unequivocal meaning that the customer opens an account. This is reflected by

A customer inserts {a card that is valid} and opens an account.

To express the alternative — though not very realistic — meaning that the card opens an account the relative pronoun *that* must be repeated, thus yielding a coordination of relative sentences.

A customer inserts a card that is valid and that opens an account.

with the interpretation

A customer inserts {a card that is valid and that opens an account}.

2.9   Interpretation Rules

However, not all ambiguities can be safely removed from ACE without rendering it artificial. To deterministically interpret otherwise syntactically correct ACE sentences we use about 20 interpretation rules. Here are some examples.

If we write

The customer inserts a card with a code.

we get the interpretation

The customer {inserts a card with a code}.

that reflects ACE's interpretation rule that a prepositional phrase always modifies the verb.

However, this is probably not what we meant to say. To express that the code is associated with the card we can employ the interpretation rule that a relative sentence always modifies the immediately preceding noun phrase, and rephrase the input as

The customer inserts a card that carries a code.

yielding the interpretation

The customer inserts { a card that carries a code}.

or — to specify that the customer inserts a card and a code — as

The customer inserts a card and a code.

Adverbs can precede or follow the verb. To disambiguate the sentence

The customer who inserts a card manually enters a code.

we employ the interpretation rule that the postverbal position has priority.

The customer who {inserts a card manually} enters a code.

2.10   Anaphoric References

Usually ACE texts consist of more than one sentence, e.g.

A customer enters a card and a code. If a code is valid then SimpleMat accepts a card. If a code is not valid then SimpleMat rejects a card.

To express that all occurrences of *card* and *code* should mean the same card and the same code, ACE provides anaphoric references via the definite article, i.e.

A customer enters a card and a code. If the code is valid then SimpleMat accepts the card. If the code is not valid then SimpleMat rejects the card.

During the processing of the ACE text all anaphoric references are replaced by the most recent and most specific accessible noun phrase that agrees in gender and number, yielding

A customer enters a card and a code. If [the code] is valid then SimpleMat accepts [the card]. If [the code] is not valid then SimpleMat rejects [the card].

What does "most recent and most specific" mean? Given the sentence

A customer enters a red card and a blue card.

then

The card is correct.

yields

[The blue card] is correct.

while

The red card is correct.

yields

[The red card] is correct.

What does "accessible" mean? According to Discourse Representation Theory noun phrases introduced in if-then sentences, universally quantified sentences or negations cannot be used anaphorically in subsequent sentences. Thus *the card* in

A customer does not enter a card. The card is correct.

cannot refer to *a card*.

Anaphoric references are also possible via personal pronouns

A customer enters a card and a code. If it is valid then SimpleMat accepts the card. If it is not valid then SimpleMat rejects the card.

or via variables

A customer enters a card CARD and a code CODE. If CODE is valid then SimpleMat accepts CARD. If CODE is not valid then SimpleMat rejects CARD.

Anaphoric references via definite articles and variables can be combined.

A customer enters a card CARD and a code CODE. If the code CODE is valid then SimpleMat accepts the card CARD. If the code CODE is not valid then SimpleMat rejects the card CARD.

Note that proper nouns like *SimpleMat* always refer to the same object.

3   Extended Discourse Representation Structures in Attempto Controlled English

3.1   Introductory Notes

The Attempto Parsing Engine (APE) translates ACE texts unambiguously into extended discourse representation structures (DRS) that have the following characteristics:

- they use only a small number of predefined predicates,
- they represent information derived from words as arguments of the predefined predicates,
- they have eventuality types,
- they use a lattice-theoretic representation of objects that allows us to encode plurals in first-order language,
- they contain quantity information.

In the following we will explain extended discourse representation structures by means of illustrative examples. Readers are referred to [2] for a practical introduction to Discourse Representation Theory.

Section 3.2 introduces the notation used in this report. Sections 3.3 to 3.11 describe discourse representation structures derived from declarative ACE sentences, and section 3.12 those derived from ACE query sentences.

3.2   Notation

APE translates an ACE text unambiguously into an internal representation using Prolog notation

```
paragraph(DRS,Text)
```

where Text stands for the predicate text/1, the only argument of which is a list of the input sentences represented as character strings. The example text

```
John enters a card. Every card is green.
```

would thus be represented as

```
text(['John enters a card.', 'Every card is green.'])
```

The discourse representation structure derived from the ACE text is stored in the first argument DRS of paragraph/2 as

```
drs(Domain,Conditions)
```

The first argument of drs/2 is a list of discourse referents, i.e. quantified variables naming objects of the domain of discourse. The second argument of drs/2 is a list of simple and complex conditions for the discourse referents. The list separator ',' stands for logical conjunction. Simple conditions are logical atoms, while complex conditions are built from other discourse representation structures with the help of the logical connectors negation '-', disjunction 'v', and implication '=>'.

```
drs([A,B],[condition(A),condition(B)])
```

is usually pretty-printed as

$$\begin{array}{|l|}\hline A\ B \\ \hline condition(A) \\ condition(B) \\ \hline \end{array}$$

The above DRS corresponds to the standard first-order logic (FOL) representation

$$\exists AB : condition(A) \land condition(B)$$

Accordingly, a negated DRS like

$$\neg \ \begin{array}{|l|}\hline A\ B \\ \hline condition(A) \\ condition(B) \\ \hline \end{array}$$

corresponds to the standard FOL representation

$$\neg \exists AB : condition(A) \land condition(B)$$

and is internally represented as

```
-drs([A,B],[condition(A),condition(B)])
```

in the Attempto system. We have defined -/1 as a prefix operator which stands for the logical '¬'.

In a DRS, all variables are thus existentially quantified unless they stand in the restrictor of an implication. The implication

$$\begin{array}{|l|}\hline A \\ \hline condition(A) \\ \hline \end{array} \Rightarrow \begin{array}{|l|}\hline B \\ \hline condition(B) \\ \hline \end{array}$$

corresponding to the standard FOL representation

$$\forall A : condition(A) \rightarrow \exists B : condition(B)$$

is internally represented as

```
drs([A],[condition(A)]) => drs([B],[condition(B)])
```

The disjunction

$$\begin{array}{|l|}\hline A \\ \hline condition(A) \\ \hline \end{array} \lor \begin{array}{|l|}\hline B \\ \hline condition(B) \\ \hline \end{array}$$

corresponding to the standard FOL notation

$$\exists A : condtion(A) \lor \exists B : condition(B)$$

is likewise internally represented as

```
drs([A],[condition(A)]) v drs([B],[condition(B)])
```

The predicates `=>/2` and `v/2` are defined as infix operators.

In nested discourse representation structures, a DRS can occur as an element of the conditions list of another DRS. Therefore

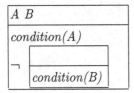

is represented as

```
drs([A,B],[condition(A),-drs([],[condition(B)])])
```

The discourse representation structure uses a reified, or 'flat' notation for logical atoms (see [4]).

For example, the noun *card* that customarily would be represented as

$$\exists A : card(A)$$

is represented here as

$$\exists A : object(A, card, object), \ldots$$

relegating the predicate 'card' to the constant 'card' used as an argument in the predefined predicate 'object'.

As a consequence, the large number of predicates in the customary representation is replaced by a small number of predefined predicates. This allows us to conveniently formulate axioms for the predefined predicates within the Attempto Reasoner RACE (see [3]).

Logical atoms occurring in `drs/2` are actually written as `Atom-I` (using an infix operator `-/2`) where the index I refers to the I-th element of the list in `text/1`, i.e. to the sentence from which `Atom` was derived.

The example text

```
John enters a card. Every card is green.
```

the DRS of which is

$$\begin{array}{|l|}
\hline
A\ B\ C\ D\ E \\
\hline
\textit{named(B,'John')} \\
\textit{object(B,named\_entity,person)} \\
\textit{structure(B,atomic)} \\
\textit{quantity(B,cardinality,count\_unit,A,eq,1)} \\
\textit{structure(D,atomic)} \\
\textit{quantity(D,cardinality,count\_unit,C,eq,1)} \\
\textit{object(D,card,object)} \\
\textit{predicate(E,event,enter,B,D)} \\
\hline
\end{array}$$

$$
\boxed{\begin{array}{l}
F\ G \\
\hline
\textit{structure(G,atomic)} \\
\textit{quantity(G,cardinality,count\_unit,F,eq,1)} \\
\textit{object(G,card,object)}
\end{array}}
\ \Rightarrow\
\boxed{\begin{array}{l}
H\ I \\
\hline
\textit{property(I,green)} \\
\textit{predicate(H,state,be,G,I)}
\end{array}}
$$

will thus internally be represented as

```
paragraph(drs([A,B,C,D,E],[named(B,'John')-1,
object(B,named_entity,person)-1,structure(B,atomic)-1,
quantity(B,cardinality,count_unit,A,eq,1)-1,structure(D,atomic)-1,
quantity(D,cardinality,count_unit,C,eq,1)-1,object(D,card,object)-1,
predicate(E,event,enter,B,D)-1,drs([F,G],[structure(G,atomic)-2,
quantity(G,cardinality,count_unit,F,eq,1)-2,
object(G,card,object)-2])=>drs([H,I],[property(I,green)-2,
predicate(H,state,be,G,I)-2])]),text(['John enters a card.',
'Every card is green.']))
```

The following sections provide the discourse representation structures for a selected number of ACE 4 sentences in the form they will be output by APE.

Using illustrative ACE 4 examples this paper describes the language of extended DRSs derived from ACE texts. For a complete description of the ACE 4 language itself please refer to the ACE 4 Language Manual found on the Attempto web site [1].

3.3   Noun Phrases

ACE noun phrases (NP) are headed by a countable noun such as *card*, a mass noun such as *bread*, or they are a proper names such as *Mary* or pronouns such as *she*. All ACE NPs except proper names and pronouns are introduced by a determiner. We also introduce special determiners called generalized quantifiers, NP conjunctions and measurement NPs.

Singular Countable Noun Phrases. Singular countable NPs are typically introduced by an existential quantifier such as *a* or a universal quantifier such as *every*. Both quantifiers can also be negated. Existentially quantified NPs are typically introduced with an indefinite article *a* if they are new discourse participants and with a definite article *the* if they refer to a referent that has been previously introduced. A noun phrase with a definite article that does not anaphorically refer to a previously introduced noun phrase is treated as if having an indefinite article, i.e. as a new discourse participant.

a card

A B
structure(B,atomic) quantity(B,cardinality,count_unit,A,eq,1) object(B,card,object)

no card

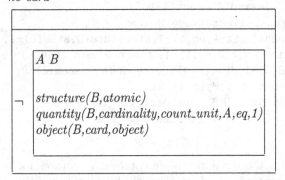

every card

not every card

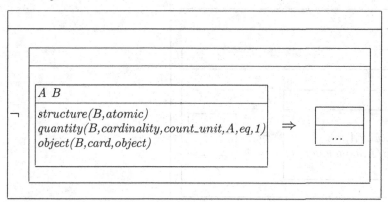

Mass Nouns. Non-countable nouns, also called mass nouns, are introduced by *some* in their existential and *all* in their universal affirmative version. Both quantifiers can also be negated.

some money

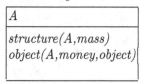

no money

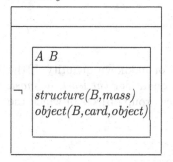

all money

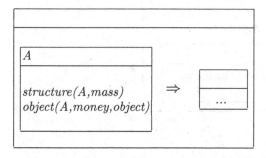

not all money

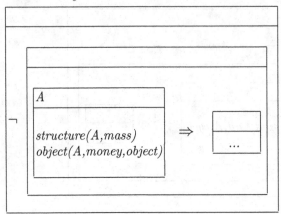

Proper Names. Proper names denote a unique object. They can be singular or plural.

John

A B
named(B, 'John') object(B,named_entity,person) structure(B,atomic) quantity(B,cardinality,count_unit,A,eq,1)

Plural Noun Phrases. Plural NPs are of known or unknown quantity. If the quantity is unknown but restricted, a generalized quantifier (*at least*, *at most*, *more than*, *less than*) can be used. Plurals introduce group objects of which the ndividual constituents form parts.

some cards

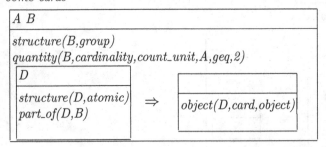

2 cards

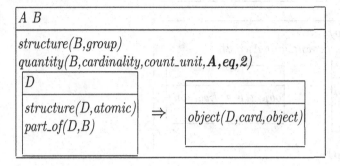

at least *2 cards*

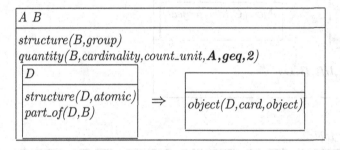

Plural Interpretations. In ACE, a plural noun phrase has a default collective reading. In order to express a distributive reading, a noun phrase has to be preceded by the marker *each of*. Since the relative scope of a quantifier corresponds to its surface position, we use *there is/are* and *for each of* to move a quantifier to the front of a sentence and thus widen its scope.

The natural English sentence

2 girls lift 2 tables.

has a multitude of readings (see [6]), eight of which can be expressed in ACE. Here we present two of these eight readings.

The first one shows the default collective reading of both *2 girls* and *2 tables*, while the second shows the distributive reading of *2 girls* and the collective reading of *2 tables*. The other six readings can be expressed analogously using *each of* and *there is/are*.

2 girls lift 2 tables.

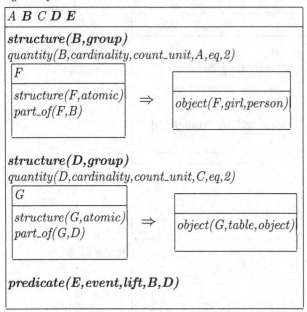

Each of 2 girls lifts 2 tables.

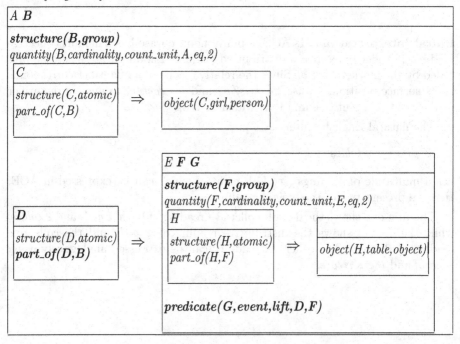

Non-anaphoric Pronouns. Anonymous objects can be introduced by non-anaphoric pronouns. They offer a natural way to express a passive voice situation in ACE.

someone / somebody / something

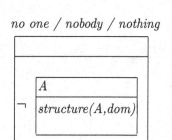

no one / nobody / nothing

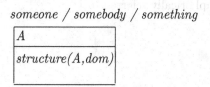

everyone / everybody / everything

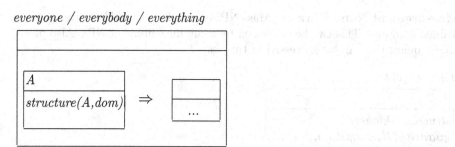

not everyone / not everybody / not everything

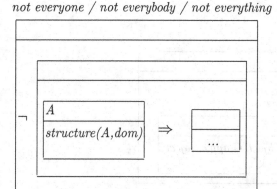

Noun Phrase Conjunction. NPs can be conjoined, introducing a plural object into the discourse. The default interpretation of conjoined plurals (e.g. *a customer and a clerk*) is that the individuals act together. Both the conjoined plural object and the individuals can be anaphorically referred to.

a customer and a clerk

A B C D E F
structure(B,group)
quantity(B,cardinality,count_unit,A,eq,2)
sum_of(B,[D,F])
structure(D,atomic)
quantity(D,cardinality,count_unit,C,eq,1)
object(D,customer,person)
proper_part_of(D,B)
structure(F,atomic)
quantity(F,cardinality,count_unit,E,eq,1)
object(F,clerk,person)
proper_part_of(F,B)

Measurement Noun Phrases. Mass NPs cannot be counted but often come in defined amounts. This can be expressed by using measurement NPs. Also plural object quantities can be expressed in this way.

*1 **kg of** gold*

A B
structure(B,mass)
quantity(B,weight,kg,A,eq,1)
object(B,gold,object)

*2 **kg of** apples*

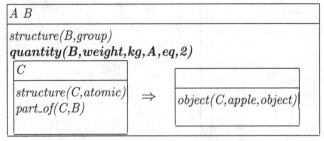

3.4   Verb Phrases

Verbs fall into classical subcategories known as intransitive (e.g. *wait*), transitive (e.g. *enter something*), and ditransitive (e.g. *give something to somebody*). ACE also knows the copula *be*. The copula can be followed by a (simple, transitive or comparative) adjective, noun phrase or a prepositional phrase.

*The customer **waits**.*

A B **C**
structure(B,atomic)
quantity(B,cardinality,count_unit,A,eq,1)
object(B,customer,person)
predicate(C,state,wait,B)

*John **enters** a card.*

A B C D **E**
named(B,'John')
object(B,named_entity,person)
structure(B,atomic)
quantity(B,cardinality,count_unit,A,eq,1)
structure(D,atomic)
quantity(D,cardinality,count_unit,C,eq,1)
object(D,card,object)
predicate(E,event,enter,B,D)

*A clerk **gives** a password **to** a customer.*

A B C D E F **G**
structure(B,atomic)
quantity(B,cardinality,count_unit,A,eq,1)
object(B,clerk,person)
structure(D,atomic)
quantity(D,cardinality,count_unit,C,eq,1)
object(D,password,object)
structure(F,atomic)
quantity(F,cardinality,count_unit,E,eq,1)
object(F,customer,person)
predicate(G,event,give_to,B,D,F)

*A card **is valid**.*

*A B **C D***
structure(B,atomic)
quantity(B,cardinality,count_unit,A,eq,1)
object(B,card,object)
predicate(C,state,be,B,D)
property(D,valid)

*A card **is valid and correct**.*

*A B **C D***
structure(B,atomic)
quantity(B,cardinality,count_unit,A,eq,1)
object(B,card,object)
predicate(C,state,be,B,D)
property(D,valid)
property(D,correct)

*2 codes **are valid**.*

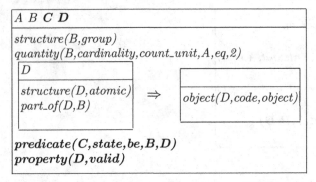

*Each of 2 codes **is valid**.*

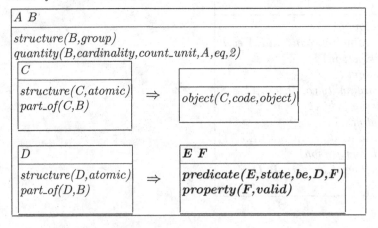

John is a rich customer.

A B C D E
named(B,'John')
object(B,named_entity,person)
structure(B,atomic)
quantity(B,cardinality,count_unit,A,eq,1)
structure(D,atomic)
quantity(D,cardinality,count_unit,C,eq,1)
object(D,customer,person)
property(D,rich)
predicate(E,state,be,B,D)

*A customer is **richer than** John.*

A B C D E F
named(B,'John')
object(B,named_entity,person)
structure(B,atomic)
quantity(B,cardinality,count_unit,A,eq,1)
structure(D,atomic)
quantity(D,cardinality,count_unit,C,eq,1)
object(D,customer,person)
property(F,richer_than,B)
predicate(E,state,be,D,F)

*John **is** in the bank.*

A B C D E
named(B,'John')
object(B,named_entity,person)
structure(B,atomic)
quantity(B,cardinality,count_unit,A,eq,1)
predicate(C,state,be,B)
structure(D,atomic)
quantity(D,cardinality,count_unit,E,eq,1)
object(D,bank,object)
modifier(C,location,in,D)

3.5   Verb Phrase Coordination

Verb phrases can be conjoined (*and*) and disjoined (*or*).

*A screen flashes **and** blinks.*

A B C D
structure(B,atomic) quantity(B,cardinality,count_unit,A,eq,1) object(B,screen,object) predicate(C,event,flash,B) predicate(D,state,blink,B)

*A screen flashes **or** blinks.*

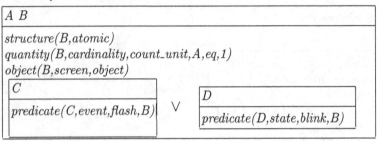

3.6   Modifying Verb Phrases

Facultative additional information detailing, for instance, how or where an action is performed is expressed by modifying the verb by an adverb or a prepositional phrase.

Adverbs can precede or follow the verb they modify. In case of ambiguity, attachment to following adverbs is preferred. Adverbs fall into semantic classes such as manner, time, location, direction.

*A customer enters a card **quickly**.*

A B C D E
structure(B,atomic) quantity(B,cardinality,count_unit,A,eq,1) object(B,customer,person) structure(D,atomic) quantity(D,cardinality,count_unit,C,eq,1) object(D,card,object) predicate(E,event,enter,B,D) **modifier(E,manner,none,quickly)**

Prepositional phrases (PPs) follow the verb they modify. The semantic class of a PP depends on the preposition of the PP as well as on the type of the noun occurring in the PP.

*John enters a card **in a bank**.*

*A B C D E **G F***
named(B,'John')   *object(B,named_entity,person)*   *structure(B,atomic)*   *quantity(B,cardinality,count_unit,A,eq,1)*   *structure(D,atomic)*   *quantity(D,cardinality,count_unit,C,eq,1)*   *object(D,card,object)*   *predicate(E,event,enter,B,D)*   ***structure(G,atomic)***   ***quantity(G,cardinality,count_unit,F,eq,1)***   ***object(G,bank,object)***   ***modifier(E,location,in,G)***

*John enters a card **in the morning**.*

*A B C D E **G F***
named(B,'John')   *object(B,named_entity,person)*   *structure(B,atomic)*   *quantity(B,cardinality,count_unit,A,eq,1)*   *structure(D,atomic)*   *quantity(D,cardinality,count_unit,C,eq,1)*   *object(D,card,object)*   *predicate(E,event,enter,B,D)*   ***structure(G,atomic)***   ***quantity(G,cardinality,count_unit,F,eq,1)***   ***object(G,morning,time)***   ***modifier(E,time,in,G)***

3.7   Modifying Nouns and Noun Phrases

ACE offers a wide range of NP modifications: adjectives, relative clauses, *of*-PPs, Saxon genitives, possessive pronouns, and appositions.

Adjectives. An adjective or a conjunction of adjectives precede a noun.

*A **rich** customer waits.*

A B C
structure(B,atomic)
quantity(B,cardinality,count_unit,A,eq,1)
property(B,rich)
object(B,customer,person)
predicate(C,state,wait,B)

*The **rich and old** customer waits.*

A B C
structure(B,atomic)
quantity(B,cardinality,count_unit,A,eq,1)
property(B,rich)
property(B,old)
object(B,customer,person)
predicate(C,state,wait,B)

Relative Sentences. Relative sentences are an important natural language option to express complex NP modification.

*A customer enters a card **which is valid**.*

A B C D E F G H
structure(B,atomic)
quantity(B,cardinality,count_unit,A,eq,1)
object(B,customer,person)
structure(E,atomic)
quantity(E,cardinality,count_unit,D,eq,1)
object(E,card,object)
property(H,valid)
predicate(F,state,be,E,H)
predicate(G,event,enter,B,E)

*A customer enters a card **which is green and which is valid**.*

```
A B C D E F G H I
```
structure(B,atomic)
quantity(B,cardinality,count_unit,A,eq,1)
object(B,customer,person)
structure(D,atomic)
quantity(D,cardinality,count_unit,C,eq,1)
object(D,card,object)
property(H,green)
predicate(E,state,be,D,H)
property(I,valid)
predicate(F,state,be,D,I)
predicate(G,event,enter,B,D)

*A customer enters a card **which is green or which is red**.*

```
A B C D G
```

structure(B,atomic)
quantity(B,cardinality,count_unit,A,eq,1)
object(B,customer,person)
structure(D,atomic)
quantity(D,cardinality,count_unit,C,eq,1)
object(D,card,object)

E H		**F I**
property(H,green) ***predicate(E,state,be,D,H)***	∨	***property(I,red)*** ***predicate(F,state,be,D,I)***

predicate(G,event,enter,B,D)

***of*-Prepositional Phrases.** NPs can be modified by *of*-PPs. Other PP modification of NPs is not possible but can be rephrased using relative sentences.

*The surface **of the card** has a green color.*

```
A B C D E F G
```
structure(B,atomic)
quantity(B,cardinality,count_unit,A,eq,1)
object(B,surface,object)
structure(D,atomic)
quantity(D,cardinality,count_unit,C,eq,1)
property(D,green)
object(D,color,object)
predicate(E,state,have,B,D)
structure(F,atomic)
quantity(F,cardinality,count_unit,G,eq,1)
object(F,card,object)
relation(B,surface,of,F)

Possessive Nouns. Possessive noun phrases are either introduced by a Saxon genitive (e.g. *Peter's*) or a possessive pronoun (e.g. *his*).

The customer's card is valid.

```
A B C D E F
structure(B,atomic)
quantity(B,cardinality,count_unit,A,eq,1)
object(B,card,object)
property(F,valid)
predicate(C,state,be,B,F)
structure(D,atomic)
quantity(D,cardinality,count_unit,E,eq,1)
object(D,customer,object)
relation(B,card,of,D)
```

Appositions. Appositions of noun phrases can be proper names, quoted strings or variables.

The customer Mr Miller enters a card.

```
A B C D E
structure(B,atomic)
quantity(B,cardinality,count_unit,A,eq,1)
object(B,customer,person)
named(B,'Mr Miller')
object(B,named_entity,person)
structure(D,atomic)
quantity(D,cardinality,count_unit,C,eq,1)
object(D,card,object)
predicate(E,event,enter,B,D)
```

A customer X enters the password "Jabberwocky".

```
A B C D E
structure(B,atomic)
quantity(B,cardinality,count_unit,A,eq,1)
object(B,customer,person)
variable(B,'X')
structure(D,atomic)
quantity(D,cardinality,count_unit,C,eq,1)
object(D,password,object)
quoted_string(D,'Jabberwocky')
predicate(E,state,enter,B,D)
```

3.8   Conditional Sentences

Conditional sentences combine two sentences by an if-then construction.

If the password is valid then the machine accepts the request.

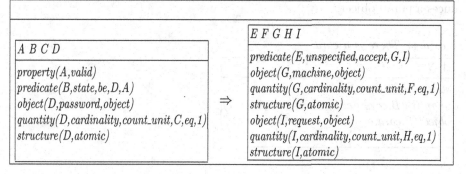

3.9   Coordinated Sentences

Coordinated sentences combine simpler sentences by *and* and *or*.

The screen blinks and John waits.

```
A  B C D E F

structure(B,atomic)
quantity(B,cardinality,count_unit,A,eq,1)
object(B,screen,object)
predicate(C,state,blink,B)
named(E, 'John')
object(E,named_entity,person)
structure(E,atomic)
quantity(E,cardinality,count_unit,D,eq,1)
predicate(F,state,wait,E)
```

A screen blinks or John waits.

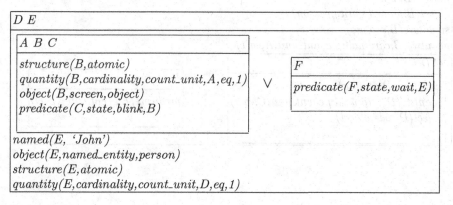

3.10   Quantified Sentences

Quantified sentences allow users to express existential quantification and universal quantification. Furthermore, a construct *there is* followed by a noun phrase introduces an existentially quantified singular object. Similarly, *there are* introduces a plural object.

a card ⇔ *There is a card.*

A B
structure(B,atomic) *quantity(B,cardinality,count_unit,A,eq,1)* *object(B,card,object)*

John enters a card.

A B C D E
named(B,'John') *object(B,named_entity,person)* *structure(B,atomic)* *quantity(B,cardinality,count_unit,A,eq,1)* *structure(D,atomic)* *quantity(D,cardinality,count_unit,C,eq,1)* *object(D,card,object)* *predicate(E,event,enter,B,D)*

John enters every code. (= If there is a code then John enters it.)

A B
named(B,'John') *object(B,named_entity,person)* *structure(B,atomic)* *quantity(B,cardinality,count_unit,A,eq,1)* ┌─ C D ──────────────────────────┐ ┌─ E ──────────────────────────┐ │ *structure(D,atomic)*   │ ⇒ │ *predicate(E,event,enter,B,D)* │ │ *quantity(D,cardinality,count_unit,C,eq,1)* │ └──────────────────────────────┘ │ *object(D,code,object)*   │ └─────────────────────────────────┘

There is a code *such that* every clerk enters it.

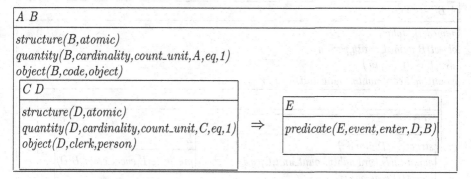

For every code *(there is)* a clerk *(such that he)* enters it.

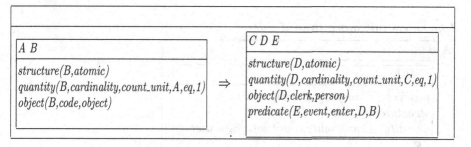

3.11   Negation

ACE offers many ways to negate noun phrases, quantified noun phrases, verb phrases and complete sentences.

John enters no code.

```
┌─────────────────────────────────────────────┐
│ A B                                           │
├─────────────────────────────────────────────┤
│ named(B,'John')                               │
│ object(B,named_entity,person)                 │
│ structure(B,atomic)                           │
│ quantity(B,cardinality,count_unit,A,eq,1)     │
│    ┌──────────────────────────────────────┐  │
│    │ C D E                                 │  │
│    ├──────────────────────────────────────┤  │
│    │ structure(D,atomic)                   │  │
│  ¬ │ quantity(D,cardinality,count_unit,C,eq,1)│
│    │ object(D,code,object)                 │  │
│    │ predicate(E,event,enter,B,D)          │  │
│    └──────────────────────────────────────┘  │
└─────────────────────────────────────────────┘
```

John enters not every code.

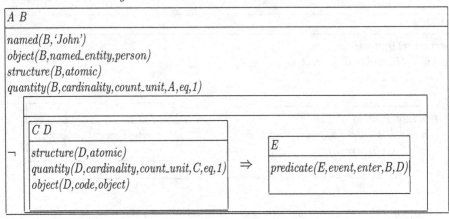

*John enters **not more than 2** codes.*

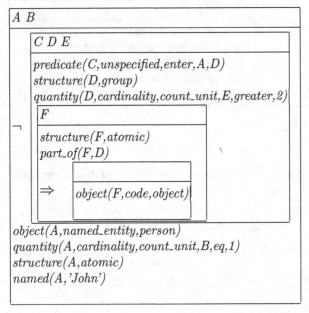

Every screen does not blink.

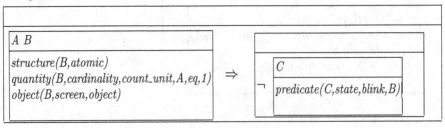

A card is not valid.

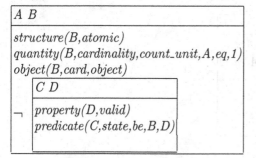

It is not the case that a screen blinks.

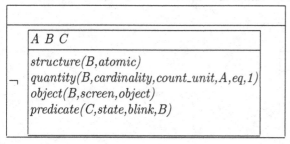

3.12   Query Sentences

Yes/no-questions ask for the existence of a state of affairs. These questions are translated exactly as their declarative counterparts.

Does John enter a card?

A B C D E
object(C,card,object)
quantity(C,cardinality,count_unit,B,eq,1)
structure(C,atomic)
predicate(D,event,enter,A,C)
object(A,named_entity,person)
quantity(A,cardinality,count_unit,E,eq,1)
structure(A,atomic)
named(A,'John')

Is the card valid?

```
A B C D

object(B,card,object)
quantity(B,cardinality,count_unit,A,eq,1)
structure(B,atomic)
property(C,valid)
predicate(D,state,be,B,C)
```

Who/What/Which-Questions. Who/what/which-questions ask for the subjects or the objects of sentences. These questions are translated as their declarative counterparts but contain additional conditions for the query words.

Who enters what?

```
A B C

query(A,who)
structure(A,dom)
query(B,what)
structure(B,dom)
predicate(C,event,enter,A,B)
```

Which customer enters a card?

```
A B C D E

query(B,which)
structure(B,atomic)
quantity(B,cardinality,count_unit,A,eq,1)
object(B,customer,person)
structure(D,atomic)
quantity(D,cardinality,count_unit,C,eq,1)
object(D,card,object)
predicate(E,event,enter,B,D)
```

Where/When/How/...-Questions. Where/when/how/...-questions ask for details of an action. These questions are translated as their declarative counterparts but contain additional conditions for the query words.

Where does John enter a card?

A B C D E F G
named(G, 'John')
structure(G, atomic)
quantity(G, cardinality, count_unit, A, eq, 1)
object(G, named_entity, person)
query(F, E, where)
modifier(B, location, F, E)
predicate(B, event, enter, G, C)
structure(C, atomic)
quantity(C, cardinality, count_unit, D, eq, 1)
object(C, card, object)

When does John enter a card?

A B C D E F G
named(G, 'John')
structure(G, atomic)
quantity(G, cardinality, count_unit, A, eq, 1)
object(G, named_entity, person)
query(F, E, when)
modifier(B, time, F, E)
predicate(B, event, enter, G, C)
structure(C, atomic)
quantity(C, cardinality, count_unit, D, eq, 1)
object(C, card, object)

How does John enter a card?

A B C D E F G
named(G, 'John')
structure(G, atomic)
quantity(G, cardinality, count_unit, A, eq, 1)
object(G, named_entity, person)
query(F, E, how)
modifier(B, manner, F, E)
predicate(B, event, enter, G, C)
structure(C, atomic)
quantity(C, cardinality, count_unit, D, eq, 1)
object(C, card, object)

3.13   Predicate Declarations

modifier(X,K,Preposition,Y/Adverb)

X   discourse referent of the event or state that is modified
K $\in$ {location, origin, direction, time, start, end, duration, instrument,
      comitative, manner, ...}
Y   discourse referent of an object, i.e. the NP of the modifying PP

named(X,ProperName)

X discourse referent of the object that is named

object(X,Noun,K)

X   discourse referent of the object that is denoted by the noun
K $\in$ {person, object, time}

part_of(X,Y)

X discourse referent of an (atomic) object
Y discourse referent of a (group) object

predicate(E,D,Verb,X)

E   discourse referent of the event or state that is denoted by the verb
D $\in$ {event, state}
X   discourse referent of the subject

predicate(E,D,Verb,X,Y)

E   discourse referent of the event or state that is denoted by the verb
D $\in$ {event, state}
X   discourse referent of the subject
Y   discourse referent of the direct object

predicate(E,D,Verb,X,Y,Z)

E   discourse referent of the event or state that is denoted by the verb
D $\in$ {event, state}
X   discourse referent of the subject
Y   discourse referent of the direct object
Z   discourse referent of the indirect object

proper_part_of(X,Y)

X discourse referent of an (atomic) object
Y discourse referent of a (group) object

property(X,IntransitiveAdjective)

X discourse referent of the object a property of which is described
   by the adjective

property(X,Comparative/TransitiveAdjective,Y)

X discourse referent of the object that is described
Y discourse referent of the object with which X is compared or the
     object of the adjective

property(X,TransitiveComparative,Y,Z)

X discourse referent of the object that is described
Y discourse referent of the object of the adjective
Z discourse referent of the object with which X is compared

quantity(X,K,I,Q,J,N)

K ∈ {cardinality, weight, size, length, volume, ...}
I ∈ {count_unit, kg, cm, liter, ...}
X discourse referent of the object the quantity of which is indicated
Q discourse referent of the (reified) quantity of X
J ∈ {eq, leq, geq, greater, less}
N a number

query(X,Q)

X discourse referent of the object that is asked for
Q ∈ {who, what, which}

query(P,Y,Q)

P preposition
Y discourse referent of an object, i.e. the NP of the modifying PP
     or an adverb
Q ∈ {where, when, how, ...}

quoted_string(X,QuotedString)

X discourse referent of the object that is denoted by the quoted
     string

relation(X,Relation,of,Y)

X discourse referent of the object that is related to Y
Y discourse referent of the object that is related to X

structure(X, D)

X discourse referent of the object the structure of which is indicated
D ∈ {atomic, group, mass, dom}

sum_of(X,L)

X discourse referent of a (group) object
L list of discourse referents of objects that are a proper part of X

variable(X,Variable)

X discourse referent of an object that is denoted by the variable

4   Conclusions

Attempto Controlled English (ACE) is a knowledge representation language with a dual face — humans can read ACE texts and machines can process them. ACE has already been used as specification language, as knowledge representation language, and as interface language to formal systems. We believe, that the attributes of ACE — specifically its ability to express business and policy rules — make it a prime candidate for the knowledge representation and query tasks of the semantic web.

5   Acknowledgment

The authors would like to thank Uta Schwertel, a former collaborator of the project Attempto, for her important contributions to the project.

References

1. Attempto Website. http://www.ifi.unizh.ch/attempto.
2. Patrick Blackburn and Johan Bos. *Working with Discourse Representation Structures*, volume 2nd of *Representation and Inference for Natural Language: A First Course in Computational Linguistics*. September 1999.
3. Norbert E. Fuchs and Uta Schwertel. Reasoning in Attempto Controlled English. In *Workshop on Principles and Practice of Semantic Web Reasoning (PPSWR 2003)*, Lecture Notes in Computer Science, Hannover, 2003. Springer.
4. Jerry R. Hobbs. Ontological Promiscuity. In *Proceedings of the 23rd Annual Meeting of the ACL*. University of Chicago, 1985.
5. Hans Kamp and Uwe Reyle. *From Discourse to Logic: Introduction to Modeltheoretic Semantics of Natural Language, Formal Logic and Discourse Representation Theory*. Kluwer, Dordrecht/Boston/London, 1993.
6. Uta Schwertel. *Plural Semantics for Natural Language Understanding — A Computational Proof-Theoretic Approach*. PhD thesis, University of Zurich, Zurich, 2003.

Rule Modeling and Markup

Gerd Wagner

Institute of Informatics, Brandenburg University of Technology at Cottbus,
P.O.Box 10 13 44, 03013 Cottbus, Germany
G.Wagner@tu-cottbus.de

Abstract. In this paper we address several issues of rule modeling on the basis of UML. We discuss the relationship between UML class models and OWL vocabularies. We show how certain rules can be specified in a class diagram with the help of OCL. We also show how rule concepts can be described, and how the abstract syntax of RDF, OWL, SWRL and RuleML can be defined, by means of UML class diagrams in a concise way.

1 Introduction

Rules play an important role not only in everyday life but also in computational formalisms and information systems. They define derived concepts as elements of the information state structure and constrain or prescribe the behavior of people and IT systems. In particular, rules are being used to express privacy protection and access control policies, both of which are important issues on the Web.

As we model the state structure and behavior of a system to be analyzed or to be designed, we also have to model the rules defining the derived elements of its information base and governing its behavior. Therefore, rule modeling is part of a general *model-driven* approach to software and information systems engineering.

Rules always come on top of a vocabulary. There is no rule without an underlying vocabulary. Consequently, for being able to see how rules can be modeled and represented in formal languages, we also have to understand how vocabularies are being modeled and expressed. in formal languages.

1.1 Specifying Vocabularies

While the recommended method for specifying domain vocabularies, as part of systems analysis, in general software engineering is to use the *Unified Modeling Language*[1] *(UML)* for making a *class model* in the semi-visual form of a *class diagram*, the W3C has recommended to use the languages *RDF* and *OWL*[2] for specifying vocabularies as part of Web applications. In particular, OWL has a great overlap with UML class models. However, while UML class models have a visual

---

[1] See http://www.uml.org/.
[2] RDF is the *Resource Description Framework* (see http://www.w3.org/RDF/). OWL is the *Web Ontology Language* (see http://www.w3.org/2004/OWL).

N. Eisinger and J. Małuszyński (Eds.): Reasoning Web 2005, LNCS 3564, pp. 251–274, 2005.

syntax and are widely used in academic and industrial software engineering activities, they don't have a formal logic semantics. OWL, on the other hand, has a formal logic semantics, but has no visual syntax and is not (yet?) widely used in industry.

Clearly, both languages can benefit from each other:

– OWL vocabularies can be captured in the user-friendly form of class diagrams. For this purpose the UML provides an extension mechanism that allows to use OWL-specific elements in a class diagram. Expressing OWL construct as elements of a UML class model gives OWL a kind of operational semantics and makes it accessible to software engineers who are not familiar with, and not willing to learn, the description logic semantics of OWL.

– UML class diagrams can be mapped to OWL vocabularies and, in this way, obtain a logical semantics.

There is yet another good reason to consider UML: UML class diagrams can also be used as a visual language to describe the vocabulary, and the abstract syntax, of all kinds of languages in a concise visual manner. The particular fragment of UML class modeling that has been proposed for this purpose by the OMG is called *Meta-Object Facility*[3] *(MOF)*; we call it *MOF/UML* in the sequel We use MOF/UML in this article for describing the abstract syntax, or the language model, of RDF, OWL, SWRL[4] and RuleML. This representation helps to identify commonalities and differences between these languages.

1.2 Modeling Rules

Since rules are based on vocabularies, it is natural to add rule constructs to the language of UML class models for obtaining a general rule modeling language. For this purpose, the UML has been supplemented by the *Object Constraint Language (OCL)*, which allows to add *integrity rules* (called *invariants*) and *derivation rules* to a class model in order to constrain or derive certain model elements. However, UML and OCL do not provide any visual syntax for rules, nor do they support other kinds of rules. In particular, the concept of *reaction* (or *event-condition-action*) rules is not supported at all in UML.

The *Model Driven Architecture*[5] *(MDA)* is a framework for software development defined by the *Object Management Group (OMG)*. It is based on a fundamental distinction between three different modeling levels:

1. the level of semi-formal business domain modeling, called *'computation-independent' modeling (CIM)*,
2. the level of platform-independent logical design modeling, in short: *platform-independent modeling (PIM)*, and
3. the level of platform-specific implementation modeling, in short: *platform-specific modeling (PIM)*.

---

[3] See http://www.omg.org/mof.
[4] See the subsection on SWRL below.
[5] See http://www.omg.org/mda.

As illustrated in Fig. 1, we consider rules at these three different abstraction levels:

1. At the **business domain (CIM) level**, rules are statements that express (certain parts of) a business/domain policy (e.g., defining terms of the domain language or defining/constraining domain operations) in a declarative manner, typically using a natural language or a visual language. Examples are:

   (R1) "The driver of a rental car must be at least 25 years old"

   (R2) "A gold customer is a customer with more than $1Million on deposit"

   (R3) "An investment is exempt from tax on profit if the stocks have been bought more than a year ago"

   (R4) "When a share price drops by more than 5% and the investment is exempt from tax on profit, then sell it"

   R1 is an *integrity rule*, R2 and R3 are *derivation rules*, and R4 is a *reaction rule* (see below for explanations of these rule categories).
2. At the platform-independent **operational design (PIM) level**, rules are formal statements, expressed in some formalism or computational paradigm, which can be directly mapped to executable statements of a software system. Examples of rule languages at this level are SQL:1999, OCL 2.0, and DOM Level 3 Event Listeners. Remarkably, SQL provides operational constructs for all three business rule categories mentioned above: *checks/assertions* operationalize a notion of integrity rules, *views* operationalize a notion of derivation rules, and *triggers* operationalize a notion of reaction rules.
3. At the platform-specific **implementation (PSM) level**, rules are statements in a language of a specific execution environment, such as Oracle 10g views, Jess 3.4, XSB 2.6 Prolog, or the Microsoft Outlook 6 Rule Wizard.

Generally, rules are self-contained knowledge units that typically involve some form of reasoning. They may, for instance, specify:

- static or dynamic integrity constraints (e.g. for constraining the state space or the execution histories of a system),
- derivations (e.g. for defining derived concepts),
- reactions (for specifying the reactive behavior of a system in response to events)

Given the linguistic richness and the complex dynamics of application domains, it should be clear that any specific mathematical account of rules, such as classical logic Horn clauses, must be viewed as a limited descriptive theory that captures just a certain fragment of the entire conceptual space of rules, and not as a definitive, normative account. Rather, we need a pluralistic approach to the heterogeneous conceptual space of rules. Therefore, the goal should be to define a family of rule languages capturing the most important types of rules. While these languages should come with a recommended standard semantics, their rule expressions may, in addition, allow alternate semantics, which are also considered acceptable. This will accommodate various formalisms based on non-standard logics, supporting temporal, fuzzy, defeasible, and other forms of reasoning.

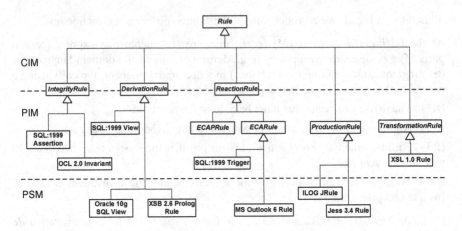

Fig. 1. Various rule concepts and rule languages at different levels of abstraction

We assume that the reader is familiar with the basic conceptual modeling constructs of UML class diagrams (types/classes, attributes, associations, role names, multiplicity constraints, aggregations, generalization) and to some degree also with OCL. We explain some of theses modeling constructs in the next section when discussing an example..

The structure of this article is as follows: after showing with an example ho to use UML class models for specifying vocabularies and rules in section 2, the foundational vocabularies of OWL/SWRL and RuleML are compared with each other in section 3. In section 4, different rule categories are discussed and modeled as class diagrams. In section 5, MOF/UML meta-models of OWL, SWRL and RuleML are presented. Finally, in section 6, the relationship between UML class models and OWL vocabularies is discussed.

2 Rule Modeling and Markup – An Example

An example, where a derived attribute in a UML class model is defined by a derivation rule, is the following:

> *A car is available for rental if it is not assigned to any rental contract and does not require service.*

This rule defines the derived Boolean-valued attribute isAvailable of the class RentalCar by means of an association isAssignedTo between cars and rental contracts and the stored Boolean-valued attribute requiresService, as shown in the UML class diagram in Fig. 2.

This class diagram specifies a vocabulary fragment consisting of

– two *basic entity types* (classes), RentalCar and RentalContract
– one *attribution fact type* that can be verbalized as: RentalCar has String as RentalCarID;

- two *subtypes* of RentalCar, AvailableRentalCar and the derived subtype RentalCarRequiringService, both being represented by Boolean-valued attributes
- an *association fact type*: RentalCar isAssignedTo RentalContract, which comes with three integrity rules and a clarification:

  1. *Functional*: It is necessary that each RentalCar isAssignedTo at most one RentalContract.
  2. *Inverse Total*: It is necessary that each RentalContract is assigned at least one RentalCar.
  3. *Inverse functional*: It is necessary that each RentalContract is assigned at least one RentalCar
  4. *Not total*: It is possible that a RentalCar isAssignedTo no RentalContract

An implicational OCL invariant, attached to the RentalCar class rectangle, is used to state that for a specific rental car whenever there is no rental contract associated with it, and it does not require service, then it must be available (for a new rental). In this OCL invariant expression, the condition RentalContract->isEmpty() means that the set of associated rental contracts must be empty.

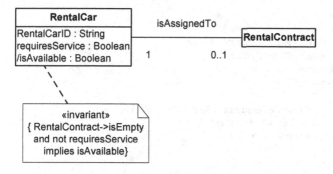

Fig. 2. An OCL invariant that constrains the derived attribute isAvailable

However, such an OCL invariant does not really define anything but rather puts a constraint on the model elements it refers to. OCL 2.0, in addition to expressing integrity rules ('invariants'), also allows to express derivation rules for defining derived elements of a class model. Using this possibility, we get the following OCL expression:

```
context RentalCar::isAvailable : Boolean derive:
RentalContract->isEmpty() and not requiresService
```

This OCL derivation rule assigns the truth value of the conjunction

```
RentalContract->isEmpty() and not requiresService
```

to the Boolean attribute isAvailable of the class RentalCar, and in this way it is a definition and not just a constraint.

We now present the concrete XML syntax of this rule according to the RuleML 0.88 syntax. Notice that the *head* element corresponds to the *Conclusion*, and the *body* element corresponds to the *Condition* of Fig. 6. It is assumed that the attribute `requiresService` is optional, that is it does not need to have a value (in case it is unknown whether a particular car requires service or not). By contrast, the attribute `isAvailable` is assumed to be mandatory.

The first condition of this rule, `RentalContract->isEmpty()`, corresponds to a negation-as-failure, which is expressed by the tag `<naf>` in RuleML, while the second condition, `not requiresService`, corresponds to a strong negation since it requires that the value of this Boolean attribute is explicitly `false`. If it would be unknown, its negation with `not` would result in unknown and not in true. So, this rule involves two kinds of negation, marked up with `<Naf>` and `<Neg>` in RuleML:

```
<Implies>
    <head>
        <Atom>
            <Rel>isAvailable</Rel>
            <Var>Car</Var>
        </Atom>
    </head>
    <body>
        <Atom>
            <Rel>RentalCar</Rel>
            <Var>Car</Var>
        </Atom>
        <Neg>
            <Atom>
                <Rel>requiresService</Rel>
                <Var>Car</Var>
            </Atom>
        </Neg>
        <Naf>
            <Atom>
            <Rel>isAssignedToRentalContract</Rel>
            <Var>Car</Var>
            </Atom>
        </Naf>
    </body>
</Implies>
```

Rule markup languages are a vehicle for using rules on the Web. They allow deploying, publishing and communicating rules on the Web. They are also converging towards a lingua franca for exchanging rules between different systems and tools.

In a narrow sense, a rule markup language is a concrete (XML-based) rule syntax for the Web. In a broader sense, it should be defined by an abstract syntax as a common basis for defining various concrete languages serving different purposes. The main purpose of a rule markup language is to permit reuse, interchange and publication of rules.

3   Foundational Concepts for Vocabularies and Rules

Rules are built on vocabularies, which include proper names designating individuals, type terms designating entity types (or classes) and fact types expressions designating fact types or predicates.

In this section, we discuss the *foundational* concepts (or *meta-concepts*) being used in this report and the terms we are using to designate them. These concepts, and their canonical designations, are described in a **foundational vocabulary**, which is also called a *foundational* (or 'upper level') *ontology*. They define a range of top-level domain-independent ontological categories, which form a general foundation for more elaborated domain-specific vocabularies. Our foundational vocabulary is based on the Unified Foundational Ontology (UFO) proposed in [1,2].

Our analysis is focused on four languages for expressing vocabularies and rules:

1. SBVR – "Semantics of Business Vocabularies and Rules", the main submission to the OMG BSBR CFP [3]
2. UML – the *Unified Modeling Language* of the OMG [4]
3. RDF – the *Resource Description Framework* of the W3C [5]
4. OWL – the *Web Ontology Language* of the W3C [6]

All these languages come with their own foundational vocabulary, employing different (or the same) designations for the same (or different) concepts. We will therefore use our own 'unified' foundational vocabulary as defined in the first column, called REWERSE I1 (after the name of the REWERSE working group on rule markup), of the terminology tables below. The I1 foundational vocabulary helps to understand the differences and overlaps among these terminologies.

For simplicity, we will not always be consistent in distinguishing the conceptual from the terminological level; we will, for instance, often say "rule" instead of "rule expression", "fact" instead of "fact statement", and "fact type" instead of "fact type expression".

3.1   Things, Sets, Entities and Individuals

A **thing** is 'anything perceivable or conceivable'. This includes concrete entities and also abstract things such as sets A **set** is a *thing* that has other *things* as *members* (in the sense of set theory).

An **entity** is a *thing* that is not a *set*; neither the set-theoretic membership relation nor the subset relation can unfold the internal structure of an entity. An **individual** is an *entity* that does not have any *instances*, i.e., that is not an *entity type*. A **data value** is a member of a *datatype*, which is a particular kind of named *set*.

3.2   Entity Types and Datatypes

An **entity type** is an *entity* that has an *extension* (the set of entities that are instances of it) and an *intension*, which includes an applicability criterion for determining if an entity is an instance of it. A **basic entity type** is an entity type whose instances are individuals. A **datatype** is a *set* whose members are *data values*.

Table 1. Different kinds of things

REWERSE-I1	UML	SBVR	RDF	OWL
thing	n.a.	Thing	n.a.	n.a.
entity			resource (an instance of rdfs:Resource)	n.a.
individual	object	individual concept		individual (an instance of owl:Thing)
data value	data value		literal (an instance of rdfs:Literal)	data value

Table 2. Different kinds of entity types

REWERSE-I1	UML	SBVR	RDF	OWL
entity type				n.a.
basic (1st order) entity type	type / class	object type / general concept	class (an instance of rdfs:Class)	class (an instance of owl:Class, which is a subclass of rdfs:Class)
datatype	datatype		datatype (an instance of rdfs:Datatype)	

In Fig. 3, the foundational vocabulary about things, sets, entities and individuals adopted by I1 from UFO is described in the form of a UML class diagram.

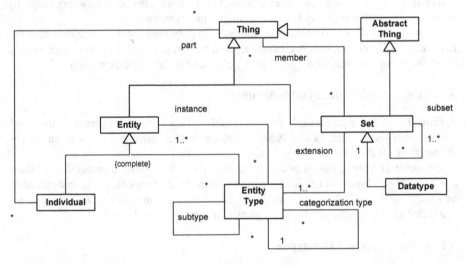

Fig. 3. The foundational vocabulary about things, sets, entities and individuals adopted by I1 from UFO

In Fig. 4 the foundational vocabulary supported by RDF(S) is summarized. Notice that rdfs:Class is an instance of itself. Fig. 5 describes the relationships between some basic RDF(S) concepts and their OWL counterparts.

3.3 Facts and Statements

We distinguish between 5 different kinds of *facts* (or atomic statements), as depicted by Table 3. In addition to the basic fact kinds of classification facts, association facts and attribution facts, we also consider categorization facts and aggregation facts. A categorization fact states that an entity, as an instance of a type, is an instance of a 'category', i.e. a subtype of that type. An aggregation fact is a part-whole statement.

3.4 Fact Types

A fact type corresponds to a predicate in predicate logic. But while there is no further distinction between different kinds of predicates in standard predicate logic, we distinguish between four different kinds of fact types as depicted in Table 4.

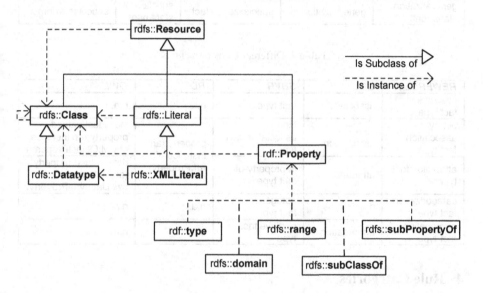

Fig. 4. The foundational vocabulary supported by RDF(S)

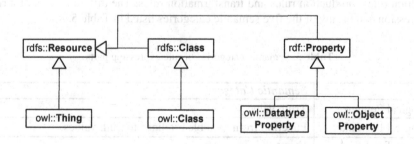

Fig. 5. The relationships between RDF(S) concepts and their OWL counterparts

Table 3. Different kinds of facts

REWERSE-I1	UML	SBVR	RDF	OWL
association fact	link	associative fact	n.a.	n.a.
binary association (reference property) fact	binary link	binary associative fact	triple, statement	individual-valued property fact
attribution fact	object-attribute-value triple	is-property-of fact		data-valued property fact
classification fact	instanceOf dependency	assortment fact	rdf:type statement	classification fact
categorization fact	n.a.	categorization fact	n.a.	n.a.
aggregation fact	aggregation link	partitive fact	n.a.	n.a.
generalization statement	generalization	specialization fact	subclassOf statement	subclass axiom

Table 4. Different kinds of fact types

REWERSE-I1	UML	SBVR	RDF	OWL
association fact type	association	fact type	n.a.	n.a.
binary association fact type	binary association	binary associative fact type	property (an instance of rdf:Property)	individual-valued property (an instance of owl:ObjectProperty)
attribution fact type	attribute	is-property-of fact type		data-valued property (an instance of owl:DatatypeProperty)
categorization fact type	n.a.	categorization fact type	n.a.	n.a.
aggregation fact type	aggregation	partitive fact type	n.a.	n.a.

4 Rule Categories

We briefly discuss the main categories of rules: integrity rules, derivation rules, reaction rules, production rules and transformation rules. The different parts of a rule expression can be any of the five semantic categories listed in Table 5.

Table 5. Semantic categories of rule expression parts

Type	Semantic Category
Logical Sentence	Truth value
Logical Formula	Function from variable bindings to truth values
Event Term	Event
Action Term	Action
Term	Can denote anything (an element from some term algebra)

4.1 Derivation Rules

Logical derivation rules (also called *deduction rules*), in general, consist of one or more *conditions* and one or more *conclusions*[6], which are both roles played by expressions of the type LogicalFormula.

For specific types of derivation rules, such as definite Horn clauses or normal logic programs, the types of condition and conclusion are specifically restricted.

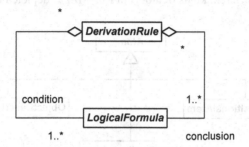

Fig. 6. The abstract concept of derivation rules

For instance, in RuleML 0.85, conditions are quantifier-free logical formulas with weak and strong negation, called *AndOrNafNeg-Formula* in Fig. 7. More precisely, they are quantifier-free predicate logic formulas with weak and strong negation, called *AndOrNafNeg-PL-Formula* (this formula class specializes the abstract class *AndOrNafNeg-Formula*, which admits also of other kinds of atoms such as OCL-like atoms, by restricting it to predicate logic atoms).

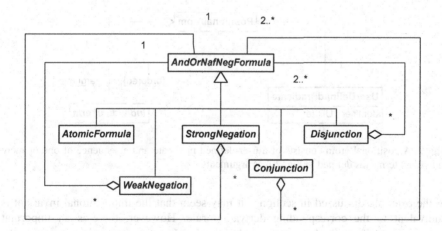

Fig. 7. Quantifier-free formulas with weak and strong negation

---

[6] Notice that we don't consider rules with no condition or no conclusion. These expressions are better not called "rules", but "facts" and "denial constraints".

The distinction between weak and strong negation is present in several computational languages: in *extended logic programs* it is present in explicit form, while it is only implicitly present in SQL and OCL. Intuitively speaking, weak negation captures the absence of positive information, while strong negation captures the presence of explicit negative information (in the sense of Kleene's 3-valued logic). Under the preferential model semantics of minimal/stable models, weak negation captures the computational concept of negation-as-failure (or closed-world negation).

There are three different kinds of atoms in RuleML, as depicted by Fig. 8.

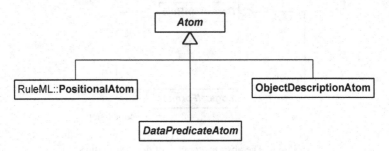

Fig. 8. Three kinds of atomic formulas in RuleML

A *positional atom* corresponds to an atomic formula in standard predicate logic. A *data predicate atom* (also called *built-in*) is formed with the help of a datatype predicate. An object description atom corresponds to an OWL individual description: it refers to an individual, classifies it, and makes a number of property-value-assertions about it, as depicted in Fig. 10.

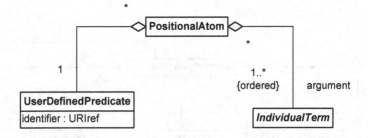

Fig. 9. A positional atom consists of a user-defined predicate and a sequence of one or more individual terms (as defined in Fig. 20) as arguments

In the example discussed in section 2 it may seem that the implicational invariant is equivalent to the corresponding derivation rule. However, there is an important conceptual difference between an implicational constraint $p \rightarrow q$ and the corresponding derivation rule *from p derive q*. While the former only constrains the logical state space (and is also satisfied by the truth of $\neg p$), it does not prescribe a derivation procedure to be applied for deriving the conclusion q. We may consider the rule *from p derive q* to be one of several possible derivation procedures that comply with the constraint $p \rightarrow q$. Another one would be the derivation procedure consisting of the two rules *from p derive r* and *from r derive q*.

Derivation rules should be semantically distinguished from implications. While an implication is an expression of a logical formula language (such as classical predicate logic or OCL), typically possessing a truth-value, a derivation rule is a meta-logical expression, which does not possess a truth-value, but has the function to generate derived sentences. There are logics, which do not have an implication connective, but which have a derivation rule concept. In standard logics (such as classical and intuitionistic logic), there is a close relationship between a derivation rule (also called "sequent") and the corresponding implicational formula: they both have the same models. For nonmonotonic rules (e.g. with negation-as-failure) this is no longer the case: the intended models of such a rule are, in general, not the same as the intended models of the corresponding implication.

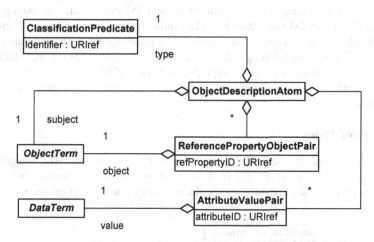

Fig. 10. An object description atom refers to an object (its 'subject'), classifies it, and makes a number of property-value-assertions about it

4.2 Integrity Rules (Constraints)

Integrity rules, also known as (integrity) constraints, consist of a constraint modality and a constraint assertion, which is a sentence in some logical language such as first-order predicate logic or OCL. This is depicted in Fig. 11. We consider two constraint modalities: the **alethic** and the **deontic** one. The alethic constraint modality can be expressed by a phrase such as "it is necessarily the case that". The deontic constraint modality can be expressed by phrases such as "it is obligatory that" or "it should be the case that". Notice that in English the phrase "it must be the case that" is ambiguous: it can denote either the alethic or the deontic modality.

The constraint assertion is a logical sentence that *must necessarily*, or that *should*, hold in all evolving states and state transition histories of the discrete dynamic system to which it applies. Notice that not only software systems, but also physical,

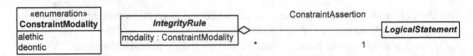

Fig. 11. The abstract concept of integrity rules

biological and social systems, such as organizations, can be viewed as discrete dynamic systems. Typically, we describe the natural and social laws that govern material (i.e. physical, biological and social) systems in the form of CIM integrity rules (at the domain modeling level). Then, when we transform the domain model into an operational design, we formalize these rules in the chosen PIM language, after which they no longer refer to the material system itself but to its computational model. So, a PIM constraint refers to the state (and execution histories) of the software system that models (or represents) the material system under consideration.

Rule R1 is an example of a (deontic) static CIM constraint. An example of a (deontic) dynamic CIM constraint is: "The confirmation of a rental reservation must lead to an allocation of a car of the requested car group for the requested date prior to that date". Well-known languages for expressing PIM constraints are SQL and OCL. In logic programming, rules with empty heads (also called "denials") corresponding to the negation of the conjunction of all body atoms are sometimes used as constraints.

4.3 Reaction Rules

Reaction rules are the second important type of rule in RuleML. Integrity and transformation rules have not received as much attention as derivation and reaction rules. Reaction rules are considered to be the most important type of business rule in [7].

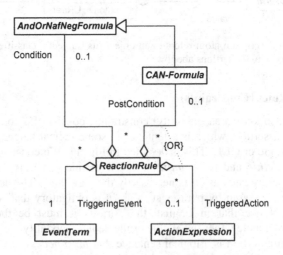

Fig. 12. The abstract concept of reaction rules

Reaction rules consist of a mandatory triggering event term, an optional condition, and a triggered action term or a post-condition (or both), which are roles of type EventTerm, LogicalFormula, ActionTerm, and LogicalFormula, respectively, as shown in Fig. 12. While the condition of a reaction rule is, exactly like the condition of a derivation rule, a quantifier-free formula, the post-condition is restricted to a conjunction of possibly negated atoms (called CAN-formula)..

Action and event terms may be composite and specified in different ways. For instance, the UML Action Semantics could be used to specify triggered actions in a platform-independent manner.

There is a little known parallel between derivation rules and reaction rules. Reaction rules are to dynamic (temporal logic) implication constraints what derivation rules are to static implication constraints.

There are basically two types of reaction rules: those that do not have a post-condition, which are the well-known *Event-Condition-Action (ECA)* rules, and those that do have a post-condition, which we call *ECAP rules*.

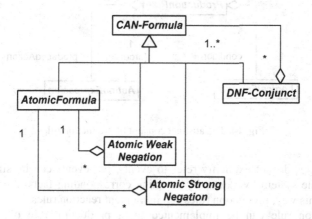

Fig. 13. The post-condition in a reaction rules is a conjunction of possibly negated atoms, also called CAN-formula

The post-condition of a reaction rule is either an atomic formula, a negation of an atomic formula or a conjunction of these (thus corresponding to a disjunctive normal form conjunct). This is called a CAN-Formula in Fig. 13. Such a definite formula specifies an update in a declarative way.

Event-Condition-Action-Postcondition (ECAP) rules extend ECA rules by adding a postcondition that accompanies the triggered action. ECAP rules allow specifying the effect of a triggered action on the system state in a declarative manner, instead of specifying this state change procedurally by means of corresponding state change operations (like SQL UPDATEs).

An application-specific ECA rule language may be used in software applications for handling application events in an automated fashion. A prominent example of this is the Microsoft Outlook rule wizard, which allows specifying email handling rules referring to incoming (or outgoing) message events.

4.4 Production Rules

Production rules consist of a condition and a produced action, which are roles of the type LogicalFormula and ActionTerm, respectively, as shown in Fig. 14. While OCL could be used in a platform-independent production rule language to specify conditions on an object-oriented system state, the UML Action Semantics could be used to specify produced actions.

These rules have become popular as a widely used technique to implement 'expert systems' in the 1980s. However, in contrast to (e.g. Prolog) derivation rules, the production rule paradigm lacks a precise theoretical foundation and does not have a formal semantics. This problem is partly due to the fact that early systems used production/ECA-like rules, where the semantic categories of a rule's events and conditions in the left-hand-side, and of its actions and effects in the right-hand-side, were mixed up.

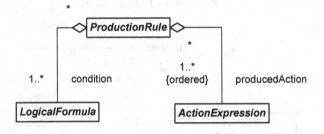

Fig. 14. The abstract concept of production rules

Production rules do not explicitly refer to events, but events can be simulated in a production rule system by externally asserting corresponding facts into the working memory. In this way, production rules can implement reaction rules.

A derivation rule can be implemented by a production rule of the form if-*Condition*-then-*assert*-*Conclusion* using the special action *assert* that changes the state of a production rule system by adding a new fact to the set of available facts.

Production rule platforms are the rule technology that is most widely used in the business rules industry. Well-known examples of production rule systems are JESS, Fair Isaac/Blaze Advisor, iLOG Rules/JRules, CA Aion, ART*Enterprise, Haley, and ESI Logist.

5 Semantics of Business Vocabularies and Rules

The *Semantics of Business Vocabularies and Rules (SBVR)* is an OMG proposal [3] for developing and structuring business vocabularies suited for business people to express business rules. A business vocabulary contains all the specialized terms and definitions of concepts that a given organization or community uses in their talking and writing in the course of doing business.

The SBVR follows a common-sense definition of 'business rule' as a *rule that is under business jurisdiction*. 'Under business jurisdiction' is taken to mean that the business can enact, revise and discontinue their business rules as they see fit.

All business rules need to be *actionable*. This means that a person who knows about a business rule could observe a relevant situation (including his or her own behavior) and decide directly whether or not the business was complying with the rule. Just because business rules are actionable, this does *not* imply they are always automatable. Many business rules, especially operative business rules, are *not* automatable in IT systems.

In SBVR, a rule is "an element of guidance that introduces an obligation or a necessity". The two fundamental categories of rule are:

- **Structural Rule** (necessities): These are rules about how the business chooses to organize (i.e., 'structure') the things it deals with. Structural Rules supplement definitions.:
- **Operative Rules** (obligations): These are rules that govern the conduct of business activity. In contrast to Structural Rules, Operative Rules are ones that can be *directly* violated by people involved in the affairs of the business.

The preferred mode of expression for vocabularies and rules is *SBVR Structured English*, a controlled English that works with verbalization patterns and font markup.

The SBVR Structured English is not meant to offer all of the variety of common English, but rather, it uses a small number of English structures and common words to provide a simple and straightforward mapping.

The following keywords are used in SBVR Structured English:

- *IF, THEN, OR, AND, NOT* – designate logical connectives
- The keyword "the": 1. Used with a designation to make a pronominal reference to a previous use of the same designation; this is formally a binding to a variable of a quantification. 2. Introduction of a name of an individual thing or of a definite description.
- The keywords "a, an": Universal or existential quantification, depending on context based on English rules.
- The keyword "that": 1. When preceding a designation for a type or role, this is a binding to a variable (as with 'the'). 2. When after a designation for a type or role and before a designation for a fact type, this is used to introduce a restriction on things denoted by the previous designation based on facts about them

Below, we use the following font types markup for the different parts of a SBVR Structured English expression:

- **type term** – designates a type (that is part of a vocabulary being used or defined)
- *type term* – This markup is applied to a type term in the special case where the term is used to name the represented concept rather than to refer to things denoted by the term. This is a reference to the concept itself.
- connecting verb phrase – designates a (user-defined) domain predicate symbol
- *predefined connecting verb phrase* – designates a predefined predicate symbol
- name – designates an individual or data value

This markup differs from the original SBVR markup, but is equivalent. The description of the SBVR Structured English is divided into sections:

- Expressions in SBVR Structured English
- Describing a Vocabulary
- Vocabulary Entries
- Specifying a Rule Set
- Rule and Clarification Entries

There are two styles of SBVR Structured English:

1. Prefixed Rule Keyword Style
2. Embedded (Mixfix) Rule Keyword Style

The Prefix Style introduces rules by prefixing a statement with keywords that convey a modality

Operative Business Rules and Clarifications	Structural Rules and Clarifications
It is obligatory that	It is necessary that
It is prohibited that	It is impossible that
It is permitted that	It is possible that

The Embedded Style features the use of rule keywords embedded (usually in front of verbs) within rules statements of appropriate kind. The following key words are used within expressions having a verb (often modified to be infinitive) to form verb complexes that add a modal operation.

Operative Business Rules and Clarifications	Structural Rules and Clarifications
... must ...	... always ...
... must not ...	... never ...
... may ...	... sometimes ...

5.1 Examples of SBVR-Style Rule Expressions

UML associations are verbalized as *association fact type expressions*. For instance, consider the binary association between the classes rental car and rental in Fig. 15. It can be verbalized by the following fact type expressions:

rental car is assigned to *a* **rental**

Rules can be verbalized on the basis of fact type expressions. For instance, the rule that defines the derived association fact type

rental car is available at **branch**

can be expressed in the following way:

IF **rental car** is stored at *the* **branch** *AND* **rental car** is *NOT a rental car scheduled for service AND* **rental car** is *NOT* assigned to *a* **rental** *THEN* **rental car** is available at *the* **branch**.

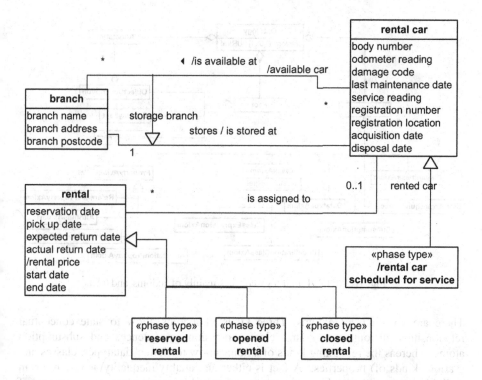

Fig. 15. A business vocabulary fragment for the domain of car rental

In OCL, this derivation rule can be expressed as:

```
context Branch::availableCar: RentalCar derive:
self.storedCar->select( c |
    not oclIsKindOf( RentalCarScheduledForService)
    and c.Rental->isEmpty())
```

6 MOF/UML Metamodels as Language Definitions

UML class models also allow to specify the abstract syntax of a language. The set of class modeling core constructs needed for this purpose is called *Meta Object Facility (MOF)*. The MOF/UML language models are also called *metamodels*. They allow a concise definition of a language in a graphical notation.

We briefly show how the abstract syntax of OWL, SWRL and RuleML can be defined by means of MOF/UML language models.

6.1 OWL

The W3C *Web Ontology Language* OWL defines an ontology as a set of axioms and a set of facts, as shown in Fig. 16.

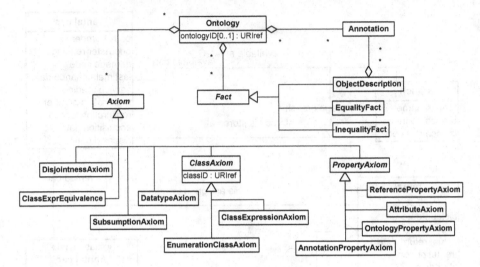

Fig. 16. An OWL ontology consists mainly of 'axioms' and 'facts'

There are six kinds of axioms. Three kinds of axioms allow to state conceptual relationships: disjointness axioms, class expression equivalences and subsumption atoms; whereas the remaining kinds of axioms allow to 'define' datatypes, classes and (various kinds of) properties.[7] A fact is either an equality/inequality assertion, or an 'individual description', which refers to an individual term and aggregates a number of classification facts and property-value-facts about it, as depicted in Fig. 17.

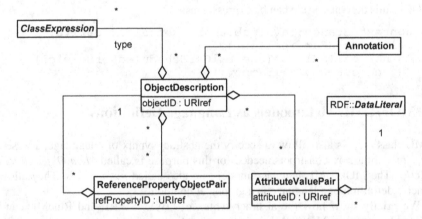

Fig. 17. An OWL 'individual description fact' is a collection of classification facts, attribution facts and binary association facts, all concerning one particular individual

---

[7] Notice that, strictly speaking, the semantics of OWL does not support the computational distinction between definition and constraint, which is reflected by the distinction between invariants and derivation rules in OCL, and which is also an essential part of the SBVR approach. Class 'definitions' in OWL are typically expressed by means of equivalence axioms.

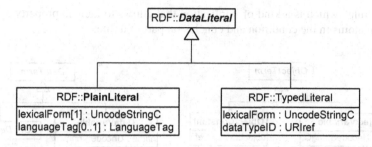

Fig. 18. An RDF data literal is either a plain literal, possibly associated with a language, or a typed literal

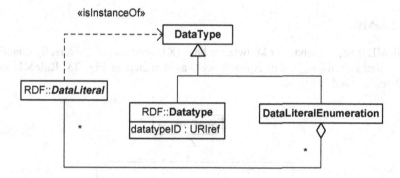

Fig. 19. A datatype in OWL is an RDF datatype or a data literal enumeration, or it is equal to the set of RDF literals

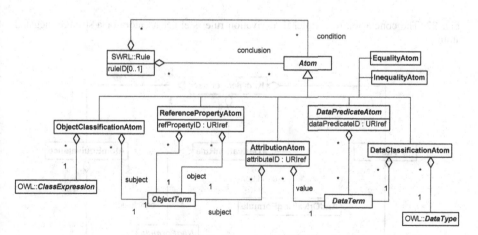

Fig. 20. The abstract syntax of SWRL rules

6.2 SWRL

The *Semantic Web Rule Language (SWRL)* extends the concept of an OWL ontology by adding a notion of logical variables and terms as well as a seventh kind of axiom, called 'rule', which is a kind of implication that allows to include property atoms and built-in atoms in the condition and conclusion part of a rule.

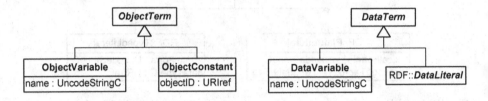

Fig. 21. There are two kinds of logical terms: object terms and data terms

6.3 RuleML

In RuleML 0.88, a rulebase or knowledge base (KB) consists of universally quantified atoms, implications and atom equivalences, as depicted in Fig. 23. RuleML atoms have been defined in Fig. 8.

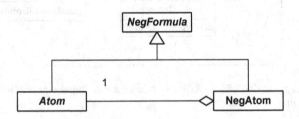

Fig. 22. The conclusion of a RuleML derivation rule is either an atom or a strongly negated atom

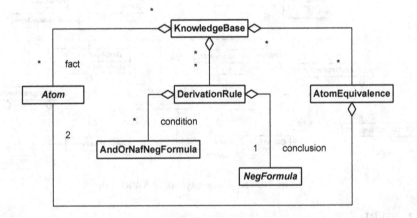

Fig. 23. A RuleML knowledge base consists of universally quantified atoms, implications and atom equivalences

7 Correspondence Between OWL and UML

As already described in Table 1, there is a close correspondence between OWL and UML. We summarize the commonalities and differences between UML and OWL in Table 6.

Table 6. Commonalities and differences between UML and OWL

UML	OWL
datatype	datatype
class	class
n.a.	class description
association	n.a.
binary association	individual-valued property (an instance of owl:ObjectProperty)
attribute	data-valued property (an instance of owl:DatatypeProperty)
aggregation	n.a.
multiplicity constraint	cardinality restriction
generalization	subsumption axiom
n.a.	class expression equivalence
n.a.	anonymous class expression

UML binary associations correspond to OWL object properties. For instance, the association

corresponds to the following OWL property axiom (expressed in the abstract syntax of OWL):

```
ObjectProperty( supplier
    domain(person) range(vendor) inverseOf(customer))
```

UML attributes correspond to OWL datatype property axioms. For instance, consider the following attributes of a class **person**:

The attribute *phone number* corresponds to the following OWL datatype property axiom:

```
DatatypeProperty( phone_number
    domain(person) range(xsd:string))
```

UML multiplicity constraints correspond to OWL cardinality restrictions. But while the graphical notation for multiplicity constraints in UML is simple and elegant, the

OWL syntax for cardinality restrictions is rather cumbersome and hard to read. A related issue is the lack of a shorthand for total properties. While properties can be declared to be functional and inverse functional, there is no corresponding shorthand construct for declaring a property to be total, resp. inverse total.

Another usability issue is the lack of a convenient mechanism in OWL to declare classes as mutually disjoint, which is the default assumption in UML

Since many core constructs of UML class models can be mapped to OWL, such a mapping provides a logical semantics for UML class models Exploiting this mapping possibility and the inference tools available for OWL, UML tools could e.g. check the consistency of a class diagram by running an OWL. inference engine.

8 Conclusions

We have shown that there is a close correspondence between the Web ontology language OWL and the vocabulary language of UML class diagrams, which can be exploited for capturing OWL ontologies with the more user-friendly graphical notation of UML. UML class diagrams, in the form of MOF/UML metamodels, can also be used to define the abstract syntax of OWL, SWRL and RuleML. These language metamodels provide a level of abstraction that allows to unify apparently distinct constructs. For instance, the metamodel for RuleML 'slot atoms' (better called *object description atoms*) shown in Fig. 10, reveals that RDF descriptions and OWL individual descriptions can be mapped to this RuleML construct.

References

[1] G. Guizzardi & G. Wagner. A Unified Foundational Ontology and some Applications of it in Business Modeling. In P. Green and M. Rosemann (Eds.), Business Systems Analysis with Ontologies, IDEA Publishing, 2005.

[2] G. Guizzardi & G. Wagner. Towards Ontological Foundations for Agent Modelling Concepts Using the Unified Foundational Ontology. In P. Bresciani et al. (Eds.): AOIS 2004, LNAI 3508, pp. 110 – 124, Springer-Verlag, 2005.

[3] Semantic of Business Vocabulary and Business Rules (SBVR). Revised Submission to OMG BEI RFP br/2003/06/03, http://www.omg.org/cgi-bin/doc?bei/2005-03-01.

[4] UML, http://www.uml.org/.

[5] G.Klyne and J.J.Caroll (Eds.), Resource Description Framework (RDF): Concepts and Abstract Syntax, W3C, 2004.

[6] OWL Web Ontology Language, http://www.w3.org/2004/OWL.

[7] Taveter K., Wagner, G.: Agent-Oriented Enterprise Modeling Based on Business Rules. In Proc. of 20th Int. Conf. on Conceptual Modeling (ER2001), Springer-Verlag, LNCS 2224, pp. 527–540, 2001.

Information Extraction for the Semantic Web

Robert Baumgartner[1], Thomas Eiter[2], Georg Gottlob[1], Marcus Herzog[1]
and Christoph Koch[1]

[1] Database and Artificial Intelligence Group,
Institute of Information Systems, Vienna University of Technology
Favoritenstrasse 9-11, 1040 Vienna, Austria
{baumgart, gottlob, herzog, koch}@dbai.tuwien.ac.at
[2] Knowledge-Based Systems Group
Institute of Information Systems, Vienna University of Technology
Favoritenstrasse 9-11, 1040 Vienna, Austria
eiter@kr.tuwien.ac.at

Abstract. The World Wide Web represents a universe of knowledge and information. Unfortunately, it is not straightforward to query and access the desired information. Languages and tools for accessing, extracting, transforming, and syndicating the desired information are required. The Web should be useful not merely for human consumption but additionally for machine communication. Therefore, powerful and user-friendly tools based on expressive languages for extracting and integrating information from various different Web sources, or in general, various heterogeneous sources are needed. The tutorial gives an introduction to Web technologies required in this context, and presents various approaches and techniques used in information extraction and integration. Moreover, sample applications in various domains motivate the discussed topics and providing data instances for the Semantic Web is illustrated[1].

Keywords: Web data extraction, Semi-structured Data, Wrapper Languages and Systems, Web data integration, Semantic Web.

1 Motivation and Global Context

1.1 Introduction

Today the Semantic Web [7] is still a vision. On the other hand, the *unstructured Web* already contains millions of documents which are not queryable as a database and heavily mix layout and structure. Moreover, they are not annotated at all. There is a huge gap between Web information and the qualified, structured data as usually required in corporate information systems. According to the vision of the Semantic Web, all information available on the Web will

---

[1] This research has been partially supported by REWERSE - Reasoning on the Web (rewerse.net), Network of Excellence, 6th European Framework Program.

N. Eisinger and J. Małuszyński (Eds.): Reasoning Web 2005, LNCS 3564, pp. 275–289, 2005.

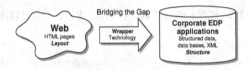

Fig. 1. Bridging the Gap

be suitably structured, annotated, and qualified in the future. However, until this goal is reached, and also, towards a faster achievement of this goal, it is absolutely necessary to (semi-)automatically extract relevant data from HTML documents and automatically translate this data into a structured format, e.g., XML. Once transformed, data can be used by applications, stored into databases or populate ontologies.

Figure 1 exhibits the gap between, on the one hand, structured databases or ontologies used for enterprise data processing, and on the other hand, the vast amount of web data optimized merely for layout and almost impossible to query. Web data extraction technology addresses these issues and enables application and system designers to bridge this gap. A program that extracts data and transforms it into another more structured format or markups the content with semantic information is usually referred to as *wrapper*. There exists a large number of different wrapping methods and software tools, and the designer of an intelligent system thus faces the problem of selecting appropriate components for designing an intelligent system embedding Web data. Our tutorial shall provide some guidance.

1.2   Wrapper Technology

Wrapper technology is a new leap forward in interacting with (especially) semi-structured and loosely structured data such as Web data. Wrapper and integration technology is often confused with search engine technology, which is, however, somewhat orthogonal. Figure 2 puts these and other different technologies concerning Web data into context with each other. The two axes of Figure 2 are the Information Complexity (horizontal) and the kind of the accessed and retrieved information (vertical); based upon the latter are the usage possibilities of the retrieved information.

- *Search engines* crawl the whole Web, but they merely return links. Documents are parsed only up to keyword indices needed as a result of the search. The search engine's result is a list of URLs.
- *Notification Tools* regularly search merely a small number of Web pages tracking for interesting changes. The Web document has to be parsed and relevant changes have to be detected. User interaction is generally required to identify relevant portions of text and structure.
- *Text Categorization Tools* rate a document, e.g. classify it as a document that belongs to a particular domain. Such tools require parsing a document and analyzing its content, and are often using statistics or natural language

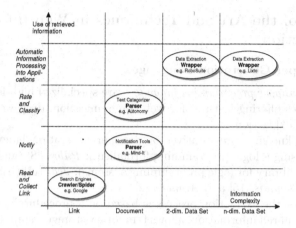

Fig. 2. Comparing Web Technologies

analysis. One of the main aspects for the end user are the possibilities of personalization.

– *Wrappers* transform data, in our case unstructured or semi-structured data into structured data. They do not simply return links or parsed and rated documents, but relevant data extracted from usually a set of similarly structured documents. One wrapper is not capable of extracting data from arbitrary Web pages, however, with the big advantage of a very structured response. Information extracted with wrappers can easily be pushed to enterprise applications, databases or ontologies.

Whereas information retrieval targets to analyze and categorize documents, information extraction collects and structures entities inside of documents.

1.3   Web Application Integration

A further step is integration of extracted data into enterprise processes. Integration brokers provide infrastructure for sharing information between applications (EAI, B2B), many of them featuring Web connectors. Business Activity Monitoring vendors strive to deliver instant awareness of business critical events to customers. Heterogeneous environments such as integration and mediation systems require a conceptual information flow model. Web Data Extraction and Integration technologies open the way to use today's Web as the largest database to provide input for business intelligence applications (including cooperative and non-cooperative sites) and to reuse data for portals and personalisation and for portal-based cross-company communication. Moreover, static Web data can be turned into dynamic Web Services.

The application areas are manifold - every vertical business domain requires to analyse, monitor and interact with Web data – a few sample cases are given in Section 5. In this tutorial we will discuss a sample scenario used in the REWERSE project.

2   State of the Art and Techniques in Web Information Extraction

2.1   Wrapper Generation Languages

Stand-alone wrapper programming languages are specialized high-level programming languages offering features for web communication, deep web navigation, and web data extraction.

Some well-known representatives of wrapper generation languages include *Florid* [26] (using a logic-programming formalism), *Pillow* [8] (an HTML/XML programming library for logic programming systems), *Jedi* [17] (using attributed grammars), *Tsimmis* [15] and *Araneus* [2].

In *Tsimmis*, the extraction process is based on a procedural program which skips to the required information, allows temporary storages, split and case statements, and to follow links. However, the wrapper output has to obey the document structure. In *Araneus*, a wrapper designer can create relational views from web pages by computationally fast and advanced text extracting and restructuring formalisms, in particular using procedural "Cut and Paste" exception handling inside regular grammars. In general, all manual wrapper generation languages are difficult to use by laypersons.

2.2   Automated Wrapper Generation Approaches

Machine learning approaches generally rely on learning from examples and counterexamples of a large number of Web pages. Very prominent approaches include *Stalker* [30] and *Wien* [22]. *Stalker* [30] specializes general *SkipTo* sequence patterns based on labelled HTML pages. An approach to maximise specific patterns is introduced by Davulcu et al. [10].

Kushmerick et al. [22] create robust wrappers based on predefined extractors; their visual support tool *WIEN* receives a set of training pages, where the wrapper designer can label relevant information and the system tries to learn a wrapper. Their approach does not use HTML parse trees. Kushmerick also contributed to the wrapper verification problem [21].

The *RoadRunner* [9] approach does not need labelled examples, but derives rules from a number of given pages by distinguishing the structure and the content. It uses an interesting generation of pattern names based on offset-criteria in addition to the applied semi-structured wrapping technology. Some approaches such as [12] offer generic wrapping techniques. Such approaches have the advantage that they can wrap arbitrary Web pages never seen before, on the other hand the disadvantage that they are restricted to particular domains (such as detecting addresses).

Other examples include *Softmealy* [16] (using finite-state transducers) and *MIA* [34] (prolog-based wrappers using anti-unification; neural networks to generalize and learn texts). *NoDoSe* [1] extracts information from plain string sources and provides a user interface for example labelling. It has restricted capabilities to deal with HTML.

In general, drawbacks of machine-learning approaches are limited expressive power and the large number of required example pages. In case of systems that do not rely on labelled examples the main drawback is the low percentage of correctness of the extracted data.

2.3 Supervised Wrapper Generation

Interactive approaches allow for semi-automatic extraction generation and offer convenient visual dialogues to generate a wrapper based on a few examples and user interaction. *Supervised interactive wrapper generation* tools include *W4F* [33], *XWrap* [24], *Wiccap* [25], *SGWrap* [27], *Wargo* [31], *DEByE* [32] and *Lixto* (Section 4).

W4F uses an SQL-like query language called HEL. Parts of the query can be generated using a visual extraction wizard which is limited to returning the full DOM tree path of an element. However, the full query must be programmed by the wrapper designer manually. Hence, *W4F* requires expertise with both HEL and HTML. HEL requires tricky use of index variables and fork constructs to correctly describe a complex pattern structure. *XWrap* uses a procedural rule system and provides limited expressive power for pattern definition. *XWrap* lacks visual facilities for imposing external or internal conditions to a pattern, but instead is rather template-based. The division into two description levels and the automatic hierarchical structure extractor limits the ways to define extraction patterns.

In general, many supervised wrapper generation tools require manual post-processing and do not offer the browser-displayed document for labelling. Additionally, many systems neglect the capabilities of Deep Web navigation such as form filling; however, in practice this is highly required, as most information is hidden somewhere in the Deep Web [6].

The area of supervised wrapping is also the one mostly explored by commercial software products such as *RoboSuite* [19], *FirstRain* and *QL2*.

3 Classifications of Wrapper Generation Systems

3.1 Existing Taxonomies

A number of classification taxonomies for wrapper development languages and environments have been introduced in various survey papers [13, 20, 23].

In [20] a detailed analysis of wrapper-generation software is given. There, an ample number of wrapping tools especially regarding extraction from HTML data are classified according to various criteria. A condensed comparison is available on the Web [36]. The paper moreover contains a detailed comparison between the freeware tool Lapis [28] and the commercial tool RoboSuite [19].

The principle differentiation of this taxonomy is between "Freeware" and "Commercial Tools," with further criteria being: Supported output formats; Availability of Java API; Open Source or availability of demo version; Language of source code; Presence of GUI; Presence of a built-in editor; Scripting language (and use of regular expressions and document object models); Connectivity to other applications; Further features; Release cycle.

Another type of classification is given in [23]. In this paper, web data extraction tools are classified as

- Languages for wrapper development;
- HTML-aware tools;
- NLP-based (Natural Language Processing) tools;
- Wrapper induction tools;
- Modeling-based tools;
- Ontology-based tools.

So, while [20] is a feature-based classification, the one in [23] stresses the mode of wrapper creation.

A classification of machine learning approaches is given in [13]. The authors compare approaches based upon the following aspects:

- the technique employed;
- the supported formats;
- complexity of extracted data structure;
- the capability to deal with missing values;
- the capability to deal with permutation of values.

Especially the capabilities to deal with missing values and permutation of values contribute to the robustness of a wrapper. Moreover, the supported formats are of high interest as is the complexity of the output data structure (and the expressiveness of a wrapper language in general). Authors of methods and systems for inductive wrapper generation usually compare their approaches using the (currently not maintained and updated) RISE wrapper repository [29]. This wrapper repository comprises an ample number of sample Web pages of various domains.

3.2   Desiderata for Wrapper Generation Tools

As extension to the taxonomies presented above we compiled a list of desiderata for a good wrapper generation system to be usable in practice.

- **High expressive power.** The system should enable the definition of complex, structurally organized patterns from Web pages and translate the corresponding data (the so-called pattern instances) into a corresponding hierarchically structured XML document.
- **Robustness.** Wrappers are generally aimed at extracting information from similarly structured Web pages of changing content. It is obvious that wrappers risk failing to deliver a correct result if the structure of the source documents changes. However, we expect a good wrapper to have a certain degree of robustness, i.e., insensibility to minor structural changes (such as introduction of a new banner).

- **Runtime Efficiency.** The method should provide efficient algorithms and the system should implement these algorithms efficiently such that the system becomes usable in practice and is highly scalable.
- **Smooth XML Interface.** The method or system should provide a smooth and user-friendly way of translating the extracted data into XML in order to make it accessible to further processing, e.g. via XML query engines or well-known transformation languages such as XSLT. Ideally, the translation to XML is done automatically on the basis of the information gathered from the designer during the process of defining extraction patterns.
- **n-Dimensional Data Structures.** In many cases it is not sufficient to generate XML data comprising two levels, i.e. representing a relational table. In general, wrapper output shall support arbitrarily nested XML output data.
- **Semantic Web Interface.** A good wrapper generation system shall be able to populate ontologies with instance data and even extend an ontology based on concepts extracted from the Web. Ideally, the extraction language is logic-based and compatible to languages used for reasoning in ontologies.
- **Semi-structured and Unstructured File Support.** Although many formats such as CSV files require to parse flat strings, it contributes to robustness if a wrapper language supports a tree model for loosely structured formats such as HTML, too. The use of both a document object model and regular expressions operating on strings form the base of a powerful extraction language.
- **Platform Independence.** For integration into a mediation framework supported platforms might be a decision criteria.

Regarding wrapper design, moreover, a few more criteria are relevant:

- **User friendliness.** It should allow a human wrapper designer to design, program, or specify wrappers in a very short time.
- **Good learnability.** The learning effort for being able to understand the method or use the system should be as small as possible. The method or system should be accessible to and usable by a non-technical content manager who is not a programmer or a computer scientist.
- **Good visual support.** It should offer the wrapper designer a GUI for specifying wrappers or XML translations. Ideally, the visual user interface allows a wrapper designer to work directly on displayed sample source documents (e.g. on HTML Web pages) and supports a purely visual way of defining extraction patterns.
- **Ease of accessibility and installation.** The system should be widely accessible and should not require particular installation efforts. Ideally, the system provides an interface so that it uses a standard Web browser.
- **Parsimony of samples.** In case the method or system uses sample pages as a basis for constructing wrappers, it should require only very few of these (a single one at best) for most applications. The reason is that, in many cases, a wrapper designer has only one or very few sample pages at hand.

We believe that *Lixto* satisfies the above criteria very well. In the next section we illustrate a sample wrapper generation based on the Lixto system.

4   Lixto

4.1   Wrapping the Web with Lixto

The Lixto data extraction project [3] was started in the year 2000 as academic project and by now led to a commercial enterprise with an established customer base, and allows us to view web wrapping from two perspectives, from the one of theory and from the one of practice. This project has engendered several fundamental questions that led to theoretical results. Lixto has a number of unique characteristics by which it distinguishes itself from the state-of-the-art in Web wrapping and which would not have been possible without foundational research using results and techniques from database theory that, however, remained focussed on producing a working, and practical, industrial-strength software system. Lixto's distinctive features are summarized in the following.

- Lixto employs a fully visual wrapper specification process, which allows for a steep learning curve and high productivity in the specification of wrappers. Neither manual fine-tuning nor knowledge of HTML or the internal wrapping language is necessary.
- With Lixto, very expressive visual wrapper generation is possible: It allows for the extraction of target patterns based on surrounding landmarks, on the content itself, on HTML attributes, on the order of appearance, and on semantic and syntactic concepts. Lixto even allows for more advanced features such as Web crawling and recursive wrapping.
- The visual specification framework is based on an internal logic-based language similar to datalog, Elog.
- Elog has been closely studied. In particular, it was shown that its core fragment captures precisely the expressiveness of monadic second-order logic (MSO) over trees it is therefore quite expressive and can still be evaluated very efficiently [14].
- High robustness: Insensitivity to minor structural changes and warnings in case of major changes.
- A Data Aggregation and Runtime Environment where wrappers are embedded (described in Section 4.3).

We believe that this presents Web wrapping as a significant new application of logic (programming) to information systems. The database programming language datalog, which has received considerable attention from the database theory community over many years but has ultimately failed to attract a large following in database practice, would deserve to experience a "rebirth" in the context of trees and the Web.

4.2   Wrapper Generation Example

In the following, we describe a step-by-step construction of a wrapper in *Lixto Visual Wrapper* from the viewpoint of an application designer who creates this application. As sample application we choose the REWERSE Personal Publication Reader (see Section 5.3) [4]. The Personal Publication Reader offers an integrated and personalized view on publication data from REWERSE project members. The publication data is extracted from the individual project members Web pages on a regular base using Lixto.

A human being tends to assign semantic meaning to parts of a Web page; a designer does not think of *table row* as of a set with text values, but rather as a *publication entry*. Therefore, the basic building block of a Lixto wrapper program is a so-called *pattern*, a container for pieces of information with the same meaning. Patterns are structured in a hierarchical fashion. In the lower half of the Visual Wrapper's UI (see Figure 3) an active example Web page is displayed for marking example instances: For each type of Web page, an own wrapper has to be created; in the following the wrapper creation for the publications of Munich is illustrated.

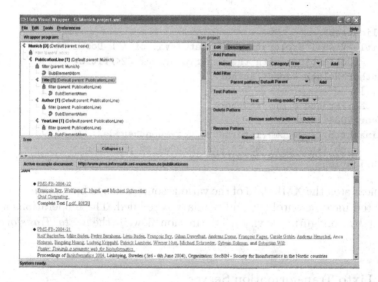

Fig. 3. Lixto Visual Wrapper: Wrapping Publication Pages

In this case, the designer identifies one of the list items (each resembling a publication) as a pattern *PublicationLine*. Once a pattern is created, the designer continues with visually defining a filter, a crucial part of the pattern which defines how to extract relevant information from its parent pattern instances. Internally, filters are represented in Elog, but the language is entirely hidden from the wrapper designer.

Defining a filter expects the designer to select an example publication with two mouse clicks on the example Web page. A filter definition continues with optional fine-tuning of properties for the generated generalization of the chosen example. It is possible to visually debug the wrapper program, i.e., to test filters. Typically, operators test filters after adding new components. Based on results, the designer decides whether to extend (i.e., add a filter) or shrink (i.e., add condition to an existing filter) the set of matched instances.

In this example, the system displays the complete list of matched publications for the so-far created filter by highlighting parts of the Web page. In cases where the system generalization does not detect all instances correctly, additional conditions can be imposed.

Next a child pattern *Title* of the just defined pattern is created and then a filter with the condition that the extracted element is in italics. The pattern *Author* on the Munich page can be easily characterized, too, by the fact that a special hyperlink is present and that the author names precede the title.

In a similar fashion the remaining patterns are defined and the wrapper is stored. The XML Companion of the publication web page that can be regularly generated by applying the wrapper is comprised of entries like the one given below:

```
<Publication>
  <Title>Visual Exploration and Retrieval of XML Document
        Collections with the Generic System X2</Title>
  <Author>Holger Meuss</Author>
  [...]
  <Author>Francois Bry</Author>
  <Year>2004</Year>
  <Link>http://www.pms.informatik.uni-muenchen.de/
        publikationen/PMS-FB/PMS-FB-2004-12.pdf</Link>
</Publication>
```

As next step the XML data of the various sources has to be combined, cleaned, syndicated into the ontology, and regulary scheduled. These operations are carried out by configuring a visual information flow in the *Lixto Transformation Server*.

4.3 Lixto Transformation Server

Heterogeneous environments such as integration and mediation systems require a conceptual information flow model. The usual setting for the creation of services based on Web wrappers is that information is obtained from multiple wrapped sources and has to be integrated; often source sites have to be monitored for changes, and changed information has to be automatically extracted and processed. Thus, push-based information systems architectures in which wrappers are connected to pipelines of post-processors and integration engines which process streams of data are a natural scenario, which is supported by the Lixto Transformation Server [5]. The overall task of information processing is composed into stages that can be used as building blocks for assembling an information processing pipeline. The stages are to

- acquire the required content from the source locations; this component resembles the Lixto Visual Wrapper plus Deep Web Navigation and Form iteration;
- integrate and transform content from a number of input channels and tasks such as finding differences,
- interact with external processes, and
- format and deliver results in various formats and channels and connectivity to other systems.

The actual data flow within the Transformation Server is realized by handing over XML documents. Each stage within the Transformation Server accepts XML documents (except for the wrapper component, which accepts HTML), performs its specific task (most components support visual generation of mappings), and produces an XML document as result. This result is put to the successor components. Boundary components have the ability to activate themselves according to a user-specified strategy and trigger the information processing on behalf of the user. From an architectural point of view, the Lixto Transformation Server may be conceived as a container-like environment of visually configured information agents. The pipe flow can model very complex unidirectional information flows (see Figure 4). Information services may be controlled and customized from outside of the server environment by various types of communication media such as Web Services.

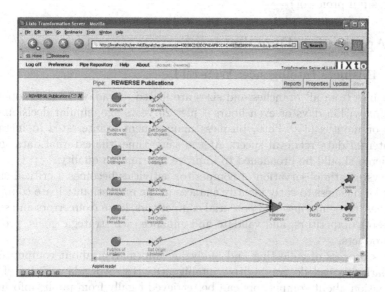

Fig. 4. Lixto Transformation Server: Rewerse Publication Data Flow

4.4   Visual Data Aggregation Example

In the Personal Publication Reader scenario, the application designer visually composes the information flow from Web sources to an RDF presentation that is handed over to the Personal Publication Reader once a week.

First, the application designer creates Source components that contain Lixto wrappers. In the source components (that are reflected as disks in Figure 4) a schedule is defined how often which Web source is queried and Deep Web navigation sequences containing logins and forms can be stored. Next, the wrapper designer can combine the XML documents by adding integration components.

In the "XSL" components publication data is harmonized to fit into a common structure, an attribute "origin" is added containing the institution's name, and author names are harmonized by being mapped to a list of names known by the system. The triangle in Figure 4 represents a data integration unit; here data from the various institutions is put together and duplicate entries are removed. IDs are assigned to each publication in the subsequent step. Finally, the XML data structure is mapped to a defined RDF structure (this happens in the lower arc symbol in Figure 4) and passed on to the Personal Publication Reader as described below. A second deliverer component delivers the XML publication data additionally.

This application can be easily enhanced by connecting further Web sources. For instance, abstracts from www.researchindex.com can be queried for each publication lacking this information and joined to each entry, too. Another possibility is to extract organization and people data from the institution's Web pages to inform the ontology to which class in the taxonomy an author belongs (such as full professor).

5   Application Domains

5.1   Business Intelligence: Web-ETL

Companies from all branches and sizes are forced nowadays to make operative decisions within days or even hours – just 25 years ago, similar decisions took weeks or months [35]. Thus, business management is interested in increasing the internal data retrieval speed. At the same time, the external data sources considered should be broadened to improve information quality.

A systematic observation of competitor activities becomes a critical success factor for business to early identify chances in the market, anticipate competitor activities, recognize new and potential competitors, learn from errors and success stories of competitors, and validate and enhance own strategic goals, processes and products.

This process of collecting and analyzing information about competitors on the market is called "competitive intelligence" [18]. Nowadays, a lot of basic information about competitors can be retrieved legally from public information sources, such as Web sites, annual reports, press releases or public data bases.

On the one hand, powerful tools for Extracting, Transforming and Loading (ETL-tools) data from source systems into a BI data warehouse are available today. They support the data extraction from *internal* applications in an efficient way. On the other hand, there is a growing need to integrate also *external* data, such as market information, into these systems. The World Wide Web, the largest database on earth, holds this huge amount of relevant information. Advanced data extraction and information integration techniques as described in this tutorial are required to process Web data automatically. Increasing demand for such data leads to the question of how this information can be extracted, transformed to a semantically useful structure, and integrated with a "Web-ETL" process into a Business Intelligence system.

5.2   Business Processes in the Automotive Industry

Many business processes in the automotive industry are carried out by means of web portal interaction. Business critical data from various divisions such as quality management, marketing and sales, engineering, procurement, supply chain management, and competitive intelligence has to be manually gathered from web portals and websites. By automation, automotive part suppliers can dramatically reduce the cost associated with these processes while at the same time improving the speed and reliability with which these processes are carried out. Instead of manually browsing and searching for results on these sites, wrapper technology automatically gathers the data and renders the results in a structured format such as XML. Data in this format is then ideally suited for processing by various enterprise applications or distributing through various communication channels. The automation of such manually performed processes can help to tremendously save time. It also enables employees to react more quickly to changes and news, paving the way to the "real-time enterprise".

5.3   Gathering Data for Semantic Web Applications

The Personal Reader Framework (www.personal-reader.de) is an environment for designing, implementing and maintaining personal Web-content Readers [11]. These personal Web-content Readers allow a user to browse information (the *Reader* part), and to access personal recommendations and contextual information on the currently regarded Web resource (the *Personal* part).

The architecture of the Personal Reader is a rigorous approach for applying recent Semantic Web technologies. It allows to design, implement and maintain Personal Web Content Readers. One application, the *Personal Publication Reader* [4] uses Lixto to extract Web data of publications and transform the data to RDF for usage in the Personal Reader Framework as illustrated above.

6   Conclusion and Summary

Extraction technologies for the web as of today help unfold the structure of the desired pieces of information from HTML documents and translate it into

XML and subsequently, into a semantic representation if desired in a very cost-effective way. This bridges the gap between unstructured Web data and structured databases, and is an important step towards the creation of the Semantic Web. Web Data Extraction and Integration technologies open the way to use today's web as the largest database to provide input for business intelligence applications (including cooperative and non-cooperative sites) and to reuse data for portals and personalisation and for portal-based cross-company communication.

References

1. B. Adelberg. NoDoSE - a tool for semi-automatically extracting semi-structured data from text documents. In *Proc. of SIGMOD*, 1998.
2. P. Atzeni and G. Mecca. Cut and paste. In *Proc. of PODS*, 1997.
3. R. Baumgartner, S. Flesca, and G. Gottlob. Visual web information extraction with Lixto. In *Proc. of VLDB*, 2001.
4. R. Baumgartner, N. Henze, and M. Herzog. The personal publication reader: Illustrating web data extraction, personalization and reasoning. In *Proc. of ESWC*, 2005.
5. R. Baumgartner, M. Herzog, and G. Gottlob. Visual programming of web data aggregation applications. In *Proc. of IIWeb-03*, 2003.
6. M. K. Bergman. The deep web: Surfacing hidden value. BrightPlanet White Paper, http://www.brightplanet.com/technology/deepweb.asp.
7. T. Berners-Lee, J. Hendler, and O. Lassila. The Semantic Web. In *Scientific American*, May 2001.
8. D. Cabeza and M. Hermenegildo. Distributed WWW programming using (Ciao-)Prolog and the PiLLoW library. *TPLP*, 1(3), 2001.
9. V. Crescenzi, G. Mecca, and P. Merialdo. Roadrunner: Towards automatic data extraction from large web sites. In *Proceedings of 27th International Conference on Very Large Data Bases*, pages 109–118, 2001.
10. H. Davulcu, G. Yang, M. Kifer, and I. Ramakrishnan. Computat. aspects of resilient data extract. from semistr. sources. In *Proc. of PODS*, 2000.
11. P. Dolog, N. Henze, W. Nejdl, and M. Sintek. The Personal Reader: Personalizing and Enriching Learning Resources using Semantic Web Technologies. In *Proceedings of the 3nd International Conference on Adaptive Hypermedia and Adaptive Web-Based Systems (AH 2004)*, Eindhoven, The Netherlands, 2004.
12. O. Etzioni, M. Cafarella, D. Downey, S. Kok, A. Popescu, T. Shaked, S. Soderland, D. S. Weld, and A. Yates. Web-Scale Information Extraction in KnowItAll (Preliminary Results). In *Proceedings of the World Wide Web Conference 2004*, 2004.
13. S. Flesca, G. Manco, E. Masciari, E. Rende, and A. Tagarelli. Web wrapper induction: a brief survey. *AI Communications Vol.17/2*, 2004.
14. G. Gottlob and C. Koch. Monadic datalog and the expressive power of languages for Web Information Extraction. In *Proc. of PODS*, 2002.
15. J. Hammer, H. Garcia-Molina, J. Cho, R. Aranha, and A. Crespo. Extracting semistructured information from the web. In *Proc. Workshop on Mang. of Semistructured Data*, 1997.
16. C.-N. Hsu and M. Dung. Generating finite-state transducers for semistructured data extraction from the web. *Information Systems*, 23/8, 1998.

17. G. Huck, P. Fankhauser, K. Aberer, and E. Neuhold. JEDI: Extracting and synthesizing information from the web. In *Proc. of COOPIS*, 1998.

18. L. Kahaner. *Competitive Intelligence: How to Gather, Analyse Information to Move your Business to the Top*. Touchstone Press, 1998.

19. Kapowtech. RoboSuite, 2003. Published on `http://www.kapowtech.com`.

20. S. Kuhlins and R. Tredwell. Toolkits for generating wrappers. In *Net.ObjectDays*, 2002.

21. N. Kushmerick. Wrapper verification. *World Wide Web Journal*, 2000.

22. N. Kushmerick, D. Weld, and R. Doorenbos. Wrapper induction for information extraction. In *Proc. of IJCAI*, 1997.

23. A. H. Laender, B. A. Ribeiro-Neto, A. S. da Silva, and J. S. Teixeira. A brief survey of web data extraction tools. In *Sigmod Record 31/2*, 2002.

24. L. Liu, C. Pu, and W. Han. XWrap: An extensible wrapper construction system for internet information. In *Proc. of ICDE*, 2000.

25. Z. Liu, F. Li, and W. K. Ng. Wiccap Data Model: Mapping Physical Websites to Logical Views. In *Proceedings of the 21st International Conference on Conceptual Modelling (ER2002)*, Tempere, Finland, October 7-11 2002.

26. W. May, R. Himmeröder, G. Lausen, and B. Ludäscher. A unified framework for wrapping, mediating and restructuring information from the web. In *WWWCM*. Sprg. LNCS 1727, 1999.

27. X. Meng, H. Wang, C. Li, and H. Kou. A schema-guided toolkit for generating wrappers. In *Proc. of WEBSA2003*, 2003.

28. R. C. Miller and B. A. Myers. LAPIS: Smart Editing with Text Structure. In *Proceedings of the CHI 2002 Conference on Human Factors in Computing Systems, Minneapolis, Minnesota, USA*, pages 496–497. ACM Press, Apr. 2002.

29. I. Muslea. RISE: Repository of Online Information Sources Used in Information Extraction Tasks, 1998. Published on `http://www.isi.edu/info-agents/RISE/`.

30. I. Muslea, S. Minton, and C. Knoblock. A hierarchical approach to wrapper induction. In *Proc. of 3rd Intern. Conf. on Autonomous Agents*, 1999.

31. J. Raposo, A. Pan, M. Alvarez, J. Hidalgo, and A. Vina. The Wargo System: Semi-Automatic Wrapper Generation in Presence of Complex Data Access Modes. In *Proceedings of DEXA 2002*, Aix-en-Provence, France, 2002.

32. B. Ribeiro-Neto, A. H. F. Laender, and A. S. da Silva. Extracting semi-structured data through examples. In *Proc. of CIKM*, 1999.

33. A. Sahuguet and F. Azavant. Building light-weight wrappers for legacy web datasources using W4F. In *Proc. of VLDB*, 1999.

34. B. Thomas. Anti-unification based learning of T-wrappers for information extraction. In *Workshop on Machine Learning for IE*, 1999.

35. E. Tiemeyer and H. E. Zsifkovitis. *Information als Führungsmittel: Executive Information Systems. Konzeption, Technologie, Produkte, Einführung*. 1st edition, 1995.

36. R. Tredwell and S. Kuhlins. Wrapper Generating Tools, 2003. Published on `http://www.wifo.uni-mannheim.de/~kuhlins/wrappertools/`.

Reuse in Semantic Applications

Uwe Aßmann

Institut für Software- und Multimediatechnik (SMT),
Technische Universität Dresden
uwe.assmann@inf.tu-dresden.de
http://www-st.inf.tu-dresden.de*

Abstract. Applications using semantic technology are not fundamentally different from other software products. As standard applications, they need a well-defined development process, an appropriate modelling technology, and, to decrease construction cost, a good reuse technology for models and components. This paper shows that employing ontologies can help to enlarge the reuse factor. Ontologies improve the refinement process in object-oriented software development, simplify design of product lines, improve interoperability in component-based systems, and help in service-based applications, such as web services. Hence, ontologies will play an important role in the future engineering of software products.

The reuse factor for software artifacts is a mission-critical figure for software-dependent companies. Mainly to save costs, applications, web services, enterprise services, and entire product families require a fair amount of reuse of models, components, and more complex frameworks. Basically, two forms of reuse can be distinguished: *refinement-based reuse*, in which domain and analysis models are successively refined to implementations, and *compositional reuse,* in which components on different abstraction levels are reused in many applications. The paper shows that ontologies help to improve the effectivity of both forms of software reuse.

Let's start with the first issue. Refinement-based reuse of ontologies plays an important role not only in the construction of singular applications, but also of product families. In the standard object-oriented design process, when dealing with one system at a time, refinements are the major development steps (Fig. 1). Requirements analysis constructs an *analysis model*, which captures the major functional and non-functional requirements of a system. Since the deliveries of a system are provided in an application domain, the requirements specification has to include a definition of a *domain vocabulary* or a *domain model* (a domain vocabulary with interrelations). Usually, this model is the result of the *domain analysis*, being constructed in interviews with the customers. Because experience shows that errors in requirement analysis are those that cost most [10] and all later steps are based on the domain model, the construction of a sound domain

---

* Work partially supported by European Community under the IST programme, contract IST-2003-506779-REWERSE [6].

N. Eisinger and J. Małuszyński (Eds.): Reasoning Web 2005, LNCS 3564, pp. 290–304, 2005.

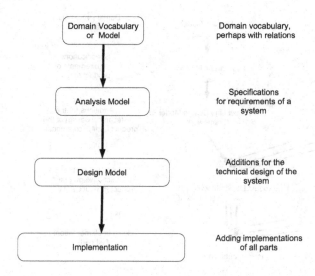

Fig. 1. Standard layout of object-oriented development

model is very important. Since ontologies play the role of standardized, approved models for application domains, how can we integrate them into the domain analysis?

In contrast to the development of one singular system, the second half of the 1990s has considered the development of *product lines* (*product families*), which consist of a set of related products that share as many common parts as possible [5]. The goal of a product line is to reuse specifications on the requirements and design level, as well as code components on the implementation level (Fig. 2). In product-line engineering, the role of the domain analysis is even more important (see top of Fig. 2): the domain model reveals commonalities for all products in the line, as well as possible variabilities, leading to specific products [9]. The domain model is reused for all products of the line, being refined to an analysis model for all products, then extended by *design variants* to designs of the specific product designs, which in turn are extended by *code components* to the product implementations. Consequently, product lines provide a planned form of reuse: product variants are foreseen, their variabilities are analyzed, and the engineering process handles the shared artefacts (the *framework*) together with all variants. Clearly, product lines will play an important role also in future web engineering. As soon as several related web services can be envisaged for an application domain, the development process should share common requirement, design, and implementation artifacts. And this raises the question how domain ontologies can be related to domain models of product lines, in particular for web service families.

Product-line-based thinking has promoted the invention of *component models*, schemas for design and implementation components, which provide a better reusability compared to standard object-oriented technology, since they follow

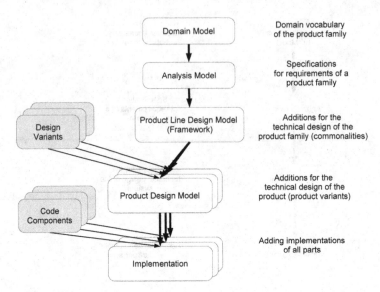

Fig. 2. Standard process to construct product line

standards (*component-based software engineering*). At the moment, component models are mainly focused on the reuse of *implementation artifacts*, i.e., they provide standard interfaces for sets of classes, objects, layers, or other software agglomerations. For instance, an Enterprise Java Bean (EJB) provides four standard interfaces for a set of enclosed classes [11]. These interfaces offer a standardized lookup service for components, hide the middleware that glues the beans together, and provide standard protocols to access their services. While EJB is a Java-focused component model, also language-interoperable models exist, such as CORBA [18], or WSDL [8]. These approaches provide a standardized way to relate interfaces of components even if they have been written in different languages. However, in language-homogeneous as well as language-heterogeneous component models, standardization has been applied to the interfaces, but not the types of component parameters, which still stem from self-made models. How can ontologies help here?

For web services, interoperability is also of vital importance, because, on the web, many different component languages are employed. Beyond that, however, service-oriented applications require a lookup-and-find of services on the intra- or internet. Obviously, standardized terminology is crucial for precise matchmaking. So, can ontologies contribute here?

This paper conjectures that ontologies will play an important role in the construction of software applications. Firstly, ontologies are being refined step by step towards the implementations (Sec. 1). Secondly, ontologies can specify constraints for the products of a product line (Sec. 2). Additionally, applications in product lines can be layered in the sense that the most general layer consists of terms of the ontology (Sec. 2.1). On the other hand, compositional reuse is more important in component-based software engineering. Here, ontologies, due to their standardization effect, increase interoperability (Sec. 3) and improve the matchmaking of components and services (Sec. 4).

1   Refinement-Based Reuse of Ontologies in the Software Development

Ontologies will play a major role in application development, both for singular applications as well as product lines. In this section, we argue that domain ontologies can be employed as domain models for software artifacts. They increase the level of standardization, because they specify shared and approved vocabulary for all applications in a domain. Hence, domain ontologies should be explicitly introduced as an integral part of the object-oriented development process, from which all development starts (Fig. 3).

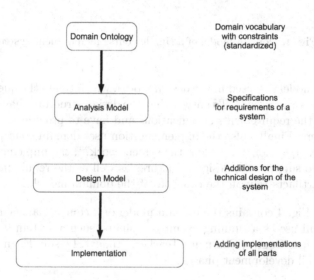

Fig. 3. Enhanced object-oriented development process, starting from a domain ontology

Let us investigate in more detail, which role a domain model plays in software development. Usually, the domain model is a base ingredient of every software product. It is put up as an integral part of the requirements analysis and contains all concepts the user of the system knows about the domain. This permits the user to talk about the functionality of the system and express her requirements. Technically, the domain model is refined to an analysis model, modelling the environment and the users of the system, the use cases, the system inputs and results. Hence, the central question of the analysis model, "what can I do with the system?", critically depends on vocabulary of the domain model. Secondly,

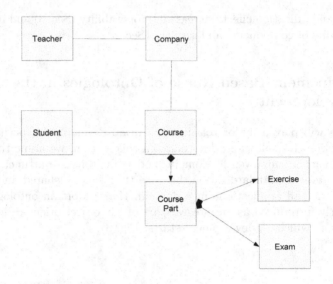

Fig. 4. Domain model of a simple course management system

the domain model is reused in the design model, which treats the question: "How is the system structured?". To answer this, the design structures have to fit to the concepts in the requirements specifications and have to provide structural solutions for them. Finally, also the implementation uses domain concepts, because, to answer the question "How does the system work?", the implementation concepts have to support the design structures as well as the requirements. Hence, all system artifacts rely on the concepts of the domain model.

Example 1. Fig. 4 contains the domain model of a course management system, which we will use as a running example. Usually, such a system has to rely on concepts such as Course, Company, Teacher, Student, Lesson, Exam, or Exercise throughout all development phases.

Ontologies resemble domain models in software engineering, but additionally provide standardization for a large group of users. This effect suggest a slightly modified software process. Instead of starting the requirements analysis by a domain analysis, an approved domain ontology can be reused.

Example 2. For the course management system, there might be off-the-shelf ontologies, such as a *course ontology* or a *business ontology* from which we can reuse concepts (Fig. 5). In this example, only the concepts Teacher, Student, Course, and Company can be reused. Missing concepts have to be added, when the analysis model is constructed, such as CoursePart, Exercise, and Exam. Also, the domain concepts will be refined, adding new features. Hence, the analysis model of the course management system contains concepts from domain ontologies and adds new, application-specific concepts, typical for the application.

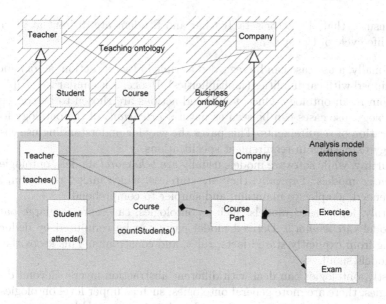

Fig. 5. Analysis model of web course, extended from ontologies

Ontologies offer several opportunities to improve the process of constructing analysis models. First of all, domain ontologies have usually been constructed by domain experts who understand the application domain. Often, when software engineers model application domains, the customer is misunderstood, and the model contains flaws. If a domain ontology is reused, this should not happen, because ontologies have been agreed on and employed by many people, so that their conceptualizations are stabilized and mature. This is not always the case with self-made analysis models.

Secondly, the ontological constraints, expressed by description logic or other more general rule languages, enable the engineer to specify integrity constraints for her models. Since these constraints are inherited to the models further down in the development chain (Fig. 3), also analysis model, design model, and implementation can be verified against the integrity constraints. Actually, such *application domain constraints* yield *system invariants* that must hold for all parts of the system and throughout its entire life time.

Thirdly, domain ontologies can be very useful, when constructing use cases. A *use case* is a use scenario of the system, putting up the relationships of a user (*actor*) with an *action (function)* of the system [17]. In an ontology-enriched analysis model, the use cases employ the standardized concepts from the ontologies for actors and actions. This does not only yield a more precise semantics for the use cases, but also inherits the ontological constraints to them.

Example 3. For instance, a disjointness constraint specifying that teachers cannot be students can be inherited from the course ontology via the analysis model to the use case diagrams, further to the design model, and the implementation.

This ensures that the actor sets Teacher and Student are disjoint at all points in the life-cycle of the system.

Additionally, a use case can be regarded a triple of (actor, action, actor) and can be equipped with cardinalities (multiplicities). Hence, it is similar to a triple, i.e., an axiom in an ontology. Once actors and actions are chosen to be concepts of an ontology, use cases can be seen as natural *extensions* of the ontology for the specification of requirements. This paves the way for understanding use cases as ontology extensions in requirement specifications.

Fourthly, while software models usually are *behavioral* models, ontologies are *declarative* models. Typically, they are stateless, which makes them simpler to be extended, simpler to maintain, and simpler to comprehend.

Fifthly, logic-based models, such as ontologies, can represent large parts of the model *intensionally*. Derived model parts can be computed by deduction, starting from explicitly stated facts, rules, and constraints. This keeps the original models small.

Lastly, ontologies can deal with different abstraction layers. Beyond domain ontologies, there are more general ontologies, such as upper level ontologies [19]. This suggests a layering of analysis models, in which several layers are made up by ontologies of different abstraction levels.

2   Ontologies and Domain Models in Product Lines

Starting from a domain ontology, also a family of applications can be constructed. Then the construction process for the entire product line inherits the advantages discussed in the last section. However, ontologies can be used for more purposes in a product line. In the following, we deal with such *product-line ontologies*.

Example 4. Fig. 6 contains two design variants of a product line for course management. Two course management systems are modeled, one for free courses and one for non-free courses. It can be seen that both variants need different design extensions of the analysis model.

Firstly, the design constraints of the product family can be specified with an ontology (see the right part of Fig. 7). Such a specification contains integrity constraints on the architecture of all products. These constraints may specify structural or behavioral invariants of products or the architectural style of the family [1]. This resembles the use of constraints in domain ontologies, however, here, the constraints do not constrain the application concepts, but the system concepts.

Example 5. Architectural styles usually constrain the kind of components and connectors that can be used. For instance, the UNIX shell provides *filter components* that are connected via the connectors *pipes* or *files* (pipe-and-filter style). Connectors are directed, and filter components have input and output ports (stdin, stdout, stderr). All these constraints can easily be specified with an OWL

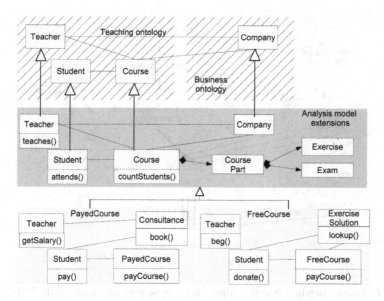

Fig. 6. Two design models in a product line for a course management system

ontology. If a product line should be built based on shell scripts, a product-line ontology can constrain their assemblage, so that only components and connectors fitting to pipe-and-filter style can be employed.

Example 6. It could be asked, whether it is justified to use the word *ontology* for a system model. Actually, the community to use a product line may be very large. Typical examples are business software product lines. They are run in thousands of sites throughout the world, involving hundreds of thousands of people. Hence, a product-line ontology defines a technical vocabulary for many people. And such a vocabulary may be very well called an ontology.

Secondly, variant selection or exclusion constraints can be specified with ontologies (see the left part of Fig. 7). The configuration space of a product line may be enormously large, can span over several stages, and must be stable over many years. Many constraints exist that distinguish product from product, specify product constraints, such as consistency criteria, or select design variants and implementation components.

Example 7. Business software product lines, being installed at many sites, are configured over several stages: pre-configuration at the software house, configuration in the deploying company, post-configuration by system consultants in the deployment company, and user-configuration by end users. In all these cases, a product-line ontology to specify configuration constraints will be of great help: it can guide the multi-stage configuration process, ensuring variant consistency for all products.

Due to these advantages, we expect that large product lines will be steered by product-line ontologies.

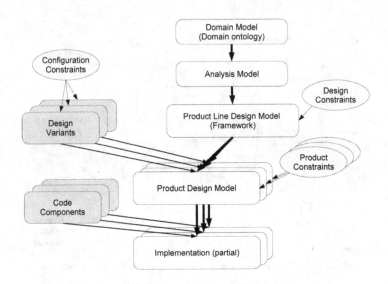

Fig. 7. Enhanced product-line development process, starting from a domain ontology, steered by design and configuration constraints in product-line ontologies

2.1 Reuse of Domain Ontologies in Layered Frameworks

A well-known architectural style for a product line is a *layered framework* [7]. In a layered framework, a layer expresses knowledge with regard to a specific application concern. An application object (often called a *business object*) cross-cuts all layers and consists of *role objects*, one per layer, that encapsulate the layer-specific knowledge. Applications are built by plugging new application specific layers on top of the layers of the framework.

Example 8. Fig. 8 contains a layered framework for an application in the course domain. There are 4 layers in an application (type in domain model, payment, topic of course, end-user device), of which the first two two are framework and the latter two are application layers. Each application object is expressed as a layered object, with role objects in all layers. For instance, it is possible to model an exam of a free English course for a PC desktop as a cross-cut through all layers, as well as a student subscribed to a course in IT basics, using a PDA.

In a layered application, upper layers depend on lower layers, but not vice versa. Application layers depend on framework layers, but framework layers are independent of application layers. Inside the framework layers, more specific layers depend on more general and abstract layers. Hence, in this scheme, because it contains the most basic knowledge of the application, the domain model will cover one or two basic layers. When integrating ontologies into the software process using layered frameworks, it is straightforward to fill one or two layers from domain ontologies. Whereas in standard object-oriented applications a domain model is *refined* towards an application model (Sec. 1), in a layered framework

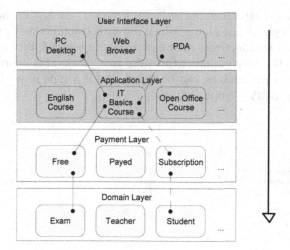

Fig. 8. Two courses, expressed as layered objects in a layered application. Left: an exam of a free English course for a PC desktop. Right: a student subscribed to a course in IT basics, using a PDA

the domain role objects are taken from ontologies and plugged together with other role objects, which stem from analysis models, design models, and implementation components.

Layered frameworks have been used for large product lines of thousands of applications [7]. They can also be applied to products on the Semantic Web, generating families of semantic applications [2]. And within such layered frameworks, ontologies will play a major role, modelling the domain roles of the application objects. Hence, also here, ontologies will play a major role for reuse.

3   Supporting Interoperability with Ontologies - Compositional Reuse

Ontologies simplify interoperability because they define shared, standardized types for an application domain. We saw in Sec. 1 that this circumstance can be used to derive refined models, starting from domain ontologies. However, there is a second use case for ontologies here: concepts from an ontology can be used as standardized types in component interfaces and concept relations can be used as standardized relations between types. Once components talk the same types and relations, they become interoperable.

Components appear on many abstraction levels, from design to code to implementation [3, 4]. On all levels, however, we can discern a component model, a composition technology, and a composition language, which glues the components together. Usually, a component model defines content and the interface concepts of the components, the composition technique describes how components are composed to larger components, and the composition language describes the system structure in-the-large. However, no matter, how diverse the component models are, no matter which reuse abstractions they provide, components receive information from their environment (*required interface*) and deliver information to their environment (*provided interface*). This information, passed through ports or parameters, can be typed, and if a type is an ontological concept, interoperability is improved.

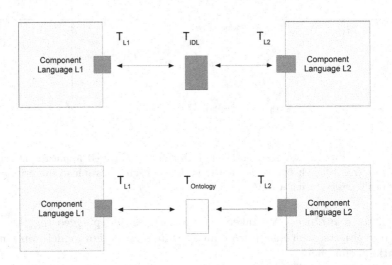

Fig. 9. Two components, exchanging information. By default, a port of a component is typed in the language of the component. Mappings can be defined to IDL specifications or ontologies

Firstly, ontological concepts can be used as types for interaction of binary components. Many classical component models, such as CORBA [18] or COM+ inside .NET [12] use a type mapping to map a type of component language L_1 to a type in an interface definition language (IDL), and another type mapping to map the IDL specification to component language L_2 (Fig. 9). Usually, from such mappings, an IDL compiler generates conversion code for the transported data. However, usually, type specifications in an IDL are not shared nor standardized for a domain. Hence, it is better to use ontologies here. If a mapping is defined from both parameter types to a type in an ontology (or a derived type model, see Sec. 1), T_{L1} and T_{L2} get a standardized meaning, agreed on by a user community. Thus, an ontology can play the role of a mediating type model between components written in different languages and for different environments.

Example 9. ECTS grades (European credit transfer system) depend on a political agreement for European educational systems. One could say, ECTS grades provide an ontology of grading in Europe. The ontology uses relative grading, grouping all students of a course into 6 quality levels (10% of the best, 20% of the best, etc.). Using the ECTS concepts as a types enables the components of course management systems to exchange course grades in a simple way.

Example 10. Also the refinement-based reuse of domain models (Sec. 1) relies on type mappings. If a domain ontology is refined to an analysis model, all ontological concepts and their relationships are extended to classes and relationships in the analysis model. Since extension is a simple form of type mapping, the domain ontology plays the role of a mediating ontology for all analysis models that are derived from it. Using the extension relationship as a type mapping, the refinement process maps the concepts of many analysis models to each other. This enables the designers to correlate analysis models of different applications. Also, they can define analysis model variants for a product line. This extends the scheme of Sec. 2 and allows for requirements variants for different products.

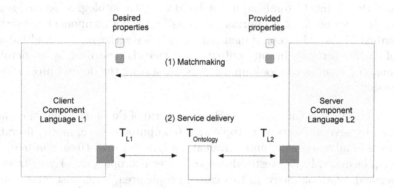

Fig. 10. Matchmaking between client and server component. The service is described by the client with a set of desired properties from a component (query). This is matched to the provided properties of the service, specified by the server

4   Ontologies in Service-Oriented Applications and Web Services

The arguments of the previous section also hold for the use of ontologies as type models for web services, because web services can be regarded as a specific component model. However, a web service has a *service-oriented* invocation protocol, differing from standard invocation protocols in that a service is not called by name, but by semantic and contextual search (Fig. 10). A service-oriented application requires that yellow page directories exist, which map semantic descriptions of services to names and location of services. In other words, yellow pages map attributes of services to names. The service-oriented architecture binds a service to a request by evaluating a query of the client (*matchmaking*). Since the name of a service is no longer a qualifying criterion for the binding, semantic descriptions should be as precise and interoperable as possible.

Ontologies simplify matchmaking. Since they provide standardized terminology and standardized ontological relations between the terms, queries can specify not only keywords with a precise, shared, and standardized meaning (*semantic search)*, but also contextual information for search in context, where the context is defined by the ontological relations of the terms. This *contextual search* seems to be one of the major advantages of a search guided by ontologies.

Example 11. A web course on IT basics can not only be queried by the standardized word *IT-basics* (being semantic search) but also in context, by relating it to courses such as *IT-advanced* or *IT-preparatory*. It is possible to say: find me an IT basics course, which has a preceding preparatory IT course and has a follow-up advanced IT course (contextual search).

In the literature, there are several approaches how to realize matchmaking for lookup of services in service-oriented architectures. Here, we present a specific approach that is most promising in combination with ontologies, *faceted matchmaking*. It relies on *faceted* information classification: a component (or service) is described in several facets, dimensions, which are orthogonal to and independent of each other [14]. In our context, each facet is described by an ontology. Matchmaking engines can look up a service by stating the desired properties for all facets.

Example 12. A course in the unified Bologna world of European education can be described by several facets, e.g., topic area (computer science, music, literature, etc.), level of advancement (undergraduate, graduate), cost (free, non-free), and country (Germany, Italy, WesternEurope, EasternEurope, etc.). Every facet can be described by an ontology, in this case on topic area, level, cost, and country. A semantic description of a course selects one value for each facet and forms a tuple. For instance, a free undergraduate music course could be described by the tuple (topic area = music, advancement = undergraduate, cost = free, country = WesternEurope). Searching a course throughout the course databases in Europe consists of comparing the tuple point-wise to database entries. The values need not match exactly, instead, subsumption in the facet ontologies can be used to deliver refinement of matchings. For example, if free-course is subsumed by non-free-course, the matcher can yield a free course, even if the client desired a non-free one. Also, a matchmaker can return a (music, undergraduate, non-free, Germany)-course which should fit the client's desires.

Facet classification has been invented in library science to simplify the description and search for books [16]. Classifications can be arranged in facets if several partitions of a group of objects exist that are orthogonal [15]. In domain modelling, this is often the case, and we conjecture, that this is also true for classifications of services. Without facets, multiple inheritance hierarchies have to be specified, which are often clumsy and error-prone. With facets, service classifications become simple.

Example 13. To describe the services of a UNIX system, [14] employed a 4-faceted scheme (function, logical object, implementation object, tool). UNIX services can be described with appropriate facet values, e.g., (function = append, logical class = line, implementation class = file, tool = text editor), which means "append a line to a file with a text editor". It is reported that facets simplified the description of the components, improved the understanding of their domain, and facilitated the search in component libraries.

Next, if every facet is described by an ontology, the service descriptions are standardized for a user group and improve understanding of service semantics. Already [14] suggested to use *controlled vocabulary* to improve the effectiveness of the search. Also, the facet classification is rather immune to extensions. Extending one facet leaves all others invariant.

Example 14. If Europe is extended with a new member state, the matchmaking algorithm can deliver new courses from the new member state, without affecting the rest of the semantic specifications at all.

Finally, the accuracy of the search can be improved by *synonym lists (thesauri)* [14]. Synonyms increase the chances for a match because they permit to search not only for keywords, but also for their synonyms. Beyond synonyms other refinement relations of concepts can be used to improve the search [13].

Example 15. Often, Great Britain is used as a synonym for England, Scotland, and Wales. Synonyms allows for matchmaking on any of the keywords, so that students looking for a course need not bother about geographic and political details.

Good matchmaking algorithms, such as facet-based search, improve the probability to find a service on the internet. In combination with ontologies, standardized conceptualizations of domains, the search will be much more effective. In turn, this will increase the reuse factor for services.

5   Conclusion

It looks like ontologies will be the basis of the future software development process, both for singular applications as well as product lines. This holds for standard applications, as well as applications on the web, including web services. In the software process, refinement is the main activity: material is added step by step to the domain ontology, which is being reused for many applications. In product families, design, product, and configuration constraints can be specified by product-line ontologies shared by the user community. Alternatively, a system can be plugged together by role layers from a layered framework, sharing domain ontology layers. Finally, ontologies increase reuse in component-based applications because they provide standardized models for mediation between components and increase the efficiency of service matchmaking algorithms.

References

1. Gregory Abowd, Robert Allen, and David Garlan. Using Style to Understand Descriptions of Software Architecture. In *Proceedings of the ACM SIGSOFT '93 Symposium on the Foundations of Software Engineering*, pages 9–20, December 1993.

2. Uwe Aßmann. Composing frameworks and components for families of semantic web applications. In *International Workshop on Principles and Practice of Semantic Web Reasoning (PPSWR 03)*, number 2901 in Lecture Notes in Computer Science, pages 1–15. Springer, December 2003.

3. Uwe Aßmann. *Invasive Software Composition*. Springer-Verlag, February 2003.

4. Uwe Aßmann. Architectural styles for active documents. In *Special Edition* Software Composition *Science of Computer Programming*. Elsevier, January 2005.

5. Don Batory, Rich Cardone, and Yannis Smaragdakis. Object-oriented frameworks and product lines. In P. Donohoe, editor, *Proceedings of the First Software Product Line Conference*, pages 227–247, August 2000.

6. Francois Bry and alia. Rules in a Semantic Web Environment (REWERSE). EU Project 6th framework. IST-2004-506779. http://www.rewerse.net.

7. Dirk Bäumer, Guido Gryczan, Rolf Knoll, Carola Lilienthal, Dirk Riehle, and Heinz Züllighoven. Framework development for large systems. *Communications of the ACM*, 40(10):52–59, oct 1997.

8. Erik Christensen, Francisco Curbera, Greg Meredith, and Sanjiva Weerawarana. Web service description language (WSDL) language definition. Technical report, W3C, 2001. http://www.w3.org/TR/wsdl.

9. Krzysztof Czarnecki and Ulrich Eisenecker. *Generative Programming: Methods, Techniques, and Applications*. Addison-Wesley, Reading, MA, 2000.

10. Albert Endres and Dieter Rombach. *A Handbook of software and systems engineering - Empirical observations, laws and theories*. Addison-Wesley, 2003.

11. JavaSoft. *Enterprise Java Beans (TM)*, April 2000. Version 2.0.

12. Juval Löwy. *COM and .NET*. O'Reilly, Sebastopol, CA, 2001.

13. Rym Mili, Ali Mili, and Roland T. Mittermeir. Storing and retrieving software components: A refinement based system. *IEEE Transactions on Software Engineering*, 23(7):445–460, July 1997.

14. Rubén Prieto-Díaz and Peter Freeman. Classifying software for reuse. *IEEE Software*, 4(1):6–16, January 1987.

15. Uta Priss. Faceted knowledge representation. *Electronic Transactions on Artificial Intelligence*, 4:21–33, 2000.

16. S. R. Ranganathan. *Elements of Library Classification*. Asia Publishing House, Bombay, 1962.

17. James Rumbaugh, Ivar Jacobson, and Grady Booch. *The Unified Modeling Language Reference Manual*. Addison-Wesley, Reading, MA, 1999.

18. Jon Siegel. OMG overview: CORBA and the OMA in enterprise computing. *Communications of the ACM*, 41(10):37–43, October 1998.

19. John F. Sowa. *Knowledge Representation: Logical, Philosophical, and Computational Foundations*. Brooks Cole Publishing Co., 2000.

Towards Types for Web Rule Languages

Włodzimierz Drabent[1,2]

[1] Institute of Computer Science, Polish Academy of Sciences,
ul. Ordona 21, Pl – 01-237 Warszawa, Poland
[2] Department of Computer and Information Science, Linköping University,
S – 581 83 Linköping, Sweden
drabent@ipipan.waw.pl

Abstract. Various schema languages have been introduced to describe (classes of) Web documents (DTD, XML Schema, Relax NG). We present mathematical treatment of their main features. We are interested in the sets of documents a schema defines; such sets will be called types. Using a mathematical formalism makes it possible to discuss chosen aspects of a schema language in a precise and simple way. Otherwise they are hidden among numerous details of a large and sophisticated schema language.

Our goal is typing of rule languages, more precisely approximately describing their semantics by means of types. Thus we are interested in formalisms for types that facilitate constructing (efficient) algorithms performing those operations on types that are needed in type checking and type inference for rules.

1 Introduction

Various schema languages have been introduced to describe (classes of) Web documents (DTD [10], XML Schema [11], Relax NG [6]). We present mathematical treatment of their main features. We are mainly interested in the sets of documents a schema defines; such sets are sometimes called types. Using a mathematical formalism makes it possible to discuss chosen aspects of a schema language in a precise and simple way. Otherwise they are hidden among numerous details of a large and sophisticated schema language.

Our main goal is typing of rule languages; by this we mean describing approximately their semantics by means of types. Such descriptions can be used for finding (certain kinds of) errors in the rules. Knowing that a rule is to be applied to data from a given type, we can compute the type of rule results. If the type is incompatible with the expectations of the programmer then there is an error in the rule. Assume that the expectations are formalized by providing a type description of the expected results. Then it can be automatically checked whether the actual results are in the given type. In other words, one can automatically check correctness of a rule with respect to an approximate specification (given by means of types). These ideas apply to sets of rules too. Sometimes the computed types are approximate and the checks are partial (answering "correct" or

N. Eisinger and J. Małuszyński (Eds.): Reasoning Web 2005, LNCS 3564, pp. 305–317, 2005.

"maybe incorrect"); still it is useful to have a possibility of automatic checking certain properties of rule programs and of obtaining hints about possible errors.

So we are interested in formalisms for specifying types that facilitate constructing (efficient) algorithms performing those operations on types that are needed in type checking and type inference for rules. Often there is a trade-off between the expressive power of a formalism and the efficiency of the related algorithms.

A related subject is typechecking of XML queries and transformations: checking whether the results of queries (or transformations) applied to XML data from a given type are within an (another) given type. Substantial theoretical work in this area has been done (see [2, 17] and references therein). That work considers formalizations of (substantial subsets of) XQuery and XSLT. Various cases of such typechecking problem have been studied, some of them shown to be undecidable, many others of non-polynomial complexity. Similar difficulties can be expected with dealing with types for Web rule languages. This suggests that one should also look for approximate, but efficient, solutions.

In the next section we introduce an abstraction of XML data as data terms. Section 3 presents a standard formalism of tree automata. Tree automata define sets of trees, or equivalently of terms, where each symbol has a fixed arity. This is too restrictive for modelling Web data, where the number of children of a tree node is not fixed. In other words, we want to deal with unranked terms. In Section 4 we present a generalization of tree automata to sets of unranked terms. The general formalism is rather powerful. It can define sets which cannot be described by means of DTD and XML Schema. Also some related algorithmic problems, for instance inclusion check, are of high complexity. In section 5 we discuss some useful restrictions of the formalism.

2   Semistructured Data

The data on the Web are presented in the form of XML documents. By database researchers a term *semistructured data* is often used [1]. This term is related to the fact that the data format does not follow any database schema; instead the data are to a certain extent self-explanatory.

XML documents can be seen as trees. From our point of view it is convenient to abstract from syntactic details of XML. We define a formal language of data terms to model tree-structured data. Our notion of data terms has been influenced by Xcerpt, a query language for Web data (see e.g. [21]). Data terms are trees. The children of a node of a data term may be ordered or unordered. We will call such trees *mixed trees* to indicate their distinction from both ordered and unordered trees. Node labels of the trees correspond to XML tags and attribute names. An attribute list of an XML tag can be modelled as an unordered set of children, as exemplified later on.

We begin with an alphabet $\mathcal{L}$ of **labels** and an alphabet $\mathcal{B}$ of **basic constants**. We assume that $\mathcal{L}$ and $\mathcal{B}$ are disjoint and countably infinite. Basic constants represent some basic values, such as numbers or strings, while labels are tree constructors, and will represent XML tags and attribute names. In contrast to function symbols of mathematical logic, the labels do not have fixed arities. The generalization of the notion of a term, allowing arbitrary number of arguments of a function symbol, is called *unranked term*. Data terms further generalize unranked terms, as in addition to argument sequences they also permit unordered sets of arguments.

From basic constants and labels we construct data terms for representing mixed trees. The linear ordering of children will be indicated by the brackets $[,]$, while unordered children are placed between the braces $\{,\}$.

Definition 1.   A **data term** is an expression defined inductively as follows:

- Any basic constant is a data term,
- if l is a label and $t_1, \ldots, t_n$ are $n \geq 0$ data terms, then $l[t_1 \cdots t_n]$ and $l\{t_1 \cdots t_n\}$ are data terms.

A data term which is not a basic constant is called **labelled**. Data terms not containing $\{,\}$ will be called **ordered**.

For a labelled data term $t = l[t_1 \cdots t_n]$ or $t = l\{t_1 \cdots t_n\}$, its **root**, denoted $root(t)$, is l. If t is a basic constant then $root(t) = t$.

Example 2. Consider the following XML element

```
<CD price="15.90" year="1994">
    Praetorius Mass
    <subtitle></subtitle>
    <artist>Gabrielli Consort and Players</artist>
</CD>
```

It can be represented as a data term

$$CD[\, attributes\{\, price[15.90]\ year[1994]\,\} \\ \text{Praetorius\_Mass} \\ subtitle[\,] \\ artist[\text{Gabrielli\_Consort\_and\_Players}] \\ ]$$

where 15.90, 1994, Praetorius_Mass, Gabrielli_Consort_and_Players are basic constants and *attributes, price, year, subtitle, artist* are labels.

The data terms $l[\,]$ or $l\{\}$ are different. One may consider it more natural not to distinguish between the empty sequence and the empty set of arguments. We have chosen to distinguish them to simplify the definition above, and some other definitions and algorithms.

Notice that the component terms are not separated by commas. This notation is intended to stress the fact that the label l in a data term $l[t_1 \cdots t_n]$ (or $l\{t_1 \cdots t_n\}$) is not an n-argument function symbol. It has rather a single argument which is a sequence (string) of data terms $t_1, \ldots, t_n$ (where $n \geq 0$).

3   Tree Automata

Finite automata (FA) are a simple, important, and well known formalism for defining sets of strings. We present tree automata [13, 7], a generalization of FA for sets of terms.

A *run* of a finite automaton M on an input string x can be seen as an assignment of states to the suffixes of x. The first suffix is x, the last one is the empty string ϵ. The suffix can be understood as the part of x not yet read by M. To the longest suffix x the run assigns the initial state of M. If a state q is assigned to a suffix ay (where a is a single symbol) then the transition function of M determines (from q and a) the state assigned to suffix y. If the state assigned to suffix ϵ is a final state then the run is *accepting*.

If M is deterministic then for each input string there exist exactly one run. This is not the case for nondeterministic finite automata. Moreover, a run of such automaton may be a partial function, not assigning any state to some suffix y of the input string (and to all the suffixes of y). The *language* defined by a FA M is the set of those strings for which there exists an accepting run.

A tree automaton (TA) deals with terms instead of strings. A basic idea is that a run assigns states to subterms of the input term (instead of suffixes of the input string of a FA). We informally describe tree automata and an equivalent formalism of regular term grammars.

We begin with a finite set of function symbols Σ, each symbol $f \in \Sigma$ has its arity $arity(f) \geq 0$. A **bottom-up tree automaton** (buTA) over Σ is a tuple $M = (Q, \Sigma, F, \Delta)$, where Q is a finite set of states, $F \subseteq Q$ is a set of final states and Δ is a set of transition rules, of the form

$$f(q_1, \ldots, q_n) \to q,$$

where $f \in \Sigma$, $q, q_1, \ldots, q_n \in Q$, and $n = arity(f)$. In particular, if f is a constant then the rule is of the form $f \to q$. A run of M on an input term t is constructed by assigning states to subterms of t. (Formally, we have to deal with subterm occurrences, as a term t' may occur many times in t, e.g. when $t = f(t', t')$. For a full definition see e.g. [7].) A state q is assigned to a subterm $f(t_1, \ldots, t_n)$ only if some states $q_1, \ldots, q_n$ are assigned respectively to the terms $t_1, \ldots, t_n$ and Δ contains the rule $f(q_1, \ldots, q_n) \to q$. If there exists such a run assigning a final state $q \in F$ to t then t is accepted by M. The set of the terms accepted by M is called the **tree language** recognized (or defined, or accepted) by M, and denoted $L(M)$.

So a computation starts with assigning states to the constants in t, by applying rules of the form $a \to q$. Then iteratively: having assigned states to to the subterms $t_1, \ldots, t_n$ of a subterm $f(t_1, \ldots, t_n)$, a rule from Δ is applied, if possible, to assign a state to $f(t_1, \ldots, t_n)$.

A bottom-up tree automaton is **deterministic** if there are no two rules with the same left hand side. It turns out that any set defined by a bottom-up tree automaton is defined by a deterministic one. (A deterministic buTA M' equivalent to a given buTA M can be obtained by a construction similar to the standard one used for FA [7]; each state of M' is a set of states of M. This construction may result in exponential growth of the number of states.)

The sets of terms defined by bottom-up tree automata are sometimes called *regular tree languages* (or recognizable tree languages).

We can consider a different kind of tree automata. Instead of starting at the leaves of the tree, the computation may start at the root. By a **top-down tree automaton** (tdTA) we mean a tuple $M = (Q, \Sigma, I, \Delta)$, where Q, Σ are as above, $I \subseteq Q$ is a set of initial states and Δ is a set of transition rules of the form

$$q \to f(q_1, \ldots, q_n),$$

(where $f \in \Sigma$, $q, q_1, \ldots, q_n \in Q$ and $n = arity(f)$). Given an input term t, a run assigns an initial state $q_0 \in I$ to t, and if a state q is assigned to a subterm $f(t_1, \ldots, t_n)$ and a rule $q \to f(q_1, \ldots, q_n)$ is in Δ then states $q_1, \ldots, q_n$ can be respectively assigned to the subterms $t_1, \ldots, t_n$. A run for t is called accepting if it assigns a state to each subterm of t. A term t is accepted by M if there exists an accepting run for t.

A top-down tree automaton is **deterministic** if it has one initial state and has no two rules with the same left hand side and the same function symbol.

The top-down and bottom-up tree automata are equivalent, they define the same class of languages. (For a proof it is sufficient to reverse the rules, and exchange the sets of final and initial states.) Notice that this transformation applied to a deterministic bottom-up automaton does not necessarily produce a deterministic top-down one. Indeed, deterministic top-down tree automata define a proper subset of regular tree languages. For instance, the set $\{f(a, b), f(b, a)\}$ is not defined by any deterministic tdTA.

It is sometimes convenient to view top-down tree automata as grammars (called *regular term grammars* or *regular tree grammars*,[1] see e.g. [8, 7]). Let $M = (Q, \Sigma, I, \Delta)$ be such an automaton. In the corresponding grammar, the states of M become non-terminal (unary) symbols of the grammar, and the initial states become start symbols. We consider terms built out of $\Sigma \cup Q$ and a derivation relation $\Rightarrow$ on such terms: $t_1 \Rightarrow t_2$ iff t_2 is obtained from t_1 by replacing an occurrence of a nonterminal q by a term $f(q_1, \ldots, q_n)$ such that the rule $q \to f(q_1, \ldots, q_n)$ is in Δ. The language generated by the grammar is

$$\{ t \mid q \Rightarrow^* t, \ q \in I, \ t \text{ does not contain symbols from } Q \}.$$

This set is equal to the language accepted by the automaton M. (We skip a proof, based on showing that an accepting run of M assigns a state q to an input term t iff $q \Rightarrow^* t$, for any term t over Σ).

The class of regular tree languages is closed under union, complement and intersection [7]. We briefly outline the proofs. To construct a buTA for the union of regular tree languages L_1, L_2, take two buTA $M_i = (Q_i, \Sigma, F_i, \Delta_i)$ $(i = 1, 2)$ respectively for L_1 and L_2, with disjoint sets of states. Automaton $(Q_1 \cup Q_2,$

---

[1] However [18] applies this name to a formalism defining sets of unranked trees.

Σ, $F_1 \cup F_2$, $\Delta_1 \cup \Delta_2$) accepts $L_1 \cup L_2$. A TA for $L_1 \cap L_2$ can be obtained by a constructing a product automaton from M_1 and M_2 (and the construction is polynomial). Exchanging the final and non final states in a deterministic buTA for a tree language L results in a buTA for the complement of L.

It can be decided in time $O(|t| \cdot |M|)$ whether a term t is accepted by a TA M (where $|t|, |M|$ are respectively the sizes of t, M). If M is a deterministic buTA (or deterministic tdTA) then the membership can be tested in linear time. Checking whether $L(M) = \emptyset$ is linear, while checking emptiness of the complement of $L(M)$ is EXPTIME-complete. Also checking whether $L(M_1) \subseteq L(M_2)$ is EXPTIME-complete. For details and proofs see [7]. For deterministic tdTA polynomial algorithms for checking $L(M_1) \subseteq L(M_2)$ exist, see e.g. [12, 9].

4   Tree Automata Generalized

Tree automata are not directly applicable to semistructured data. They deal with terms in which each symbol has a fixed arity, while in semistructured data the number of arguments of a symbol is not fixed.

A straightforward solution is to apply a standard way of representing trees as binary trees [16]. In such a binary tree the first child of a node n represents the list of children of n in the original tree, while the second child represents the (tail of the list of) siblings of n.

$$
\begin{array}{ccc}
\downarrow & & \\
n & \to \text{ sister of } n \to & \cdots \\
\downarrow & \downarrow & \\
& \cdots & \\
\text{daughter of } n & \to \text{ daughter of } n \to & \cdots \\
\downarrow & \downarrow & \\
\cdots & \cdots &
\end{array}
$$

Such representation is used for instance by [15]. A disadvantage is that the representation obscures the structure of the original tree; the (next) sibling of n is treated in the same way as its (first) child, while the children of n are treated differently. It seems more elegant and clear to provide a formalism to directly describe semistructured data. It turns out that such approach has some actual technical advantages.

There exist various equivalent generalizations of tree automata to unranked terms [18, 3, 15]. They follow a common main idea. In tree automata (or regular tree grammars) the children of a node are described by a single sequence (of states or nonterminals). The generalizations replace a single sequence by a regular language. In this way the formalism is able to specify a set of tree sequences, which are allowed as the children of a given tree node.

Some of the formalisms are formulated as defining sets of trees (e.g. [18]), some other as defining sets of sequences of trees (in other words of ordered forests, or of hedges, e.g. [3, 15]). This difference is inessential, as we may express a sequence $t_1, \ldots, t_n$ of trees as a tree $f(t_1, \ldots, t_n)$, where f is a selected new symbol. The grammatical formalism described below defines sets of trees.

As our abstraction of semistructured data we choose data terms (cf. Section 2). The purpose of this paper is to discuss defining sets of data terms, so we do not consider a way of specifying sets of basic constants. Instead we assume that we have an alphabet $\mathcal{C}$ of **type constants**, and for each $C \in \mathcal{C}$ a corresponding set $[\![C]\!]$ of basic constants is given. The formalism also employs an alphabet $\mathcal{V}$ of **type variables**. The symbols from $\mathcal{V} \cup \mathcal{C}$ will play the role of grammar nonterminals, they will be called **type names**.

A regular language (of strings) over $\mathcal{V} \cup \mathcal{C}$ will be called a *regular type language*. As a way of specifying regular type languages we choose regular expressions; they may be replaced by other formalisms, like (deterministic or nondeterministic) finite automata. By a **regular type expression** we mean a regular expression over the alphabet $\mathcal{V} \cup \mathcal{C}$. Thus ε, ϕ and any type constant or type variable T are regular type expressions, and if τ, τ_1, τ_2, are type expressions then $(\tau_1\tau_2)$, $(\tau_1|\tau_2)$ and (τ^*) are regular type expressions. As usually, every regular type expression τ denotes a *regular language* $L(\tau)$ over the alphabet $\mathcal{V} \cup \mathcal{C}$: $L(\varepsilon) = \{\varepsilon\}$, $L(\phi) = \emptyset$, $L(T) = \{T\}$, $L((\tau_1\tau_2)) = L(\tau_1)L(\tau_2)$, $L((\tau_1|\tau_2)) = L(\tau_1) \cup L(\tau_2)$, and $L((\tau^*)) = L(\tau)^*$. We adopt the usual notational conventions [14], where the parentheses are suppressed by assuming the following priorities of operators: $*$, concatenation, $|$.

As syntactic sugar for regular expressions we will also use the following notation:

- $\tau(n : m)$, or $\tau^{(n:m)}$, where $n \le m$, as a shorthand for $\tau^n|\tau^{n+1}|\cdots|\tau^m$, notice that τ^* can be seen as $\tau(0 : \infty)$
- τ^+ as a shorthand for $\tau\tau^*$,
- $\tau^?$ as a shorthand $\tau(0 : 1)$,

where τ is a regular expression and n is a natural number and m is a natural number or ∞.

Definition 3. A **type definition** D is a finite set of rules of the form

$$T \to l[\tau] \quad \text{or} \quad T \to l\{\tau\}$$

where T is a type variable, l is a label, τ a regular expression over $\mathcal{V} \cup \mathcal{C}$ (i.e. a regular type expression), and no two rules with the same T and l occur in D.

The regular expression τ is called the *content model* of the rule. A rule beginning with a type name T is said to be a *rule for T*. The form of the content models in rules of the form $T \to l\{\tau\}$ is restricted, as explained below.

The two kinds of rules are used to distinguish ordered and unordered arguments of a label. A rule $T \to l[\tau]$ describes a family of data terms where the children of the root l are ordered and their sequence is described by the regular expression τ. In the second case the children of l are unordered and we abstract from the order of symbols in the strings from $L(\tau)$. Thus the full power of regular expressions is not needed here. We will usually require that the regular expressions in the rules of the form $T \to l\{\tau\}$ are **multiplicity lists**, i.e. they are of the form $s_1^{(n_1:m_1)} \cdots s_k^{(n_k:m_k)}$ where $k \geq 0$ and $s_1, \ldots, s_k$ are distinct type names. A different kind of restrictions is considered in [20, 2].

A type definition defines a set of data terms by means of rewriting of data patterns.

Definition 4.   A **data pattern** is inductively defined as follows

- a type variable, a type constant, and a basic constant are data patterns,
- if $d_1, \ldots, d_n$ for $n \geq 0$ are data patterns and l is a label then $l[d_1 \cdots d_n]$ and $l\{d_1 \cdots d_n\}$ are data patterns.

Thus data terms are data patterns, and data patterns may be seen as data terms with some subterms replaced by type names. Now we are ready to define the rewriting relation of a type definition.

Definition 5 (of $\rightarrow_D$). Let D be a type definition and d, d' be data patterns. $d \rightarrow_D d'$ iff one of the following holds:

1. For some type variable T
   - there exists a rule $T \rightarrow l[r]$ in D and a string $s \in L(r)$, or
   - there exists a rule $T \rightarrow l\{r\}$ in D, a string $s_0 \in L(r)$, and a permutation s of s_0

   such that d' is obtained from d by replacing an occurrence of T in d, respectively, by $l[s]$ or by $l\{s\}$.
2. d' is obtained from d by replacing an occurrence of a type constant S by a basic constant in $[\![S]\!]$.

As usually, a sequence $d_1 \rightarrow_D \cdots \rightarrow_D d_n$ is called a derivation of D. Derivation may end with a data term. This gives the semantics for type definitions:

Definition 6.   Let D be a type definition. The **type** $[\![T]\!]_D$ associated with a type name T by D is defined as the set of all data terms t that can be obtained from T:

$$[\![T]\!]_D = \{\, t \mid T \rightarrow_D^* t \text{ and } t \text{ is a data term}\,\}.$$

Additionally we define the set of data terms specified by a given data pattern d, and by a given regular expression τ:

$$[\![d]\!]_D = \{\, t \mid d \rightarrow_D^* t \text{ and } t \text{ is a data term}\,\},$$
$$[\![\tau]\!]_D = \{\, t_1 \cdots t_k \mid t_1 \in [\![T_1]\!]_D, \ldots, t_k \in [\![T_k]\!]_D \text{ for some } T_1 \cdots T_k \in L(\tau)\,\}.$$

A set S of data terms is called a **type** or a **regular** set if $S = [\![T]\!]_D$ for some type definition D and type name T.

Notice that type definitions generalize regular term grammars. Assuming a fixed arity $arity(l)$ for each label l, a type definition containing only rules of the form $T \rightarrow l[T_1 \cdots T_{arity(l)}]$ is a regular term grammar.

Example 7. Assume that $\#name \in C$ and consider the following type definition D:

$$Person \rightarrow person[Name \ (M|F) \ Person^{(0:2)}]$$
$$Name \rightarrow name[\#name]$$
$$M \rightarrow m[\,]$$
$$F \rightarrow f[\,]$$

Let john, mary, bob $\in [\![\#name]\!]$. Extending the derivation

$$Person \rightarrow person[Name \ M \ Person] \rightarrow^* person[name[\#name] \ m[\,] \ Person]$$

one can check that the following data term is in $[\![Person]\!]$

$$person[name[\text{john}] \ m[\,] \ person[name[\text{mary}] \ f[\,] \ person[name[\text{bob}] \ m[\,]]]].$$

5 Useful Restrictions of Type Definitions

The formalism of type definitions introduced in the previous section is rather general. This has some disadvantages. For instance, inclusion checking for sets defined by type definitions is EXPTIME-hard. It is interesting to find out classes of type definitions for which some problems can be solved more efficiently. This section presents a few such classes; it is mainly based on the classification proposed by Murata, Lee, and Mani [18]. (A newer version of that paper is [19].) That classification is made from the point of view of membership checking, but it is also useful when other problems are considered. The work [18,19] dealt only with ordered trees (in our formalism this means ordered data terms). We provide a straightforward generalization of the classification of [18,19] to mixed trees (i.e. arbitrary data terms).

In what follows we also explain briefly the relation between the discussed classes of definitions, and DTD and XML Schema. It should also be mentioned that the schema language Relax NG [6] is able to define any regular set of ordered data terms (formally, any set of XML documents corresponding to such data term set).

There is already a restriction imposed in the Definition 3, namely that there are no two rules for the same type variable T and with the same label l. This restriction is not severe, as any two rules $T \rightarrow l\alpha\tau_1\beta$, $T \rightarrow l\alpha\tau_2\beta$ with the same T, l and the same parentheses $\alpha\beta$ are equivalent to one rule $T \rightarrow l\alpha\tau_1|\tau_2\beta$. However the restriction implies that in a type $[\![T]\!]_D$ defined by a type definition there cannot occur data terms of the form $l\{\tau\}$ and of the form $l[\tau]$ (with the same l). We expect that that this restriction is not important from a practical point of view.

A natural question arises whether we need multiple rules for one type name.

Definition 8. A type definition D will be called **single-label** if D contains at most one rule for each type name T.

We show that the sets defined by type definitions are finite unions of sets defined by single-label type definitions.

Proposition 9. Let D be a type definition. There exists a single-label definition D' such that for each type variable T occurring in D we have $[\![T]\!]_D = [\![T_1|\cdots|T_n]\!]_{D'}$ for some type names $T_1, \ldots, T_n$.

Proof. Let $T \to l_i\alpha_i\tau_i\beta_i$ $(i = 1, \ldots, n)$ be the rules from D for a type variable T (where $\alpha_i\beta_i$ are parentheses [] or {}). By Definition 3 the labels $l_1, \ldots, l_n$ are distinct. Introduce new type variables $T_1, \ldots, T_n$. Replace the i-th rule above by $T_i \to l_i\alpha_i\tau_i\beta_i$. Replace each occurrence of T in the content model of a rule by $(T_1|\cdots|T_n)$. For the resulting type definition D_T we have $[\![T]\!]_D = [\![T_1|\cdots|T_n]\!]_{D_T}$ and $[\![U]\!]_D = [\![U]\!]_{D_T}$ for all the other type names occurring in D. D' is obtained by repeating this transformation for all the type variables for which rules in D exist.

Consider a type definition D. Following [18] we define a notion of competing type names. Distinct type variables T_1, T_2 are **competing** (w.r.t. D) if D contains rules with T_1 and T_2 as the left hand sides and with the same label l. Distinct type constants C_1, C_2 are *competing* if $[\![C_1]\!] \cap [\![C_2]\!] \neq \emptyset$.

Definition 10. A type definition is called **local** if it does not contain competing type names.

Example 11. Consider a type definition

$$D = \{\, Book \to book[Author^*],\ Author \to man[\#],\ Author \to woman[\#] \,\},$$

where $Book, Author \in \mathcal{V}$, $\# \in \mathcal{C}$, and $book, man, woman \in \mathcal{L}$. No two type names of D are competing, thus D is local. D is not single-label; removing one of the rules for $Author$ results in a single-label definition.

The intention for introducing local definitions is simplifying the membership check. If D is local then for any data term t there is at most one type name T_t (occurring in D) such that $t \in [\![T_t]\!]_D$. Thus to check whether $l[t_1 \cdots t_n] \in [\![T]\!]_D$ it is sufficient to check, for a single sequence $T_{t_1}, \ldots, T_{t_n}$, whether $t_i \in [\![T_{t_i}]\!]_D$ for $i = 1, \ldots, n$, whether a rule $T \to l[\tau]$ exists in D, and whether $T_{t_1} \cdots T_{t_n} \in L(\tau)$. Checking if $l\{t_1 \cdots t_n\} \in [\![T]\!]_D$ is similar.

Sections 3.2 and 5.1 of [18] point out correspondence between DTD's [10] and local type definitions. Indeed, any DTD represented as a data definition is local. This is due to not distinguishing between type variables and labels; each rule of the data definition is of the form $l \to l[\tau]$. On the other hand local definitions are more general than DTD, as they allow different labels for the same type variable, like in Ex. 11. (Papers [18, 19] do not discuss this issue and all the example definitions they use are single-label). So it is more accurate to state that DTD's correspond to data definitions which are local, single-label and do not contain rules with {}.

Example 12. Consider the type definition D from Example 11 and assume that $[\![\#]\!]$ is the set of character strings. Removing the last rule from D results in a type definition D' corresponding to the DTD: `<!ELEMENT book (man*)>` `<!ELEMENT man (#PCDATA)>` .

Definition D does not correspond to any DTD, as $[Author]$ contains data terms with two roots, *man* and *woman*. Transforming D into a single-label definition as in the proof of Proposition 9 results in a definition which is not local.

The conditions on local type definitions can be weakened without requiring any substantial modifications of the outlined membership checking algorithm. Namely it is sufficient that, for a given t, in any content model of D there is at most one T such that $t \in [T]_D$.

Definition 13. A type definition D is called **single-type** if no content model in a rule of D contains competing type names [18]. A type definition D is **proper** if it is single-type and single-label [22, 5].

Example 14. Consider the type definition D from Example 11 and rules

$$D' = \{ \, Library \rightarrow lib\{Reader^*\}, \ Reader \rightarrow man[\#], \ Reader \rightarrow woman[\#] \, \}.$$

Definition $D \cup D'$ is single-type but not proper and not local. Removing from $D \cup D'$ the two rules with label *man* results in a proper definition.

Paper [18, 19] explains that the sets defined by XML Schema [11], with exclusion of a few constructs, can be defined by single-type type definitions. One of the excluded constructs is the mechanism of *xsi:type*. Actually, "single-type" can be replaced here by "proper", as all the elements of a set defined by an XML Schema have the same main tag.

An important property is that inclusion of sets defined by proper type definitions can be checked in polynomial time. More precisely, [5] presents an algorithm which checks whether $[T_1]_{D_1} \subseteq [T_2]_{D_2}$, where D_2 is proper and D_1 is arbitrary. (Definition D_1 is required to be single-label, but this restriction can be abandoned.) The algorithm works in time polynomial w.r.t. the sizes of D_1, D_2 and the sizes of deterministic finite automata equivalent to the content models of D_1, D_2. Unfortunately, the latter are exponential w.r.t. the sizes of regular expressions. It is known that construction of deterministic FA is of linear time for *1-unambiguous* regular expressions [4]. Thus inclusion can be checked in polynomial time for type definitions D_1, D_2 with 1-unambiguous content models, where D_2 is proper.

The restrictions above can be further weakened for rules with parentheses [ ], by considering the positions on which type names occur in the strings from $L(\tau)$. We do not discuss this issue here.

The classes discussed in this section can be parameterized by the way the regular languages in the content models are specified. As the discussion above on inclusion checking for proper definitions suggests, an important class of type definitions is that with content models given by deterministic FA (or by regular expressions which can be transformed to such automata in linear or polynomial time). This class is also distinguished in the work on complexity of XML transformations (cf. [17] and the references therein). That work also introduces a class of *bottom-up deterministic* (unranked) tree automata, which in our approach correspond to type definitions such that whenever a definition contains rules $T_1 \to l\alpha_1\tau_1\beta_1$ and $T_2 \to l\alpha_2\tau_2\beta_2$ for distinct T_1, T_2 then $L(\tau_1) \cap L(\tau_2) = \emptyset$.

The class of regular sets of data terms is closed under intersection, union and complementation. The classes of the sets defined by local, single-type and proper type definitions are closed under intersection but not under union (hence not under complementation) [18, 19, 5].

Conclusions

The intention of this text is to introduce the reader to formalisms for defining sets of trees; the intended application is typechecking of rule languages for Web applications. First we presented tree automata as a generalization of finite automata for strings. Tree automata define sets of terms where each function symbol has a fixed arity. This is too restrictive from the point of view of modelling Web data. For this task unranked terms are needed, where arity of symbols is not fixed. We deal with a slightly more general concept of data terms, where the arguments of a symbol can be ordered or unordered. A generalization (called type definitions) of tree automata for data terms is shown in Section 4. Some algorithmic problems, like inclusion check, are of non polynomial complexity already for tree automata. We outlined some restrictions of the formalism; for such restrictions more efficient algorithms exist. We briefly discussed the correspondence of these restrictions to DTD and XML Schema.

Acknowledgement. This research has been partially funded by the European Commission and by the Swiss Federal Office for Education and Science within the 6th Framework Programme project REWERSE number 506779 (cf. http://rewerse.net).

References

1. S. Abiteboul, P. Buneman, and D. Suciu. *Data on the Web: From Relations to Semistructured Data and XML*. Morgan Kaufmann, 1999.
2. N. Alon, T. Milo, F. Neven, D. Suciu, and V. Vianu. XML with data values: Typechecking revisited. *J. Comput. Syst. Sci.*, 66(4):688–727, 2003.
3. A. Brüggemann-Klein, M. Murata, and D. Wood. Regular tree and regular hedge languages over unranked alphabets. Technical Report HKUST-TCSC-2001-0, The Hongkong University of Science and Technology, April 2001.
4. A. Brüggemann-Klein and D. Wood. One-unambiguous regular languages. *Information and Computation*, 142(2):182–206, May 1998.
5. François Bry, Włodzimierz Drabent, and Jan Małuszyński. On subtyping of tree-structured data: A polynomial approach. In Hans Jürgen Ohlbach and Sebastian Schaffert, editors, *Principles and Practice of Semantic Web Reasoning, Second International Workshop (PPSWR 2004)*, volume 3208 of *Lecture Notes in Computer Science*, pages 1–18. Springer-Verlag, 2004.

6. J. Clark and M. Murata (editors). RELAX NG specification, December 2001. http://www.oasis-open.org/committees/relax-ng/spec-20011203.html.

7. H. Common, M. Dauchet, R. Gilleron, F. Jacquemard, D. Lugiez, S. Tison, and M. Tommasi. Tree automata techniques and applications. http://www.grappa.univ-lille3.fr/tata/, 2002.

8. P. Dart and J. Zobel. A regular type language for logic programs. In F. Pfenning, editor, *Types in Logic Programming*, pages 157–187. The MIT Press, 1992.

9. W. Drabent, J. Maluszynski, and P. Pietrzak. Using parametric set constraints for locating errors in CLP programs. *Theory and Practice of Logic Programming*, 2(4–5):549–610, 2002.

10. Extensible markup language (XML) 1.0 (second edition), W3C recommendation 6 October 2000. http://www.w3.org/TR/REC-xml.

11. D. C. Fallside (ed.). XML Schema part 0: Primer. W3C Recommendation, http://www.w3.org/TR/xmlschema-0/, 2001.

12. J. Gallagher and D. A. de Waal. Fast and precise regular approximations of logic programs. In P. Van Hentenryck, editor, *Proc. of the Eleventh International Conference on Logic Programming*, pages 599–613. The MIT Press, 1994.

13. F. Gécseg and M. Steinby. Tree languages. In G. Rozenberg and A. Salomaa, editors, *Handbook of Formal Languages*, volume 3, Beyond Words. Springer-Verlag, 1997.

14. J. E. Hopcroft, R. Motwani, and J. D. Ullman. *Introduction to Automata Theory, Languages and Computation*. Addison-Wesley, 2nd edition, 2001.

15. H. Hosoya, J. Vouillon, and B. C. Pierce. Regular expression types for XML. In *ICFP 2000*, pages 11–22, 2000.

16. Donald E. Knuth. *Fundamental Algorithms*, volume 1 of *The Art of Computer Programming*. Addison-Wesley, Reading, Massachusetts, second edition, 1973.

17. W. Martens and F. Neven. Frontiers of tractability for typechecking simple XML transformations. In *PODS 2004*, pages 23–34, 2004.

18. M. Murata, D. Lee, and M. Mani. Taxonomy of XML schema languages using formal language theory. In *Extreme Markup Langages*, Montreal, Canada, 2001. http://www.cs.ucla.edu/~dongwon/paper/.

19. M. Murata, D. Lee, M. Mani, and K. Kawaguchi. Taxonomy of XML schema languages using formal language theory. Submitted, 2003.

20. F. Neven and T. Schwentick. XML schemas without order. Unpublished, 1999.

21. Sebastian Schaffert and François Bry. Querying the Web Reconsidered: A Practical Introduction to Xcerpt. In *Proceedings of Extreme Markup Languages 2004, Montreal, Quebec, Canada (2nd–6th August 2004)*, 2004.

22. A. Wilk and W. Drabent. On types for XML query language Xcerpt. In *International Workshop, PPSWR 2003, Mumbai, India, December 8, 2003, Proceedings*, number 2901 in LNCS, pages 128–145. Springer-Verlag, 2003.

Author Index

Alferes, José Júlio   134
Antoniou, Grigoris   1
Aßmann, Uwe   290

Bailey, James   35
Baldoni, Matteo   173
Baroglio, Cristina   173
Baumgartner, Robert   275
Bry, François   35

Drabent, Włodzimierz   305

Eiter, Thomas   275

Franconi, Enrico   1
Fuchs, Norbert E.   213
Furche, Tim   35

Gottlob, Georg   275

Henze, Nicola   173
Herzog, Marcus   275
Höfler, Stefan   213

Kaljurand, Kaarel   213
Kifer, Michael   22
Koch, Christoph   275

May, Wolfgang   134

Rinaldi, Fabio   213

Schaffert, Sebastian   35
Schneider, Gerold   213

van Harmelen, Frank   1

Wagner, Gerd   251

Lecture Notes in Computer Science

For information about Vols. 1–3483

please contact your bookseller or Springer

Vol. 3596: F. Dau, M.-L. Mugnier, G. Stumme (Eds.), Conceptual Structures: Common Semantics for Sharing Knowledge. XI, 467 pages. 2005. (Subseries LNAI).

Vol. 3587: P. Perner, A. Imiya (Eds.), Machine Learning and Data Mining in Pattern Recognition. XVII, 695 pages. 2005. (Subseries LNAI).

Vol. 3582: J. Fitzgerald, I.J. Hayes, A. Tarlecki (Eds.), FM 2005: Formal Methods. XIV, 558 pages. 2005.

Vol. 3580: L. Caires, G.F. Italiano, L. Monteiro, C. Palamidessi, M. Yung (Eds.), Automata, Languages and Programming. XXV, 1477 pages. 2005.

Vol. 3578: M. Gallagher, J. Hogan, F. Maire (Eds.), Intelligent Data Engineering and Automated Learning - IDEAL 2005. XVI, 599 pages. 2005.

Vol. 3576: K. Etessami, S.K. Rajamani (Eds.), Computer Aided Verification. XV, 564 pages. 2005.

Vol. 3575: S. Wermter, G. Palm, M. Elshaw (Eds.), Biomimetic Neural Learning for Intelligent Robots. IX, 383 pages. 2005. (Subseries LNAI).

Vol. 3574: C. Boyd, J.M. González Nieto (Eds.), Information Security and Privacy. XIII, 586 pages. 2005.

Vol. 3573: S. Etalle (Ed.), Logic Based Program Synthesis and Transformation. VIII, 279 pages. 2005.

Vol. 3572: C. De Felice, A. Restivo (Eds.), Developments in Language Theory. XI, 409 pages. 2005.

Vol. 3571: L. Godo (Ed.), Symbolic and Quantitative Approaches to Reasoning with Uncertainty. XVI, 1028 pages. 2005. (Subseries LNAI).

Vol. 3570: A. S. Patrick, M. Yung (Eds.), Financial Cryptography and Data Security. XII, 376 pages. 2005.

Vol. 3569: F. Bacchus, T. Walsh (Eds.), Theory and Applications of Satisfiability Testing. XII, 492 pages. 2005.

Vol. 3568: W.K. Leow, M.S. Lew, T.-S. Chua, W.-Y. Ma, L. Chaisorn, E.M. Bakker (Eds.), Image and Video Retrieval. XVII, 672 pages. 2005.

Vol. 3567: M. Jackson, D. Nelson, S. Stirk (Eds.), Database: Enterprise, Skills and Innovation. XII, 185 pages. 2005.

Vol. 3565: G.E. Christensen, M. Sonka (Eds.), Information Processing in Medical Imaging. XXI, 777 pages. 2005.

Vol. 3564: N. Eisinger, J. Małuszyński (Eds.), Reasoning Web. IX, 319 pages. 2005.

Vol. 3562: J. Mira, J.R. Álvarez (Eds.), Artificial Intelligence and Knowledge Engineering Applications: A Bioinspired Approach, Part II. XXIV, 636 pages. 2005.

Vol. 3561: J. Mira, J.R. Álvarez (Eds.), Mechanisms, Symbols, and Models Underlying Cognition, Part I. XXIV, 532 pages. 2005.

Vol. 3560: V.K. Prasanna, S. Iyengar, P.G. Spirakis, M. Welsh (Eds.), Distributed Computing in Sensor Systems. XV, 423 pages. 2005.

Vol. 3559: P. Auer, R. Meir (Eds.), Learning Theory. XI, 692 pages. 2005. (Subseries LNAI).

Vol. 3557: H. Gilbert, H. Handschuh (Eds.), Fast Software Encryption. XI, 443 pages. 2005.

Vol. 3556: H. Baumeister, M. Marchesi, M. Holcombe (Eds.), Extreme Programming and Agile Processes in Software Engineering. XIV, 332 pages. 2005.

Vol. 3555: T. Vardanega, A. Wellings (Eds.), Reliable Software Technology – Ada-Europe 2005. XV, 273 pages. 2005.

Vol. 3554: A. Dey, B. Kokinov, D. Leake, R. Turner (Eds.), Modeling and Using Context. XIV, 572 pages. 2005. (Subseries LNAI).

Vol. 3553: T.D. Hämäläinen, A.D. Pimentel, J. Takala, S. Vassiliadis (Eds.), Embedded Computer Systems: Architectures, Modeling, and Simulation. XV, 476 pages. 2005.

Vol. 3552: H. de Meer, N. Bhatti (Eds.), Quality of Service – IWQoS 2005. XVIII, 400 pages. 2005.

Vol. 3551: T. Härder, W. Lehner (Eds.), Data Management in a Connected World. XIX, 371 pages. 2005.

Vol. 3548: K. Julisch, C. Kruegel (Eds.), Intrusion and Malware Detection and Vulnerability Assessment. X, 241 pages. 2005.

Vol. 3547: F. Bomarius, S. Komi-Sirviö (Eds.), Product Focused Software Process Improvement. XIII, 588 pages. 2005.

Vol. 3543: L. Kutvonen, N. Alonistioti (Eds.), Distributed Applications and Interoperable Systems. XI, 235 pages. 2005.

Vol. 3542: H.H. Hoos, D.G. Mitchell (Eds.), Theory and Applications of Satisfiability Testing. XIII, 393 pages. 2005.

Vol. 3541: N.C. Oza, R. Polikar, J. Kittler, F. Roli (Eds.), Multiple Classifier Systems. XII, 430 pages. 2005.

Vol. 3540: H. Kalviainen, J. Parkkinen, A. Kaarna (Eds.), Image Analysis. XXII, 1270 pages. 2005.

Vol. 3537: A. Apostolico, M. Crochemore, K. Park (Eds.), Combinatorial Pattern Matching. XI, 444 pages. 2005.

Vol. 3536: G. Ciardo, P. Darondeau (Eds.), Applications and Theory of Petri Nets 2005. XI, 470 pages. 2005.

Vol. 3535: M. Steffen, G. Zavattaro (Eds.), Formal Methods for Open Object-Based Distributed Systems. X, 323 pages. 2005.

Vol. 3533: M. Ali, F. Esposito (Eds.), Innovations in Applied Artificial Intelligence. XX, 858 pages. 2005. (Subseries LNAI).

Vol. 3532: A. Gómez-Pérez, J. Euzenat (Eds.), The Semantic Web: Research and Applications. XV, 728 pages. 2005.

Vol. 3531: J. Ioannidis, A. Keromytis, M. Yung (Eds.), Applied Cryptography and Network Security. XI, 530 pages. 2005.

Vol. 3530: A. Prinz, R. Reed, J. Reed (Eds.), SDL 2005: Model Driven. XI, 361 pages. 2005.

Vol. 3528: P.S. Szczepaniak, J. Kacprzyk, A. Niewiadomski (Eds.), Advances in Web Intelligence. XVII, 513 pages. 2005. (Subseries LNAI).

Vol. 3527: R. Morrison, F. Oquendo (Eds.), Software Architecture. XII, 263 pages. 2005.

Vol. 3526: S.B. Cooper, B. Löwe, L. Torenvliet (Eds.), New Computational Paradigms. XVII, 574 pages. 2005.

Vol. 3525: A.E. Abdallah, C.B. Jones, J.W. Sanders (Eds.), Communicating Sequential Processes. XIV, 321 pages. 2005.

Vol. 3524: R. Barták, M. Milano (Eds.), Integration of AI and OR Techniques in Constraint Programming for Combinatorial Optimization Problems. XI, 320 pages. 2005.

Vol. 3523: J.S. Marques, N. Pérez de la Blanca, P. Pina (Eds.), Pattern Recognition and Image Analysis, Part II. XXVI, 733 pages. 2005.

Vol. 3522: J.S. Marques, N. Pérez de la Blanca, P. Pina (Eds.), Pattern Recognition and Image Analysis, Part I. XXVI, 703 pages. 2005.

Vol. 3521: N. Megiddo, Y. Xu, B. Zhu (Eds.), Algorithmic Applications in Management. XIII, 484 pages. 2005.

Vol. 3520: O. Pastor, J. Falcão e Cunha (Eds.), Advanced Information Systems Engineering. XVI, 584 pages. 2005.

Vol. 3519: H. Li, P. J. Olver, G. Sommer (Eds.), Computer Algebra and Geometric Algebra with Applications. IX, 449 pages. 2005.

Vol. 3518: T.B. Ho, D. Cheung, H. Liu (Eds.), Advances in Knowledge Discovery and Data Mining. XXI, 864 pages. 2005. (Subseries LNAI).

Vol. 3517: H.S. Baird, D.P. Lopresti (Eds.), Human Interactive Proofs. IX, 143 pages. 2005.

Vol. 3516: V.S. Sunderam, G.D.v. Albada, P.M.A. Sloot, J.J. Dongarra (Eds.), Computational Science – ICCS 2005, Part III. LXIII, 1143 pages. 2005.

Vol. 3515: V.S. Sunderam, G.D.v. Albada, P.M.A. Sloot, J.J. Dongarra (Eds.), Computational Science – ICCS 2005, Part II. LXIII, 1101 pages. 2005.

Vol. 3514: V.S. Sunderam, G.D.v. Albada, P.M.A. Sloot, J.J. Dongarra (Eds.), Computational Science – ICCS 2005, Part I. LXIII, 1089 pages. 2005.

Vol. 3513: A. Montoyo, R. Muñoz, E. Métais (Eds.), Natural Language Processing and Information Systems. XII, 408 pages. 2005.

Vol. 3512: J. Cabestany, A. Prieto, F. Sandoval (Eds.), Computational Intelligence and Bioinspired Systems. XXV, 1260 pages. 2005.

Vol. 3511: U.K. Wiil (Ed.), Metainformatics. VIII, 221 pages. 2005.

Vol. 3510: T. Braun, G. Carle, Y. Koucheryavy, V. Tsaoussidis (Eds.), Wired/Wireless Internet Communications. XIV, 366 pages. 2005.

Vol. 3509: M. Jünger, V. Kaibel (Eds.), Integer Programming and Combinatorial Optimization. XI, 484 pages. 2005.

Vol. 3508: P. Bresciani, P. Giorgini, B. Henderson-Sellers, G. Low, M. Winikoff (Eds.), Agent-Oriented Information Systems II. X, 227 pages. 2005. (Subseries LNAI).

Vol. 3507: F. Crestani, I. Ruthven (Eds.), Information Context: Nature, Impact, and Role. XIII, 253 pages. 2005.

Vol. 3506: C. Park, S. Chee (Eds.), Information Security and Cryptology – ICISC 2004. XIV, 490 pages. 2005.

Vol. 3505: V. Gorodetsky, J. Liu, V. A. Skormin (Eds.), Autonomous Intelligent Systems: Agents and Data Mining. XIII, 303 pages. 2005. (Subseries LNAI).

Vol. 3504: A.F. Frangi, P.I. Radeva, A. Santos, M. Hernandez (Eds.), Functional Imaging and Modeling of the Heart. XV, 489 pages. 2005.

Vol. 3503: S.E. Nikoletseas (Ed.), Experimental and Efficient Algorithms. XV, 624 pages. 2005.

Vol. 3502: F. Khendek, R. Dssouli (Eds.), Testing of Communicating Systems. X, 381 pages. 2005.

Vol. 3501: B. Kégl, G. Lapalme (Eds.), Advances in Artificial Intelligence. XV, 458 pages. 2005. (Subseries LNAI).

Vol. 3500: S. Miyano, J. Mesirov, S. Kasif, S. Istrail, P. Pevzner, M. Waterman (Eds.), Research in Computational Molecular Biology. XVII, 632 pages. 2005. (Subseries LNBI).

Vol. 3499: A. Pelc, M. Raynal (Eds.), Structural Information and Communication Complexity. X, 323 pages. 2005.

Vol. 3498: J. Wang, X. Liao, Z. Yi (Eds.), Advances in Neural Networks – ISNN 2005, Part III. XLIX, 1077 pages. 2005.

Vol. 3497: J. Wang, X. Liao, Z. Yi (Eds.), Advances in Neural Networks – ISNN 2005, Part II. XLIX, 947 pages. 2005.

Vol. 3496: J. Wang, X. Liao, Z. Yi (Eds.), Advances in Neural Networks – ISNN 2005, Part II. L, 1055 pages. 2005.

Vol. 3495: P. Kantor, G. Muresan, F. Roberts, D.D. Zeng, F.-Y. Wang, H. Chen, R.C. Merkle (Eds.), Intelligence and Security Informatics. XVIII, 674 pages. 2005.

Vol. 3494: R. Cramer (Ed.), Advances in Cryptology – EUROCRYPT 2005. XIV, 576 pages. 2005.

Vol. 3493: N. Fuhr, M. Lalmas, S. Malik, Z. Szlávik (Eds.), Advances in XML Information Retrieval. XI, 438 pages. 2005.

Vol. 3492: P. Blache, E. Stabler, J. Busquets, R. Moot (Eds.), Logical Aspects of Computational Linguistics. X, 363 pages. 2005. (Subseries LNAI).

Vol. 3489: G.T. Heineman, I. Crnkovic, H.W. Schmidt, J.A. Stafford, C. Szyperski, K. Wallnau (Eds.), Component-Based Software Engineering. XI, 358 pages. 2005.

Vol. 3488: M.-S. Hacid, N.V. Murray, Z.W. Raś, S. Tsumoto (Eds.), Foundations of Intelligent Systems. XIII, 700 pages. 2005. (Subseries LNAI).

Vol. 3486: T. Helleseth, D. Sarwate, H.-Y. Song, K. Yang (Eds.), Sequences and Their Applications - SETA 2004. XII, 451 pages. 2005.